SPIES FOR HIRE

THE SECRET WORLD OF INTELLIGENCE OUTSOURCING

Tim Shorrock

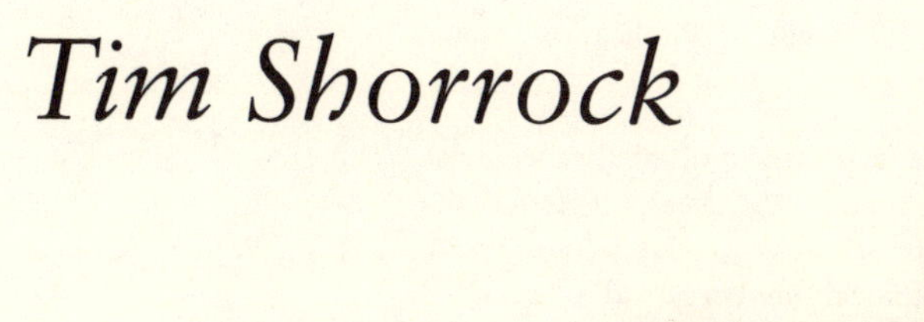

SIMON & SCHUSTER New York • London • Toronto • Sydney

SIMON & SCHUSTER
1230 Avenue of the Americas
New York, NY 10020

First Simon & Schuster hardcover edition May 2008

Designed by Dana Sloan

Manufactured in the United States of America

10 9 8 7 6 5 4 3 2 1

Library of Congress Cataloging-in-Publication Data

Shorrock, Tim.
Spies for hire : the secret world of intelligence outsourcing / Tim Shorrock.—1st Simon & Schuster hardcover ed.
p. cm.
Includes bibliographical references and index.
1. Intelligence service—Contracting out—United States. 2. Intelligence service—United States. 3. National security—United States. 4. United States—Foreign relations—1989–. 5. United States—Military policy. I. Title.
JK468.I6S49 2008
327.1273—dc22 2008006900
ISBN-13: 978-0-7432-8224-6
ISBN-10: 0-7432-8224-8

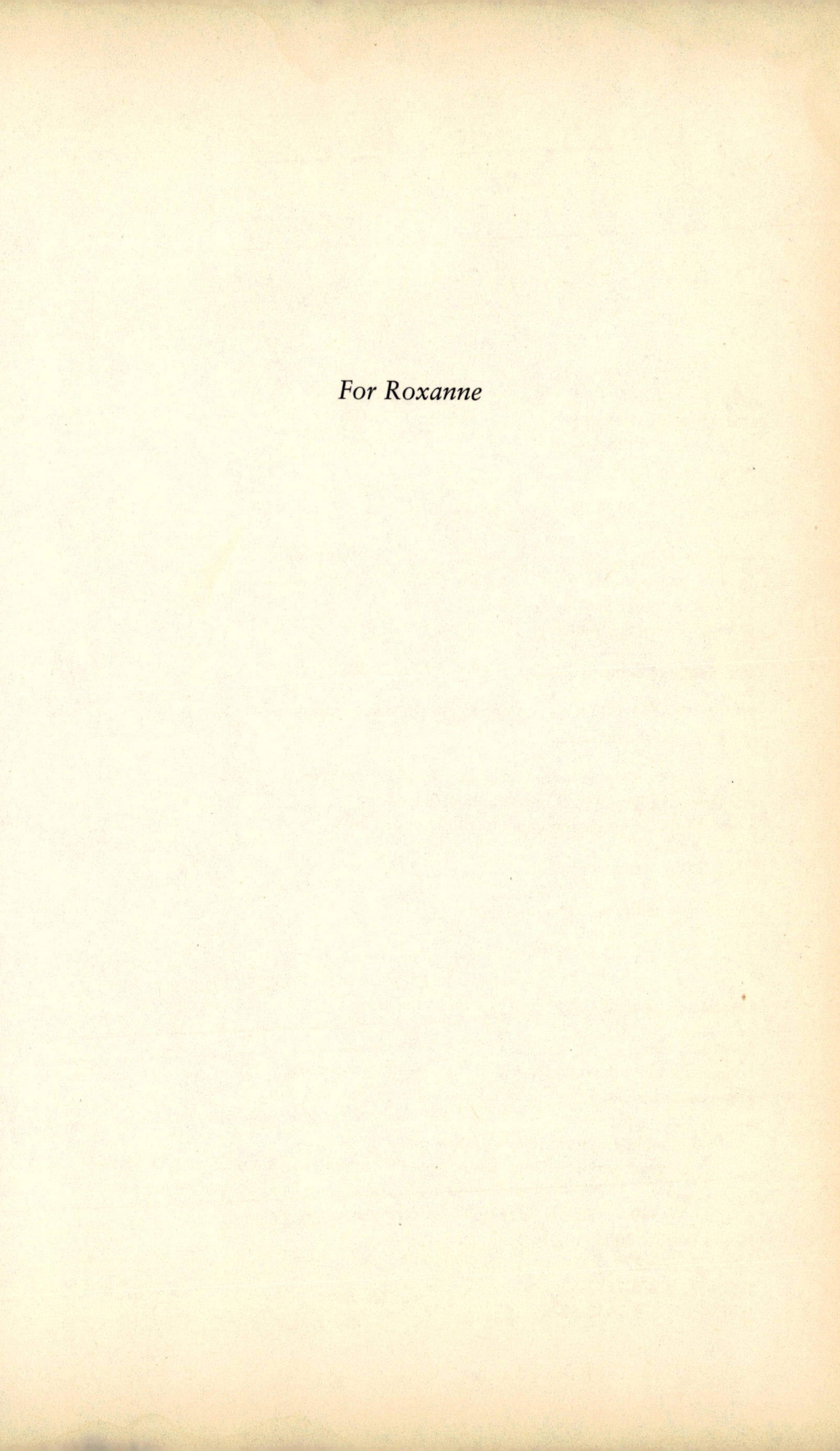

For Roxanne

CONTENTS

PROLOGUE 1

1. The Intelligence-Industrial Complex 9
2. Booz Allen Hamilton and "The Shadow IC" 38
3. A Short History of Intelligence Outsourcing 72
4. The CIA and the Sacrifice of Professionalism 115
5. The Role of the Pentagon 154
6. The NSA, 9/11, and the Business of Data Mining 185
7. Intelligence Disneyland 228
8. The Pure Plays 261
9. The Rise of the National Surveillance State 304
10. Conclusion: Ideology, Oversight, and the Costs of Secrecy 356

ACKNOWLEDGMENTS 383

NOTES 391

INDEX 423

Prologue

ON MAY 9, 2006, John Humphrey, a former CIA officer making his way up the management ladder of one of the nation's largest intelligence contractors, made a stunning disclosure to Intelcon, a national intelligence conference and exhibition at a hotel in Bethesda, Maryland. Outsourcing, Humphrey declared, was out of control. Contractors deployed in Iraq and other hotspots overseas were making decisions and handling documents that, in earlier times, had been the sole responsibility of U.S. military and intelligence officers. This had caused a "paradigm shift" in the relationship between government and the private sector, and left companies like his in an untenable position.

Five years ago, "you'd never have a contractor supporting an operation on the field where they're making a recommendation to an officer," said Humphrey. Nor would you find a contractor "making little contributions here and there" in the reports intelligence officers sent back to Washington. "This concerns me a lot, the way these lines are blurring," he went on. "We shouldn't be involved in some of these intelligence operations, or the planning, or the interrogations and what have you."[1] Unless government started taking more responsibility in the field, he warned, the "blowback" for the contracting industry could be profound.

The intelligence professionals in the room looked stunned. They had just sat through two days of upbeat discussions about the annual $10-billion expansion of U.S. intelligence budgets and the opportunities that money presented for defense contractors, information technology vendors, and former national security officials who still held their top secret security clearances. Upstairs in the exhibition hall, thirty-five companies were displaying the latest high-tech spying equipment and competing to recruit new employees, who could earn up to three times government pay by migrating to the private sector. Words like "blowback" did not come easily at such gatherings.

But this speaker, and the corporation he represented, had an exceptional story to tell. Humphrey was employed by CACI International Inc., a $1.8-billion information technology (IT) company that does more than 70 percent of its business with the Department of Defense. For many years, CACI had been one of the Pentagon's favorite contractors. It was particularly respected for its professional evaluations of software and IT products supplied to the military by outside vendors. During the late 1990s, CACI moved heavily into military intelligence when the Pentagon, its budget reduced by nearly 30 percent from the days of the Cold War and unhappy with the quality of intelligence it was getting from the CIA, began bringing in private sector analysts for the first time.

This proved to be a prescient move for CACI when nineteen Muslim fanatics linked to Al Qaeda, the global terrorist organization then based in Afghanistan, steered three hijacked jetliners into the World Trade Center and the Pentagon on September 11, 2001. In the aftermath of the worst terrorist attack in American history, the Intelligence Community began scouring Washington for analysts, covert operatives, translators, and interrogators it could deploy in the hunt for the perpetrators, and to fill the ranks of hastily organized counterintelligence centers at the Central Intelligence Agency and other government agencies. CACI, which already had a small army of trained and cleared intelligence specialists holding security clearances, was perfectly positioned to pick up the slack.

Between 2002 and 2006, CACI signed dozens of new contracts, acquired twelve companies, and more than tripled its revenue, from $564 million a year to nearly $2 billion. Its astonishing growth catapulted the company from a bit role in IT to one of the key players in what has become a $50-billion-a-year Intelligence-Industrial Complex. "CACI is a cash-flow story," Dave Dragics, CACI's chief operating officer, boasted to investors in 2006. "Whenever you hear bad news, it's usually good news for us."[2]

But along the road to this gravy train, CACI stumbled. The trouble began in the summer of 2003, when Donald Rumsfeld's Pentagon, shocked by the resistance to its occupation of Iraq, began filling Iraqi prisons with thousands of people suspected of participating in the insurgency. The U.S. Army, however, was desperately short of interrogators, particularly anyone with military experience. Through the Department of the Interior, which had subcontracted management of the Pentagon's IT contracts in 2001, the Army renewed several contracts it had signed during the Bosnian war with Premier Technology Group, a small intelligence shop that CACI acquired in 2003. Within weeks of CACI's acquisition, its PTG unit dispatched two dozen former military interrogators and prison guards to Baghdad's Abu Ghraib prison. Many of them were unaware of the nature of the work they would face.

Tasked with the job of rooting out the leaders of the insurgency, some CACI employees directed military interrogators to use techniques on Iraqi prisoners that were, to put it mildly, far outside the norm of civilized conduct. Reports of the mistreatment soon made their way to U.S. commanders in Iraq, who appointed an Army general to investigate conditions at the prison. In the spring of 2004, CACI was thrust into the public limelight when the Army's report, along with hundreds of graphic photographs of Iraqis being tortured and humiliated, were leaked to the press. The Bush administration was thrust into one of its most serious foreign policy crises. After leaving the Pentagon in 2006,

Rumsfeld would call Abu Ghraib the worst thing that happened during his five and a half years as secretary of defense (despite being the architect of the U.S. occupation of Iraq, however, he never took responsibility for the actions of his soldiers and contractors).

The details of what CACI's people did at Abu Ghraib were the subject of an insightful book, *Chain of Command: The Road from 9/11 to Abu Ghraib*, by Seymour Hersh, the reporter who broke the Abu Ghraib story, and the events recalled in excruciating detail by former Iraqi prisoners in a 2007 film made by Hollywood producer Robert Greenwald called *Iraq for Sale: The War Profiteers*. Two internal Army reports concluded that CACI's contract interrogators introduced some of the most brutal practices employed at the prison, including the use of attack dogs. The images of one naked prisoner, cringing in terror as a German shepherd snapped his teeth just inches from the man's genitals, horrified the world. Combined with the testimony of several guards who followed the orders of the CACI and Army interrogators, the pictures convinced U.S. military tribunals to convict two of the dog handlers for assault. But no case was ever made against CACI's men: even though one of CACI's employees, a former prison guard named Steven Stefanowicz, was identified at trial as suggesting the use of the dogs, he has never been charged with a crime. Nor has CACI itself.

Instead, J. P. "Jack" London, CACI's chairman and CEO, made it his life's mission to exonerate his company from any wrongdoing. From the moment the Abu Ghraib story broke in 2004, London fought back with a vengeance, attacking journalists who printed stories about the scandal, and generally castigating anyone who dared to suggest that CACI bore any responsibility for the abuse.* At the other extreme, London called Steven Stefanowicz, the man who helped introduce the use of

---

* Among those on the receiving end of London's wrath were Peter Singer, a prominent expert on private military companies who had penned a mild critique of CACI in the *Washington Post;* former California state treasurer and gubernatorial candidate Phil Angilides, who dared to question CACI's tactics at Abu Ghraib during a public hearing of the California Public Employees' Retirement System's investment committee (CalPERS, as an investor in CACI, had a legal right and a fiduciary duty to study the issue); and Randi Rhodes, a talk show host on Air America Radio, who was sued by CACI for comments she made about the company on the air.

attack dogs at Abu Ghraib, a model employee and praised him for doing "a damned fine job" in Iraq.

The Pentagon, far from chastising its wayward client, continues to reward CACI: despite the unresolved issues involving CACI's role at Abu Ghraib, the Department of Defense has awarded CACI millions of dollars in new contracts, including a three-year, $156 million contract signed in 2006 to provide IT support and training to instructors at the Army's Intelligence School in Fort Huachuca, Arizona. The Office of the Secretary of Defense has hired CACI for two contracts, worth more than $20 million in total, to support the Pentagon's transformation initiatives and manage its classified and unclassified computer networks supporting homeland security and the global "war on terror."[3] In a lucrative arrangement announced in December 2006, the Army placed CACI in an elite group of companies allowed to bid on $35 billion worth of IT and logistics contracts over the next twenty years.

In his remarks to the intelligence conference,* Humphrey, who had worked as a CIA agent in Europe for more than ten years before joining CACI, was careful not to accept, or even apportion, any blame for what happened at the prison. The individuals involved in the "Abu Ghraib incidents," as he called them, "had the best intentions." A contractor at an internment camp is in "a very stressful situation. You're being told you have to do this, that you're the only one who can do this." Contractors, he concluded, "need to settle back down to being in a supportive role." Inside the government, "there's a little too much right now of 'let's get a contractor and life is good.' There needs to be more of a setting of a line." To date, his speech is the most detailed and honest analysis of Abu Ghraib to come from CACI.

I asked CACI if I could interview London or another executive about Humphrey's allegations and the company's work in Iraq. Jody Brown, CACI's vice president for corporate communications, replied by e-mail. CACI, she said, could not confirm information regarding "em-

---

* Intelcon was supposed to be an annual event, but was held only twice, in 2005 and 2006. The sessions attracted hundreds of contractors, national security officials, think tank analysts, and journalists. In 2007, however, the conference was suspended without explanation by its organizers.

ployees, vendors, or anyone associated with the company," and has posted a "comprehensive" report on its Web site called *Facts About CACI in Iraq*. "The subject you have selected for your book is interesting and quite timely," Brown added. "As you seem to be aware, considering your interest and coverage of the company over the past two years, we provide high-value critical information technology services to the U.S. government. Our services are aligned with the nation's highest priorities to prevail in the war on terrorism, secure our homeland and improve government services to our citizens. Most of the services we provide in this area are classified and therefore by contract we cannot discuss them."

What happened at Abu Ghraib, and CACI's refusal to discuss it, stands as a kind of high-water mark for intelligence contracting. In 2006, the year Humphrey delivered his comments, the cost of America's spying and surveillance activities outsourced to contractors reached $42 billion, or about 70 percent of the estimated $60 billion the government spends every year on foreign and domestic intelligence. Unfortunately, we cannot know the true extent of outsourcing, for two reasons. First, in 2007, the Office of the Director of National Intelligence (ODNI) refused to release an internal report on contracting out of fear that its disclosure would harm U.S. national security interests. Second, most intelligence contracts are classified, allowing companies like CACI to hide their activities behind a veil of secrecy.

This book is an attempt to pierce that veil.

Our story will begin with a broad overview of America's new Intelligence-Industrial Complex, the agencies it serves, its key industrial players, and the former high-ranking national security officials who run its largest companies. After that, we'll take a close look at Booz Allen Hamilton, one of the government's most important contractors, and learn how retired Navy Admiral J. Michael McConnell, the former director of Booz Allen's intelligence business, is remaking the nation's intelligence agenda as director of national intelligence. Next, we'll turn to the history of outsourcing in intelligence, focusing primarily on how contracting advanced during the administration of Bill Clinton and the reign of former CIA director George J. Tenet over national intelligence.

After that, we'll bore in on the key intelligence agencies—the CIA, the many agencies under the command and control system of the Pentagon, the National Security Agency (NSA), and the National Geospatial-Intelligence Agency (NGA). We'll then take a closer look at the companies, such as CACI and ManTech International, that depend almost entirely on intelligence contracts for their revenues. That will bring us to domestic intelligence and the role of the private sector in the NSA's warrantless surveillance program. In the final chapter, we'll also look at the process of oversight in Congress, particularly as the new Democratic majorities in the House and Senate have tried to shed light on the Bush administration's actions and the role contractors have played in them.

Before embarking on the narrative, allow me to state a major caveat. This is a book about the *business of intelligence*. It doesn't claim to be an authoritative study of intelligence under the Bush administration. Nor do I claim any special expertise in the inner working of the Intelligence Community. I leave that job to the many excellent reporters out there covering intelligence as a daily beat. But that aside, contracting provides a unique window into intelligence. By ferreting out companies and what they do, we will learn much about how U.S. intelligence operates and what the CIA, the NSA, and other agencies have been up to over the past ten years, both at home and abroad.

1

The Intelligence-Industrial Complex

"We can't spy . . . If we can't buy."

—Terri Everett, senior procurement executive in the Office of the Director of National Intelligence, in a presentation to a conference organized by the Defense Intelligence Agency, May 14, 2007

SOMEWHERE IN Northern Virginia, tucked inside an innocuous and unmarked office complex called Liberty Crossing, is a cavernous room loaded with high-tech communications and computer gear and staffed 24/7 by analysts and action officers from all sixteen agencies that comprise the Intelligence Community. The monitors and video screens in the room cast an eerie glow as the staffers pore through classified reports and images flowing into the room from every corner of the globe. The few reporters who've been allowed to enter this secure facility are sworn not to disclose its exact location. When they do talk about it, they inevitably compare it to the fictional headquarters of the Counter Terrorism Unit in the Fox hit series *24* or the mock intelligence station in *The Bourne Ultimatum*, the Matt Damon thriller that depicts a rogue

CIA officer relentlessly pursuing a dissident agent around the world using the latest in digital surveillance and eavesdropping technology.[1]

This is the National Counterterrorism Center (NCTC), the electronic hub of the U.S. Intelligence Community and the heart of the national security state established by the administration of President George W. Bush in the aftermath of September 11. Since opening its doors in 2005, the NCTC has been the government's central collection point for monitoring global threats to national security. Its analysts have at their disposal more than thirty separate government computer networks, each carrying more than eighty unique sources of data. As they go about their tasks, they draw on human intelligence from the Central Intelligence Agency, communications intercepts from the National Security Agency, and domestic reports from the Department of Homeland Security, the FBI, and local law enforcement agencies around the country.[2]

The center's chief product, the Threat Matrix, is a highly classified status report that forms the centerpiece of a daily eight A.M. teleconference led by the NCTC's director, former federal prosecutor Michael Leiter. That meeting is beamed, via secure video, to the White House, the CIA, the NSA, and other key offices in and around Washington. The center also maintains the nation's central repository of known and suspected terrorists, and compiles highly classified briefing books for the Office of the Director of National Intelligence and the White House. In the fight against terrorism, "the best asset we have is the people represented right here in this building," President George W. Bush declared during a visit to Liberty Crossing in 2006.* Behind him in the shadows, dozens of men and women dressed in suits and military garb stood at attention next to their computer stations. It was an impressive sight, designed to convince a skeptical public that the U.S. government was drawing on all its resources to prevent another 9/11 and protect the American people.

---

* Despite the government's attempt to keep its location a secret, the NCTC would not be hard to find. According to the *Washington Times*, it is located in Tysons Corner, Virginia, in the same complex that houses the CIA Counterterrorism Center and the Pentagon's Joint Intelligence Task Force–Combating Terrorism center. See Cryptome, http://eyeball-series.org/nctc/nctc-birdseye.htm. And Mike McConnell, the DNI, scoffs at the comparison between NCTC and the Bourne movies. "We can't do that," he told *The New Yorker*'s Lawrence Wright in January 2008. "That's all horse pucky."

But it was all a charade. More than half of the people working in the center, then as now, are private sector contract employees, working not for the government but for the dozens of companies that do business with the Intelligence Community.* Most of them are employees of large defense contractors that dominate the intelligence landscape, such as Booz Allen Hamilton, Science Applications International Corporation (SAIC), BAE Systems, and Lockheed Martin. Others work for the dozens of small and medium-sized information technology companies that have crowded into Washington to feed its insatiable appetite for outsourced government services. And quite a few have walked out of the NCTC as government employees and walked back in as contract employees.

The center's terrorist database, for example, is maintained by The Analysis Corporation (TAC), an intelligence contractor in nearby Fairfax, Virginia, run by John O. Brennan, the former chief of staff of the CIA and the NCTC's first director. TAC, in turn, has subcontracted the collection activities for the database to CACI International, the same company that provided contract interrogators to the U.S. military prison at Abu Ghraib in Iraq. In 2007, to strengthen its ties with the center, CACI hired retired Navy Vice Admiral Albert Calland, the NCTC's former deputy director for strategic operational planning, as its executive vice president for security and intelligence integration.[3] Far from displaying government resolve, the NCTC is a powerful symbol of American capitalism and a stark example of the way the United States organizes its national security infrastructure in the twenty-first century.

Over the past ten years, the private sector has become a major supplier of tools and brainpower to the Intelligence Community. The CIA, the NSA, and other agencies once renowned for their analysis of intelligence and for their technical prowess in covert operations, electronic surveillance, and overhead reconnaissance have outsourced many of

* The NCTC control room itself was designed by engineers from Walt Disney Imagineering, which is normally in the business of developing theme parks. See Lawrence Wright, "The Spymaster," *The New Yorker,* January 21, 2008.

their core tasks to private intelligence armies. As a result, spying has blossomed into a domestic market worth nearly $50 billion a year.

Tasks that are now outsourced include running spy networks out of embassies, intelligence analysis, signals intelligence (SIGINT) collection, covert operations, and the interrogation of enemy prisoners. Private companies analyze intelligence collected by satellites and low-flying unmanned aerial vehicles (UAVs), and write reports that are passed up the line to high-ranking officials and policy-makers in government. They supply and maintain software programs that are used to manipulate and visualize data. They provide collaboration tools to help individual agencies communicate with each other, and they supply security tools to protect classified computer networks from outside tampering. Throughout the Intelligence Community, contractors manage the work of other contractors and, in some cases, the work of government employees. They also draft budgets for government agencies and write Statements of Work that define the tasks that they and other contractors carry out for the government.

The bulk of this $50 billion market is serviced by one hundred companies, ranging in size from multibillion-dollar defense behemoths to small technology shops funded by venture capitalists that have yet to turn a profit. At one end of the scale is Lockheed Martin, whose $40 billion in revenue and 52,000 cleared IT personnel make it the largest defense contractor and private intelligence force in the world. At the other is SpecTal of Reston, Virginia, a privately held company that employs three hundred specialists with top secret security clearances who perform intelligence missions in Afghanistan and Iraq. In between are dozens of firms, some well known (IBM) and some obscure (Scitor), who make up a business that has grown so large that even its champions aren't afraid to borrow a weighted term from President Dwight Eisenhower to describe it. "Call it the Intelligence-Industrial Complex," says retired Vice Admiral Herbert A. Browne, who served from 2002 to 2007 as executive director of the Armed Forces Communications and Electronics Association (AFCEA), the largest industry association in the intelligence business.

The analogy between the intelligence industry and the military-industrial complex famously described by President Eisenhower in

1961 is fitting. By 2006, according to the Office of the Director of National Intelligence, 70 percent, or almost three-quarters, of the intelligence budget was spent on contracts.[4] That astounding figure, which I first reported in June 2007, means that the vast majority of the money spent by the Intelligence Community is not going into building an expert cadre within government but to creating a secret army of analysts and action officers inside the private sector.

From the contractors' perspective, that shift represents the triumph of capitalist innovation and the coming of a new age in business-government cooperation. "The fact that we can have a professional intelligence organization *outside* of the government to *support* the government is no more offensive to me than the fact that we have 80 percent of our military communications traveling on commercial satellites or commercial fiber optics," says Browne, who left the military in 2000 to work for the defense intelligence division of AT&T. "In fact, I find it very healthy for the nation."[5]

But critics of the industry don't see it that way, particularly in view of the intelligence debacles of the past six years. "Contracting has simply gone crazy," says Eugene Fidell, the president of the National Institute for Military Justice, the nation's largest organization of military lawyers. He is most troubled about the CIA's and the Pentagon's use of contractors to interrogate enemy prisoners. "That's really playing with fire," he says. "That kind of activity, which so closely entails the national interest and exposes the country to terrible opprobrium, is something that ought to be done only by people who are government employees."[6]

There's a lot of daylight between those two perspectives. But whatever one's position on outsourcing, there is little doubt that spying for hire has become a way of life in twenty-first-century America.

- Since 9/11, the Central Intelligence Agency has been spending 50 to 60 percent of its budget on for-profit contractors, or about $2.5 billion a year, and its number of contract employees now exceeds the agency's full-time workforce of 17,500. Outsourcing has also spread to human intelligence. At the CIA, contractors help staff overseas stations and provide disguises used by agents working undercover.

Contractors make up more than half the workforce of the CIA's National Clandestine Service (formerly the Directorate of Operations), which conducts covert operations and recruits spies abroad. According to Robert Baer, a former CIA officer who worked undercover in the Middle East for many years, a contractor stationed in Iraq even supervises where CIA agents go in Baghdad and who they meet. "It's a completely different culture from the way the CIA used to be run, when a case officer determined where and when agents would go," he told me. "Everyone I know in the CIA is leaving and going into contracting whether they're retired or not."[7]

- The National Security Agency, once so secretive it was jokingly called No Such Agency, has become one of the largest users of contractors in the federal government. The agency began reaching out to the private sector in the late 1990s to help it cope with the massive amount of information it was scooping up from its global eavesdropping network, the largest and most powerful spying operation on earth. After the 9/11 terrorist attacks, the need for such information increased drastically. To feed the NSA's insatiable demand for data and information technology, the industrial base of contractors seeking to do business with the agency grew from 144 companies in 2001 to more than 5,400 in 2006. "Partnerships with industry," NSA official Deborah Walker says, are now "vital to mission success."[8]

- Intelligence outsourcing has mushroomed at the Department of Defense, which controls more than 85 percent of the U.S. intelligence budget. On the battlefields of Iraq and Afghanistan, civilian intelligence specialists under contract to the NSA and the National Geospatial-Intelligence Agency operate signals intelligence and imagery equipment for Army and Marine units on the move against Iraqi insurgents and Islamic militias. NSA contractors also capture electronic signals emanating from enemy weapons, determine the exact type of weapons being fired, and relay that information to Air Force Airborne Warning and Control System (AWACS) aircraft flying overhead. At least 35 percent of the staff at the Defense Intelligence Agency (DIA), which provides intelligence to the Secretary of Defense and the Joint Chiefs of Staff, are employed by contractors. At the Counterintelligence Field Activity, a Pentagon agency that was criticized by Congress in 2005 for spying on American citizens, the figure is 70 percent.

- With contractors deeply imbedded in the CIA, the NSA, and the Pentagon, substantial portions of the President's Daily Brief, the most sensitive document in government, are based on the work of private sector analysts. It is well established that about 70 percent of the brief is drawn from telephone and e-mail intercepts provided by the NSA, which relies heavily on SAIC, CACI International, Northrop Grumman, and other companies for the analysis and interpretation of signals intelligence. The same is true for the Office of the Director of National Intelligence, which prepares the final draft of the president's brief, and the DIA, which supplies much of the president's intelligence about foreign military forces. This adds even more contracted intelligence to the presidential mix, and dilutes the significance of the DNI seal on the President's Daily Brief. At best, that seal is misleading, says R. J. Hillhouse, an intelligence expert and the author of a popular blog on outsourcing. "For full disclosure, the PDB really should look more like NASCAR with corporate logos plastered all over it."[9]

- As they did in Abu Ghraib, private interrogators working at the U.S. military prison in Guantánamo Bay, Cuba, have led the questioning of enemy prisoners from the Middle East and South Asia. That puts contractors at the heart of one of the darkest chapters in the history of the war on terror: the CIA's use of extreme measures to coerce suspected terrorists to confess to their crimes. At Guantánamo, according to *New Yorker* reporter Jane Mayer, the CIA hired a group of outside contractors who implemented "a regime of techniques" described acidly by a former adviser to the U.S. Intelligence Community as a *Clockwork Orange* type of approach. The contractors, Mayer learned, were retired military psychologists who had trained U.S. Special Forces soldiers in how to survive torture.[10] (As of this writing, none of the actual companies has been identified.) Meanwhile, at the U.S. Army's Intelligence Center in Fort Huachuca, Arizona, even the training of military interrogators has been turned over to corporations, which supply private instructors to lead classes in interrogation techniques for young Army recruits.

- At the National Reconnaissance Office (NRO), the agency in charge of launching and maintaining the nation's photoreconnaissance and eavesdropping satellites, almost the entire workforce is composed of contract employees working for companies. According to Donald M. Kerr, who directed the NRO from 2005 to 2007, "ninety-five percent of the resources over which we have stewardship in fact go out on a contract to our industrial base. It's an important thing to recognize that we cannot function without this highly integrated industrial government team."[11] With an estimated $8 billion annual budget, the largest in the IC, contractors control about $7 billion worth of business at the NRO, giving the spy satellite industry the distinction of being the most privatized part of the Intelligence Community.

- The CIA itself has even become part of the intelligence contracting industry by creating its own investment fund. In-Q-Tel, started under CIA director George Tenet in 1999, works with the CIA's Directorate of Science and Technology to find companies that produce software and other products with intelligence applications, and then buys equity positions in these firms—many of which are managed by former intelligence officials. By 2007, In-Q-Tel had invested in more than ninety companies. Among them was a company called Keyhole Inc., which had created a three-dimensional computer map of the world that allowed users to zoom in and out of cities. It was later acquired by Google, and is now the key software for Google Earth, one of the most popular programs on the Internet and in the news business.

- The intelligence contracting industry has grown so large that there are no fewer than three business associations representing intelligence contractors. The one with the closest ties to the government is the Intelligence and National Security Alliance (INSA), which primarily represents contractors working for the NSA and the CIA. From 2005 to 2007, its chairman was J. Michael McConnell, the former executive vice president of Booz Allen Hamilton, who left his company and INSA to become DNI—the government's top intelligence officer and principal intelligence adviser to the president—in February 2007. The largest by membership is the Armed Forces Communications and Electronics Association, which claims to represent over one thousand companies involved in defense intelligence. The United States Geospatial Intelligence Foundation represents several hundred companies that provide software and networking services to the National Geospatial-Intelligence Agency, the newest member of the Intelligence Community.

Because intelligence budgets and most intelligence contracts are classified, quantifying how much outsourcing goes on in the IC has been difficult. In 2005, writing in *Mother Jones* magazine, I estimated that at least 50 percent of the intelligence budget was spent on outsourcing.[12] That number, based on interviews with prominent intelligence experts in Washington, turned out to be a low estimate; but it came to be used widely in Congress and in subsequent articles about outsourcing by other journalists. As I researched this topic over the next two years, I stuck to the 50 percent figure because it seemed to accurately reflect what I was learning about contracting at the NSA, the CIA, and the rest of the Intelligence Community. But I still needed hard numbers to make my case that more than half of intelligence spending went to contractors. In 2006 it finally looked like I might get my wish.

That summer, the Office of the Director of National Intelligence ordered the first comprehensive survey of the IC's use of contractors since 9/11. The survey was triggered by two factors: the growing demands from Congress for information about contractors; and a realization within the ODNI that its agencies had become a training camp for the private sector. The Intelligence Community increasingly "finds itself in competition with its contractors for our own employees," the ODNI said in a 2006 report on human capital. "Confronted by arbitrary staffing ceilings and uncertain funding, components are left with no choice but to use contractors for work that may be borderline 'inherently governmental'—only to find that to do that work, those same contractors recruit our own employees, already cleared and trained at government expense, and then 'lease' them back to us at considerably greater expense."[13]

Under the survey ordered up as a result of those findings, sixteen agencies were asked to turn over their contracting records to the DNI. "We have to come to some conclusion about what our core intelligence mission is, and how many [full-time employees] it's going to take to accomplish that mission," Ronald Sanders, the DNI's chief human capital officer, explained to the *Los Angeles Times*.[14] The survey's final report, dubbed the "IC Core Contractor Inventory," was completed in the spring of 2007 and sent to the House and Senate committees with jurisdiction over intelligence budgets.

But when the time came to declassify its findings for the public, the ODNI and its member agencies got cold feet, and refused to release it on the grounds the information would help America's enemies. "I can't give you anything that would allow you to impute the size of the IC civilian work force," Sanders announced.[15] The ODNI later reiterated its concerns in a press release, saying that "the overall Intelligence Community budget and its components are classified to protect the national security interests of the United States."[16] Luckily, my search didn't end there.

In May 2007, I obtained an unclassified PowerPoint presentation prepared by Terri Everett, the DNI's senior procurement executive, for a Defense Intelligence Agency acquisition conference in Colorado.[17] When I opened the slides, I was stunned to see a pie chart with the figures I'd been looking for: *no less than 70 percent of the nation's intelligence budget was being spent on contracts*. Everett's slides disclosed for the first time the true extent of intelligence outsourcing. They also included a series of bar graphs revealing that contracting had *more than* *doubled* between 1998 and 2006, the most recent year for the DNI statistics.[18] *

In 1998, the slides showed, U.S. intelligence agencies spent $18 billion on contracts; in 2001, the number had increased to nearly $22 billion. Over the next two years, as the Bush administration and Congress vastly increased the defense and intelligence budgets in response to 9/11, contract spending jumped by $20 billion, to $43.5 billion in 2003, where it stayed for the next three years. As one of Everett's slides put it, "non-core functions" of intelligence that were done "in-house" during the Cold War era were now being "outsourced" in the twenty-first century. Another slide declared simply: "We can't spy . . . If we can't buy." By 2007, that had become, literally and figuratively, the new slogan of U.S. intelligence.

The findings were startling, even to veteran outside observers of the intelligence budget. The 70 percent figure "represents a transformation of the Cold War intelligence bureaucracy into something new and dif-

---

* I discovered the underlying figures quite by accident. As I was studying the DNI slides, I used my mouse to right-click on the slide showing the 70 percent figure. At that, a series of bar graphs popped up showing the aggregate spending on contracts over the past decade. When my story about the contracting figures appeared in *Salon,* we posted a link to Everett's presentation, which was still posted on the DIA's Web site. Later that week, R. J. Hillhouse, the intelligence blogger, used the $42 billion contracting figure to extrapolate on the broader intelligence budget. By reverse engineering the numbers in data imbedded in the PowerPoint slides, she found that the budget of the sixteen U.S. intelligence agencies in 2006 was $60 billion, almost 25 percent higher than most analysts believed. By inadvertently releasing the keys to that number in the PowerPoint presentation, she said, the ODNI had revealed "one of the government's most guarded secrets." ("Exclusive: Office of Nation's Top Spy Inadvertently Reveals Key to Classified Intel Budget," *The Spy Who Billed Me* [blog], June 4, 2007.) In response, the ODNI issued a highly unusual statement. "In recent reports, information contained in an unclassified [ODNI] presentation at a government acquisitions conference has been mistakenly assumed to be representative of the overall budget of the U.S. Intelligence Community," said Ellen Cioccio, the ODNI's acting director of public affairs, in a statement issued on June 19, 2007. "The slides and accompanying presentation were designed to illustrate general trends in Intelligence Community contracting for conference participants. They concerned overall procurement award trends; they did not address the issue of Intelligence Community contractors (personnel under contract) or the size of the Intelligence Budget, in relative or actual terms." Cioccio added that the bar graphs and their underlying data were based on a "small, anecdotal sample" of a portion of the IC's contracting activities and therefore could not "be used to derive either the overall [IC] budget or a breakdown of any portion of the budget."

ferent that is literally dominated by contractor interests," said Steven Aftergood, the director of the Project on Government Secrecy at the Federation of American Scientists.

That contractor-dominated bureaucracy now spends close to $60 billion a year, according to ODNI data and estimates from contractors and intelligence analysts. The money is divided among sixteen agencies, which fall into two categories of spending; the numbers that follow are estimates based on the 2007 intelligence budget.

The National Intelligence Program (NIP) receives about 80 percent of the total intelligence budget. It includes the intelligence activities of the National Reconnaissance Office ($8 billion); the National Security Agency ($8 billion); the National Geospatial-Intelligence Agency ($3 billion); the Central Intelligence Agency ($6 billion); the FBI ($1.5 billion); the Department of Homeland Security ($12 million); the State Department's Bureau of Intelligence and Research ($60 million); and the Treasury Department ($60 million).

The Joint Military Program (MIP) funds two agencies that provide intelligence for all elements of the U.S. military. The largest of these are the Defense Advanced Research Projects Agency ($3.5 billion) and the Defense Intelligence Agency ($2 billion). Both answer to the secretary of defense (in a quirk in the intelligence system that we'll explore in Chapter 5, three of the national agencies, the NSA, the NRO, and the NGA, are considered combat support agencies and receive some funding through the MIP). This program also includes the intelligence units of the Army ($6 billion), the Navy ($4 billion), the Air Force ($8 billion), and other service branches, such as the Marines ($2 billion). These units fall under the authority of the DIA and the undersecretary of defense for intelligence.

Budgets for these programs are drafted and approved in classified hearings of the House Select Committee on Intelligence and included in the annual defense appropriations bills passed by the House Armed Services Committee and then the full House. The legislation is then considered by the Senate and approved by House-Senate conference committees. The line items for the NSA, the NGA, the DIA, and the NRO (and even subagencies like the Pentagon's Counterintelligence Field Activity office) can be clearly seen in the defense budget, but the actual amounts are left blank and marked CLASSIFIED. The CIA budget is harder to find; John Pike, the director of GlobalSecurity.org and a highly respected intelligence expert, has concluded that the agency's annual appropriation is hidden in a section of the Air Force budget devoted to "other procurement aircraft."

Secrecy, however, comes at a cost. "The problem is the lack of transparency," says Scott Amey, the general counsel for the Project on Government Oversight, a Washington public interest group. "We have billions of dollars in spending going out that has little or no oversight" by Congress.[19] Other critics of the system point out that budgetary information about individual agencies is available to contractors, who are at liberty to lobby members of Congress about those budgets. Yet the public is completely excluded when these appropriations are discussed in Congress, skewing policy in favor of the private sector.

"It's not like a debate when someone loses," says Aftergood, who is a leading advocate for declassifying the intelligence budget. "There *is* no debate. And the more work that migrates to the private sector, the less effective congressional oversight is going to be." From that secretive process, he added, "there's only a short distance to the Duke Cunninghams of the world and the corruption of the process in the interest of private corporations."[20] He was referring to the case of Randy "Duke" Cunningham, a former Republican congressman from California, who was sentenced in 2006 to eight years in prison after pleading guilty of accepting more than $2 million in bribes from executives with MZM Inc., a prominent San Diego defense contractor. In return for the bribes, Cunningham used his position on the House appropriations and intelligence committees to win tens of millions of dollars' worth of contracts for MZM at the CIA and the Pentagon's CIFA office.

Secrecy can also be problematic for the many contractors that trade their shares on Wall Street. The Securities and Exchange Commission requires publicly traded companies to report "material events," which includes important contracts signed or canceled. At the same time, companies hoping to drive their share prices up have an interest in telling investors that they've won an important contract. The problems emerge when the agency awarding a contract wants it to remain secret. "It's a bit of a tug-of-war," explains Leonard Moodispaw, the CEO of Essex Corporation, a key NSA contractor recently acquired by Northrop Grumman. "Investors want to know about your contracts, how likely it is you'll lose this contract, and so on. If they can't look it up in the defense budget, they don't feel comfortable about it." Although it's impossible to be completely transparent, he says, "you overcome that by performance—by them getting to trust you, doing what you say you're going to do." [21]

To make things easier for agencies and companies alike, John Negroponte, Mike McConnell's predecessor as DNI, issued an edict in 2005 that gave publicly traded contractors the right to exclude certain "material events" from their public filings with the SEC, including the signing of a new contract with the CIA or the NSA. As a result, it's now up to the companies to decide for themselves what's material, and announcements of new contracts are frequently crafted with extremely vague language. In 2006, for example, ManTech announced a new contract worth $130 million to "support intelligence missions that help fight the Global War on Terrorism," and CACI said it had obtained a $230 million contract "designed to increase the capabilities of federal agencies directly engaged in providing homeland security and waging the war on terrorism." [22] Exactly what those contracts entailed was left to the reader's imagination.

The lack of transparency also makes it almost impossible to create an accurate list of intelligence contractors, ranked by size and market share, as you might see for the defense or homeland security industries. The closest thing to a Top 100 list are the annual rankings published by *Washington Technology* and other newspapers of the market leaders in defense and federal information technology, the two sectors where most intelligence contracting takes place. Creating an intelligence industry ranking, therefore, requires drawing from the defense and IT rankings as well as culling information from every public source imaginable—press releases, annual reports, public filings with the Securities and Exchange Commission, corporate brochures, industry association newsletters, company presentations at investor conferences, and speeches and press conferences by intelligence agency officials. Out of this riot of data we can start to see the outlines of the intelligence contracting industry as it looks in 2008. Here's how it shakes out.

At the top tier are the "systems integrators" that manage mega-projects for government agencies and supply the large armies of cleared analysts and technicians who fill slots at the CIA, the National Counterterrorism Center, and other agencies. The leading companies are SAIC and Booz Allen Hamilton, which stand together like a private colossus across the whole intelligence industry. Of SAIC's 42,000 employees, more than twenty thousand hold U.S. government security clearances; Booz Allen commands a private intelligence army at least ten thousand strong. Both companies are deeply involved in the operations of all the major collection agencies, particularly the NSA, the NGA, and the CIA. Each employs an executive vice president with authority over all intelligence matters; by the nature of their companies and the scope of their work, these executives should probably be considered deputy directors of national intelligence—with the proviso that they answer to shareholders instead of the government. At SAIC, that man is retired Army Major General John D. Thomas, the company's senior vice president and general manager of operations, intelligence, and security. Until recently, his counterpart at Booz Allen was Mike McConnell, who is now the director of national intelligence.*

The systems integrators, whose ranks also include Lockheed Martin, Northrop Grumman, Raytheon, Computer Sciences Corporation

---

* McConnell himself made the comparison between himself and SAIC's Thomas. In August 2007, during a public speech at an intelligence conference in El Paso, Texas, McConnell recalled to an audience of intelligence professionals his circumstances when he was asked by the Bush administration to consider taking over as DNI. "Quite frankly, I was enjoying supporting this community from, shall we say, an executive position in industry," he said. Without identifying any companies, he added: "General Thomas and I had similar positions, he in one company and me in another." See "Remarks by DNI Michael McConnell at the 2007 Border Security Conference, as released by the DNI," Federal News Service, August 14, 2007.

(CSC), General Dynamics Advanced Information Systems, and BAE Systems, separately earn total revenues of at least $4 billion a year. They provide much of the software and systems engineering required for agencies such as the NSA to share intelligence with military commanders and other members of the IC. SAIC, for example, managed one of the NSA's largest efforts in recent years, the $3 billion Project Trailblazer, which attempted (and failed, as we shall see) to create actionable intelligence from the cacophony of telephone calls, fax messages, and e-mails picked up by the NSA every day. Booz Allen plays an instrumental role as an adviser on technology to the DNI as well as the National Security Agency. The top tier companies are involved in every aspect of intelligence, from signals to imagery to open source human intelligence (HUMINT): they are the giants of the spying industry. Their ties with the agencies are so close that top executives encourage their people to think of themselves as extensions of the government. "Everyone talks about the Intelligence Community as 'those guys in government,' whether it's the people in the military or the people in the agencies," Ben Romero, the director of Intelligence and Homeland Security Programs for Lockheed Martin, told a roomful of contractors in 2005. "Well, guess what? You are all part of the Intelligence Community. In fact, you probably make up the largest part of it."[23]

The second tier is composed of companies with combined total revenues of between $1 billion and $2 billion a year, nearly all of it—95 percent in some cases—from contracts with the Pentagon and the national intelligence collection agencies: the NSA, the NGA, and the NRO. These companies provide the specialized technical IT services and analytical services that are essential to agencies such as the CIA and the NSA, and often work as subcontractors to the systems integrators. The largest and best known of the second tier companies is CACI International. Its chief competitor, ManTech International, is well-known in the homeland security market for making a key software program that allows national agencies to share classified and unclassified intelligence with the FBI and local law enforcement agencies.

Like the larger systems integrators, the midlevel firms often have satellite operations near important intelligence outposts. In addition to holding down the fort in Washington, a typical contractor might have an office in Dayton, Ohio, near Wright-Patterson Air Force Base; in Huntsville, Alabama, near the U.S. Army's Missile Defense Agency; or in San Diego, the headquarters for some of the Navy's most classified operations. The latest area to experience an intelligence boom in recent years is Colorado, where the Pentagon's Northern Command and its Counterintelligence Field Activity office conduct many of their domestic intelligence operations.

The third tier of companies in the industry are the small technical shops established around Washington to provide specialized technology or services to one or more of the intelligence agencies. They are often called "Beltway bandits" because of their proximity to the interstate highway that encircles the capital city. Since 9/11, literally thousands of such companies have started up, primarily to service the IC's enormous appetite for technology—any technology—that will help find meaning in the flood of data sweeping through the intelligence system.

"Perhaps nowhere is unstructured data piling up faster than at American security organizations tasked with winning the war on terrorism," the Chesapeake Innovation Center, a Maryland business "incubator" funded in part by the National Security Agency, said in a 2005 report.[24] "They are inundated with an unprecedented 'volume, velocity and variety,' or '3Vs,' of data, causing massive 'information overload.' " To ease that overload, the NSA might turn to a company like Attensity Inc., a California firm that was one of the first companies financed by In-Q-Tel. Its product line includes a software program called PowerDrill, which allows analysts to "drill quickly and deeply into written information and uncover important patterns and relationships, including patterns of behavior by a person or organization."[25] That might prove extremely useful to the NSA as it analyzes phone calls and dialing patterns, domestically or internationally.

The fourth tier of the intelligence contracting industry is made up of companies, large and small, that are known primarily for their achievements in information technology, communications, or satellites but have made major inroads as the Intelligence Community has opened up to contracting. Here's where we find Google, which has created a major niche by selling its powerful search engine technology to government agencies. Accenture, the global consulting company that was formerly a branch of Andersen Consulting, does financial planning and audits for intelligence agencies, and recently began providing information-sharing and collaboration tools to the IC; its customers, according to Accenture literature distributed at industry gatherings, include the NSA, the DIA, the NGA and the NRO. Microsoft sells classified versions of its operating systems to the IC and also cooperates with the NSA in such areas as encryption and computer security (if you're using a PC with Microsoft's XP system, your system was tested extensively by the NSA before it was placed on the market). BearingPoint, another major federal contractor, does a considerable amount of business with the NSA.

The last tier also includes telecommunications companies, such as AT&T, which has had a long relationship with U.S. intelligence because of its leading role as a telephone and Internet services provider. It reportedly allowed the NSA to gain access to its huge customer databases as part of the Bush administration's warrantless surveillance program, when the NSA was given the power to monitor international telephone conversations involving U.S. persons—either a U.S. citizen or a foreign resident of the United States—in which one participant was considered to be a member or supporter of Al Qaeda or another terrorist group. AT&T also supplies technology and expertise to help intelligence agencies secure their communications systems and classified operations from outside attacks and intrusions. IBM is a player in the industry as well, in part as a major provider of computer systems to the Pentagon and the NSA, and in part because of its acquisition in 2005 of a company called SRD, which was funded by In-Q-Tel to help intelligence agencies track terrorists after the 9/11 attacks.

Winning a contract from an intelligence agency can be a long and arduous process, even when a company is the only bidder (that's a common occurrence at the highest levels of intelligence, particularly at the NSA). The process begins at the bidding stage, where prospective contractors must have at their command a sizable number of employees with high-level security clearances. That has made security clearances—and the people who hold them—a precious commodity. "Top security clearances are actually marketable," says Robert Baer, the former CIA officer. As a result, contractor executives frequently begin presentations to investors with facts about their workforce. At a 2006 conference on defense and homeland security investing that I attended, the numbers on cleared employees flew like statistics at a ball game: at CACI, 70 percent of its employees held top secret clearances; at SI International and NCI Information Systems, which both hold NSA contracts, the figures were 83 percent and 65 percent, respectively.

New companies to the market must also be prepared for a lengthy procurement process made worse by the "risk-adverse, slow-moving bureaucracies" in the Intelligence Community, warns John Elstner, the founding CEO of the Chesapeake Innovation Center.[26] The slow pace works to the advantage of incumbent contractors and is "especially onerous" for small companies that "may not have the resources to last several months" of procurement meetings, says Elstner, who is now the managing director of the Convergent Security Group, a Maryland investment firm that raises capital for homeland security and intelligence contractors.

But once a contract is signed, a company can be assured of strong revenues well into the future. "Intelligence is a very robust market because the contracts are typically very long—at least five to ten years," says Steve Waechter, who was the chief financial officer at CACI International from 1999 to 2007. "That makes intelligence a very attractive place to invest." * And once a company is ensconced at an agency, a long-term relationship is almost assured because the government becomes reliant on that service. "If you're really doing something mission-critical and you take over that function for the government, it's pretty hard to replace you if you're doing a good job," explains Thomas E. Dunn, the executive vice president and chief financial officer of SI International, a key NSA contractor. "And, frankly, [officials] are not motivated to do that."[27]

---

* There's a flip side to this: because contracting is dependent on government budgets, predicting future revenues can be tricky. Waechter discovered this the hard way. Confident that CACI would continue its winning ways, he predicted in 2006 that company earnings would likely surpass $2 billion in 2007. When that didn't happen, CACI had to downgrade its earnings predictions, leading many investors to sell and dropping the price of CACI's stock. As a result, Waechter soon found himself out of a job.

• • •

Like any other industry, the Intelligence-Industrial Complex has a distinct culture and history. As we begin to peer into different parts of the community—human intelligence, direct aid to the war-fighter, signals intelligence, imagery, and domestic security—we will notice many points in common. But one point of reference is shared by every agency: the revolving door.

Perhaps in no other area of business are former high-ranking officials as ubiquitous as they are in intelligence. From SAIC to ManTech to the smallest Beltway bandit, companies involved in the intelligence business seek out former intelligence and national security officials as both managers and directors. For the most part, these are people who have served for decades at the pinnacle of national power. Their lives have been defined by secret briefings, classified documents, covert wars, and sensitive intelligence missions. Many of them have kept their security clearances and maintain a hand in government by serving as advisers to high-level advisory bodies at the Pentagon, the CIA, the National Security Agency, and the White House.

Now, with their government careers behind them, they make their living by rendering strategic advice to the dozens of IT vendors and intelligence contractors headquartered along the banks of the Potomac River and the byways of Washington's Beltway. In these new jobs, they continue to fight terrorist threats and protect the "homeland," as they once did while working in government—but now they do it for profit, in the form of lucrative stock options, director and consultant fees, and executive salaries. By fusing their politics with business, these former officials have brought moneymaking into the highest reaches of national security and created a new class of capitalist policy-makers the likes of which have never been seen before.

Take the case of George Tenet, who retired as CIA director in 2004. As he was writing his memoirs and preparing for a new career as a professor at Georgetown University, Tenet quietly began cutting deals with companies that earn much of their revenue from contracts with the Intelligence Community. By the summer of 2007, he had made nearly $3 million in director fees and other compensation from his service as a director and adviser to four companies, including QinetiQ, the British defense research company that was privatized in 2003 and acquired by the well-known Carlyle Group.

Many of Tenet's closest aides at the CIA have gone into business as well. Joan A. Dempsey, who was Tenet's representative to the rest of the IC as the CIA's director of community management, is now a vice president of Booz Allen Hamilton, where she works with another former CIA director, R. James Woolsey. Another Tenet aide who's gone into the intelligence business is retired Air Force General John A. Gordon, the CIA's deputy director from 1996 to 2000. He is an adviser to Abraxas, a Virginia contractor that became notorious in the CIA for recruiting new employees in the CIA cafeteria, and a director of Detica Inc., a British defense and intelligence contractor that has rapidly expanded its U.S. business over the past two years.*

Connections with the private sector are especially close at the NSA, where outsourcing has grown rapidly since the late 1990s. Retired Admiral Mike McConnell went directly from his director's post at the NSA to Booz Allen, and has now jumped back to the government as director of national intelligence. Retired Air Force Lieutenant General Kenneth A. Minihan, McConnell's predecessor at the NSA, is now a member of the board of directors of six major intelligence contractors, including ManTech International, BAE Systems, and MTC Technologies Inc. Another former NSA director, William O. Studeman, was vice president of Northrop Grumman from 2002 to 2005, and Barbara McNamara, a

---

* One of the more spectacular transitions from intelligence to business has taken place at Blackwater, which operates one of the world's largest private security firms. One of its first contracts was a secret no-bid $5.4 million deal with the CIA. Within two years of signing, Blackwater hired as its vice chairman Cofer Black, the CIA's former top counterterrorism official. Days after 9/11, Black was dispatched to the White House to brief President Bush and his advisers on the CIA's plans for overthrowing the Taliban in Afghanistan; his orders to the CIA paramilitaries sent to Afghanistan were to "bring him Osama bin Laden's head on a stick." Rob Richer, the CIA's former associate deputy director of operations and, before that, head of its Near East division, became Blackwater's vice president of intelligence, and later went to work for a private intelligence company. Erik Prince, the millionaire former Navy SEAL who founded Blackwater, is reportedly on "very tight" terms with top CIA officials and meets frequently with the CIA's covert operations division. See Ken Silverstein, "Revolving Door to Blackwater Causes Alarm at CIA," *Harper's* On-Line, September 12, 2006.

former deputy director, is on the board of directors of CACI International. Essex Corporation, an important NSA contractor we will meet in Chapter 6, was founded and almost entirely staffed by former NSA officials and scientists.

Being part of the revolving door doesn't necessarily require support for the war in Iraq. Richard L. Armitage, who was deputy secretary of state during the first four years of the George W. Bush administration, is a stellar example. Armitage is best known as the "nonpartisan gunslinger" * who accidentally leaked the fact that Valerie Plame, the wife of Iraq war critic Joseph Wilson, was working undercover for the CIA. After 9/11, he was Colin Powell's closest ally during the bitter disputes inside the Bush administration over the war. His opposition to Bush's policies, however, hasn't stopped him from cashing in on his government service.

A few months after leaving the State Department in 2005, Armitage joined the board of directors of ManTech International, an important intelligence contractor that has an extensive presence in Iraq and Afghanistan. Previously, during the 1990s, he'd served on ManTech's advisory board and was also on the board of directors of CACI International, a key ManTech competitor in the market for outsourced intelligence services. More recently, Armitage—who earns most of his income from his eponymous consulting firm—has become active in private equity funds, which provide much of the venture capital for intelligence start-ups. From 2005 to 2007, Armitage was on the Defense and Aerospace Advisory Council of Veritas Capital, which owns DynCorp International and several other military and intelligence contractors. In 2007, he joined the advisory board of DC Capital Partners, a defense- and intelligence-oriented buyout firm with some $200 million in assets. One of its first acquisitions after Armitage came on board was Omen Inc., a Maryland company that provides IT services to the NSA; the fund has since combined Omen with two other acquisitions to form a new company called National Interests Security Company LLC, which

* The actual term was "not a partisan gunslinger." That's how columnist Robert Novak described Armitage, then an anonymous source, in the story that exposed Valerie Plame as a CIA officer working under nonofficial cover as a financial consultant.

will have more than 350 employees, many of them with top secret or higher security clearances.[28]*

In all of these positions, Armitage is in good company. ManTech's board includes two former high-ranking intelligence officials: Richard J. Kerr, a thirty-two-year veteran of the CIA, where he last served as deputy director; and retired Vice Admiral David E. Jeremiah, the former vice chairman of Colin Powell's Joint Chiefs of Staff, who now sits on the President's Foreign Intelligence Advisory Board and is a paid adviser to the National Reconnaissance Office. At DC Capital, his fellow advisers include Jeffrey Smith, the CIA's former general counsel. And at Veritas Capital, he rubbed shoulders with retired Army General Barry McCaffrey and retired Marine Corps General Anthony Zinni.

Former high-ranking officials bring tremendous value to a government contractor seeking new work or a private equity fund looking for companies to buy. "You understand the decision-making process inside the Beltway, and that is liquid gold," said Roger Cressey, who worked in President Clinton's National Security Council as deputy director of counterterrorism and is now a partner in Good Harbor Consulting, a company he founded with his former boss at the NSC, Richard Clarke. Cressey, who is a terrorism consultant for NBC News, adds that the influence of a retired official lasts only a limited period of time after he or she leaves office. "You have eighteen to twenty-four months to translate your Rolodex into real services," he told an intelligence conference in 2005.[29]

But the value of a CIA director or national security official goes much further than a Rolodex. Because high-ranking officials have been privy to classified and top secret information for years, they have details

---

* There was a touch of irony in this. During Armitage's time at the State Department, his open battles with the neoconservative hawks around President Bush and Vice President Dick Cheney became legendary inside Washington. According to the *Washington Post*'s Bob Woodward, Armitage advised Powell on more than one occasion to tell the neocons to "go fuck themselves," and, at one point, even refused to deliver a speech about Iraq drafted for him by Cheney's office. "Armitage exceeds even his own former boss and current best friend Colin Powell in visceral hatred of the neoconservatives," Christopher Hitchens, the cranky British columnist for *Vanity Fair,* once wrote ("The End of the Affair," *Slate,* July 17, 2006). Yet here he was, two years after those battles, working for companies making money directly from the war his former nemeses had started. Whichever side Armitage was on, he'd clearly learned an important lesson: you don't need a neocon to know which way the wind blows.

about intelligence programs, covert operations, and the internal affairs of other countries that few others can claim. George Tenet, for example, has extensive inside knowledge about intelligence services in Saudi Arabia, the United Kingdom, and Pakistan, as well as secret U.S. operations in Iraq, Afghanistan, and Somalia; that would be extremely useful information for companies hoping to win contracts from the CIA, the NSA, and other agencies working in those countries.

Booz Allen's Joan Dempsey received some of her early training as a naval intelligence officer listening to Soviet bomber and submarine traffic at Misawa Air Base in Japan, a key NSA listening post. During that time, she told an industry reception in 2004, her agency fought "huge battles" with the NSA over information sharing. Her Naval Security Group, she said, "wanted to get near real-time intelligence we were collecting on the Soviet fleet out to our naval battle groups operating in the Pacific, but NSA felt that dissemination would put its sources at risk. That was my first experience with data owners believing that controlling intelligence was more important than using it." Experiences like that would be valuable to Booz Allen, where Dempsey advises the Office of the DNI on these very issues.[30]

Moving back and forth between industry and government is a long tradition in Washington, and perfectly legal: the only restriction senior government officials face in accepting private sector employment is a one-year prohibition from contacting their agency. But that, many analysts say, is a thin reed of protection for a public concerned about undue influence on the political process. "The way they get around some of this is, you don't get hired, you go on the board," says Lawrence Korb, a former assistant secretary of defense with the administration of Ronald Reagan. When someone is placed on a board of directors, Korb explains, "you don't even need the lobbying restriction because, theoretically, you're not working for the company, you're on the board."[31]

Inside the industry, former high-ranking officials like Tenet and Dempsey are seen as rainmakers—that is, as people with the knowledge and contacts to bring in contracts from government agencies. The key to understanding contracting, I was told, is that it's not about agencies contracting with a company so much as an agency contracting with an individual they know and trust; in a sense, the company is irrelevant. "Contracting officers contract with individuals," said R. J. Hillhouse, who studied the intelligence contracting industry for several years in preparation for writing her espionage thriller, *Outsourced*. "When that person moves, his contract niche moves with him, unless overridden by a boss who likes someone else better. So it's not about favoring large or small companies, but which ones are able to attract a rainmaker."[32]

An industry insider described to me how the system worked. "To compete and win, the primes hire former top government and military officials in business development roles," said the insider, who spoke to me in May 2007 on the condition of anonymity. "That's how the game is played. It's all about relationships. Without them, any government contractor will go out of business, no matter how good its product or service is. Tenet was not hired by a contractor because he's smart. He was hired because he still has relationships, influence, access, and favors to call in." (Tenet, through a spokesman, declined to comment, and his co-author and spokesperson, Bill Harlow, told me all of Tenet's business ties "were a matter of public record.")

As we'll soon see in Chapter 3, intelligence contracting is best understood as part of the federal government's embrace of outsourcing and the Pentagon's use of private firms to carry out some of the tasks of war fighting and empire building. Intelligence "is like everything else," says David Isenberg, an independent national security analyst who has closely studied the phenomenon of military contracting. "In the new, slimmed-down post–Cold War military, the phrase of art is, we will concentrate on our core competencies, and anything other than firing an artillery round, firing a tank, firing an M-16, or dropping a bomb is not a core competency. Everything else is up for grabs."[33]

The fruits of that philosophy can be seen most clearly in the Middle East. Over the past six years, corporate names such as Halliburton, Bechtel, and Blackwater have become as familiar to the public as the mountain villages of Korea and the jungle hamlets of Vietnam were to earlier generations of Americans. In Iraq and Afghanistan, the enormously complex job of nation building was outsourced to these and other large U.S. corporations—a practice that would have been unthinkable during the postwar occupations of Japan and Germany, which were planned years in advance.

And as the war intensified in Iraq, escalating into a full-blown insurgency in 2003, the Pentagon turned to private military companies to provide basic security to U.S. diplomats and the contractors supporting the occupation. Today, more than 180,000 civilians, including Americans, foreigners, and Iraqis, are working in Iraq under contract to the U.S. government, compared to 160,000 U.S. soldiers, and a few thousand civilian government employees.[34] In September 2007, in a notorious incident that underscored the dangers of relying on private security forces, a squad of armed security guards working for Blackwater USA opened fire on a car carrying civilians in downtown Baghdad, killing nearly two dozen people.

Meanwhile, back on the home front, the government has relied on contractors to manage everything from hurricane relief to border security. Some of the same companies hired by the Bush administration to rebuild Iraq's infrastructure were sent by the Department of Homeland Security to rebuild New Orleans and the Gulf Coast after Hurricane Katrina; neither plan succeeded, and both were suffused with cost overruns and corruption. The big defense contractors that build and operate classified IT systems for the Intelligence Community provide the same products and software for the Department of Homeland Security, which spends more than half of its $42-billion budget for outsourced services.

By 2007, contractors were so ubiquitous in Washington that they had become a virtual shadow government, and the total number of contracts was valued at $400 billion a year—more than double what it was in 2000. Even the government's online database for tracking contracts, the Federal Procurement Data System, had been outsourced.[35] With 40 percent of the federal workforce expected to retire between 2007 and 2012, contractors believe that these trends could continue almost indefinitely. The government "must outsource as a means of survival," Kenneth C. Dahlberg, SAIC's chairman and chief executive, assured investors in a 2007 conference call. Because the federal government "must deliver safety to the people," Dahlberg added, the market for government outsourcing is likely to increase 3 to 5 percent a year well into the decade.

The recent big surge in intelligence contracting was fueled by record spending on national security programs after September 11, 2001. The Bush administration and Congress, determined to prevent further terrorist attacks, ordered a major increase in intelligence spending and organized new institutions to fight the war on terror, such as the NCTC. To beef up these organizations, the CIA and other agencies were authorized to hire thousands of analysts and human intelligence specialists. Partly because of budget and personnel cuts made during the 1990s, however, many of the people with the skills and security clearances to do that work were in the private sector. As a result, contracting grew by leaps and bounds as intelligence agencies rushed to fill the gap.

Timothy R. Sample, a former CIA case officer and the executive director of the Intelligence and National Security Alliance, blames decisions made by the George H. W. Bush and Bill Clinton administrations for that gap. "After the Cold War, we as a government decided, wrongly I think, to build down our intelligence capability, and we have yet to recover from that," he says—a view shared by many of his colleagues. "So when people get excited and react to the level of contracting within the IC, they tend to forget that, especially post-9/11, the major issue was speed," he adds. "After 9/11, where do you go? You go to where that expertise resides when government decided it didn't need you anymore, and that's within industry. So I have a hard time with the concept that massive contracting for intelligence is a problem."[36] (Sample speaks from experience: he left the CIA to take a job with General Dynamics Information Technology, a major CIA contractor.)

But technology played a crucial role as well. By the 1990s, commercial developments in encryption, information technology, imagery, and satellites had outpaced the government's considerable efforts in these areas, and intelligence agencies began to turn to the private sector for technologies they had once created and developed in-house. "At the end of the day, outsourcing ended up being a reaction to the reality of the marketplace," says Stan Soloway, the executive director of the Professional Services Council, the primary lobby for federal contractors. "Over the last thirty-five years, the ownership of technology has changed almost entirely in this country, from primarily government-driven and government-run, to privately created and privately owned. When that happens, the workforce and the skill sets typically go with it. If you wanted to do development science in the old days, you'd go to NASA or the Defense Department. Now you can go to any one of hundreds of R&D firms around the country." The government, he says, is "now competing in the open market for talent with everybody else."[37]

But, as we shall see, the problem with this "open market" is that contractors, whether in intelligence, defense, or homeland security, owe their allegiance to their company, and not the taxpayer. "There's something civil servants have that the private sector doesn't," David M. Walker, the comptroller general of the United States, told the *New York Times* in an extraordinary interview in 2007. "And that is the duty of loyalty to the greater good—the duty of loyalty to the collective best interest of all rather than the interest of a few. Companies have duties of loyalty to their shareholders, not to the country."[38]

Ironically, the Intelligence Community, one of the government's largest users of contractors, has reached the same conclusion. Among the many slides posted by the Defense Intelligence Agency during its May 2007 conference on acquisition was one titled "Government Employee vs. Contractor Employee." Two items were high on the first list: people working for the government, the DIA said, had a "fiduciary obligation to serve the public good" and "no profit motive." In contrast, contractors have a "fiduciary duty to [their] employer only," and operate out of a "profit motive." At a time when the Intelligence Community is under fire for politicizing intelligence, those are critical differences.

"It's hard enough for a government analyst to tell it like it is and be just one step removed from the president," says Raymond McGovern, a twenty-seven-year veteran of the CIA's analytic division who once delivered the CIA's daily briefing to President George H. W. Bush. "But think how much more difficult it is for an analyst who's working for Booz

Allen Hamilton or SAIC. There's pressure there; there's much more freedom for people to tailor their analysis to something they think the contracting officer would like." The problem with outsourcing is simple, he says: "Contractors are in it for the money."[39] If that is the case, few companies have been as skilled in profiting from intelligence as Booz Allen Hamilton. That's where we begin our story.

2

Booz Allen Hamilton and "The Shadow IC"

WHEN MIKE MCCONNELL was appointed by President George W. Bush as the director of national intelligence in January 2007, he appeared to be the ideal candidate to replace John Negroponte, the first DNI, a diplomat more accustomed to the public art of statesmanship than to the dark and dirty worlds of espionage and surveillance. In contrast, McConnell's spying credentials were impeccable: for five years during the Clinton administration, he had been the director of the National Security Agency and, before that, had served as Colin Powell's chief intelligence officer when Powell headed the Joint Chiefs of Staff during the first Gulf War. McConnell had also worked closely with Vice President Dick Cheney during his earlier incarnation as secretary of defense, and Cheney, President Bush's viceroy for intelligence matters, had played a critical role in his appointment as DNI.

Part of McConnell's attraction to Cheney was his background in military operations. McConnell had devoted his career to expanding the reach of intelligence to front-line soldiers, and was perfectly aligned with the Pentagon's strategy to harness the NSA and the other national collection agencies in providing overhead imagery and signals intelligence to war-fighters on the ground in Iraq and Afghanistan. The admiral's martial background won strong praise from President Bush, who introduced McConnell to the nation as a man with "decades of experience ensuring that our military forces had the intelligence they need to fight and win wars."[1] Bush further noted that his new DNI had "worked with the Congress and with the White House to strengthen our defenses against threats to our information systems," and said McConnell would offer "the best information and analysis that America's intelligence community can provide." Intentional or not, however, the president failed to mention the most significant part of the retired admiral's experience.

McConnell is the first contractor ever to be named to lead the Intelligence Community. Never, in the sixty years since the creation of the CIA and the national security state in 1947, has someone gone directly from a top position with industry into the most senior leadership position in the nation's spy system. A transition of this sort would have been notable in any era; but at a time when 70 percent of the U.S. intelligence budget was being spent on contracts, it was highly significant. Moreover, McConnell didn't come from just any company: during the ten years prior to his appointment, he had worked for Booz Allen Hamilton, one of the nation's premier intelligence contractors.

As executive vice president, McConnell had managed Booz Allen's extensive assignments in military intelligence and consulted with a wide range of clients, including U.S. Unified Combatant Commands and the directors of the three national collection agencies: the NSA, the National Geospatial-Intelligence Agency, and the National Reconnaissance Office. Even the Office of the DNI, which had steadfastly refused to say how extensive contracting had become by the time of McConnell's appointment, was forced to concede that Booz Allen was a "huge" supplier of intelligence contracting.[2]

McConnell, a tall, bookish man from South Carolina who speaks with a slight Southern drawl, briefly alluded to his private sector experience after being sworn in as DNI in a ceremony at Bolling Air Force Base on February 20, 2007. "My work over the past ten years after leaving government has allowed me to stay focused on the national security and intelligence communities as a strategist and as a consultant," he said. "Therefore, in many respects, I never left."[3] But that was a vast understatement: under McConnell's watch, Booz Allen, as we'll see in this chapter, was directly involved in the most sensitive initiatives taken by U.S. intelligence and the Pentagon during the war on terror.

McConnell, in other words, was not a mere consultant: he and his company were high-ranking players in a community where power was shared, almost equally, between the private sector and the agents of the state. By appointing McConnell to run the Intelligence Community, Bush and Cheney sent a powerful signal to the rest of the government, particularly the Department of Defense, that private corporations were now the de facto managers of the nation's intelligence system. McConnell's actions since taking the post only deepened that perception. His firm, and the company he would keep, are the natural starting places for our study of the privatization of U.S. intelligence.

Booz Allen Hamilton was founded in 1914 in Chicago by three businessmen who gave the firm its name. In 1940, after more than three decades as a consultant to the top-ranking companies in America's manufacturing economy, it started working for the U.S. military. According to a corporate history posted on its Web site, Booz Allen was hired that year by the Navy and Army "to help prepare the nation for war, and later for peace," and during World War II, it used "leading-edge management principles to help the US government run its war effort." In 1947, Booz Allen got its first Air Force contract, which led to millions of dollars in consulting work in electronic intelligence and for major aircraft manufacturers. Over the next fifty years, the company would be involved in every aspect of national security, from the military to the highest reaches of national intelligence. By 2006, the privately held company had a global staff of 18,000 and annual revenues of $3.7 billion.* Work for U.S. government agencies now accounts for more than 50 percent of its business.[4]

---

* Booz Allen is involved as a consultant in more than twenty industries, from energy to chemicals to consumer goods. But it seems most at home advising governments on how to out-

Throughout the period of the Cold War, Booz Allen was involved in U.S. government efforts to win "hearts and minds" in developing countries where anti-colonial movements threatened U.S. economic and political interests. In 1953, Booz Allen was hired by the U.S. Agency for International Development (AID) to study and reorganize land ownership records in the Philippines. The study was carried out just after the CIA, under the direction of Edward Lansdale, a CIA case officer who had served in the Philippines during World War II, led a campaign for the Philippine government to defeat the Huks, a revolutionary movement that drew its strength from landless peasants.* Long after this brutal campaign, the Philippines remained an important focus for Booz Allen. In 1984, under a contract with the CIA, Booz Allen was paying academics to gather information about the New People's Army, the armed wing of the Maoist Communist Party of the Philippines.[5]

Later, the company brought its social network analysis—the mapping and measuring of relationships between people, social organizations, and governments—to Central America. Just before U.S. forces were dispatched to Haiti during a period of intense social unrest in 1994, the Pentagon's Atlantic Command commissioned Booz Allen to devise a computer model of Haitian society. The model, according to an extensive report published in *The Nation* magazine, sought to identify Haitian organizations that might oppose the U.S. invasion. It was seen by human rights groups as part of a U.S. "divide-and-conquer strategy" designed to weaken grassroots leftist groups and shore up "moderate" forces that welcomed a long-term U.S. presence.[6] During the first Gulf War, Booz Allen developed a similar "Power Relationship Matrix" on Iraqi society for the U.S. Central Command.

Booz Allen's engagement with Iraq dates back to the 1950s, and

---

source public agencies. The company contracts with governments all over the world, with the bulk of its clients in Europe and Asia. Its services, it says on its Web site, are "increasingly valuable" outside the United States "as government-led monopoly operations privatize and begin to compete in both their local markets and the global market." Privatization is Booz Allen's watchword at home as well, particularly in its dealings with the Department of Defense.

* Roy Prosterman, a controversial U.S. academic who managed that program and later introduced U.S.-style land reform to South Vietnam and El Salvador, was hired by Booz Allen in the 1990s to conduct an AID study of land rights in post-communist Moldova.

involves one of the most colorful characters in the history of U.S. intelligence—Miles Copeland. Copeland was a trumpet player and jazz musician who was recruited into the Office of Strategic Services (OSS), the precursor to the CIA, in 1941. After World War II, Copeland joined the CIA and was assigned to the Middle East, where he spent much of his career as a CIA operative in Syria (where he was the CIA station chief), Egypt, Lebanon, Iran, and Iraq. For much of that time, according to his own and other accounts, Copeland was employed by Booz Allen Hamilton, where he worked under "nonofficial cover" for the CIA. (Booz Allen could not locate any records on Copeland and informed me that "his tenure is too old for us to confirm.")

One of Copeland's first jobs in the Middle East was to install a pro-American colonel as the leader of Syria.[7] A few years later, he reorganized parts of the Egyptian government on behalf of Egyptian President Gamal Abdel Nasser. During the 1950s, as Nasser's status rose throughout the Arab world, Copeland was "loaned" to Nasser by the CIA to organize the Egyptian secret intelligence service, the Mukhabarat. He "soon became Nasser's closest western adviser," according to a biography of Copeland posted on the Web site of his son and namesake, who is a well-known entertainment executive.[8] While working for Booz Allen, the senior Copeland was also involved in the CIA-engineered 1953 overthrow of the Mossadegh government in Iran and helped the CIA bring Saddam Hussein and the Baath Party to power in Iraq in 1963.

Copeland is also credited with organizing some of the first war games in the U.S. Intelligence Community. As head of a five-man political action unit in Washington, he ran a "games room" where international problems, particularly those concerning the Middle East, could be played out. War games remain one of Booz Allen's specialties; former CIA director James Woolsey, Booz Allen's expert on protecting critical infrastructure from terrorist attacks, has run several such scenarios for Booz Allen's corporate clients and the Department of Homeland Security.*

* After his retirement, Copeland published several best-selling books, and in 1988 wrote an article ("Spooks for Bush") endorsing George H. W. Bush for president. Although he criticized CIA paramilitary operations like the Bay of Pigs, he ended his life as an unapologetic

Booz Allen describes itself as "the one firm that helps government and commercial clients solve their toughest problems with services in strategy, operations, organization and change, and information technology." The largest part of its business is supporting U.S. national security clients, including the Intelligence Community and the Department of Defense.[9] That work increased substantially after McConnell was hired to manage the company's military intelligence business in 1996. Since then, its contracts with the U.S. government have risen dramatically, from $626,000 in 2000 to $1.6 billion in 2006. Most of the latter figure, $932 million, was with the Department of Defense, where Booz Allen's major customers included the NSA, the Army, the Air Force, the Defense Logistics Agency, and the National Guard. In 2006, it was one of seven firms awarded a ten-year contract to bid on up to $20 billion worth of work in command, control, communications, computers, intelligence, surveillance, and reconnaisance—a mouthful of a term usually referred to as C4ISR—for the Army's Communications and Electronics Command, which is based in Fort Monmouth, New Jersey. "From Army Transformation, to current operations, to the Global War on Terror—we will provide results that endure for our Army clients," Booz Allen vice president Gary Mather boasted in a press release.[10]

But it is in intelligence that Booz Allen has made its mark. In 2002, *Information Week* reported that Booz Allen had more than one thousand former intelligence officers on its staff.[11] Four years later, I asked the company if it could confirm that number or provide a more accurate one, and received an answer from spokesman George Farrar by e-mail: "It is certainly possible, but as a privately held corporation we consider that information to be proprietary and do not disclose." Buried deep on the company's Web site, however, I found an explanation of a Booz Allen IT contract with the Defense Intelligence Agency, which carries out intelligence for the Joint Chiefs of Staff and the Office of the Secre-

---

supporter of the agency and U.S. foreign policy in general. "I am 100 percent capitalist and imperialist, a believer in Mom, apple pie, baseball, the corner drugstore, and even American-style democracy for us, even if I doubt its relevance in many of the alien cultures in which I've worked," he wrote in his autobiography, *The Game Player*.

tary of Defense. It stated that the Booz Allen team "employs more than 10,000 TS/SCI cleared personnel." TS/SCI stands for Top Secret/ Sensitive Compartmented Information, the highest possible security rating in the IC. This would make Booz Allen one of the largest employers of cleared personnel in the United States. Booz Allen has "the biggest chunk of recent former CIA people of any of the corporations" involved in contracting, says John Gannon, the former director of the CIA's National Intelligence Council, who is now a senior executive with BAE Systems, a major competitor with Booz Allen.[12]

Booz Allen's executive ranks are filled with people with decades of experience in the Intelligence Community. Keith Hall, one of the company's three hundred vice presidents (who are the primary owners of the privately held company),[13] is emblematic of this trend. He began his career as a U.S. Army intelligence officer, and later served as a professional staffer of the Senate Select Committee on Intelligence. In the early 1990s, he was hired by the CIA, where he managed budgets and policy development for Director of Central Intelligence Robert Gates; during that time, as we will see, he played an instrumental role in creating the National Imagery and Mapping Agency, which was later renamed the National Geospatial-Intelligence Agency. He then moved to the Pentagon, where he was deputy assistant secretary of defense for intelligence and security.

During the Clinton administration, Hall was named assistant secretary of the Air Force for space programs and, simultaneously, director of the NRO, the agency that manages the nation's military satellite program. Since 2002, when he left the government, he has led a "strategic intelligence initiative" at Booz Allen that integrates the company's extensive contracting activities for the NRO and the NGA. One of his most important tasks involved chairing the 2005 homeland security study group mentioned earlier, which recommended to the government a major expansion of information and data sharing between U.S. spy agencies and the FBI and domestic law enforcement. Without such a plan, Hall wrote, the "ultimate effect" would be "missed opportunities to collect, exploit and disseminate domestic information critical to fighting the war on terrorism, preparing for, responding to, and recovering from disasters natural and man-made." [14] That report later formed the basis of a plan, put in place at the DNI by McConnell in 2007, to allow the NGA to share classified imagery with the FBI and other domestic agencies.

Woolsey, the former director of the CIA, was another key hire from the Intelligence Community. In 2002, he was brought in as a vice president in Booz Allen's Global Strategic Security service, where his job is to work with the CEOs of major corporations to integrate security into their strategic business planning. (Woolsey's team, the company notes, includes "former leaders of the nation's highest security and intelligence agencies, as well as experts in cyber-security, global-supply chain management and wargame-scenario planning." [15])

Woolsey also provides an important link to the foreign policy apparatus of the George W. Bush administration. He is one of the chief ideologists of the neoconservative movement behind Bush's aggressive military and national security policies, and is famous in Washington for his fanatical devotion to the cause of regime change in Iraq and his outspoken views on the war on terror, which he describes in apocalyptic terms as "World War IV." His political views brought important dividends to Booz Allen: from 2001 to 2006, he was a key member of Donald Rumsfeld's Defense Policy Board. Shortly after the 9/11 attacks, he was dispatched by Paul Wolfowitz, then Rumsfeld's deputy, to Europe to find a connection between Saddam Hussein and the events of 9/11. He also served for five years on an advisory group that met monthly with former CIA director George Tenet to discuss policy issues. Through Woolsey, Booz Allen had a ringside seat on the war on terror and the invasion of Iraq, which created enormous contracting opportunities for the consulting firm and its many corporate clients.*

---

* Woolsey is also the chairman and chief spokesman for the reborn Committee on the Present Danger, a right-wing policy group that advocates "total victory" in the war against terrorism, and was a founding member and senior adviser to the Libby Legal Defense Trust, a group of conservatives who raised money to help former Cheney adviser I. Lewis "Scooter" Libby defend himself against charges that he lied to a grand jury investigating the outing of former CIA operative Valerie Plame. (Woolsey definitely puts his money where his mouth is: in addition to his job at Booz Allen, he sits on the boards of several prominent defense-oriented information technology firms, and is a principal with the Paladin Capital Group, the

Perhaps the most representative of Booz Allen's intelligence elite is Joan Dempsey, a career U.S. intelligence official who was hired in 2005 as a Booz Allen vice president. Dempsey, a steely-looking blonde, rose up the ranks to become one of the few women in the top tier of the Intelligence Community. Over the years, she slowly worked her way up the intelligence chain of command at the Pentagon, from Naval Intelligence to the Defense Intelligence Agency. In 1997, she was appointed deputy assistant secretary of defense for intelligence and security in the Clinton administration, the highest civilian intelligence position in the Department of Defense at the time. There, she had responsibility over the NSA, the NGA, and the NRO, the three national collection agencies controlled by the Pentagon, as well as the DoD's tactical command, control, communications, and intelligence (C3I) efforts.

In 1998, Dempsey was chosen by CIA director George Tenet as his deputy director of community management, where her primary job was to protect the pet technical projects of the national intelligence agencies from congressional budget-cutters. In 1999, she won the everlasting support of those agencies—and their growing armies of contractors—when she led negotiations with the Republican-led Congress that added $1.2 billion to the intelligence budget—one of the largest single-year increases in the history of the National Foreign Intelligence Program. Five years later, in recognition of this feat, Dempsey was given the William O. Baker Award for meritorious intelligence service by the Security Affairs Support Association (SASA), which from 1979 to 2005 represented the largest prime contractors at the NSA and the CIA. Her remarks at that ceremony, which were published in SASA's in-house publication, *Colloquy*, underscored the close ties between contractors and the Intelligence Community and serve as a kind of leitmotif for the outsourcing phenomenon in intelligence.

---

first private equity fund to focus exclusively on the homeland security marketplace.) Other former intelligence officials at Booz Allen include Dale Watson, the former counterterrorism director at the FBI, and Richard Wilhelm, the first director of the NSA's Information Warfare office. Booz Allen's work for the Pentagon and other global defense clients is managed by Dov Zakheim, who served in Rumsfeld's Pentagon as comptroller and chief financial officer from 2001 to 2004.

In her acceptance speech, Dempsey paid effusive praise to the corporations she had known over the years, many of whom had purchased tables for the event: General Dynamics, Essex Corporation, Oracle Corporation, Computer Sciences Corporation, AT&T Government Solutions, ManTech International, and Lockheed Martin.[16] She thanked her "Pentagon friends" from L-3 Communications Inc., the nation's sixth largest defense contractor, with whom she had worked "on my favorite program of all time, the U-2" spy plane. She spoke of her pride in working with the Boeing Company on the Future Imagery Architecture, an expensive project by the NRO and the NGA to build and operate the next generation of imagery satellites.* At the CIA, Dempsey said, she had "benefited enormously" from her work with Booz Allen Hamilton and SAIC.

Then she went slightly off-script: "I like to call Booz Allen the Shadow IC," she said, because it has "more former secretaries of this and directors of that" than the entire government. That must have caused some chuckles at the lead table, where Woolsey was sitting. But Dempsey got the last laugh. Fifteen months later, she joined the "Shadow IC" herself as a vice president. In her job at Booz Allen, she "provides strategy consulting services to the US government, including the national security and civil sectors, as well as commercial industry," according to company spokesman George Farrar. Then, in January 2007, Dempsey's joke came full circle when McConnell, her boss at Booz Allen, succeeded John Negroponte as director of national intelligence. In the space of a few years, Booz Allen had been transformed from a "shadow" IC into the real thing.

It was most intriguing, then, to hear what Dempsey is actually doing in her new job. In the spring of 2006, just a few months after she joined the consulting firm, Dempsey was invited to speak to a seminar on intelligence reform at Harvard University.[17] Asked to describe her role at the company, Dempsey disclosed that her office at Booz Allen was evaluat-

---

* The future imagery project was killed in 2005 after a loss of more than $4 billion. See Philip Taubman, "In Death of Spy Satellite Program, Lofty Plans and Unrealistic Bids," *New York Times*, November 11, 2007.

ing the entire decision-making process within the intelligence community. After going to her fellow Booz Allen vice presidents "who control the money and got investment dollars to do this," said Dempsey, she began "studying the implications of the many decisions that are being made on a daily basis right now all over the intelligence community and the departments in which pieces of the community reside, to include the DNI's staff. No one has thought through the implications of those decisions in a strategic or aggregate sense for the future." The problem, she explained, is that the DNI's staff is "putting out dictates daily on things that it wants the community to do." Booz Allen is aiding that process by "trying to forecast what they mean for the intelligence community of the future—what it's going to look like, how it's going to operate—along a trend line."

It was a remarkable circumstance: Booz Allen was conducting a study for the director of national intelligence, a position that was about to be filled by one of the company's own—Mike McConnell. The shadow IC was now helping the real IC prepare for an immediate future when the real IC would be led by the shadow IC. This was more than a revolving door: the private and the public sides of intelligence were now sharing the same room.

McConnell came to Booz Allen in 1995 after a long career in Naval Intelligence. He began his service in Vietnam as an officer on a riverboat operating in the Mekong Delta. Later, he was assigned to Navy counterintelligence work in Yokosuka, Japan, home of the U.S. Seventh Fleet. He liked the work, and by the late 1970s was serving as an intelligence officer on ships stationed in the Persian Gulf and Indian Ocean. That's where he was introduced to the esoteric world of signals intelligence, SIGINT. His Navy experience "changed my understanding, respect for, and use of SIGINT for the rest of my life," he told the author James Bamford.[18] McConnell later served as commander of the Navy's Middle East Force Operations and as a top assistant to the director of naval intelligence. He first gained national attention when he was working in the Pentagon for Colin Powell and Dick Cheney during the administration of the first President Bush. His work during the Gulf War so impressed the two men that, when Admiral William Studeman left his director's job at the NSA in 1992 to take a position at the CIA, Cheney ordered the Pentagon to elevate McConnell from a one-star admiral to a three-star vice admiral so he could take Studeman's place at the top secret agency. It was one of the fastest career boosts in Navy history, and sparked a long friendship between McConnell and the future vice president.[19] Fifteen years later, when McConnell was considering the DNI position in the administration of the second President Bush, Cheney once again reached out to his former aide with what *Newsweek* called a "direct, personal approach," and convinced him to take the job.[20]

McConnell took over the NSA just after the collapse of the Soviet Union and at a time of deep budget cuts in defense and intelligence. The consensus among intelligence historians is that he managed effectively and staved off deeper cuts,[21] but some critics claim that he allowed R&D efforts to stall as a result. At the NSA, McConnell developed a deep interest in information security, which is one of the primary tasks of the agency. According to Booz Allen, McConnell was one of the first officials to identify information assurance as a strategic issue "in our increasingly networked society." People who worked with him say that he understood before many of his peers how the development of the Internet would affect intelligence and counterintelligence. That was important during his most trying years at the NSA, when McConnell presided over a contentious debate with the telecommunications and computer industries over export controls on encryption technology that the NSA wanted to impose on business.

Encryption is the process of transforming information into codes so it can't be read by outsiders, and makes it possible for spies, armies, banks, retailers, and individuals to share confidential information and transact business affairs electronically. Until the late 1970s, the NSA was the sole source of advanced cryptology used in the United States, and provided the secure communications links used by the White House, the Department of Defense, other intelligence agencies, and the diplomatic corps to transmit private and classified messages. By the early 1990s, however, U.S. and foreign computer manufacturers had developed encryption chips so sophisticated that the NSA was having trouble cracking the codes for intelligence purposes; in response, the Clinton administration, with McConnell in the lead, barred U.S. companies from exporting the technology. That put the U.S. firms at a disadvantage over their Japanese and European competitors, who had no such restraints. In the end, McConnell and the NSA settled for a compromise that allowed U.S. companies such as IBM and AT&T to export sophisticated encryption systems so long as they provided the government with "keys" that would allow the NSA to access the systems under a lawful court order.

That experience would serve McConnell well. A few months after leaving the NSA in 1996, McConnell was hired by Booz Allen as a senior vice president. During his first years at the company, his work primarily involved issues revolving around protecting "critical infrastructure," such as the nation's transportation and communications networks. McConnell led the firm's support to President Clinton's Commission on Critical Infrastructure Protection, which focused on the vulnerabilities of the banking and financial sector, and worked closely with the Pentagon and the NSA on defending the nation's computer networks from hostile attacks. On a trip to Australia in 2003, he warned that, without a "cyber-9/11" or "something that serves as a forcing issue," governments and businesses would not be prepared for an attack on their information systems. "We are inviting cyber terrorism," he said.[22] Altogether, McConnell's cyber-security team won nearly $300 million in government contracts for Booz Allen.[23]

At the time of his trip to Australia, McConnell was director of Booz Allen's Infrastructure Assurance Center of Excellence, the company's research laboratory for the Intelligence Community. The center is just one piece of an extensive intelligence contracting operation that provides expertise to the IC in nearly every aspect of spying, or what is known as the "black" world. Topics available for research, according to the intelligence page on Booz Allen's Web site, include information warfare, signals intelligence, systems engineering and solutions, multisource intelligence analysis, imagery and geospatial systems, cryptographic design and analysis, systems integration, and "outsourcing/privatization strategy and planning." Much of that work is done for the NSA. Under McConnell, Booz Allen was hired by his former agency to manage the largest intelligence outsourcing project ever undertaken by the IC: the $3-billion Project Groundbreaker, which rebuilt the agency's internal communications systems (this project is described in detail later).

The terrorist attacks of September 11, 2001, underscored Booz Allen's deep connections to the military. Three Booz Allen consultants meeting with Army clients were killed when the hijacked commercial airliner crashed into the Pentagon. The tragedy quickly became opportunity, however. In the months after the attacks, Booz Allen substantially increased its defense and intelligence work and moved aggressively to capture both public and private contracts in homeland security. Ralph Shrader, Booz Allen's CEO, described the response in the company's 2002 annual report. Within hours of the attacks, he recalled, "our officers and staff fanned out through Washington, helping clients ranging from the Department of Defense to the Federal Bureau of Investigation deal with an abruptly and forever-changed environment." That work, he said, included helping the Department of Justice "redirect scarce resources to counterterrorism efforts" and aiding the Immigration and Naturalization Service as it prepared a new visa policy.

At the Pentagon, Booz Allen had a strong ally in Donald Rumsfeld, who ran the Department of Defense for the first six years of the Bush administration and came to the office with intimate knowledge of Booz Allen's capabilities. In the 1970s, as director of the Office of Economic Opportunity during Richard Nixon's administration, he had hired Booz Allen to reorganize OEO and kill or outsource many of its programs. Under Rumsfeld, Booz Allen was so trusted that it was hired in 2004 to help prepare President Bush's national defense budget[24] and to perform war gaming for the Quadrennial Defense Review, one of the most sensitive documents produced by the Pentagon. The company also provided assessments of the U.S. space industrial base and performed "cybersecurity strategy, design and implementation" for the Department of Defense.[25] And as a consultant to Central Command, the company was at the center of the first preemptive war in U.S. history.

As part of its contribution to the war on terror, Booz Allen helped develop the Blue Force Tracking system, which allows the Pentagon to determine, in real time, the precise location and status of military units, vehicles, and aircraft as well as individual soldiers; the system was first used in a combat situation in Afghanistan. Booz Allen also won several Pentagon contracts in post-invasion Iraq, including as a subcontractor on a telecommunications project managed by Lucent Technologies. And in 2003, shortly after the U.S. invasion, Booz Allen organized a major conference on rebuilding Iraq that attracted hundreds of corporations eager to cash in on the billions of dollars in contracts about to be awarded by the Bush administration.

The event followed the lead of President Bush himself, who had characterized his plan to transform Iraq along free market lines as a "generational challenge" that would combine the economic scope of the Marshall Plan with the moral clarity of the civil rights movement. Held in the conference room of the Center for Strategic and International Studies in Washington, it featured a string of Pentagon and White House officials, who spelled out to the assembled businessmen how they were rewriting Iraq's business, property, and trade laws "in a way very conducive to foreign investment," as David Taylor, a top Treasury official, put it. Woolsey delivered the keynote address in the only off-the-record part of the conference. He bluntly told the assembled businessmen that American firms would receive the majority of contracts in Iraq as representatives of the only world power with the will to stage a preemptive strike on Iraq. "Basically, he said to hell with France, to hell with Germany, and to hell with the United Nations; the United States is going to do this alone," an Arab banker who asked not to be identified told me after the meeting.

The Pentagon also turned to Booz Allen to manage the controversial Total Information Awareness (TIA) plan to use information technology to counter terrorist threats. In 2002, the Defense Advanced Research Projects Agency (DARPA), the Pentagon's R&D agency, hired retired Navy Rear Admiral John Poindexter to manage a project that would sift through public databases storing credit card purchases, rental agreements, medical histories, e-mails, airline reservations, and phone calls for electronic "footprints" that might indicate a terrorist plot in the making. Poindexter was a curious choice: he'd been under a cloud since 1987, when he resigned as the national security adviser to President Reagan to take the blame for the Iran-contra scandal, which involved selling arms to Iran and using the proceeds to fund an illegal war in Nicaragua. Nevertheless, he was given a mandate that was breathtaking in scope: to "imagine, develop, apply, integrate, demonstrate and transition" IT systems that would "counter asymmetric threats"—meaning challenges from terrorist groups like Al Qaeda and insurgencies like the one in Iraq—"by achieving total information awareness." Booz Allen and Science Applications International Corporation were hired as the prime contractors, with Booz Allen winning over $63 million worth of contracts.[26] McConnell was a key figure in the outsourcing arrangement, according to a former NSA official interviewed by *Newsweek*. "I think Poindexter probably respected Mike [McConnell] and probably entrusted the TIA program to him as a result," the former official said.[27]

When TIA came to light in 2003, Congress acted quickly to defund the program. Part of the problem was the involvement of Poindexter, who had been convicted of five felony charges for his involvement in the Iran-contra affair (the convictions were later reversed on a technicality). But many lawmakers saw in TIA an attempt to create a national surveillance system. Others were shocked at Poindexter's plan to create a national betting parlor on terrorism that would harness the "anonymous forces of market capitalism" to predict the likelihood of acts of terrorism, much as commodity traders speculate on the future price of pork or electric power. The Pentagon's justification, that "markets are extremely efficient, effective and timely aggregators of dispersed and even hidden information," didn't sell, and the TIA program was killed.[28] The program was kept alive, however, in secret NSA accounts long after 2003, and remained a profit center for Booz Allen throughout McConnell's tenure.

As a trusted ally of the Bush administration, Booz Allen was also chosen to audit a secret program, run by the CIA and the Treasury Department, that gave U.S. officials access to millions of records of international financial transactions to search for terrorist-controlled money. The transactions were handled by SWIFT, a Belgium-based industry cooperative that routes trillions of dollars every day between banks, brokerages, investment houses, and other financial institutions in 208 countries around the world. In 2006, the *New York Times* revealed that, after 9/11, SWIFT had agreed to turn over large portions of its database to the CIA in response to a series of subpoenas issued by the Treasury Department.[29] Although Booz Allen was brought in as an "outside" auditor for the program, its impartiality was questioned by a European Union panel, which recommended independent supervision and declared "we don't see such independent supervision under the current situation."[30] In 2006, the American Civil Liberties Union and Privacy International, an organization that monitors government intrusion, issued a scathing report on the issue. "Though Booz Allen's role is to verify that the access to the SWIFT data is not abused, its relationship with the US government calls its objectivity significantly into question," the two organizations said.[31] Booz Allen rejected the charge. "What clients are buying from us is independence and objectivity," spokeswoman Marie Lerch told the *New York Times*.[32] But the company's close ties to the IC through such former high-ranking officials as McConnell, Dempsey, and Woolsey make it difficult to see where that independence might be found.

A more pressing issue, given the degree of collaboration between Booz Allen and the NSA, is whether McConnell and his company knowingly cooperated with the NSA on its warrantless domestic surveillance program. As one of a handful of contractors working with the NSA to integrate its data systems with those of other members of the Intelligence Community, Booz Allen very likely had some involvement in what the Bush administration called the Terrorist Surveillance Program. It is known, for example, that the NSA passed information gleaned from its warrantless intercepts of phone calls to both the Defense Intelligence Agency and the FBI. Booz Allen, according to its own Web site, was "a key member of the team managing the entire NSA infrastructure" and is a major DIA and FBI contractor. As we will see in the chapter on the NSA and its domestic surveillance programs, McConnell was able to discuss intimate details of the NSA's eavesdropping capabilities within weeks of his confirmation as director of national intelligence. And it was only a few months into his tenure as DNI that he informed the Bush administration—and the nation—that technological changes in telecommunications had vastly increased the amount of global telephone traffic moving through the United States, thus making it more difficult for the NSA, which is bound to legal strictures on tapping U.S. phone lines, to spy. "The intelligence director, Admiral Mike McConnell, alerted us to the intelligence gap, and we asked Congress to fix the law," Vice President Cheney pointed out in January 2008, on the eve of an important Senate vote on NSA surveillance.[33] It's hard to escape the conclusion that McConnell's experience at Booz Allen was critical as he prepared for his tasks as the nation's spymaster.

But McConnell is not simply a yes-man, as some observers have called him. He has expressed concerns about potential abuses of America's democratic system by the Intelligence Community. In 2006, in an off-the-record address to an intelligence conference in Washington, he noted that spy agencies in most countries around the world are seen as "an evil thing, a secret police." "We all want security, but won't give up our privacy," he said. Without being specific, he added: "So we have to rethink intelligence, reshape it, and we're not there yet." On the issue of domestic spying and eavesdropping, which had just emerged as a national issue in the aftermath of the *New York Times*'s revelations about the NSA, McConnell indicated he might be "a little more liberal" than the Bush administration. "Any bureaucracy can do evil," he concluded. "There must be oversight."[34]

Later that year, he told Stephen F. Hayes, a reporter with the conservative *Weekly Standard* who recently published a favorable book about Dick Cheney, that he had lost some of his respect for the vice president because of the administration's attempts to influence the IC's prewar intelligence on Iraq. "My sense of it is their political faith and convictions influenced how they took information and interpreted [it] as well as how they picked up and interpreted outside events," McConnell told Hayes, adding that the results in his view "have been disastrous"[35] (he added a qualifier, suggesting to Hayes that Cheney should have been used more as a propagandist because "he has such a way of making it simple and compelling"). In December 2007, McConnell pulled another surprise by releasing a National Intelligence Estimate concluding that Iran had halted its nuclear weapons program in 2003, directly contradicting assertions made by Cheney and Bush during the past year. That greatly enhanced his reputation as an independent thinker and actor. But, as we will see later in the book, McConnell's stature as someone who can speak truth to power would suffer greatly during his first year as DNI, particularly during the intense debate over NSA spying.

As McConnell's confirmation hearing for that position approached in early 2007, Senator Ron Wyden, D-Oregon, and other lawmakers concerned about the Bush administration's intelligence policies and Booz Allen's role in them assured the public that they would grill him about contracting. "It's a critical concern," Wyden told *USA Today*.[36] But the hearing turned out to be a desultory affair, with few probing questions from the Democrats running the Senate Intelligence Committee. At one point, Senator Wyden asked the former admiral about his role in Poindexter's Total Information Awareness program. McConnell responded by defending the concept of TIA and downplaying his role in it. The program, he told Wyden, was primarily a response to the use by terrorists of global information networks to plot against the United States. "What's happening today is the terrorists are using those very systems for their own benefit—think of it as command and control for remote terrorists, who have a particular ideology they're attempting to spread so they can communicate around the globe," he said. DARPA, he explained, merely wanted to use data mining to keep ahead of the game. As for his own involvement, McConnell said, "I was more of an operational adviser." He recalled urging Poindexter to "talk about how information could be used and to be very clear about how it could be applied under today's laws, rules, values, Constitution [and] regulation"; his argument, he told the senators, "did not persuade." That explanation seemed to satisfy Wyden, who told McConnell a few minutes later that he would support his nomination.[37]

Given McConnell's expansive role in domestic intelligence after taking over as DNI, the most significant part of his confirmation hearing concerned homeland security. "We know that terrorist organizations today are making plans for attacks on our citizens inside our borders," McConnell told the committee, and later referred to "the current planning by Al Qaeda to attack inside" U.S. borders. In recent years, he said, the Intelligence Community "focused almost exclusively on foreign threats outside our borders. What is new is the need to focus on these threats inside our borders. . . . This ability to think domestically is, I believe, one of the biggest challenges for the DNI and for the community." That statement was welcomed by the committee chairman, Senator John D. "Jay" Rockefeller, D–West Virginia, who ended the hearing with a plea for the future DNI to make frequent visits to his state to meet local law enforcement officials.

McConnell's role as a contractor did come up at least once during the hearing, when Wyden asked about it. But contrary to his prehearing pledge, the Oregon lawmaker didn't attempt to flesh out Booz Allen's role in intelligence gathering and analysis. Instead, he pleaded ignorance, observing that the Senate committee "doesn't even know how many contractors are employed by the intelligence community" because, so far, the DNI hadn't come up with any numbers. McConnell didn't have the figures, either, but described contracting as a sign of "the goodness of the American system." "The private sector maintains a significant capability," he said. "Post-9/11, the government found itself in need of special skills and special talent, and they were not available inside the government. So the government turned to the private sector." Wyden didn't ask any obvious follow-ups: If this capability is so badly missing in government, why do companies like yours spend hundreds of millions of dollars to lobby the government to expand contracted jobs? And if it's so great for the country, why can't you or the government tell us how much contracting is really going on? The senators' abdication of their oversight role over the Intelligence Community that McConnell was about to head would have serious consequences.

After leaving Booz Allen and taking over as DNI in the spring of 2007, McConnell moved quickly to shore up his ties with the private sector and express his fealty to the industry from which he'd come. One of his early decisions was to keep secret the long-awaited report on intelligence outsourcing, described in Chapter 1, that had been commissioned in 2006 by his predecessor, John Negroponte. By preventing disclosure of the report's findings, McConnell saved the Intelligence Community and its largest contractors, including his old company, from the scrutiny that would have inevitably followed in Congress and the press if the true magnitude and scope of outsourcing had been revealed.

In April 2007, only a few weeks after he'd moved into DNI headquarters, McConnell declared a hundred-day plan to improve collaboration between agencies throughout the Intelligence Community. One of the top items on the plan's to-do list was to streamline the DNI's acquisition process by reducing the amount of time it takes to bring "complex intelligence platforms" online; this program, promised McConnell, would "dramatically change how the IC does business." McConnell also pledged to create an Intelligence Advanced Research Projects Agency, modeled after the Pentagon's DARPA, to fund technical innovations, particularly "blue sky," futuristic concepts that individual agencies might not budget for. Significantly, the plan's focus on acquisitions was listed ahead of several other goals—including integrating foreign and domestic intelligence, accelerating information sharing across agency lines, and clarifying the authority of the DNI—that had been the hallmarks of intelligence reform since the 9/11 attacks. The DNI, McConnell was saying, was now wide open for business.

To make sure that contractors got the message, McConnell created a new DNI position, deputy director for acquisition, and appointed Alden V. Munson, an industry veteran, to fill it. Munson, like McConnell himself, was no ordinary executive. As the former vice president of TRW, he had been involved with highly classified black operations for decades, and, in 2000, had been honored by the National Reconnaissance Office for developing what the NRO described as a "fully automatic electronic intelligence system" to support U.S. military forces in the field. As a partner with the Windsor Group, a defense-oriented investment bank with a large clientele in the intelligence industry, Munson had played an important advisory role in scores of mergers and acquisitions over the past decade.* He was also on the board of directors of bd Systems, Inc., an intelligence contractor specializing in data mining that was acquired in 2006 by Science Applications International Corporation. Munson's selection signaled the DNI's determination to leverage the corporate side of intelligence, and its constant litany of buyouts and mergers, to the IC's advantage. Munson's "business experience with large acquisitions," McConnell announced, "will be invaluable as we work to increase our technological agility."[38]

McConnell's most important gesture to the contracting industry involved a little known business association known as the Intelligence and National Security Alliance. Originally founded in 1979 as a forum for informal discussions between the NSA and its contractors, INSA was reorganized in 2005 by a group of prominent contracting executives to serve as a bridge between the industry and the leaders of national intelligence. Those executives, representing Booz Allen, SAIC, Computer Sciences Corporation, and ManTech International, among others, elected McConnell the chairman of INSA in 2005—a relationship that was completely overlooked by the media in its coverage of McConnell's accession to the DNI.

That was a significant oversight, because shortly after taking over as intelligence chief, McConnell elevated INSA into a virtual partnership with the Office of the DNI, and used its nonprofit status to promote a dialogue within the broader IC on domestic intelligence. When it first began, that dialogue seemed innocent enough; who could argue with developing an industry consensus on this volatile issue? But as we will see later in the book, as McConnell's term at DNI progressed, he became the leader within the Bush administration of a drive to greatly expand the domestic reach of the NSA and convince Congress to grant immunity to companies that collaborated with the NSA in its surveillance program from its inception in the months after 9/11 to the present day. Seen in this light, McConnell's experience with INSA, and the role

* Among the companies Windsor advised were CACI International, MTC Technologies, ManTech International, Analex, Anteon, BAE Systems, Dynamic Research Corporation, and L-3 Communications. All of them are major intelligence contractors and do extensive business with the DNI.

of his company in the Bush-Cheney intelligence regime, take on greater significance.

For years, the most important contractor organization in the Intelligence Community was the Security Affairs Support Association (SASA). Founded in 1979, SASA was the premier industry group for companies doing classified work in what IC insiders call "the intelligence space"—the CIA, the NSA, and the NRO. One of its founders was Leonard Moodispaw, the CEO of Essex Corporation and one of the best-known contractors in the intelligence business. While working at the NSA in the late 1970s, Moodispaw told me, he became frustrated with his inability to speak openly with contractors "in a generic sense." Strict agency acquisition rules required companies working at the NSA to communicate only with NSA contracting officers. The contractors "could talk to me privately, but didn't want to talk to the contracting officer because it would become adversarial," Moodispaw explained. "That's how SASA was born. I said, 'there has to be a way to get everybody together without it being us pissing on each other.' "[39] He took the idea to Navy Admiral Bobby Ray Inman, the NSA director at the time, and won approval to start an organization to discuss broad issues of concern to both the agency and its contractors. SASA's first project was to conduct an internal study of the NSA's acquisitions methods. A new public-private partnership was launched; but, as usual, the actual public was nowhere to be seen.

SASA's primary function was to create a way for contractors and their government employers to schmooze in peace. Over the years, according to SASA newsletters, many of its events were held at highly secure intelligence facilities normally reserved for meetings of high-level national security officials. In 1988, for example, the CIA allowed the association to hold a seminar, "Technical Shortfalls in Intelligence Architecture," in its top secret war room at Langley. "The bubble was packed" for the event, *Colloquy,* SASA's in-house publication, reported. "It is fair to observe that it was one of the most stimulating programs in which SASA has ever been involved." Later that year, the DIA made its Defense Intelligence Analysis Center at Bolling Air Force Base in Virginia available to SASA for an award ceremony for Dr. Edwin Land, who had developed the Polaroid camera for the Intelligence Community. "Many of his countless achievements remain beyond the public domain," CIA director William Webster said in presenting the award, underscoring the still secretive nature of the industry.

Reading through the lists of speakers at past SASA events is a voyage through the revolving door. In 1991, Duane P. Andrews, then the assistant secretary of defense under Dick Cheney, delivered a keynote speech at a SASA conference; after leaving the Pentagon, he was hired by SAIC and, later, QinetiQ North America, a British-owned defense and intelligence contractor, where he is now the chairman and CEO. Lieutenant General Patrick M. Hughes, the former director of the DIA, once addressed a SASA symposium on "the role of modeling and simulation in the 21st century." Ten years later, he was a key executive with L-3 Communications and an outspoken advocate for the contracting business. Most of the organization's past presidents have become major players in the industry as well. Edward C. "Pete" Aldridge, SASA's president from 1989 to 1992, served in the George H. W. Bush administration as undersecretary of defense for acquisition, technology, and logistics, and is now on the board of directors of Lockheed Martin. SASA's president in 1999 was retired Air Force Lieutenant General James R. Clapper, who went on to head the NGA and later joined the board of GeoEye, a major NGA contractor; now he is back at the Pentagon as the undersecretary of defense for intelligence.

The organization's biggest event was its annual presentation of the Baker Award for contributions to the Intelligence Community. The award was named after William O. Baker, the legendary former director of Bell Labs. It was once the Intelligence Community's primary R&D center, and was responsible over the years for many key technologies, including sonar tracking systems used by Navy submarines, listening devices for the NSA, and encrypted telephones used by the president and other high-ranking national security officials. The Baker Award typically represents the consensus in government and business of the most influential figure in the IC, and the award dinner was the social event of the year for agencies and contractors alike.

The way SASA chose the recipients was instructive. Every year, the organization invited the departments and agencies of the Intelligence Community, the President's Foreign Intelligence Advisory Board, and the IC's scientific, industrial, and academic communities to submit names for nomination. These were reviewed by an awards panel selected by SASA as well as representatives of the secretaries of state and defense and officials with the President's advisory board and the CIA. The award was traditionally handed out by the director of the CIA. In 2005, it went to retired Air Force Lieutenant General Brent Scowcroft, who ran the intelligence board for President George H. W. Bush until he was pushed aside in a dispute with Dick Cheney over the Pentagon's role in intelligence. Other recipients include former CIA director George Tenet; former NGA director Clapper; Charles Allen, a former top CIA officer who is now the intelligence director for the Department of Homeland Security; and, as we saw earlier, Booz Allen's Joan Dempsey. The awards are now being handed out by INSA, SASA's successor organization.

In 2005, SASA went through a major shake-up. Its members were trying to figure out the organization's identity. Was it a networking organization? Or was it a trade association, like the airline groups, all about industry? The collective answer, Tim Sample, INSA's executive director, told me, was to make SASA a "more professional association" that promoted "collaboration, that partnership between industry, the private sector, academia, and government, for the betterment of what you were trying to do for national security." In November 2005, SASA was renamed the Intelligence and National Security Alliance, and McConnell, then the executive vice president of Booz Allen, was chosen to spearhead the new organization as chairman of its board of directors.

INSA's founding corporations included many of the major brand names in intelligence, as well as a few new entries to the industry. Each one, according to the INSA in-house newsletter, made initial investments of between $50,000 and $150,000, and pledged at least $25,000 in membership contributions every year. They are listed on INSA's Web site: BAE Systems, Computer Sciences Corporation (CSC), General Dynamics Advanced Information Systems, Lockheed Martin, Booz Allen Hamilton, ManTech International, SAIC, and the Potomac Institute, a Washington think tank with close links to the Intelligence Community.

The other two founding companies, Hewlett-Packard and Microsoft, never belonged to SASA, as the others did. Their presence in the new organization underscores the central role that information technology now plays in the broader national security industry. "[Information technology] is now a huge part of intelligence," says INSA spokesperson Jason Kello. Asked why the two IT giants joined an organization dedicated to intelligence, he cited INSA's shift in 2005 from a networking association to a public policy forum. "That's when Microsoft and Hewlett-Packard stepped forward and helped provide the founding efforts for INSA, monetarily as well as with expertise," he said.[40] HP, which earned $181 million from defense contracts in 2006, is represented on INSA's board by Tom Hempfield, its vice president for federal sales. Microsoft, which doesn't break out its federal government earnings, is represented by Linda K. Zecher, vice president for the U.S. public sector. Both executives declined to comment on their companies' ties with INSA.

Given INSA's deep roots in the national collection agencies, McConnell was a logical choice for INSA's first chairman. When he left the organization to take the reins of the Office of the DNI in February 2007, INSA spent several months searching for a successor, and in April chose John Brennan, the president and CEO of The Analysis Corporation. Brennan, whose activities as a contractor are described in more detail later, had extensive experience in the Intelligence Community; he served for more than thirty years at the CIA, and was the first director of the National Counterterrorism Center when it opened in 2004. His breadth of contacts outside of the intelligence mainstream was apparently the key to his selection. "INSA's board believes that John's experience in reaching out to departments and agencies in the days immediately after 9/11, including at the state and local levels, best fit INSA's role of supporting the United States intelligence and national security communities," INSA stated in a press release. "If anything," Kello added in an interview, Brennan "understands that intelligence means more than just the federal area. We want to start reaching out to chiefs of police. He comes from a background with the NCTC, understanding intelligence as not just being a Washington-centric policy discussion, like how does this affect people in Kansas City and Miami, that kind of thing." Brennan is pushing within INSA to expand the reach of U.S. intelligence to the domestic sphere, just as McConnell is doing at the DNI.

The man who manages INSA's day-to-day activities is Tim Sample, who is himself a second-generation spook. Sample's father was one of the original members of Army counterintelligence, and spent the years immediately after World War II debriefing Russians at a U.S. Army base in Otsu, Japan. Sample's career personifies the cozy relationship between the IC and its contractors. After service with intelligence units within the Air Force, he joined the CIA, where he eventually became director of the CIA's Nonproliferation Center. He went on to become staff director for the House Permanent Select Committee on Intelligence, where he worked closely for five years with Porter Goss, R-Florida, the former chairman of the committee who briefly served as CIA director in 2005. Sample left Congress to take a job as vice president for strategic intelligence at Veridian, a major intelligence contractor that was acquired by General Dynamics in 2005.

Under the leadership of Sample and Brennan, INSA now holds regular discussions with the DNI as well as the leadership of the NSA and the CIA about industry and national security issues. In June 2006, while McConnell was still INSA's chairman, the Office of the DNI met with INSA to explore "long-term challenges and priorities" facing the Intelligence Community as spelled out in the DNI's Quadrennial Intelligence Community Review (that review, INSA noted in its newsletter, "previously had not been briefed to the private sector"). The meeting, held at the Northrop Grumman Heritage Conference Center in Chantilly, Virginia, provided a "unique opportunity" for INSA members to "contribute directly to those who are doing the strategic planning and outlining the priorities for the DNI for the next five-to-ten years, a critical time for the Intelligence Community," according to a press release posted on INSA's Web site. The event was open only to those holding secret security clearances.

These discussions, Sample assured me in an interview, build "trust" between contractors and the agencies they serve. Private industry and the government "come at things differently, especially in today's world," he said. "So it's an issue of creating that trusted environment, where there can be collaboration and conversation, and where there's benefits to both sides without a lot of concern about tainting, if you will, industry or government along the way." He didn't say much about what these "collaborations and conversations" are about. But he explained, when I asked, that there are things "we want to make sure happen the right way," because in today's world "there tends to be a lot of knee-jerk reactions until people understand what the issues are and the goals are. So what we do is try to provide an environment where some of these discussions can be had and people feel fairly comfortable and protected." But protected from what? Congress? An inquisitive public, concerned about the lack of oversight in defense and intelligence? That isn't clear.

What *is* clear is INSA's desire to stay below the radar screen. In the "trusted environment" it has created, it's difficult to tell who is from the government and who represents the private sector. On a section of its Web site listing INSA's board, only the names of directors appear—not their business and government affiliations. Board members, Sample explained, are "selected for their expertise and understanding of intelligence and national security, and serve only in their personal capacities." That may be true; but their government agency and corporate affiliations are exactly why they're in the organization. Because only someone on extremely familiar terms with the Intelligence Community would even recognize their names, the nondisclosure looks much more like an attempt to conceal than anything else.

INSA, in fact, is one of the only business associations in Washington that include current government officials on their board of directors. Kello stoutly denies this: "There's government officials on the board of the Boy Scouts, AMA, on all kinds of nonprofits," he says. But in those organizations, the high-ranking government officials are there in ceremonial, honorary roles, and don't play a role in decision making. Major business organizations, such as the U.S. Chamber of Commerce and the Business Roundtable, are led by corporate executives—Fortune 500 types—not by government bureaucrats. The three other associations representing intelligence contractors, including the Armed Forces Communications and Electronics Association (AFCEA), the United States Geospatial Intelligence Foundation (USGIF), and the National Defense Industrial Association (NDIA), are all managed by boards of directors composed only of corporate executives. Government agencies may belong as dues-paying members, but their representatives don't hold positions as directors.

Yet at INSA, they make up a huge proportion of the board. The CIA holds two seats; also represented are the Defense Intelligence Agency, the Office of the Secretary of Defense, Army Counterintelligence, the NSA, the Department of Homeland Security, and the FBI.* In addition to the founding companies named earlier, the board also includes representatives from The Analysis Corporation, SI International, SRA International, CACI International, Northrop Grumman, Microsoft, and Hewlett-Packard. In recent years, the INSA board has included a number of "seniors" within the wider intelligence community and some of the most well-connected contractors in the private sector. Among them are quite a few people we will encounter later in this book: Robert A. Coleman, the chairman of ManTech; Harry Gatanas, a former NSA acquisitions official, now with the NSA contractor SI International; and Barbara McNamara, the former deputy director of the NSA, now on the board of directors of CACI International. Booz Allen has been particularly well represented: INSA's board now includes Booz Allen vice presidents Keith Hall, the former director of the NRO; Leo A. Hazlewood, a former top imagery analyst with the CIA who helped found the NGA; and Joan Dempsey.

---

* These were the government agency representatives on INSA's board in September 2007. From the CIA, Carmen Medina, associate deputy director for intelligence, and Caryn Wagner, executive director of intelligence community affairs. From the DIA, Barbara A. Duckworth, chief of staff. From the Office of the Secretary of Defense, Terrance M. Ford, assistant deputy chief of staff, G-2 (Intelligence). From Army Counterintelligence, Thomas Gandy, director for human intelligence, foreign disclosure, and security in the Office of the Army's Deputy Chief of Staff for Intelligence. From the NSA, Richard C. Schaeffer, information assurance director. From DHS, James F. Sloan, assistant commandant for intelligence and criminal investigations, U.S. Coast Guard. And from the FBI, Donna Bucella, director, Terrorist Screening Center.

In 2007, as part of its efforts to broaden its impact within the wider Intelligence Community, INSA incorporated into its membership the National Correlation Working Group, a shadowy organization of military intelligence operatives led by retired Air Force Lieutenant General Lincoln D. Faurer, who directed the NSA from 1981 to 1985. The correlation group, which is now a council within INSA, keeps a low profile: it doesn't have a Web site, and Google searches about the group yield virtually nothing. According to Jason Kello, it sponsors classified-level conferences and symposiums that focus on putting real-time intelligence into strategic use on the battlefield. An NCWG pamphlet in his office described its members as "highly experienced professionals, well-versed in defense tactics and combat decision-making, and dedicated to getting verified information to the warfighter with absolute speed and with no compromise to informational integrity."

Many of the group's members are retired Air Force generals. And like INSA, its board of directors is dominated by contractors: Faurer, the working group's chairman, sits on the board of directors of Analex Inc., a company owned by the British firm QinetiQ that does extensive business with the CIA and NSA. William R. Usher, the former Air Force general who chairs INSA's NCWG Council, was for many years the director of Lockheed Martin's Washington Special Projects Office; he now runs his own eponymous consulting firm. Other board members with deep roots in the industry include Larry Cox, a former NSA technician now working for SAIC, and William Crowell, the former deputy director of the NSA under McConnell, and a senior executive with Narus Inc., a Silicon Valley firm well known in the telecom industry for its eavesdropping technologies. Jeffrey K. Harris, one of its board members, previously served with the CIA and as director of the NRO and is now a senior executive with Lockheed Martin. The working group, said Kello, used to be part of the National Defense Industrial Association but "decided to move over to INSA because we fit more with their mission, which was to be a public policy forum. We were part of a thought-leadership effort, as opposed to an industrial effort."

The well-connected executives and former officials who make up INSA's leadership have collectively decided that INSA should act as a kind of promoter for the DNI. One of INSA's first projects, launched while McConnell was chairman, was to work with the DNI to improve the "information sharing environment" within the Intelligence Community. This was one of the recommendations made by the National Commission on Terrorist Attacks upon the United States (also known as the 9/11 Commission), and it was written into the 2004 intelligence reform bill that created the DNI. According to an INSA press release from February 2006, Booz Allen was hired in August 2005 to support the government "with research and analysis to help identify solutions to critical issues" involving information sharing. Based on this research, the DNI was to submit an information sharing plan to Congress, and "INSA and Booz Allen will support the plan's construction." According to the plan, as outlined in the press release, the information sharing would "go beyond the IC" to include federal, state, and local governments.

To further its mission along, INSA launched the Council on Domestic Intelligence in the fall of 2006. The idea behind the council, Sample told me, was to "help promote the right debate so we can aim toward the right level of oversight." The council is co-chaired by two INSA board members, retired Army Major General Robert A. Harding and Kathleen L. Kiernan. Harding, another former DIA official, runs a consulting firm that works closely with the DIA and has, according to company literature, "become the premier government contractor for counterintelligence, human intelligence, homeland security and MASINT solutions to support our country's fight against terrorism" (MASINT is measurement and signatures intelligence, a highly classified school of intelligence that can, through the use of sensors, detect chemicals and other materials in the air). Kiernan, the former assistant director for strategic intelligence for the Bureau of Alcohol, Tobacco, Firearms and Explosives (ATF), also runs her own consulting firm. According to Sample, INSA's domestic security council includes both industry and intelligence officials, and is "sanctioned by the FBI."

The council is a transparent attempt to shape public discussions about civil liberties and issues related to domestic surveillance. This, I think, is what Sample meant by having "the right debate." Once you say domestic intelligence, he observed, you read stories about "whether it's what NSA's doing, or what information phone companies are giving out, right? Usually these things are played out in the media, and people speaking on them are usually at the extremes of the issues, and you rarely get a substantive basis for the argument. And you rarely get a good solid debate on what we should be doing." At the same time, he says, in polls taken after the *New York Times* disclosed the NSA's warrantless domestic surveillance program, "generally the American people thought it was not such a bad thing if it catches terrorists." That's why INSA wants to "promote the right debate," he repeated. With a membership that includes many of the companies that provide technical support to the NSA's eavesdropping and data mining capabilities, it's not hard to guess what the debate, or the proper conclusions, should be.

In the spring of 2007, after Brennan was elected chairman of INSA and McConnell was firmly in control at the DNI, the pace of cooperation between the Office of the DNI and INSA stepped up dramatically. Since that time, the ODNI and INSA have jointly sponsored a series of "outreach workshops," most of them open only to government officials and contractors holding security clearances, on a wide range of subjects relevant to the Intelligence Community. On May 30, 2007, for example, the ODNI and INSA held a workshop on "insider threats" that "ODNI has identified as issues on which it seeks engagement, including insider criminal vulnerability, insider criminal activities, insider economic espionage, and insider terrorist activity," INSA explained in the announcement for the event, posted on its Web site. Companies interested in the DNI workshop were asked to send their information to INSA.

In June 2007, the ODNI and INSA co-sponsored a DNI Industry Day, where contractors were invited to hear DNI officials "address budget priorities and the near-term and long-term strategy," and "learn from the ODNI about how your company can help achieve the national intelligence strategy alignment." The event, sponsored in part by BAE Systems, Booz Allen, ManTech, Microsoft, SAIC, and Raytheon, cost $350 for INSA members and $425 for nonmembers. It was open to government agencies and contractors with secret clearances; "innovative companies" who did not have clearances were invited to attend a separate event with agency procurement officials. The speakers included most of the leadership of the Intelligence Community, including NSA director Lieutenant General Keith B. Alexander, NRO director Donald Kerr, DIA director Lieutenant General Michael Maples, and NGA director Vice Admiral Robert B. Murrett (Alden Munson, the new acquisitions man at the DNI, also made an appearance).

Other ODNI-INSA events have focused on open source intelligence gained from analyzing information openly published in other countries, such as local newspapers and scientific journals; political and economic stability in India and China; and intelligence, surveillance, and reconnaissance. In September 2007, INSA was the chief sponsor of a week of events commemorating the sixtieth anniversary of the National Security Act of 1947 "and the creation of our nation's modern intelligence and national security establishments." It included an "anniversary gala" at Georgetown University—where INSA has endowed a special chair on intelligence studies—that was co-sponsored by the Office of the DNI (the anniversary events and the open source conference were both open to the public).

Although INSA is a nonprofit, some of these activities are money-making ventures that bring in considerable revenue to INSA (the organization's 2005 tax return shows program services revenues of $1.4 million for the year). Yet there is no competition for these contracts; they are essentially sole-source contracts that appear to be awarded at the discretion of the DNI (the DNI press office would not comment on the DNI's ties with INSA). Moreover, these projects seem to make INSA itself a contractor—something that the organization strenuously denies. "INSA is a nonprofit," Kello, INSA's spokesperson, stressed to me. While the organization collects sponsorship and attendance fees, "ODNI does not pay us," he said. "We help promote the mission INSA has, which is as a forum for enhancing intelligence policy."

INSA's joint programs with the DNI have alarmed some intelligence veterans, who wonder if INSA has become a way for contractors and intelligence officials to create policy in secret, without oversight from

Congress. "Evidently, DNI McConnell has made it an early priority to stand up INSA as the preeminent nonprofit association serving the ODNI," an industry insider told me, on condition of anonymity. "While INSA has created multiple levels of memberships and a large connected board of both government and industry leaders, the real control remains with the big-dollar founding primes. I wonder if it's even legal for these officials to sit on an actual board of an industry trade association."

That is not entirely clear. Scott Amey, the counsel for the Project on Government Oversight, a public interest group that monitors federal contracting, said the DNI's relationship with INSA certainly raises serious ethical questions. If government officials are attending INSA meetings on a regular basis, he said, those meetings may be subject to open meeting rules, which would require them to be open to the public. The fact that contractors and intelligence officials are meeting under the cover of a business association—despite the fact that they are supposedly there as individuals—points to the need to expand the oversight of intelligence to include contracting. "This sounds like a self-policing program," said Amey. "At that point, who's really minding the store?"[41]

That's a question that will be raised again and again as we investigate the secret world of intelligence outsourcing. Before we open those doors, however, let's take a journey into the origins of intelligence outsourcing, and try to understand why so many spies are working for hire these days.

3

A Short History of Intelligence Outsourcing

"I remember when NSA stood for No Such Agency. I remember a time before newspapers had reporters regularly assigned to the intelligence beat. I remember a time when congressional oversight consisted of an hour's worth of conversation with the friendly House and Senate Armed Forces Committee chairmen. I even knew a time when the idea of using 'contractors' to help solve intelligence gathering or analytical problems was regarded with disdain."

—ANN CARACRISTI, THE FORMER DEPUTY DIRECTOR OF THE NATIONAL SECURITY AGENCY, ACCEPTING THE WILLIAM O. BAKER AWARD FOR LIFELONG CONTRIBUTIONS TO THE INTELLIGENCE COMMUNITY, MAY 27, 1999

IT'S BECOME AN article of faith on the American left today that the outsourcing of government and military services is intrinsically part of a "Bush agenda," rooted in part in a neoconservative drive to siphon U.S. spending on defense, national security, and social programs to large corporations friendly with the Bush administration. While there's some truth to this trope, it's a misleading analysis of the dynamics of capitalism and the peculiar way state and capital have mixed in the national security arena in the years before and after 9/11. American corporations have rarely acquiesced to political dictates, either from the right or the left. Instead, they grasp opportunities presented by government policy, and then move as quickly as possible to maximize profits and minimize risk in a given market. And in the case of the defense and intelligence industries, those opportunities appeared long before George W. Bush was elected president and 9/11 brought terrorism to the top of the national security agenda.

The big government contractors of today are the direct beneficiaries of privatization policies set in motion by the Reagan and Clinton administrations, sanctioned by the Department of Defense and the Intelligence Community, and embraced and ultimately funded by a Republican-led Congress anxious to bring market discipline to government agencies. Bill Clinton, one of the most liberal presidents in the nation's history, picked up the privatization cudgel where the conservative Ronald Reagan left off and—for reasons we will explore in this chapter—took it deep into services once considered inherently governmental, including high-risk military operations and intelligence functions once reserved only for government agencies. By the end of his term, more than 100,000 Pentagon jobs had been transferred to companies in the private sector—among them thousands of jobs in intelligence.

"People forget what happened under President Clinton," says Stan Soloway, the president of the Professional Services Council, the chief Washington lobbyist for U.S. government contractors. "I'm not trying to brag here, but in the Clinton administration, we did a substantial amount [of privatization] and the current Bush administration took it to the next level. That's the reality." [1] Soloway speaks from personal experience. As president of the PSC, he represents some of the nation's largest intelligence contractors, from Booz Allen Hamilton to Northrop Grumman to L-3's Titan Group. During the Clinton administration, he was the deputy undersecretary of defense for acquisition, where he played an important role in the Pentagon's campaign to streamline its operations by privatizing agencies and outsourcing functions no longer deemed important enough for government work.

In arguing that intelligence outsourcing got its start during the Clinton administration, I don't intend to minimize the subsequent actions of the Bush administration. As we've already seen, outsourcing and contracting of essential national security functions has risen dramatically under President Bush, and without a doubt Vice President Dick Cheney's old employer, Halliburton, and dozens of companies with close ties to the administration, benefited handsomely from the radical brand of foreign policy practiced by Bush and his neoconservative allies in government. But the evidence is clear that Bush and Cheney pursued policies that built on Clinton's legacy of outsourcing and privatization to siphon billions of dollars in federal money to the private sector. Let's start from the beginning.

In a sense, outsourcing has always been part of the U.S. spying enterprise. Former CIA director George Tenet, who now earns a significant amount of his income from companies involved in intelligence contracting, knows that history well. "Our private sector has stepped forward for over half a century to offer the best technology and expertise" to the Intelligence Community, he said in a speech to intelligence professionals in 2003. "They are part of our intelligence family because they share our same passion for our mission—to safeguard the freedoms that make America great. Throughout our history, American industry has given every DCI the tools needed to solve our greatest challenges—and we need them now more than ever."[2]

During the Eisenhower administration, the CIA contracted with Lockheed Corporation to build the U-2, the famous high-flying spy plane that provided unprecedented surveillance of forbidden areas in the Soviet Union and the People's Republic of China and is still in service today. By the 1960s, TRW, General Electric, Eastman Kodak, Itek Corporation, and Polaroid were legendary in the black world for building spy satellites, cameras, and other reconnaissance aircraft to keep watch on America's enemies. Those tools and systems, managed by the

CIA, the Air Force, and the super-secret National Reconnaissance Office, allowed U.S. intelligence to photograph Soviet military installations from outer space at incredible detail. One of the most famous systems was the CIA's CORONA photoreconnaissance satellites, supplied by Lockheed, General Electric, and Itek, a small high-tech company financed by a member of the Rockefeller family.

CORONA greatly expanded the CIA's reach, taking thousands of pictures from space and dropping them back to earth in an eighty-four-pound gold-plated pod suspended beneath a huge orange-and-white parachute (according to a 1958 top secret CIA report on CORONA declassified nearly fifty years later, the surveillance equipment and recoverable film cassettes were "procured covertly" by the CIA, primarily from Lockheed, and their products were "compartmentalized" among several companies). These collection systems helped dispel fears of a "missile gap" and, by 1964, had photographed all Soviet ICBM complexes and allowed U.S. intelligence to catalogue Soviet air defense and antiballistic missile sites, nuclear weapons facilities, and submarine bases, as well as airbases and military facilities in China and Eastern Europe.[3] The United States didn't acknowledge the existence of its spy satellites until President Jimmy Carter disclosed "the fact of" U.S. photoreconnaissance satellites in a speech at the Kennedy Space Center on October 1, 1978. "Photoreconnaissance satellites have become an important stabilizing factor in world affairs in the monitoring of arms control agreements," Carter said, according to documents unearthed by the National Security Archive in 2007. "They make an immense contribution to the security of all nations. We shall continue to develop them."[4] The existence of the CORONA satellites was finally declassified in 1993.*

The National Security Agency, too, has maintained close ties with the private sector. From the late 1940s to the mid-1970s, Western Union, AT&T, and several other communications companies allowed

* John McMahon, one of the CIA officials who supervised CORONA, is now a registered lobbyist for Lockheed Martin. In 2005, he filed a lobbying disclosure report with Congress saying that he had represented Lockheed in obtaining "funding for classified programs."

the NSA to read and listen in on every international telegram and phone call placed to the United States. AT&T also cooperated closely with the CIA, on occasion handing over phone records to the agency.* Beginning in the 1950s, information technology and communications companies such as IBM, Bell Labs, and Cray developed the first supercomputers and encryption equipment used by the NSA to crack coded diplomatic and military messages and convert the huge volumes of signals intelligence into actionable intelligence.

And to keep its global network of listening posts humming and assist covert CIA operatives working overseas, the NSA always had a small coterie of electronics and communications suppliers ready to assist. Those companies maintained NSA equipment and traveled to all corners of the globe, from U.S. bases in Japan to CIA safe houses in Beirut. "If you had problems with your radio, you wanted Motorola to send the repairman out, not the CIA," recalls Robert Baer, a former CIA agent who worked undercover in Iraq and Lebanon.[5]

Many of the companies that dominate the intelligence industry today got their start by providing technical services and products to the Intelligence Community. Unlike the present day, when Booz Allen, SAIC, and other companies operate openly as intelligence contractors, the firms that dominated the industry during the Cold War stayed in the shadows, and their actions only came to light through leaks or as the result of a crisis.

During the 1970s, for example, when Iran under the Shah became the largest foreign customer for U.S. arms sales, Rockwell International was the prime contractor on a $500 million project to build a huge intelligence collection system along Iran's borders with Iraq and the Soviet Union. The project, called IBEX, was jointly managed by the CIA

---

* A document released by the CIA in 2007 as part of its collection of past misdeeds called the "family jewels" describes an incident in 1972 when the CIA asked an official of AT&T for copies of telephone call slips relating to U.S.-China calls. According to the note, the operation "lasted for three or four months and then dried up." Agency officials concluded that "the collection of these slips did not violate the Communications Act"—which prohibits companies from giving the government customer records without a warrant—"since eavesdropping was not involved."

and the NSA with SAVAK, the Shah's secret police, and recruited many of its executives from U.S. intelligence agencies. The plan was to use both airborne and ground-based receiving and recording equipment to monitor communications and radar signals from countries on Iran's borders.

IBEX was kept secret until August 1976, when three American civilians working for Rockwell were assassinated on the streets of Tehran by an underground organization opposed to the Shah's dictatorial rule. Even though the project was never completed, the list of bidders tells us how large the contracting industry had grown by this time. Among the companies competing for the project were Boeing, the aircraft and electronics manufacturer, which eventually acquired Rockwell's intelligence operations and merged them with its Integrated Defense Systems unit; E-Systems, which was later incorporated into Argon ST, a key NSA contractor we will meet later on; ITT Corporation, one of the largest suppliers to the IC of high-resolution cameras used on satellites; and GTE Sylvania, an aerospace company later acquired by General Dynamics.*

During the 1980s, the spying industry received a huge, multibillion-dollar stimulus from a highly classified government project that wasn't fully exposed until the early twenty-first century. This was the "continuity of government" task force initiated by the Reagan administration to protect the nation's leadership in case of a nuclear attack. In the early 1980s, President Reagan appointed a select group of former high-ranking officials to periodically gather in secret locations around the country to practice setting up an underground government in case Washington was destroyed in a Soviet nuclear attack.

Some of the participants in the program, which was known by the

---

* Bob Woodward, writing in the *Washington Post*, called IBEX "a project of truly Buck Rogers proportions." According to his report, former CIA director Richard M. Helms, then the American ambassador to Iran, initially described the Raytheon killings as a "professional" job carried out with Polish machine guns and a pistol stolen from the U.S. military mission to Iran. Iranian newspapers initially claimed the hit was the work of Islamic terrorists, but the Shah told "an American" that "the Russians" were behind it. "Two hours later," wrote Woodward, "Helms told the same American he agreed with the Shah." See "IBEX: Deadly Symbol of U.S. Arms Sales Problems," *Washington Post*, January 2, 1977.

acronym COG and referred to as the Armageddon Project, would later take key positions in the George W. Bush administration or as supporters of the Bush foreign policy agenda. They included Donald Rumsfeld and Dick Cheney, who had both served as chief of staff for President Gerald Ford, and James Woolsey, who was CIA director under President Clinton. Participants in the exercises were pulled from their jobs in the private sector and dispatched, without a word to their families and very little notice, to secret locations around the country, such as the huge Greenbrier Hotel in West Virginia and a farmhouse in rural Pennsylvania.

Once in position, the shadow government was joined by sitting members of the president's cabinet as well as members of Congress, the CIA, and various domestic agencies, and ran through exercises that would, at a time of war, maintain a governmental structure to fight on through the holocaust. Many of the details about the program were first disclosed in 2002 by the journalist James Mann in his excellent book on the Bush war cabinet, *Rise of the Vulcans*.

The COG program was abandoned during the Clinton administration; but, according to Mann, a version of it was put into play on September 11, 2001, when members of the Bush administration joined senior lawmakers and top officials with the CIA and other intelligence agencies at secret government locations in the hills of Pennsylvania and Virginia to plan the U.S. response to the terrorist attacks (Cheney and Rumsfeld "were familiar with the Armageddon exercises of the Reagan era," Mann wrote. "They themselves had practiced all the old drills."[6]). For Woolsey, the experience provided valuable background for the homeland security exercises he would later run for corporations and government agencies as vice president of Booz Allen Hamilton.[7]

The Armageddon Project served as a catalyst for outsourcing in much the same way that the war on terror does today. To manage the mock operations, the Reagan administration created a secret agency called the Defense Mobilization Planning Systems Agency, which reported to Vice President George H. W. Bush. Four agencies were charged with executing the plan: the CIA, the Departments of State and Defense, and the Federal Emergency Management Agency (FEMA). In

1989, the journalist Steven Emerson, who would later become well-known as an expert on Islamic terrorism, wrote about some of the technical plans for the agency.

In the event of a nuclear attack, he reported in *U.S. News & World Report,* special teams equipped with war plans, military and security codes, and data on all aspects of government were to accompany designated presidential successors and their cabinets to secret command posts scattered around the country.[8] A CNN special investigation later discovered that the communications and logistics part of the plan was managed by a super-secret agency called the National Program Office, which was headquartered in Fort Huachuca, Arizona, the headquarters for Army intelligence. It reported that as much as $8 billion was spent on the program, including spending to manufacture secure, mobile command, control, and communications links for the secret plan.[9]

To build those systems, CNN reported, FEMA hired the Harris Corporation, an important intelligence contractor based in Florida, the CIA hired McDonnell Douglas (this was before its merger with Boeing), and the Pentagon hired TRW, an important intelligence contractor that was acquired in 2002 by Northrop Grumman. The military's contracting tasks were assigned to the Army's Information Systems Command based at Fort Huachuca, Arizona, where the project was managed by the late Major General Eugene Renzi, the deputy chief for operations at the base and the senior national program officer at the Army systems command. In a practice that would be repeated during the Bush administration, his office awarded contracts "worth tens of millions of dollars to former military officials who worked on COG while they were in the Pentagon,"[10] Emerson reported.

One of the biggest winners was Betac Corporation, a consulting firm composed of former intelligence and communications specialists from the Pentagon.[11] Betac, which was eventually sold to ACS Government Solutions Group and is now a unit of Lockheed Martin, was one of the largest government contractors of its day and, with TRW and Lockheed, dominated the intelligence contracting industry from the mid-1980s until the late 1990s.[12] Its first project for the continuity of government plan was a sole-source contract to devise and maintain security for the system. Between 1983 and 1985, the contract expanded from $316,000 to nearly $3 million; and by 1988, Emerson found, Betac "had multiple COG contracts worth $22 million." [13]

These contracts would become the source of the first major scandal involving the intelligence contracting industry when a whistle-blower inside the National Program Office reported that Betac had benefited from its ties with General Renzi, the commandant at Fort Huachuca, whose son, a future congressman from Arizona, worked for Betac. We'll pick up that thread later in the book, when we focus on Renzi's current employer, the NSA contractor ManTech International.

Together, the IBEX and Armageddon projects pumped hundreds of millions of dollars into the intelligence contracting business, which by the 1980s was beginning to take on a life of its own, separate from the broader defense industry. One of the first signs of this emerging industry was the formation in 1979 of the Security Affairs Support Association. SASA, as mentioned earlier, provided a mechanism for companies involved in intelligence to come together with intelligence officials to exchange views on common issues and problems, and in recent years has become a voice for the most powerful players in the Intelligence Community.

Three of SASA's thirty-four founding members were contractors in the Armageddon Project: Harris, Betac, and TRW. Several others, including Boeing, Hughes Aircraft, Lockheed, and Ford Aerospace, were major defense contractors with a stake in the intelligence business. But the majority were specialized companies that provided surveillance and eavesdropping technology that the CIA, the NSA, and other spy agencies couldn't produce themselves, and most of them have either gone out of business or disappeared as corporate entities. Only four of SASA's thirty-four founding companies—Booz Allen Hamilton, IBM, SAIC, and Northrop Grumman—are still around today.*

Yet somehow an obscure industry with just three dozen members

---

* The other twenty-nine firms were swallowed up in the wave of mergers that swept through the defense industry in the late 1980s and early 1990s. One of SASA's earliest benefactors, a company called California Microwave Systems, operated satellite earth stations, microwave

evolved, in twenty years, into a booming spy market of $50 billion a year. To learn how that happened, we will analyze four developments: the privatization revolution that started during the Reagan administration but reached full fruition during the Clinton years; the great leap in defense outsourcing that occurred in the late 1990s, largely as a result of Clinton's policies; the surge in intelligence spending negotiated at the turn of the century by CIA director George Tenet after years of budget cuts and personnel reductions; and the post-9/11 expansion of the intelligence industry. Out of that milieu, the full force of privatization and outsourcing came into existence. Bush, as the lobbyist said earlier, simply took it to the next level.

In 1982, President Reagan appointed J. Peter Grace, a conservative industrialist, to head the Private Sector Survey on Cost Control. Reagan directed its members to "work like tireless bloodhounds to root out government inefficiency and waste of tax dollars."[14] The survey group, better known as the Grace Commission, marked the start of a grand experiment in privatization and outsourcing that would eventually turn over large sectors of the government, including military and intelligence services, to the private sector. It was the perfect expression of Reagan's ideological fixation on "big government," and reflected his belief that capitalism and free markets were the answer to society's problems.

Grace was the ideal man to lead Reagan's charge. He was the founder and CEO of W. R. Grace & Company, one of the largest chemical companies in the world. As the head of a major foreign investor in Latin America, where governments at that time played a key role in eco-

---

radio networks, and surveillance aircraft for U.S. intelligence agencies. It was later sold to Northrop Grumman, and in 2003, three of its pilots working in Colombia were captured by Marxist guerrillas after their plane was shot down (they are still being held more than four years later). Northrop Grumman acquired three other SASA founders: Essex, BDM, and TRW. Loral Electronic Systems and McDonnell Douglas were later acquired by Lockheed Martin. Intercon USA, a consulting firm, made a splash in 1997 when it hired Oleg Kalugin, a retired KGB general, for its staff, but never made it into the news again. Quarry Hill, another consulting firm, went out of business after its president died in 1978. The other companies simply went belly-up or disappeared as corporate entities. I obtained this information from back issues of SASA's in-house magazine, *Colloquy*.

nomic development, he had firsthand experience in dealing with bureaucracies and state planning agencies. Like Reagan, he believed that the U.S. government had grown so large that it was teetering on socialism, and he viewed free enterprise and private property as sacrosanct.* "The government is run horribly," he declared in 1984. "There is no company I know of, except maybe IBM, that could survive if they ran it this way."[15]

Over a period of four years, the Grace Commission methodically surveyed every government service that might conceivably be provided more efficiently and cheaply by the private sector. In a report issued in 1984, it made 2,500 recommendations, including the sale or lease of dozens of government agencies to the private sector. The commission called for the sale of most of the government's dams and hydropower stations in the Pacific Northwest and for the privatization of parts of the U.S. Postal Service, the Coast Guard, the Federal Aviation Administration, and the two federally run airports near Washington, D.C., Dulles and National. It proposed exposing 500,000 federal jobs to private competition under an Office of Management and Budget Circular, A-76, that was first issued in 1966 but had been basically ignored until 1980.

Reagan heartily endorsed the commission's recommendations and made privatization the centerpiece of his campaign to reduce the size of government. Even before the Grace Commission had finished its work, Reagan proposed privatizing millions of acres of public lands, primarily

---

* Grace also had a special relationship with organized labor, which had a huge political and economic stake in the heavily unionized federal government and opposed many of the changes he tried to implement. For many years, Grace was the chairman of the Agency for International Free Labor Development (AIFLD), which was founded in 1962 by the U.S. government and the AFL-CIO to finance and train pro-American "free trade unions" in Latin America. Under the cover of anti-communism, AIFLD's real purpose was to undercut leftist labor unions more attuned to the state-led economic development so popular in the Third World at the time; it also played a role in U.S.-supported coups in Guyana, Brazil, and Chile. Throughout its sordid history, AIFLD maintained close ties with the CIA, which covertly funded some of its activities in Latin America. With the AFL-CIO, through AIFLD, on his side, Grace was in a position to ease labor's opposition to the privatization drive he was about to launch with Reagan, who greatly weakened the power of organized labor by firing nine thousand air traffic controllers who went on strike in 1981. For more on AIFLD and its relationship with the CIA, see my article "Labor's Cold War," in *The Nation,* May 1, 2003.

in the West, as a way to stimulate resource extraction and reduce U.S. dependence on foreign oil. In 1987, declaring that the government "should not compete with the private sector to perform 'commercial type operations,' " Reagan proposed selling off the Naval Petroleum Reserve in California, the Federal Housing Administration, and the Power Marketing Administration, the government agency that markets electricity generated by federal dams.[16]

That same year, the administration completed its first major sale of a government entity by auctioning off the assets of Conrail, the Northeastern freight railroad, for $1.6 billion. During Reagan's second term, the Pentagon also outsourced the U.S. Navy's fleet of cargo ships and tankers, which delivered oil, fuel, military supplies, and weapons to hundreds of U.S. bases scattered around the world. Starting in the mid-1980s, the operation and management of these ships was passed from the Pentagon to private shipping companies.

But that was about it; Reagan's venture in privatization proved to be more illusory than real. Many government agencies resisted his privatization and outsourcing edicts. Congress, which remained under Democratic control for most of his presidency, stoutly resisted the program as well; many statutes were written to discourage and even prohibit privatization.[17] Nor did the public embrace it. In fact, many Americans, including some of the president's closest supporters, were appalled at Reagan's proposal to sell off public lands. At the same time, Reagan did little to promote his program to the public, in the mistaken belief that his ideological commitment to free markets would bring the people along. By the end of Reagan's presidency, only two government agencies had actually been sold—Conrail and the National Consumer Cooperative Bank. That left radical proponents of privatization deeply disappointed.

Reagan's reputation as a champion of privatization "is largely a misconception," Robert Poole, the founder of the libertarian Reason Foundation and a former Reagan adviser, wrote in 2004. "While [Reagan] was generally positive about privatization, he viewed it as a remedy for fixing what was wrong with socialist countries, not as a key pillar of economic reform in the USA. . . . Ironically, there was more real privatization during the Clinton administration than the Reagan administration."[18] Stan Soloway, the contracting lobbyist, agrees with that assessment. "If you look at the numbers, very little privatization took place in the Reagan administration, and none under [the elder] Bush," he says.[19]

In fact, as president, George H. W. Bush had little interest in privatizing government agencies, and devoted some of his time to studying "whether the private sector was doing *too much* relative to government," Peter Fairman, an academic specialist on privatization, wrote in an unpublished study that compares the Reagan and Clinton approaches to privatization. Bush, according to Fairman, reversed some of Reagan's policies and gutted the federal privatization office; it would fall on Clinton's shoulders to push forward the privatization agenda and expand contracting into defense and intelligence.[20]

Bill Clinton began his presidency on extremely poor footing with the Pentagon. The fact that he had avoided the draft and opposed the Vietnam War during the 1960s was bad enough for the generals who ran the armed services. Even worse was his attempt in his first year of office to lift the ban on gays serving openly in the military and the perceived arrogance of his young, liberal staff, who had a tendency to boss people around in the agencies they managed from the White House. Uniformed officers didn't even like the way Clinton saluted, and viewed his proposals to slash military and intelligence spending as dangerous and naive. "I had the feeling the White House wanted the Department of Defense to cease to be part of the United States government," a high-ranking Pentagon official told the *New York Times* in 1996. "We had terrible relations with the White House. They did not understand national defense."[21]

Making war was not high on Bill Clinton's agenda—or the country's, for that matter—when he took power after defeating the senior Bush in the 1992 election. The country was just beginning to emerge from the bipolar world and mind-set of the Cold War. The Soviet Union had ceased to exist, and China and the newly independent countries of

Eastern Europe had embraced capitalism with surprising fervor. In the early 1990s, President George H. W. Bush had tried to create a new "world order" in the aftermath of the Soviet Union's collapse and America's awesome military victory in the first Gulf War. By this time, the defense and intelligence budgets, which began to be slashed in 1990, had reached a post–Cold War low. At the CIA, the cuts resulted in a 30 percent decline in funding for the Directorate of Operations, which ran the agency's clandestine services, and an overall personnel reduction of about 20 percent.[22] "From the Berlin Wall falling and the Soviet Union collapsing, by around 1992 or so the budgets really started to plummet," recalls Jacques Gansler, a former Pentagon acquisition official. "It was called the Peace Dividend." Defense procurement was cut by $60 billion and total acquisition by $100 billion. As a result, Gansler told me, "there were significant cuts across the board in government employment, and intelligence was certainly one of the areas that suffered significantly."[23]

With fears of nuclear and even conventional war fading, many Americans questioned the need for a huge military. Moreover, Clinton, the first baby-boomer and the first antiwar activist to become president, had little initial interest in intelligence. Early on, he dropped the practice of having a CIA official personally deliver the president's traditional morning security briefing. James Woolsey, his first CIA director, saw Clinton so little that, when a deranged man crashed a small plane onto the White House lawn in 1995, tongues wagged in Washington that it was Woolsey, trying to see his commander-in-chief.

It wasn't that Clinton didn't believe in the use of American power, or downgraded the issue of national security. The invasion of Haiti in 1994, the use of airpower in 1999 to drive the Serbs out of Kosovo, and the tightening of economic sanctions on Iraq in the last years of his administration made that clear. He, and many of his contemporaries in government, simply believed that the nexus of American power had shifted away from weapons and spying systems to technology and international trade. The shift in priorities was symbolized by Clinton's creation of the National Economic Council, chaired by the treasury secretary, as an equal to the National Security Council. The idea was to use

American financial power to build high-technology industries that would replace the fading textile, garment, and steel industries and harness the government to make it happen. "It's the economy, stupid," was not only a Clinton campaign slogan, it was national policy.

The signature issue of Clinton's first term was his Reinventing Government initiative run by Vice President Al Gore. It was designed to reduce the size of government and create government agencies that, in Gore's words, would "work better and cost less."[24] Starting in 1993, Gore initiated National Performance Reviews throughout the government to determine what services various agencies provided and whether or not they could be done more efficiently in the private sector. He simultaneously ordered federal government managers to reduce total federal employment by 100,000. The Clinton administration ended up transforming many agencies and subagencies into businesses, and handing out more strategic work to private companies than any administration in history. By the end of its term in 2001, the administration had cut 386,000 jobs from the federal payroll and the government was spending 44 percent more on contractors than it had in 1993.[25]

The Gore initiative really picked up steam after the 1994 midterm elections, when the Republicans captured Congress and took power in the House for the first time in forty-three years. Flush with his success at the polls, House Speaker Newt Gingrich immediately started calling for deeper cuts in the federal workforce and a radical program of privatization. Clinton's response was to come up with a compromise that met the Republicans halfway while still keeping his promise of making government more "responsive" to the public. Out of this coalescence of interests came the outsourcing of defense and intelligence functions that would reach its peak, or nadir, during the administration of George W. Bush.

Two weeks after the 1994 election, Vice President Gore sent a memo to all government departments ordering them to justify every program under their jurisdiction or risk either termination or privatization of those services.[26] Within a month, he had negotiated deep cuts, totaling nearly $20 billion, in the Departments of Energy, Transportation, and Housing. When Gingrich introduced a bill making privatization mandatory in most agencies, Clinton and Gore denounced it as a rigid piece of legislation that would limit competition and government flexibility.

After two years of negotiations, the administration and the Republican congressional leadership agreed on a bill that required agencies to annually publish a list of jobs that are not "inherently governmental" and put them up for bid. The compromise elated conservatives, who had been waiting for such legislation for decades. When Clinton spelled out the details in his 1996 budget, the Heritage Foundation hailed it as the "boldest privatization agenda put forth by any American president to date," and the Reason Foundation called it "the highlight of the year for privatization."[27]

It was an amazing feat: even as Gingrich and his Republican colleagues were hammering Clinton for having an affair with a White House intern and over his foreign policies in Haiti and North Korea, they were working closely with him on privatization. In 1995, Joshua Wolf Shenk, a reporter for the liberal *Washington Monthly,* caught the zeitgeist in an article that described outsourcing as a virtual joint venture between Gingrich and Clinton. "Privatization—involving the private sector in public services, or selling state assets outright—is hot," he wrote. "In particular, contracting out—hiring a business or non-profit to do the public's work at taxpayer expense—is the vogue, bipartisan answer to all sort of governmental problems. The Internal Revenue Service wants private firms to hound those in debt to the government; the Bureau of Prisons wants private firms to lock up prisoners of the state; the Central Intelligence Agency want private firms to, well, 'gather intelligence.'"[28]

That would come, in time. But overall, the number of government agencies that were privatized during the Clinton administration is astounding. One of the first government services to be sold to private interests was the vast computer network known as the Internet, which had started initially as a defense project linking government research institutes in different states. In 1993, the Clinton administration turned over the registration of domain names—the addresses that are used for e-mail and Web sites—to a private company called Network Solutions (perhaps this was what Gore meant in 2000 when he claimed to be the "inventor" of the Internet). A few years later, when the company's government-sanctioned monopoly became controversial, management of the Web was handed over to an international consortium called the Internet Corporation for Assigned Names and Numbers, or ICANN.

Five years after the Internet sale, the Clinton administration privatized the U.S. Enrichment Corporation, which processed uranium into fuel for nuclear power plants, and then sold the shares to private investors in an initial public offering that brought in $1.9 billion. That was the biggest sale of a government agency since the Reagan administration unloaded Conrail; at the time, the corporation had operations in fourteen countries, large enrichment plants in Kentucky and Ohio, and held a 40 percent share of the world market for processed uranium (the *Washington Post* called USEP "a major player in the country's national security and a linchpin of global nuclear proliferation").[29] Also in 1998, the Department of Energy sold the Elk Hills Naval Petroleum Reserve to Occidental Oil & Gas Corporation for $3.65 billion. The reserve was the nation's eleventh largest oilfield, and had served since the early 1900s as an emergency supply for the U.S. Navy's oil-fired ships.

The last two sales alone brought in twice as much revenue as the Reagan administration earned from privatization deals in its entire eight years in office. The Clinton administration also auctioned off parts of the government-owned broadcast spectrum, for $8 billion; outsourced the management of over one hundred air traffic control towers administered by the Federal Aviation Administration; and backed the privatization of four of the nation's five Power Marketing Administrations, which sell electricity generated by 129 federal hydropower facilities (that action was blocked by Congress). In his memoir, Clinton took pains to give his Reinventing Government (or "Rego," as he called it) programs a liberal spin. "All the Rego changes were developed according to a simple credo: protect people, not bureaucracy; promote results, not rules; get action, not rhetoric," he wrote. "Al Gore's highly successful initiative confounded our adversaries, elated our allies, and escaped the notice of the public because it was neither sensational nor controversial."[30]

Starting in 1997, Clinton's administration began focusing its privatization energies on the military and intelligence communities. But he had to be careful: by this time, Clinton had alienated much of those communities by backing Congress in its defunding of the black budget—cuts that were fought every step of the way by Jim Woolsey, his CIA director. Clinton and Woolsey were not only on different pages politically, they worked at complete opposite ends of the street when it came to the budget. That was largely Clinton's fault, however, because his staff apparently had no clue, when Woolsey was hired, that he was as close to the high-tech spying industry as any CIA director in history.

Woolsey had been around the national security establishment since 1969, when he began working as a systems analyst at the Pentagon. One of his first jobs there, according to an early profile of him in the *New York Times,* was studying "supersecret spy satellite programs inside a Pentagon vault."[31] For the next fifteen years, Woolsey made his way up the policy chain, serving as an undersecretary of the Navy and an arms control negotiator for two administrations. Along the way, he had become good friends with Richard Perle, his future comrade-in-arms in the campaign to topple Saddam Hussein. Perle at the time was an anti-Soviet hard-liner working on the staff of Senator Henry M. "Scoop" Jackson. Perle later brought Woolsey onto the staff of the Senate Armed Services Committee as its general counsel.

Over time, Woolsey became a hard-liner on foreign policy and maintained close ties with neocons who'd gotten their start opposing détente and arms control during the Ford administration (among his early contacts were Dick Cheney and Donald Rumsfeld, who served with Woolsey on the secret Armageddon Project). Once he turned rightward, he never looked back: during the Iran-contra affair in 1987, Woolsey represented Michael Ledeen, the man who brought Oliver North, a Marine colonel on the White House staff and Reagan's National Security Council, into contact with Manucher Ghorbanifar, the Iranian arms dealer who acted as a middleman between the government of Iran and the Reagan administration (Ledeen had developed those contacts through his relationship with extreme rightists in Italy's intelligence service).[32] But Woolsey's true interests lay in intelligence and the satellite imagery he had learned so much about as an arms control negotiator, a job that required close contacts with the CIA and its secret photo-reconnaissance units. Long before he was appointed director of the CIA by President Clinton, Woolsey had found a home in the Intelligence-Industrial Complex.

In the early 1980s, as a corporate lawyer, Woolsey was recruited to the board of directors of Titan Corporation, a firm represented by his law firm that is now an intelligence subsidiary of L-3 Communications. Titan had many classified contracts in defense electronics and missile programs that Woolsey knew so much about as an arms negotiator. It was founded by J. Sidney Webb, the retired vice chairman of TRW, and Gene W. Ray, once the top strategic planner in the Air Force, who had developed computer programs that could simulate the outcomes of nuclear wars. By 1987, Titan had assembled a science and management team that *BusinessWeek* called "the envy of the defense establishment." Seventy-one percent of its $4 million in revenues that year were from federal contracts.[33]

In 1991, Woolsey was elected to the board of Martin Marietta, one of the nation's largest rocket manufacturers and a major contractor for the NRO (it merged with Lockheed in 1996), and a year later to the board of British Aerospace, which was just beginning its rise to the top ranks of the U.S. defense industry (it's now known as BAE Systems). His experience in the industry clearly shaped his views toward intelligence. In its 1993 profile written when Woolsey was nominated to be CIA director, the *New York Times* noted that "though American intelligence organizations have already begun to focus more on the spread of weapons and regional tensions after the cold war, Mr. Woolsey is likely to go further by directing that more reconnaissance satellites, electronic interception capabilities and human intelligence sources be focused" on the "arc of unstable and heavily armed nations" running from the Middle East to Northeast Asia.[34] Clearly, Woolsey had strong grounds to oppose cutting the intelligence budget.

But President Clinton and his aides didn't have a clue about

Woolsey's background. According to the late David Halberstam, who chronicled the Clinton administration's national security policies in his book *War in a Time of Peace,* Woolsey was "added to the [Clinton] team at the last minute as a necessary concession to the Reagan Democrats," and "was always a bad fit."[35] Clinton, in his autobiography, says he first met Woolsey at a 1991 conference organized by Samuel "Sandy" Berger, Clinton's old friend from the George McGovern presidential campaign of 1972. Berger, who later served as Clinton's second national security adviser, organized a meeting for the future president with a group of Democrats and independents who had, according to Clinton, "more robust views on national security and defense than our party typically projected." (Woolsey and Berger now work together at the private equity fund Paladin Capital Group, which invests in homeland security companies.) Clinton offered Woolsey the CIA post after one interview, and, as mentioned earlier, rarely saw him after he was confirmed.

Accounts of Woolsey's two years at the CIA portray him as an arrogant intellectual who browbeat intelligence critics in Congress but was outmaneuvered because of his lack of presidential support. "Many of Woolsey's friends and supporters blame his troubles on what they see as his argumentative and sometimes abrasive personal style," R. Jeffrey Smith, a reporter at the *Washington Post,* wrote in 1994. "An ambitious, driven litigator, Woolsey is frequently said to be unable or unwilling to strike a compromise."[36] But part of the problem was that Woolsey strongly disagreed with Clinton's desire to cut technical intelligence spending and wanted to continue a rebuilding program that Robert Gates, his predecessor as CIA director, had started under the first President Bush.

The CIA's official history of Woolsey's tenure at the agency, titled "Uncompromising Defender," underscores that point, saying that Woolsey "identified more with sustaining elements of continuity in intelligence between the Bush and Clinton administrations than with calls for reining it in or changing its direction, and over time his lack of political allies or support led to his fighting increasingly lonely battles and eventually departing."[37] The CIA history dryly notes that Woolsey "did not enjoy a relationship of trust and mutual confidence with the president he served, Bill Clinton, who chose him as his DCI on the recommendation of foreign policy advisers. Their lack of a prior relationship did not foreordain distance between them, but unfortunately no bond developed in the 23 months that Woolsey served as DCI."

In any case, Woolsey didn't seem much interested in the CIA's core competency, human intelligence. According to Melissa Boyle Mahle, a former CIA operative who wrote a memoir of her years at the agency called *Denial and Deception,* Woolsey reduced the number of large overseas CIA stations by more than 60 percent, and cut the number of deployed case officers working overseas by more than 30 percent. Much of this was in response to Al Gore's National Performance Review of the Intelligence Community, which concluded that the IC's biggest problem was its failure to work together as a team, and "called upon the community to find ways to share resources, be more efficient and effective, and reduce overhead."[38]

In contrast, Woolsey was ferocious in defending the IC's technical budget. He fought vigorously to increase spending on expensive high-technology programs—precisely the vehicles that were funding the great leaps being made at the time by Titan, Martin Marietta, and other companies he advised before going to the CIA (as required, Woolsey resigned all of his board seats upon taking over as DCI). Woolsey, according to the CIA, also "pressed for progress" in developing unmanned aerial vehicles for reconnaissance as part of a broader plan to demonstrate the utility of UAVs to the U.S. military. During his tenure at the CIA, the Pentagon created the Defense Airborne Reconnaissance Office to pursue the idea.

"In effect," the CIA history says, "the NRO could now concentrate on space systems, and airborne programs enjoyed separate status and support" within the Department of Defense (as a footnote, the CIA adds that "Woolsey loved the science and technology aspects of defense and intelligence matters"). The UAVs developed under Woolsey's watch were the predecessors of the Predator, which has been used extensively by the U.S. military and the CIA in the wars in Afghanistan and Iraq. Its primary manufacturers are Northrop Grumman and General Atomics of San Diego.

But Congress was not receptive to Woolsey's pitch for investments in technical systems. In 1994, the Senate cut $300 million from Woolsey's $1 billion request for accelerated development of a new generation of classified spy satellites. Senators urged him to pay more attention to human intelligence, and reminded him that spending on satellites had already tripled during the 1980s.[39] This did not sit well with Woolsey. In one hearing, according to an account in the *Washington Post,* he "sternly instructed senators—pointer in hand—how their budget cuts had 'decimated' the spy agency's operations and would have to be reversed."[40] Woolsey also riled lawmakers when he opposed creation of a congressionally mandated commission on the future of intelligence and lobbied against legislation that would have resolved some of the turf battles between the CIA and the FBI.[41]

In the end, Woolsey's demise was caused by his refusal to fire anyone inside the CIA over the damage caused to the nation by Aldrich Ames, a CIA agent who spied for the Soviet Union for eleven years. Ames, a notorious drunk who lived a lavish lifestyle that included fancy cars and houses, was arrested in 1994. He admitted to handing over to the Soviets the names of thirty-four American spies in the Soviet Union, at least ten of whom were later executed. All Woolsey managed to do in response was hand out letters of reprimand to eleven CIA officials—eight of them retired—for allowing Ames to operate despite years of living beyond his means and being denied promotions because of his alcoholism. But he adamantly refused to fire anyone, saying "that's not the American way." No officials were docked pay or forced to change jobs.

Woolsey's mild response infuriated many in Congress, including some of his Republican supporters in the Senate. The final factor may have been a CNN interview in which Ames bragged about how easy it was to spy at the CIA. In 1995, two months after the Senate Intelligence Committee criticized Woolsey for being too lenient in the Ames case, he resigned. "People were killed, after all," said Senator Dennis DeConcini, the Arizona Democrat who was his fiercest critic in Congress.[42] Some in the CIA never forgave him. In 2005, Michael Scheuer, who once directed the CIA's Osama bin Laden unit, described Woolsey as "the pariah of President Clinton's first-term national security team and the man who failed to punish those who ignored the suspicious behavior of Aldrich Ames, thereby letting that traitor destroy the CIA's network of human assets in the Soviet Union." Woolsey was among several directors who "lacked the courage to take the disciplinary action needed to clean up after CIA disasters," Scheuer concluded.[43]

Woolsey was succeeded by John M. Deutch and, in 1997, by George Tenet.* Deutch, who served for less than two years, played an instrumental role in the creation of the National Imagery and Mapping Agency, the predecessor to the NGA, but otherwise had little impact on intelligence policy. Under Tenet, however, the CIA and the rest of the Intelligence Community began outsourcing tasks that had previously been done by government employees. Clinton's Reinventing Government project played a key role; but this time around, the administration was getting deeply involved in military conflicts overseas, and defense spending was on the rise. With the Pentagon and Intelligence Community pared down because of the post–Cold War budget cuts, outsourcing became a convenient way to keep up with military demands for logistics, security, and, ultimately, intelligence.

By Clinton's second term, he had used military force several times, primarily in Bosnia and Haiti, and had come close to launching bombing strikes on North Korea during the 1994 standoff over that country's threat to develop nuclear weapons. He had also softened a bit on

---

* After leaving the CIA, Woolsey returned to his old Washington law firm of Shea & Gardner. There, he became actively involved in supporting Iraqi opposition figures, including Ahmed Chalabi of the Iraqi National Congress, who had gathered in Washington to press for U.S. help in overthrowing the government of Saddam Hussein. In 1998, he joined the Project for the New American Century, an advocacy group founded by prominent neoconservatives, and was one of eighteen people to sign the organization's open letter to President Clinton urging him to use military action to topple the Saddam Hussein regime (other signers who figure in this book include Donald Rumsfeld, Richard Perle, and Richard Armitage). He lobbied for passage of the Iraq Liberation Act, which endorsed the concept of regime change and

defense spending. In 1996, after threatening to veto an $11 billion spending increase passed by the Republican Congress, a sum that was greater than what the Pentagon said it needed, he went ahead and signed it. And after the disastrous tenure of former congressman Les Aspin as Clinton's first secretary of defense, the president had smoothed relations with the military by appointing William J. Perry, a former defense undersecretary with considerable experience in the defense electronics industry, to replace him. After winning reelection in 1996, Clinton and Gore were in a position to begin implementing their "reinvention" initiatives in defense and intelligence.

These efforts coincided with a raft of mergers and acquisitions in the defense industry. The M&A boom was encouraged by the administration, which recognized that the Pentagon would not be ordering enough ships, planes, missiles, and other weapons systems to sustain the number of companies that had flourished during Reagan's huge military buildup of the 1980s. Lockheed Martin, for example, was created through a merger of Lockheed's aircraft division with Martin Marietta, Loral Defense, and the General Dynamics combat aircraft division. In the end, five huge firms were left standing: Lockheed Martin, Northrop Grumman, Raytheon, Boeing, and General Dynamics.

In response to the changes sweeping through the industry, the Defense Science Board, which advises the Pentagon on acquisition, technical, and manufacturing issues, convened a special task force to find ways in which the Department of Defense could use outsourcing and privatization as tools in reducing the costs of the defense support structure. The task force was chaired by Philip A. Odeen, the president and CEO of BDM International Inc., a major defense and intelligence contractor, and filled primarily with representatives from the largest de-

---

allocated $100 million to Iraqi opposition parties, including Chalabi's INC. Woolsey was moving right, and fast. But he also maintained his interest in the intelligence business. During the 1990s, Woolsey joined the board of, and was given a substantial share of stock in, Yurie Systems Inc., a data networking company founded by Jeong H. Kim, a former naval officer who had worked in the black world of fast-attack nuclear submarines. Woolsey's involvement in Yurie turned out to be fortuitous in 1998, when the company was acquired by defense and intelligence contractor Lucent Technologies for nearly $1 billion. In 2006, Kim, by then the CEO of Lucent, appointed Woolsey to the board of a separate U.S. subsidiary for Lucent's classified work with intelligence agencies after its acquisition by France's Alcatal.

fense companies, including SAIC, Boeing, and Lockheed Martin. Not surprisingly, given its makeup, the task force recommended a major expansion in outsourcing.

"The Task Force believes that all DoD support functions should be contracted out to private vendors except those functions which are inherently governmental, are directly involved in warfighting, or for which no adequate private sector capability exists or can be expected to be established," Odeen wrote in the final report. The report recommended that the Pentagon establish a target for 2002 to "generate up to $10 billion or more in outsourcing related savings to fund the badly needed expansion of investment programs for DoD," and estimated that outsourcing would provide the Pentagon with savings of 30 to 40 percent.[44] The report, however, failed to identify which defense functions were "inherently governmental."*

Odeen chaired a second task force that was convened by Secretary of Defense William S. Cohen, Perry's successor at the Pentagon, in 1997. The National Defense Panel was formed under a congressional mandate to study future challenges for U.S. defense and national security and also endorsed outsourcing as a way to provide "effective combat support services." The Department of Defense, it concluded, "must embrace a new paradigm" that will "fully leverage the capabilities, technologies, and business practices of the commercial sector, adapted to the unique mission and special circumstances of the military environment."[45]

That panel, too, was dominated by contractors. They included retired Marine Corps General Richard D. Hearney, the vice president of military aircraft and missile systems for the Boeing Company; retired Army General Robert W. RisCassi, an executive with Lockheed Martin and a future board member of the defense intelligence contractors ATK Inc. and L-3 Communications; and Richard Armitage, a former under-

* "Needless to say, [the task force members] offered inadequate evidence to support [their] multibillion-dollar savings estimates," Ann Markusen, an economist at the University of Minnesota and an expert on defense acquisition, wrote about the study. Nevertheless, it served as a blueprint for the outsourcing boom that followed. See Ann Markusen, "The Case Against Privatizing National Security," *Dollars & Sense*, May/June 2004.

secretary of defense who had recently been named to the advisory boards of two companies that were just entering the intelligence contracting field, ManTech International and CACI International.

In November 1997, just before the defense panel unveiled its report, Secretary Cohen and Vice President Gore jointly announced a "revolution in business affairs" at the Pentagon. The plan, said Gore, would "bring America's defense into the next century—efficient, effective, the strongest in the world." It proposed slashing 25 percent of the department's workforce and for the Pentagon to begin to identify functions that could be performed by the private sector and open them to market competition. Altogether, more than thirty thousand jobs were eliminated by the plan. "What we are doing is providing a corporate vision for the Defense Department," said Cohen.[46] Jacques Gansler, who ranked third in the Pentagon hierarchy, served as point man for the program. "To meet the challenge of modernization," he said in one speech, the Pentagon "must do business more like private business. My top priority as Undersecretary of Defense is to make the Pentagon look much more like a dynamic, restructured, reengineered, world-class commercial sector business."[47]

After Cohen and Gore announced their downsizing plans for the Pentagon, a group of CEOs represented by an organization called Business Executives for National Security (BENS) announced that they would lobby Congress and the White House on behalf of Gore's defense reform initiative.* It put together a high-profile commission to promote

---

* Based in Washington with offices in major metropolitan centers, such as Atlanta and St. Louis, BENS describes itself as a "non-partisan group of business leaders." It started out, according to Ken Beeks, its current vice president for policy, with a "left-leaning, anti-nuke tilt," and did some of its earliest lobbying on arms control, such as the chemical weapons treaty ratified by the U.S. Senate in April 1997. But over time, it evolved into a conservative advocacy group that monitors government spending on weapons and intelligence systems and works with the Pentagon and the Intelligence Community to improve their business practices in procurement and acquisition. Charles G. Boyd, BENS's president and CEO, is a retired Air Force general who was a prisoner of war in Vietnam and, during the 1990s, served as a defense consultant to Speaker of the House Newt Gingrich. Its board of directors has historically included chief executives from the nation's best-known and largest corporations, including major government contractors such as Lockheed Martin and DynCorp. Its current chairman, Steven Cheney, was a close aide (but no relation) to Dick Cheney when he was secretary of defense in the George H. W. Bush administration.

outsourcing, privatization, and acquisition reform in the defense industry and promote the Clinton administration's plans to force the military to compete with the private sector for support work.[48] The program was called the "tail to tooth" commission. The idea, says Ken Beeks, BENS's current vice president for policy, was to convince the U.S. government to get out of the tail, or the support side of defense, and "get back to the tooth, the fighting side."[49] Like Odeen's two Pentagon study groups, the commission was stacked with privatization promoters and defense contractors. It was co-chaired by former senator Warren Rudman, R–New Hampshire, who had once proposed the most sweeping privatization legislation in the history of Congress, and advised by two former secretaries of defense with deep roots in the defense and intelligence industries, Frank C. Carlucci and William Perry.

Both men were working for companies that had much to gain from the Pentagon's outsourcing programs. Since leaving the Reagan administration, where he served in the top two positions at the Pentagon and as national security adviser, Carlucci had been chairman of the Carlyle Group, the defense-oriented private equity fund. There, he managed an acquisition drive that transformed Carlyle from a small boutique investment bank into the eleventh largest defense contractor, with holdings in aerospace, armaments, and intelligence. When he took on his advisory role at BENS, Carlucci was on the boards of four major defense contractors: Westinghouse Electric, Kaman Corporation, Ashland Oil, and the RAND Corporation, the military think tank funded by the Air Force. Perry, who'd served in the Carter administration as the primary intelligence adviser to Secretary of Defense Harold Brown, had been director of several contractors, including ESL Inc., which specialized in signal processing systems and was one of the first outside contractors at the NSA (it was later sold to TRW). Perry later served as a director of Boeing, United Technologies, and SAIC.

After three years of study, the Carlucci-Perry commission proposed a sweeping array of changes that, it claimed, would save an estimated $30 billion a year if enacted. They included the full privatization of the Pentagon's long-haul defense communications and its supply chain management. In a circular pattern of backslapping, the private study was then used by the Clinton administration and the Pentagon as a basis for selling their own programs to Congress. The administration's point man in this effort was Jacques Gansler, who was the undersecretary of defense for acquisition, technology, and logistics from 1997 to 2001. During this period, Gansler spoke frequently about the need to expose noninherently governmental work to competition and pushed the Pentagon to encourage both public-private competition and partnerships. He was particularly interested in proposals to expand the outsourcing of logistics. "Since we spend more than $80 billion annually on logistics and yet don't match world-class performance (in either responsiveness or costs), there is enormous potential here," he said in a 1999 speech to defense contractors.[50]

Expanding the outsourcing of logistics was especially welcome news to the Kellogg Brown & Root (KBR) subsidiary of Halliburton, which had been quietly expanding its government services business behind the leadership of Halliburton's new CEO, former secretary of defense Dick Cheney. During the waning days of the administration of the first President Bush, Cheney had spearheaded a major effort at the Pentagon to expand the private sector role in defense into logistics. In 1991, under his direction, the Department of Defense paid $9 million to Halliburton's KBR subsidiary to study whether the private sector should handle all of the military's logistics, such as transporting materials to battlefields and providing food and housing to front-line troops. The idea was seen at the time as the logical extension of the policies enacted under the Reagan administration to outsource the Navy's supply lines. KBR, not surprisingly, responded positively, and in August 1992, it won the Pentagon's first Logistics Civilian Augmentation Program contract, also known as LOGCAP. Under the terms of the contract, KBR was to provide logistics support wherever U.S. forces were engaged around the world.

Halliburton's work on LOGCAP began with a relatively modest $4-million contract, but mushroomed in size as the Clinton administration began deploying U.S. troops to various hot spots around the world. Between 1992 and 2000, KBR sent its contract employees to Bosnia, Kosovo, Macedonia, Hungary, Albania, Croatia, Greece, Italy, Somalia, Zaire, Haiti, and Southwest Asia to support U.S. Army operations. The first LOGCAP contract ended up with a value of $815 million.[51] In 1997, KBR lost the LOGCAP contract to DynCorp, a private military contractor now owned by Veritas Capital. But with U.S. forces heavily committed in Bosnia, the Army carved out a separate contract for KBR in the Balkans. There, the company became legendary for its vast array of services. "In effect, the firm was the US force's supply and engineering corps wrapped into one corporate element," Peter Singer wrote in his brilliant book, *Corporate Warriors*.[52] Ultimately, KBR earned more than $800 million for its work in the Balkans.[53] Other companies winning contracts there included Raytheon and Bell Helicopters, which provided "critical aviation assets" and support to the U.S. peacekeeping effort in Bosnia.[54] In addition, the Army handed out contracts to AT&T and Sprint to provide radio links between U.S. commanders and peacekeeping troops deployed in Bosnia and Croatia.

Like KBR, some of the companies that won military contracts in Bosnia had advised the Pentagon on outsourcing. Most of the interpreters used by the U.S. Army in Bosnia, for example, were employees of BDM, where Philip Odeen, who had managed two Pentagon task forces that recommended an expansion of outsourcing, was the CEO. At the time of its contract award, BDM was owned by Carlyle, whose chairman, former Secretary of Defense Frank Carlucci, had publicly urged the Pentagon to expand contracting as adviser to the "tail to tooth" commission. Carlyle, through its United Defense Industries subsidiary, also won a contract in Bosnia to provide maintenance support for U.S. Army ground vehicles. Its biggest payoff came in 1996: in one of the first big defense-related privatizations completed by the Clinton administration, Carlyle acquired the investigation service arm of the Office of Personnel Management. Renamed US Investigations Service, USIS remained in Carlyle's hands until 2007, and is the largest provider of security investigations for employees and contractors hired by the Pentagon, the National Security Agency, and other U.S. government agencies.

Direct contracting wasn't the only way that privatization expanded. Some of the military contracts signed during that time were drawn up after many U.S. bases were either closed or reduced in size as part of the

Defense Reform Initiative. In 1999, for example, a team of contractors led by Lockheed Martin won a fifteen-year, $10.2 billion contract to maintain aircraft engines for the U.S. Air Force; the work was put out for bid after President Clinton blocked a recommendation from an independent commission to close Kelly Air Force Base in San Antonio, Texas, but agreed instead to the outsourcing of some of the base's work. "In its place, engine work being handled there by Air Force personnel is now being done by private companies," the *Washington Post* reported. "For Lockheed, the contract is another in a series of privatization deals in which the giant aerospace company has been taking on work once performed by the government."[55] In 1997, Hughes Electronics Corporation won a contract to design and build electronics gear for Navy planes after the Pentagon closed the Naval Air Warfare Center in Indianapolis, Indiana.[56]

Another area where defense outsourcing blossomed during the Clinton administration was in overseas military training. The origins of this practice date back to the early 1980s, when Vinnell Corporation, which had worked for the Pentagon in Vietnam, won a contract to train Saudi Arabia's National Guard, a 75,000-man army that enforced domestic security for that country's authoritarian government (at the time, Vinnell was owned by the BDM subsidiary of Carlyle, which had close ties to the Saudi royal family).[57] Meanwhile, SAIC was training the Saudi navy and bringing Saudi military personnel to company headquarters in San Diego for further study.[58] Under contract with the U.S. Navy and Marines, Booz Allen Hamilton was managing the Saudi Marine Corps and running the Saudi Armed Forces Staff College. The biggest player in this business was Military Professional Resources Inc. (MPRI), a company founded in 1987 by several retired U.S. Army generals. In 1995, in what the company said was a private deal with the government of Croatia, MPRI was hired to train the Croatian army,* and later signed a con-

* The Clinton administration denied charges, voiced primarily in Europe, that MPRI's project was an attempt to circumvent the international arms embargo imposed on the former Yugoslav states. "Nonetheless," concluded the *Washington Post*, "MPRI's involvement appears in keeping with US interests in creating a Croatian military counterweight to Serbian domination in the Balkans and promoting democratic practices in former communist states." See Bradley Graham, "US Firm Exports Military Expertise," *Washington Post*, August 11, 1995.

tract to train the Bosnian armed forces after winning a bidding war against SAIC and BDM.[59]

Ken Silverstein, who is currently the Washington editor for *Harper's,* was one of the first journalists to write about the corporate role in overseas military training. "For the Pentagon, the privatization of military training programs is a win-win situation," he wrote in his 2000 book *Private Warriors*. "In addition to providing plausible deniability about overseas entanglements, it allows Washington to shed military personnel while simultaneously retaining the capacity to influence and direct huge missions." Moreover, he added, "Retired generals and private companies have far more leeway in evading questions from Congress or the press."[60]

Many of these companies remain closely entwined with U.S. training programs. MPRI, for example, is one of the largest private military contractors operating in Iraq (it is now part of L-3 Communications' intelligence division). In 2007, L-3/MPRI was recruiting former U.S. military officers for work in Equatorial Guinea, which receives military aid from the United States, to "advise and assist the transformation of the security forces, starting with the Ministry of Defense (MOD), Maritime Force and National Police."[61] Here again we can see a direct link between practices that originated during the Clinton administration and those that flourish under President George W. Bush. Few people outside the Intelligence Community, however, noticed that outsourcing had also expanded to include intelligence operations and analysis.

One of the companies that capitalized on this development was ManTech International. During the 1990s, ManTech, as we will examine in more detail later, blossomed as an intelligence contractor for the first time. During Operations Desert Storm and Desert Shield, the company provided technical support to Army intelligence and electronic warfare units, and in 1994 provided similar services to U.S. forces in Haiti. One of its first contracts was to provide support services for Army intelligence units in Bosnia, Kosovo, and Albania.[62] Under Clinton, ManTech also helped the U.S. Air Force and the National Security Agency pick up signals intelligence from F-16 fighter jets and worked with Booz Allen Hamilton on a $43-million contract with the U.S. Army's Intelligence and Security Command (the Army wing of the NSA) to support the Army's intelligence "master plan."[63] During the late 1990s and into 2000, ManTech also supported military intelligence units in Kuwait and East Timor, and after 9/11 sent its signals intelligence support units into Afghanistan and Iraq.

It was also during the Balkans war that military intelligence officers first started leaving the Army to form companies on their own. Premier Technology Group (PTG), for example, was started by a group of retired G-2 Army intelligence officers with U.S. Army V Corps stationed in Heidelberg, Germany. After being deployed in Bosnia, "they created PTG to go back and do exactly what they were doing because they realized there was nobody else there to replace them," recalls William D. Golden, a former National Security Agency officer who founded a recruitment firm that helped companies like PTG find some of their first employees.[64] Five years later, PTG was acquired by CACI International and became the basis for CACI's interrogation contract at Abu Ghraib.

The changes that occurred under Clinton, particularly in the intelligence arena, were directly related to shifts in technology. By the 1990s, commercial developments in encryption, information technology, imagery, and satellites had outpaced the government's considerable efforts in these areas, and intelligence agencies began to turn to the private sector for technologies they once made in-house. One of their vehicles was the Defense Advanced Research Projects Agency (DARPA), the central R&D organization for the Department of Defense, which President Clinton had endorsed early in his administration as an important vehicle for improving the competitiveness of U.S. high-tech industries. Under its new acronym, ARPA (the "D" for defense was dropped in 1993, only to be restored three years later), the agency began pouring research money into projects useful to the Intelligence Community.

Researchers at Wright-Patterson Air Force Base in Ohio, for example, developed the first unmanned aerial vehicles, which later evolved into the Global Hawk and Predator used extensively today in the battlefields of Iraq and Afghanistan. ARPA was also involved in the early stages of the NSA's Project Groundbreaker, a huge program to outsource the NSA's internal communications system, and began signing contracts with small Beltway bandits that were hiring former intelligence analysts and scientists leaving the NSA, the CIA, and other agencies. ARPA money also funded some of the NSA's first data mining programs. "Nineteen ninety-eight and 1999 is when it really began," says former NSA officer Golden. "This was when you had the big push in intelligence to outsource, outsource, outsource." The ARPA research programs, he adds, marked the first "shift of people in the private sector actually doing intelligence."[65]

Clinton officials involved in these programs say they acted out of a belief that private companies were more efficient than the government. "There's a large body of empirical data that shows that using the commercial market versus doing it in-house in a monopoly environment results in much better performance at much lower cost as long as it is work that is not inherently governmental," Jacques Gansler, the former Pentagon official, told me.[66] "And that's very important, that distinction." To keep the private and public sector completely separate, Gansler said the Clinton administration made sure that the *management* of government contracts remained under government control. "The person who makes the decisions as to which contractor gets the work, how much is budgeted, and does the oversight—things like that are inherently governmental," he said. There, he was drawing a sharp line between his definition of outsourcing and that of Bush and Cheney, who presided over a contract administration that itself outsourced its acquisition functions to systems integrators like Lockheed Martin and CACI International.

Gansler himself was deeply involved in a little-known incident in which the Clinton administration put a cap on intelligence outsourcing. In 1999, when U.S. and British forces were engaged in NATO's intervention in the Balkans, the Pentagon grew concerned over a British plan to privatize its Defence Evaluation Research Agency (DERA). As the British equivalent to the Defense Advanced Research Projects Agency, DERA was one of the primary channels of communication between U.S. and British intelligence. Privatizing a national asset like that was too much for Clinton's Department of Defense. That fall, U.S. officials threatened to suspend sharing of top secret satellite intelligence with Britain if the deal went through. In October 1999, Gansler sent a strongly worded letter to his British counterparts demanding that the plans be scrapped. DERA's privatization, he warned, could "produce an environment in which the special National Reconnaissance Office relationship with the DERA . . . would not be possible."[67]

I was told by Gansler, who retired from government in 2001 and teaches public policy at the University of Maryland, that the Pentagon's opposition to the British plans for DERA focused on "very sensitive intelligence issues" and the fact that some of DERA's work involving satellite reconnaissance and signals intelligence "involved the United States government as well." The British, in his view, had breached the firewall that defined "inherently governmental." So the Clinton administration leaned on British officials to keep DERA's core intelligence functions within government. "We didn't want all of DERA to be instantly transferred to the private sector. That was the concern," said Gansler. As a result of those discussions, "some work was kept in the government and the rest was spun off. In other words they assented to our request."[68] DERA's privatization, however, didn't actually occur until after the transition from the Clinton to the Bush administration. In 2003, DERA was fully privatized, renamed QinetiQ, and its assets were sold to Frank Carlucci's Carlyle Group.

By 1999, however, the momentum toward outsourcing was being fueled by new demands for intelligence and surveillance from the conservative, pro-defense Republicans leading the House and Senate. Despite Newt Gingrich's willingness to work with Clinton on "reinventing government," he and his allies had little stomach for Clinton's national security policies. As they rode the crest of their power sweep in the 1994 elections, the Republicans began agitating for increased spending on spy satellites and reconnaissance systems. They believed that the crown jewels of U.S. intelligence were being squandered by the Clinton administration, and won strong support for this position from the Project for the New American Century, a group of neoconservatives who spent much of the 1990s making the case for a more aggressive posture overseas, based on military strength and "moral clarity." In a famous declaration that became the basis for the foreign policies of the George W. Bush administration, twenty-five PNAC members, including Donald Rumsfeld, Dick Cheney, and Paul Wolfowitz, wrote in 1997 that "cuts in foreign affairs and defense spending, inattention to the tools of statecraft, and inconstant leadership are making it increasingly difficult to sustain American influence around the world. As a consequence, we are jeopardizing the nation's ability to meet present threats and to deal with potentially greater challenges that lie ahead."[69]

Those words were particularly significant to Cheney, who had taken extraordinary efforts to save intelligence from the big wave of cuts that occurred at the end of the Cold War. When Cheney was secretary of defense, he worked closely with CIA director Bob Gates to reform the intelligence apparatus. The decade of the 1990s, the two men believed, was the perfect time to create the kind of intelligence service needed for an era in which the United States would be the undisputed superpower. "It was as if we were being given a gift," says Richard L. Haver, the vice president of intelligence strategy at Northrop Grumman, who was Cheney's senior intelligence adviser at the Pentagon from 1989 to 1992. "The Cold War was over, and the chaotic new world was going to take a decade to fully form itself and manifest itself as problems on our doorstep." Cheney, said Haver, felt that "what we needed to do was to take a deep breath inside the national security apparatus, particularly inside the defense establishment."[70]

Both Cheney and Gates, he said, fought for a common objective: to preserve as much of the intelligence budget as they could from the onslaught of congressional doves intent on creating a real peace dividend. "Cheney believed we shouldn't be putting less money into intelligence; we should be putting more money into intelligence," said Haver. And by manipulating the Pentagon budget, that's exactly what Cheney did. According to Haver, "if anybody has access to the classified budgets" and could compare the line items in the late 1980s and early 1990s, they will see that "the Defense Department gave up nearly twice as much money as it should have to protect cuts in intelligence"—in other words, the intelligence budget was cut at half the rate of the defense budget. The idea, said Haver, was to chop out the "Cold War deadwood" and start reinvesting for the future. But the effort was stopped in its tracks when Bill Clinton moved into the White House. Clinton came to office vowing to slash the intelligence budget by $7 billion, and Congress, as we've seen, backed his efforts. As a result, said Haver, little of the reinvestment favored by Cheney and Gates was ever made.*

Now, six years into Clinton's term, many members of PNAC and the neoconservative right believed that cuts in defense spending—the source of more than 80 percent of the intelligence budget—had greatly reduced the ability of the United States to spy on other countries, particularly those so-called rogue states that were threatening to build nuclear weapons. Moreover, PNAC's leaders, particularly people like Cheney and Rumsfeld, were deeply suspicious of the CIA, and believed that it was underestimating the threat of ballistic missiles from North Korea, Iraq, and Iran as well as China. Their suspicions of the CIA were rekindled in 1995, when the agency produced a National Intelligence Estimate predicting that no country outside of the five major nuclear powers was capable of developing or acquiring a ballistic missile over the next fifteen years that could threaten the lower forty-eight states or Canada. In response, advocates of a missile defense system in the House introduced legislation to create a commission to study the issue. Gingrich, the House speaker, appointed Rumsfeld to chair the committee; another key member was James Woolsey, fresh from his frustrating tenure at the CIA.

Rumsfeld came to the task determined to prove that the CIA had lost its way, and his experience on the commission apparently deepened

---

* Haver, the former vice president and director of intelligence for TRW's Information Technology Group, remains extremely bitter about the outcome. Speaking to an intelligence conference in 2006, he said: "If you want to know the origins of our community's problems, if you want to know why there's a 9/11 Commission and a WMD Commission, and all the rest of this, don't look in 2001, or 2002, or even the 2000s—look at 1995, 1996, and 1997. If you are going to be a major player in the intelligence community five or ten years from now, you'll still be paying for some of those decisions."

his suspicions. The committee's first report, released in July 1998, flatly declared that the CIA's NIE of 1995 was wrong, and argued that the potential for U.S. adversaries acquiring a long-range missile threat was much sooner than fifteen years. "The threat to the United States posed by these emerging capabilities is broader, more mature and evolving more rapidly than has been reported in estimates and reports by the Intelligence Community," the committee said. Among other recommendations, it urged the Pentagon to exert greater control over the nation's spy satellites through the National Reconnaissance Office, and spend more on collection systems to minimize the ability of other countries to conceal their military activities.[71] Gingrich hailed the conclusions as "the most important warning about our national security since the end of the Cold War."[72]

Critics of the commission accused Rumsfeld of cooking his data. The commission "basically massaged existing U.S. intelligence data to come up with new conclusions that fit the political needs of its creators for a quasi-official endorsement of their exaggerated views of the missile threat to the United States," military expert William D. Hartung wrote.[73] Many Democratic lawmakers familiar with intelligence were unimpressed, particularly by the commission's emphasis on the NRO: in January 1996, a congressional investigation had revealed that the satellite agency had lost track of a $2 billion slush fund because, according to the journalist Robert Dreyfuss, "it was so highly classified even top intelligence officials had no control over it."[74] Nevertheless, Republicans seized on the Rumsfeld report, and began pressing for increased spending on missile defense and satellite reconnaissance. They were backed by a phalanx of pro-military think tanks, such as the Center for Security Policy, whose national security advisory council was co-chaired by Jim Woolsey. Its corporate contributors at the time included Boeing, General Dynamics, Lockheed Martin, Northrop Grumman, and TRW—"all major weapons contractors that benefit from the policies advocated by the Center," Hartung pointed out in a 2004 study.[75]

Then, just as the rhetoric over the missile threat was reaching fever pitch, the Intelligence Community was caught flat-footed once again. In

May 1998, the CIA failed to detect a series of nuclear weapons tests in India; worse, CIA and DIA analysts had discounted the very idea that the Indian government was contemplating its first test since 1974. Once again, Republicans blasted the Clinton administration and the IC. Senator Richard Shelby, R-Alabama, the chairman of the Senate Intelligence Committee, called the CIA's misjudgment a colossal failure. Chastened by the critique, CIA director George Tenet appointed his own commission to study the failure.

Led by retired Vice Admiral David Jeremiah, a former vice chairman of the Joint Chiefs of Staff, it recommended that the director of central intelligence take "direct charge" of intelligence collection—almost the opposite of what Rumsfeld had proposed. "We have an imbalance today between the human skills associated with reading photography, looking at reports, understanding what goes on in a nation, and the ability to technically collect that information," Jeremiah said in an interview with PBS's *NewsHour with Jim Lehrer*. "In everyday language that means there's an awful lot of stuff on the cutting room floor at the end of the day that we have not seen."[76] Tenet responded by revamping the CIA's internal organization with two key appointments: John C. Gannon as assistant director for analysis and production, and Joan Dempsey as director of community affairs.* With his new team in place, Tenet promised major changes for the IC. "I'm going to take direct charge of how our community collects information, how collection and analysis are lashed together to ensure that the kind of event that occurred here will not occur again," he told reporters.[77]

As this debate around the IC's spying abilities was taking place, the CIA was fighting—or trying to fight—a battle against Al Qaeda. In 1993, the World Trade Center was attacked for the first time, and in 1998, Al Qaeda terrorists destroyed the U.S. embassies in Kenya and Tanzania. Tenet and his Republican allies were now seeking funds for both collections and human intelligence. But the White House wasn't

---

* The three key figures in Tenet's reforms ended up in the private sector. Jeremiah, as we'll see further on, emerged during the Bush administration as a key adviser to the intelligence contracting industry. Both Gannon and Dempsey now work for major CIA contractors—the former at BAE Systems, the latter, as we've seen, at Booz Allen Hamilton.

receptive: "In the fall of 1998," Tenet recalled in his memoir, "I asked the administration for a budget increase of more than two billion annually for the entire intelligence budget over the next five years. Alas, only a small portion of that increase was granted." Believing that "we were desperately short of needed resources," Tenet decided to go around his chain of command and "struck up a relationship" with Gingrich. With the assistance of Dempsey, who managed the negotiations with the House, Gingrich "pushed through" a supplemental bill for the 1999 fiscal year that provided a "significant increase" in the IC's baseline funding, Tenet wrote.[78]

In 2007, Tenet disclosed the actual amount of that increase—$1.2 billion. That turned out to be the largest ever supplemental increase in the intelligence budget up to that point, and helped expand an already growing industry.* Using the ODNI's historical figures on intelligence spending I obtained in 2007, it's now possible to show how much money went into the coffers of the private sector during those years. In 1995, the IC spent $18 billion on contracts. Four years later, that spending reached $22 billion. It dropped to $18 billion in 2000, and rose again to $22 billion in the final year of the Clinton administration. Even in 1990s dollars, that was big money; and by 1999, the intelligence contracting industry—led by TRW, SAIC, Boeing, and Betac Corporation—had arrived.

In line with its new importance, the industry held its first major conference in 1999, with a focus on "Commercial Support to Intelligence." The event was sponsored by the Armed Forces Communications and Electronics Association (AFCEA), which represents the nation's largest military and intelligence contractors. It was a classified symposium, open only to officials and contractors with Top Secret/Special Intelli-

---

* Even though this money was raised to counter the terrorist threat, much of it was diverted to other projects that had nothing to do with counterterrorism. According to the CIA's Office of Inspector General, which conducted an internal study of the CIA's accountability for 9/11 in 2005, CIA managers "moved funds from the base budgets of the Counterterrorist Center and other counterterrorism programs to meet other corporate and Director of Operations (DO) needs." Some of these funds went to "strengthen the infrastructure" of the DO and other money went to programs "unrelated to terrorism." No explanation was given of what these "corporate" funds were. The top secret IG report was declassified in August 2007. See "OIG Report on CIA Accountability with Respect to the 9/11 Attacks," CIA, June 2005.

gence clearances, and held at the Defense Intelligence Analysis Center at Bolling Air Force Base near Washington, D.C. The agenda, which was available on the Internet for nearly eight years before being taken down in 2007, was a case study in the deep links between the Intelligence Community and the private sector. The event itself was chaired by Robert Juengling, a vice president of Betac. In his opening remarks, he laid out the reasons that intelligence agencies had been outsourcing their analytical and IT functions.

"As you well know," he said, "the Intelligence Community is awash in huge amounts of unprocessed, raw data. Collection technology continues to outpace the ability to process, let alone catalogue, the growing volume. In concert (and often in conflict) with the information explosion is the trend toward downsizing throughout the federal government, including the IC. In this challenging environment, increasing attention is being focused on ways to augment the IC to help it accomplish its mission." The conference, he said, would focus on the "interface" between the IC and the private sector. To that end, the organizers invited the new leadership of the IC to address the conference. The keynote was delivered by Joan Dempsey, then deputy director of central intelligence for community management. Another speaker, Keith Hall, the director of the National Reconnaissance Office, now works with Dempsey at Booz Allen Hamilton. And a third, John Gannon, the chairman of the National Intelligence Council, the Intelligence Community's primary think tank, is now a senior executive of BAE Systems, which holds many contracts with the CIA and other elements of the community. The conference underscores how important outsourcing had become prior to Bush's election and the events of 9/11.

Nobody was more interested in these developments than Bill Golden, the former NSA officer we met earlier. A friendly, outgoing man who loves soccer, Golden spent twenty-two years with the U.S. Army. The highlight of his career was the ten years he spent at the NSA listening post at Misawa Air Base in northern Japan. In 1996, after he completed his assignment at Misawa, Golden brought his family back to

Northern Virginia. This was a time when the agency's mission was being revised and its workforce drastically reduced: during the 1990s, the NSA shut down twenty of its forty-two listening posts around the world, and the agency's overseas workforce of military personnel was cut in half.[79]

Upon his return to the United States, Golden was transferred to Fort Belvoir in Virginia, a U.S. Army intelligence center, for what he calls "an intelligence special mission."[80] But it was mostly a desk job, and boring at that, so Golden decided to retire from the Army. To keep the money flowing, he applied for a job at ARPA, and was placed with a small company doing research with ARPA funds on artificial intelligence. While working there, Golden learned how politicized the budget process can be in Washington. As disputes mounted in Washington between Republican congressional leaders and President Clinton over spending, Congress began doling out funds in ninety-day increments. This had a direct impact on Golden: just as his company was hired to build a new program for the Navy, he was fired.

What could have been a crisis turned into opportunity when, a few months later, he began getting phone calls from former colleagues at the NSA and other parts of the Intelligence Community affected by the short-term budgets, asking him for leads on people like himself who had secret or top secret clearances and might be able to work on a temporary basis. So he began tracking intelligence jobs on a laptop and matching his contacts with potential employers. The NSA was one of his first clients, but mostly the calls came from contractors—Betac, Lockheed, Booz Allen, BAE Systems, CACI International, and other companies all needed people to fill the demand. The work was so good that, in 1997, Golden went into it full-time, and started a company: IntelligenceCareers.com. "I made so much money that I never went back," he says. But so many former intelligence officers joined the private sector that, by the turn of the century, the institutional memory of the U.S. Intelligence Community now resided in the private sector. That's pretty much where things stood on September 11, 2001.

• • •

Even before the smoke had cleared from the World Trade Center and the Pentagon, the Bush administration had turned to U.S. intelligence for answers and information. Over the next few months, as the White House and then Congress began pumping money into the agencies and the new counterterrorism centers where intelligence and law enforcement were supposed to meet, the Intelligence Community had no alternative but to seek help from contractors. The 9/11 attacks sparked a huge increase in both the intelligence budget and in contracts: the IC's spending on contracts soared to $32 billion in 2002 and peaked at $43.5 billion in 2005. It wasn't until 2005 and 2006 that the government made a concerted effort to start hiring at the agencies themselves.

But even if the Bush administration had chosen early on to allow agencies to hire people directly, it was too late: the people they needed immediately—that is, the hundreds of cleared and experienced intelligence professionals with the skills and background to start looking for the terrorists responsible for 9/11 and to prevent future attacks—were working in the private sector. And any new hires would take five to seven years to get up to speed. As a result, from 2001 on, the Washington area became a free-for-all for contractors. From the CIA to the Department of Homeland Security, longtime intelligence officers watched as thousands of contractors from companies like SAIC, Booz Allen Hamilton, and CACI came to work next to the analysts, doing essentially the same jobs, but for twice the pay.

For many intelligence officers let go in the late 1990s, the contracting binge was sweet revenge. At least that's the way Golden tells it. "During the late 1990s, they'd told all these people, 'you're a dinosaur, you're a Cold Warrior without a purpose,' " he recalls. "Well, now they needed them, because they had the institutional knowledge." And because contractors often had more experience than the people they were working for, they were put in situations where they had no supervision or oversight. Out of that came the situation at Abu Ghraib. The responsibility for that, argues Golden, sits squarely on the shoulders of the men in the Pentagon and the White House who brought them to Iraq in the first place. "If any company got in trouble, it was because of a lack of adult supervision," continues Golden. "Because the government was suffering from a brain drain, it basically went in and told the contractors—'hey, this is the person in uniform who's here to baby-sit you, but you need to tell them what to do because they're clueless. Now you're the experts, and you make it happen. We have to go after Al Qaeda, and, oh, by the way, we don't know how to do that anymore, but you do because you're the contractor, and we pay you money, and you need to make this happen.' "

One agency—the CIA—understood that logic more than any other. During the 1990s, it had experienced huge personnel cuts; but now, in the wake of the worst terrorist attack in U.S. history, it was being asked to explain what happened, find and go after the perpetrators, and staff the counterterrorism centers, all at the same time. To do that, the CIA turned to private sector contractors, which soon became the new face of U.S. intelligence.

4

The CIA and the Sacrifice of Professionalism

WHEN MOST AMERICANS think about spies, the Central Intelligence Agency is the organization that first comes to mind. The CIA led the first strikes against Al Qaeda in Afghanistan after 9/11, and a CIA agent was the first American to die in what the Bush administration would call the global war on terror. The CIA was also the lead agency for the interrogation of Al Qaeda suspects captured on the battlefield and, as the American public learned in December 2007, used extremely harsh tactics to elicit information from them. Long before President George W. Bush announced U.S. intentions to overthrow the Saddam Hussein regime, CIA agents were in Iraq trying to organize resistance within the ruling elite. The agency remained center stage when the Bush administration sold the Iraq War to Congress and the American public. Its analysts were responsible for one of the most crucial documents of that period: the October 2002 National Intelligence Estimate, which concluded that Iraq possessed chemical and biological weapons and had the capacity to use them. The report was issued on the eve of a congressional vote authorizing the war, and George Tenet, the CIA's director at the time, famously called its conclusions a "slam dunk." His reputation, and that of the CIA, remain tarnished, even by the standards of the agency's own Office of Inspector General, which called in 2007 for an investigation into Tenet's failure to disrupt the Al Qaeda network prior to 9/11 and what the IG called a "systemic breakdown" within the CIA's Counterterrorism Center.[1]

But even as the Iraq debacle played out before the public, the CIA found itself at odds with both the Bush administration and the neoconservative right over matters of policy. In the months preceding the March 2003 attack on Iraq, CIA employees were incensed when the Pentagon, with the support of the office of Vice President Dick Cheney, who was unhappy with the information he was getting from the CIA, established its own intelligence network to compete with the agency's, and leaned heavily on the CIA to tailor its findings to administration demands. At the same time, Bush supporters were angered by the CIA's repudiation of evidence purporting to link Saddam with Al Qaeda and by the hostility of some CIA officials to the upcoming war in Iraq and to other parts of the president's foreign policy agenda. Later, the CIA workforce was shattered when administration officials leaked the identity of an undercover CIA agent, Valerie Plame, to discredit her husband, former ambassador Joseph Wilson, a prominent critic of the Iraq War.

By 2007, the rift between the CIA and the neoconservative right seemed irreparable. That February, Michael Rubin, a fellow at the American Enterprise Institute and a former Pentagon adviser in Iraq, openly called for the privatization of the CIA. "The poor quality of the CIA's analytical products is an open secret among intelligence consumers [and] seldom more analytical or detailed than published newspaper accounts," he wrote in *The Weekly Standard,* the neocons' most influential voice in Washington. Rather than expand the CIA, "the government should privatize much of its analysis." Already, Rubin noted, "Beltway firms like SAIC and Booz Allen Hamilton operate streamlined intelligence shops. Their analysts hold the highest security clearances. So do many think-tank scholars and some university academics. Many private-sector analysts have language abilities and experience their government counterparts lack."[2]

Ironically, long before Rubin wrote his column, the CIA had already turned over more of its analytical work to the private sector than any other agency in the Intelligence Community. The CIA, according to more than a dozen former CIA officers, currently spends between 50 and 60 percent of its annual $5 billion budget on contractors. Greenbadgers, as these contractors are known, now outnumber the agency's full-time workforce of 17,500. They are doing almost everything career agents are doing. Contractors collect human intelligence, HUMINT, out in the field. They analyze raw, classified intelligence traffic coming in from stations overseas, and write reports that form the basis of finished intelligence estimates that are sent up the chain of command. They work in information technology, writing specialized computer applications, and creating charts that are used in classified briefings. One company even prepares false identities for CIA officers working undercover overseas. According to a groundbreaking 2006 report in the *Los Angeles Times,* at CIA headquarters in Langley, Virginia, "senior officials say it is routine for career officers to look around the table during meetings on secret operations and be surrounded by so-called greenbadgers—nonagency employees who carry special colored IDs."[3]

On the operational side, CIA contractors have fought alongside CIA officers and Special Forces in Afghanistan and, according to outsourcing expert R. J. Hillhouse, make up more than half of the workforce of the CIA's National Clandestine Service, which runs the covert operations that differentiate the CIA from the rest of the Intelligence Community—the recruitment of spies in foreign governments and hostile organizations, and the launching of offensive military operations in places like Afghanistan. "The role of CIA employees has been largely reduced to contract managers and support administrators, supervising and supporting corporate program managers, who in turn oversee staff from other firms," Hillhouse reported in 2007. "Virtually entire branches of the NCS have been privatized."[4] CIA front companies were also used in the secret "extraordinary renditions" program that sent many terrorist suspects to CIA-operated interrogation cells outside the United States. According to *New Yorker* reporter Jane Mayer, Jeppesen International Trip Planning, a wholly owned subsidiary of Boeing, handled "many of the logistical and navigational details for these trips, including flight plans, clearance to fly over other countries, hotel reservations, and ground-crew arrangements."[5]*

Overseas, contractors have been assigned to jobs as sensitive as deputy station chief, and have been used to open many of the stations closed because of budget cuts during the 1990s. Amazingly, in the intelligence hotbed that is Pakistan, a full three-quarters of the officers posted at the CIA station in Islamabad since 9/11 have been contractors.[6] In Baghdad, where the CIA operates its largest overseas station, contractors have sometimes outnumbered paid government employees. Robert Baer, a former CIA field officer stationed in the Middle East, claimed in a 2007 article in *Time* that a private company working for the agency in Iraq was even deciding where CIA officers could go and who they could meet, "essentially determining who the CIA's sources are."[7] I later learned that the company in question was Blackwater Worldwide, the private military contractor, which has a contract to provide security and analytical services to the CIA station in Baghdad.

"This is a completely different culture from the way the CIA used to be run," Baer, who spent a total of twenty-four years in the CIA, told me. "Everyone I know in the CIA is leaving and going into contracting whether they're retired or not."[8] Many of the green-badgers, he said, are former CIA employees, often returning to the same jobs they had before they retired, and earning double or triple the salaries they made as government employees. The companies doing the hiring are scattered throughout the Northern Virginia suburbs of Washington, running from the business parks near Dulles Airport to the huge office and shopping complex at Tysons Corner. ("The Dulles Corridor," Baer wrote in *Blow the House Down*, a novel based on his experience with the CIA, "was thick with Agency retirees working for Beltway Bandits with CIA

---

* Jeppesen is also involved as a contractor in geospatial intelligence. A Boeing handout at a 2007 intelligence symposium in San Antonio lists "Jeppesen Government and Military Services" as one of four subsidiaries of Boeing's Space and Intelligence Systems unit, which provides "prime contractor support to government customers that require diverse geospatial intelligence services"—a designation that could include the CIA as well as the NGA and other Pentagon agencies. Jeppesen and the other subsidiaries, Boeing says, work "in specialized organizations with broad resources to meet the time-critical requirements of today's warfighter."

contracts: SAIC, Booz Allen, Dyncorp, Titan, McDonnell Douglas. Everyone I knew seemed to be doing it once they hit the magic fifty: Retire on a Friday, back in the building Monday morning with a shiny new green badge."[9]) A typical salary for a contracted analyst is $200,000 a year, but that is only half of the $400,000 charged by the companies for each slot, Baer and other former officers said.

"We're talking about a huge industry in terms of independent contractors, who are represented in all the offices of the CIA and throughout the building in Langley," said Melvin A. Goodman, a thirty-five-year veteran of the agency who is now a senior fellow in the national security program of the Center for International Policy, a liberal think tank in Washington. Goodman contrasts the outsourcing of analysis today to earlier times, when the CIA's Directorate of Science and Technology hired corporations like Lockheed and TRW to make the satellites and spy planes that produced overhead photography that CIA analysts used to determine if the Soviets were meeting their arms control obligations. "You could make the case that you had to go to Lockheed or the Skunk Works" where U-2 and SR-71 spy planes were manufactured, he told me. "But I'm not sure you can make that case now in terms of analysis and the training of analysts. There's incredible waste going on. There isn't a single office within the CIA that I'm aware of that hasn't hired contractors."[10]

The CIA, which has been extremely hesitant in discussing its dependence on contractors, disagreed. "I can say with certainty that those figures are way off the mark," a CIA press officer who did not want his name used told me. However, the actual number, along with the identity of any company that supplies contractor employees, is classified, he said. The agency's overall assessment is that "contractors perform a vital mission to the CIA, and other intelligence agencies for that matter. They're usually hired for specific skill sets for a short period of time to provide the agency flexibility in performing our mission." The spokesperson *did* confirm that many of the green-badgers working at the CIA are former employees. "Many of our contractors have long experience with this agency in particular," he said. "There are individuals who are hired who spent their entire careers with the CIA. Contractors provide mission-critical work, they're hired for specific reasons, and they're highly experienced in the missions they're asked to perform." Asked about the high salaries paid to contractors, the CIA man said: "Government salaries are very competitive. Clearly, there is a marketplace in the contracting space. I can't say what the figures are, but salaries do vary."

In May 2007, a few weeks after this interview, CIA director Michael V. Hayden, an Air Force general, announced the completion of a review of the agency's use of private contractors he'd ordered in the fall of 2006. By that time, Hayden had grown concerned about the early resignations of employees who receive CIA training and then leave their jobs, only to return at higher rates of pay as green-badgers; in an interview with the Associated Press, he'd remarked that the CIA was beginning to look like "the farm system for contractors." While these companies played "a vital role" in the CIA's mission, he concluded, the agency had "not efficiently managed our contractor workforce, which grew out of staff hiring freezes in the 1990s and our greatly expanded ops tempo after 9/11." Without giving any details, he said the agency had identified jobs that "must or should be filled primarily by staff officers" and those that can be done by contractors. In a first for an intelligence agency, he ordered the CIA to reduce the number of contractors by 10 percent by the end of 2008, and barred contracting firms from bidding for CIA employees within eighteen months of their departure from the agency, if they leave before retirement age. He also encouraged contractors to become staff employees in jobs requiring a higher proportion of government staff. "We will expedite the process for moving from a green to a blue badge worn by CIA employees," he said.[11]

Even though green-badgers are generally hired through companies such as Booz Allen Hamilton or SAIC, some negotiate their own contracts with the agency, former officers said. The CIA wouldn't discuss how its contracts are structured. But in the spring of 2007, the agency released a few intriguing details about its personnel regulations as part of its legal defense against charges from a former covert employee, identified only as "Peter B.," who claims he was wrongfully terminated by the CIA. The court document, which was heavily redacted, described three categories of contract employees at the CIA: career associates who perform duties—"usually clandestine and operational"—on a career basis; internal contract employees, who are hired for a specific term "and normally work inside Agency installations"; and external employees hired for a specific term who normally work "outside Agency installations."[12] That seemed to cover contractors in all four of the CIA's areas of operations.

The most prominent of these is the National Clandestine Service, which was previously known as the Directorate of Operations and employs some 1,200 case officers around the world—more than half of whom are green-badgers, as mentioned earlier. The Directorate of Intelligence, the analytic branch of the CIA, employs the largest group of analysts in the federal government, according to director Hayden.[13] The other two directorates are Science and Technology, which directs the CIA's investments in innovative technology, and Support, which provides security, cover stories, financing, and other services to CIA missions. Contractors are hired in all four directorates, according to the agency. "We have no figures on the distribution of our contractors," the CIA spokesperson told me. "But it's safe to assume that our contractors perform a wide variety of missions across the agency." Some analysts believe that the number of contractors in these divisions exceeds 70 percent of the workforce—about par for the Intelligence Community, as we know now from the ODNI's own figures.[14]

The CIA's big contracting push during the Bush administration was triggered by the events of September 11. The next morning, the Special Activities division of the CIA's operations directorate began recruiting contractors to be sent into Afghanistan to start chasing Al Qaeda. The man making the calls was Cofer Black, the director of the CIA's counterintelligence unit, who organized the CIA's first effort at leading U.S. troops into battle. Black "got his orders from an all-night meeting at Camp David," Billy Waugh, a veteran CIA contractor who first worked for the CIA in Vietnam, told the journalist Robert Young Pelton. After meeting with Bush's war cabinet, Black came back with the understanding that "things were different," he added. "They wanted people killed.

They weren't going to fire off some missile and hit some friggin' dust pile. They wanted some dead bodies on the ground."[15]

Over the next few weeks, the CIA fielded a force of about one hundred fighters, including about sixty contractors, who joined up with a few U.S. Special Forces personnel and fragmented units from the pro–United States Northern Alliance and other Afghan groups opposed to the Taliban, the Afghan ruling party and an ally of Al Qaeda. In doing so, said Pelton, the CIA began "a new era of joint operations where military, intelligence, paramilitary, indigenous, mercenary, and even civilian contractors were working in unison with full lethal capabilities."[16] Six months later, the CIA-led force had defeated the Taliban and driven Al Qaeda into hiding. Its resources strained, the CIA's security division, known as the Global Response Staff, signed a six-month, $5.4-million contract with Blackwater, then an unknown private military contractor based in North Carolina, to provide security to the CIA's newly established station in Kabul. Within three years, bolstered by contracts with the U.S. occupation forces in Iraq and the State Department, Blackwater had become one of the world's largest private military companies. Since 2004, its president has been Cofer Black, who left the counterterrorism division to join Blackwater. Dozens of other former CIA officials and lower-level officers followed him into the company.

The surge in CIA contracting in the other divisions occurred in the eighteen months after the attacks, when Congress and the administration created several new institutions to deal with the new terrorist threat and thwart the next attack. In 2002, in the largest reorganization of government since 1947, the Department of Homeland Security was formed by combining twenty-two disparate federal agencies. From the beginning, it included its own intelligence and analysis division. It was headed by a longtime CIA veteran, Charles Allen, who was recruited to the position from his job as assistant director of central intelligence for collection. In January 2003, the Bush administration created the Terrorist Threat Integration Center (TTIC). It combined elements of the DHS, the Department of Defense, and the counterterrorism divisions of the FBI and the CIA, with a mission to "fuse" and analyze all information related to terrorism in one place. John Brennan, its first director, was a twenty-five-year veteran of the CIA whose last job was as chief of staff to CIA director George Tenet. Under Brennan, the TTIC was spun out of the CIA and renamed the National Counterterrorism Center.

These organizations placed tremendous strains on the CIA, which sent many of its top analysts to staff them. At the same time, the Department of Homeland Security and the NCTC needed an immediate infusion of analysts with security clearances and experience in the intelligence business. With most of the agencies already stretched and many cleared intelligence veterans working in the private sector, the only place to go for recruits was the big companies. By 2004, about 70 percent of the analysts and subject matter experts working at the NCTC were contractors, according to former CIA officials.

The use of contractors, particularly in the analytic branch of the agency, was a major shift from the past. Until recently, contracting "was very, very limited," Larry Johnson, a former CIA officer, told me. Johnson worked in the CIA's Directorate of Operations in the late 1980s and read hundreds of classified CIA reports while serving as deputy director of the State Department's Office of Counterterrorism in the early 1990s. "On the analysis side, [a contractor] would be asked to come to make a presentation or review a particular publication," he said. "It was used very sparingly. And it really wasn't used very much on the DO [Directorate of Operations] side, either."[17] Ray McGovern, an outspoken critic of the Iraq War who served in the CIA's analytic division from 1963 to 1990, had a similar experience. "Very little was outsourced," he told me. Technical data on weapons or economic models were occasionally proofed by outsiders, and CIA analysts often communicated with academic and think tank specialists. "But no contractor was involved in actually analyzing this data and presenting it to our consumers, first and foremost the president," he said. "It was always in the hands of analysts, who massaged it and compared it to what else we knew from covert sources."[18]

That was true until the early 1990s. As we saw in the previous chapter, the outsourcing of intelligence analysis grew rapidly in the decade that followed the end of the Cold War. Intelligence budgets were cut and the entire government came under pressure from the Clinton administration to streamline operations and save money by transferring jobs that were not "inherently governmental" to the private sector.[19] The Directorate of Operations was particularly hard hit by the cuts. "The Clandestine Service felt the impact of the post–Cold War peace dividend, with cuts beginning in 1992," the 9/11 Commission wrote in its 2002 report on the intelligence failures that led up to the 9/11 terrorist attacks. "As the number of officers declined and overseas facilities were closed, the DCI and his managers responded to developing crises in the Balkans or in Africa by 'surging,' or taking officers from across the service to use on the immediate problem." The Directorate of Operations' "nadir," the commission said, was in 1995, "when only 25 trainees became new officers."[20]

One factor in the CIA's increasing use of outside analysts was the congressional demands for information and analysis on new, emerging threats following the collapse of the Soviet Union. According to John Gannon, a vice president at BAE Systems who held the CIA's seniormost analytical position for most of the 1990s, Congress had very different priorities in intelligence during the Clinton administration than it does today. Specifically, after the Republicans swept the midterm elections in 1994, congressional leaders began pressing the Intelligence Community to focus on national missile defense and China's militarization; terrorism was more of a "tertiary kind of priority." That translated into big spending increases for technology to collect and analyze missile data, as opposed to human intelligence. At the same time, as the confrontation with the Soviet Union faded and other issues took its place, the CIA itself was turning outside for expertise. "For the half-century of the Soviet threat, a lot of the IC's expertise of the Soviet Union was inside the community," said Gannon. "But if you look at the cyber-threat, the threat of bioterrorism, or even Russia today, the center of gravity of experience is *outside* of the IC." In many cases, that turned out to be industry. "When I was chairman of the National Intelligence Council, even on issues like the ballistic missile threat, if we really wanted to do quality analysis, we discovered the best analysis was being done by the aerospace industry," according to Gannon. "So we worked with them."[21]

But missing in all of this is the greed factor. Many CIA officials and officers, knowing they could earn up to three times as much as a private sector contractor, left the agency in droves after 9/11 to either start their own companies or join established ones. "On the analytic side, everybody ran for the terrorism dollars," says Johnson, the former CIA officer. "That rush for the private sector will be the legacy of the Bush administration." One recent migrant from the CIA to the private sector provides a good illustration of the pattern: John Brennan, the first director of the National Counterterrorism Center. Brennan, who spent nearly thirty-five years at the CIA, retired from the government in November 2005 and immediately joined The Analysis Corporation, a Fairfax, Virginia, government contractor, as president and chief executive officer. TAC, which is owned by a defense contractor, SFA Inc., employs over 140 people, who, according to company literature, support the work of intelligence, law enforcement, and homeland security agencies "with heavy emphasis on counterterrorism." Much of TAC's business is with the NCTC itself, where Brennan worked for three years. In fact, the NCTC is one of the company's largest customers, and TAC provides counterterrorism support to "most of the agencies within the Intelligence Community," according to a company press release.

During the 1990s, before Brennan came aboard, TAC developed the U.S. government's first terrorist database, called Tipoff, on behalf of the State Department. The database was initially conceived as a tool to help U.S. consular officials and customs inspectors determine if foreigners wanting to enter the United States were known or suspected terrorists. In 2003, management of the database, which received information collected by a large number of agencies, including the CIA, the NSA, and the FBI, was transferred to Brennan's TTIC and, later, to the National Counterterrorism Center.[22] In 2005, Tipoff was expanded and renamed the Terrorist Identities Datamart Environment, or TIDE, and fingerprint and facial recognition software was added to make it easier to identify suspects as they crossed U.S. borders.

TAC remains an important NCTC contractor: in 2005, it won a $2.3 million contract in a partnership with CACI International to integrate information from the Defense Intelligence Agency into the TIDE database.[23] TIDE is now "the wellspring for watch lists distributed to airlines, law enforcement, border posts and US consulates," with nearly half a million names in the database, and it is also the first intelligence database to include both foreigners and U.S. citizens, according to the *Washington Post*.[24]* TAC has become a critical private sector player in the nation's counterterrorism efforts; in the five years after 9/11, its income quintupled, from less than $5 million in 2001 to $24 million in 2006.[25]

In 2006, TAC increased its visibility in the Intelligence Community by creating a "senior advisory board" that included three heavy hitters from the CIA: former director George Tenet, former chief information officer Alan Wade, and former senior analyst John P. Young. "We will want to tap into their expertise, they are part of the brain trust here," Brennan told the *Washington Post*[26] (Tenet, in a statement released by TAC, said he would help the company "address critical needs as government and industry work together to fight terrorism"[27]). According to a former contractor familiar with TAC, Brennan is one of Tenet's closest friends and confidants, and hired Tenet primarily as a rainmaker to bring new business and contracts to the firm. A former CIA officer who served in the Middle East said Brennan's close ties with Tenet go back to the early 1990s, when Brennan was the chief of station in Riyadh, Saudi Arabia, a country that Tenet visited frequently as director of central intelligence. TAC did not return phone calls or reply to e-mails. Brennan's prominence in the intelligence industry was underscored in 2007 when he was elected chairman of the Intelligence and National Security Alliance, the contractor organization formerly headed by Director of National Intelligence Mike McConnell.

Tenet has cashed in on his CIA experience in other ways, and has become a wealthy man as a result. In 2006, he earned more than $2 million in director's fees, stock, and other compensation from his work for three corporations that provide the U.S. government with technology, equipment, and personnel used for the war in Iraq as well as the broader war on terror.

---

* The *Post* also reported that TIDE has created significant concerns about secrecy and privacy, with innocent civilians frequently mistaken for terrorist sympathizers and some individuals remaining on the list long after they've been cleared by their own governments.

In 2006, Tenet was elected to the board of directors of L-1 Identity Solutions, a major supplier of biometric identification software used by the U.S. military and intelligence agencies to monitor terrorists, insurgents, and the general populace in Iraq and Afghanistan. Longtime defense executive Robert LaPenta, one of the three "L's" who founded L-3 Communications, is the chairman of the board and CEO of L-1, which was formed by the merger of the five top companies in the biometric industry. L-1's software, which can store millions of ID records based on fingerprints and eye and facial characteristics, helps the Pentagon and U.S. intelligence "in the fight against terrorism by providing technology for insurgent registration [and] combatant identification," the company says on its Web site. L-1 technology is employed by the State Department and the Department of Homeland Security for U.S. passports, visas, driver's licenses, and transportation worker ID cards; key customers also include intelligence contractors Booz Allen Hamilton, Northrop Grumman, Lockheed Martin, and SAIC.

L-1 clearly hired Tenet for the business he could secure at the CIA. "We want the board to contribute in a meaningful way to the success of the company," LaPenta told financial analysts during a 2006 earnings conference call. "You know, we're interested in the CIA, and we have George Tenet." The former CIA director has been particularly useful to L-1 as the company has expanded its markets in the Middle East. "George Tenet: a phone call gets us in to see whoever we want," LaPenta said in a 2007 analyst's briefing. In the months after Tenet joined L-1, the company moved heavily into intelligence outsourcing by acquiring two of the CIA's hottest contractors, SpecTal and Advanced Concepts Inc.

SpecTal, which has three hundred employees with top secret security clearances, was an interesting choice for L-1. Its Web site reads like something out of a spy novel. "From the situation rooms of Washington, D.C., to the back alleys of the Third World, SpecTal employees have devoted their lives to handling America's most daunting security and intelligence challenges." Prior to its acquisition by L-1, SpecTal was working closely with the CIA in Afghanistan on a number of classified missions that Tenet, as CIA director, was apparently quite familiar with. In November 2006, several L-1 executives met with Tenet to discuss potential business in Afghanistan. During the course of that conversation, LaPenta told investors, Tenet urged L-1 to "call the SpecTal guys" because "they know everybody in every one of these ministries that you need to go talk to."[28] In May 2007, L-1 picked up another intelligence contractor, Advanced Concepts Inc. (ACI), where 80 percent of its three hundred employees have top secret clearances. ACI, according to LaPenta, is a systems engineering firm that, among other things, protects computer systems for the National Security Agency, making it "a great complement for SpecTal."[29] By combining the two companies, LaPenta told analysts, he hoped that SpecTal might get some of its "training and analysis and ops people" hired at the NSA, and get work for ACI's IT and systems people at the CIA.

Tenet has been amply rewarded for opening doors for L-1. According to company filings with the Securities and Exchange Commission, he was provided with eighty thousand shares of L-1 stock in 2006 when the company acquired Viisage, where Tenet was also a director. Valued at the company's price in the spring of 2007 ($20), those shares were worth more than $1.5 million. According to another SEC filing, Tenet received director's compensation of $129,337, and $332,030 worth of stock in 2006. "George has amazing experience," Doni Fordyce, L-1's executive vice president for communications, told me. "We're in the security business, right? So he's a tremendous asset." In 2006, L-1 earned $164.4 million, up from $66.2 million in 2005.

Tenet is also the only American director on the board of QinetiQ Group PLC, the British defense and intelligence research firm that was controlled from 2003 to 2007 by the Carlyle Group, the well-known (and well-connected) private equity fund headquartered in Washington, D.C. QinetiQ is the privatized unit of Britain's Defense Evaluation Research Agency. It was once one of the most secretive parts of Britain's Ministry of Defence, and got its inspiration from Q, the legendary British intelligence technician immortalized on film in James Bond movies ("Think about Q in the Bond movies," Carlyle executive Douglas Franz once explained to a group of investors. "These guys do that stuff."[30]). The company employs more than ten thousand people, about the same number as CACI International; seven thousand of them are scientists and engineers.[31]

In 2003, Carlyle invested $73 million to buy a 33 percent stake in QinetiQ.* The Ministry of Defence retained the other 66 percent. But in an unusual arrangement, Carlyle was granted 51 percent of the voting shares, which meant that Carlyle and its appointed executives had effective control over the company. After this, under the close supervision of Carlyle, QinetiQ moved aggressively into North America, buying up five U.S. companies. Carlyle sold off its remaining shares in February 2007, making a $470 million profit on its original investment. In accepting his appointment at QinetiQ, Tenet said he was "especially interested in the capacity of the company's technologies to meet a number of the challenges faced by our nations' military and intelligence personnel."[32] According to QinetiQ's annual report and accounts for 2006, nonexecutive directors such as Tenet are paid a minimum of $70,000, with some paid up to more than a quarter-million dollars (we will learn more about QinetiQ later).

Here, too, Tenet profited from involvement in Iraq and the broader war on terror. QinetiQ's other acquisitions in the U.S. market include defense contractor Foster-Miller Inc., which makes the so-called TALON robots used by U.S. forces in Iraq to neutralize IEDs, improvised explosive devices. QinetiQ also controls Analex Corp., an information technology and engineering company that earns 70 percent of its revenue from the Pentagon. Among the clients listed on Analex's Web site are the National Reconnaissance Office, which manages the nation's spy satellites, and the Pentagon's Counterintelligence Field Activity office—a secretive agency that has been criticized by members of Congress for collecting intelligence on American antiwar activists. At QinetiQ, Tenet is working with Duane Andrews, a former assistant secretary of defense who was the chief intelligence adviser to Dick Cheney when he was secretary of defense in the early 1990s.[33] Prior to joining QinetiQ North America (QNA) as its CEO, Andrews served for thirteen years as a senior executive with intelligence contractor Science Applications International Corporation.

Also in 2006, Tenet joined the board of directors of Guidance Soft-

---

* See chapter 3, page 105.

ware. One of Guidance's products, EnCase, has been used extensively by U.S. law enforcement, intelligence, and military agencies to collect evidence in criminal and counterterrorism cases, including the prosecution of Enron executives and the British "shoe bomber," Richard Reid. Tenet's "years of experience fighting terrorism and extensive knowledge of potential and existing threats will expand Guidance's unparalleled expertise in computer forensics and network investigations," the company noted in a press release.[34] According to SEC records, Tenet earned $58,112 in 2006 as a director and, in 2007, held 9,700 shares of company stock worth more than $124,000.

In his 2007 memoir *At the Center of the Storm,* Tenet doesn't mention his new post-government career as an intelligence contractor and adviser.

The companies that work for the CIA include both big names and the relatively unknown, and range in size from large systems integrators like SAIC and Booz Allen to smaller shops like TAC and SpecTal. No matter what their size, all of these companies have one thing in common: they are extremely secretive about what they do for the agency. CIA companies, in fact, are even less willing to talk about their classified work than companies that contract for the National Security Agency, long considered the most secretive of the sixteen agencies in the Intelligence Community. Only in rare exceptions, as in the recent bribery investigation of the CIA contractor MZM Inc., does the government admit that a company has a relationship with the CIA. Obtaining useful details about the contractors working for what is often called the "other government agency," or OGA, is frustrating and almost impossible. To obtain the brief background interview with a CIA spokesperson I described earlier, I had to call the agency's press office more than a dozen times.

Part of that opaqueness reflects the CIA's own cult of secrecy. The agency, unlike the NSA, has never issued a press release or given a press conference to publicly discuss a major contract. And CIA director Michael Hayden, who presided over the NSA's opening to the private sector and allowed his top aides to brief the press about major outsourcing projects at the agency, has shown no willingness to do the same at the CIA. Within the intelligence industry, the CIA is also notorious for its refusal to acknowledge that it even employed a specific person. This has become problematic for agencies and contractors trying to obtain or confirm security clearances for new employees. Former CIA officers who obtained their security clearance from the CIA often find that the agency has refused to confirm the fact that they once had a CIA clearance, even when the employer seeking the information is the NSA. "They really carry secrecy to extremes," a contractor who deals with both agencies told me.

The CIA's secrecy carries over to the information that contractors share with the public. While the NSA, the DIA, the NRO, and the National Geospatial-Intelligence Agency are frequently listed as customers on contractor Web sites and in investor information, the name of the CIA almost never appears on these sites. CACI International is a rare exception to the rule: in a slide presentation for investors in 2007, it listed the CIA among its intelligence customers. Its Web site, however, provided no details about its work with the CIA; yet, as we'll see further on, CACI's work in signals intelligence is discussed in detail on its site. Providing information about the CIA is clearly off-limits for the company. Asked in 2003 on CNN's *Moneyline* what CACI does for the CIA, CEO Jack London replied, a little testily: "I wouldn't dare tell you."* Despite these obstacles, however, it *is* possible to describe, in some detail, what some private companies do for the CIA. We'll start with the obvious companies—the systems integrators.

One of the few companies to go public about its contracting relationship with the CIA is General Dynamics, the nation's fourth largest federal contractor. Best known as a defense conglomerate that makes destroyers, submarines, tanks, and armored combat vehicles, General Dynamics in recent years has branched out heavily into intelligence and information technology. In 2006, it acquired Anteon International

---

* A CACI job opening in Sarajevo in 2004 provided a hint, however; it advertised for a chief of human intelligence with eight years experience in all-source intelligence analytical work, with knowledge of counterintelligence, collections, and information management and dissemination.

Corp., a major intelligence and IT company that ranked as the twelfth largest federal contractor in 2006. Anteon, whose contracts included training U.S. military interrogators and managing NATO's intelligence network, was combined with General Dynamics' existing IT units to create General Dynamics Information Technology. It employs over 4,500 cleared employees and is now the fastest-growing unit within General Dynamics, earning 37 percent of the company's $7.8 billion in revenue in 2005.[35] According to General Dynamics Information Technology literature I obtained at an industry conference, the IT unit "provides qualified, cleared staff to augment the US Central Intelligence Agency (CIA) critical intelligence missions." The pamphlet is unusual in the detail it provides about the company's work for the CIA and what the agency has outsourced in recent years.

General Dynamics' contracts with the CIA are held by its Mission Support Group, a "customer-focused organization of over 200 professional personnel, with full lifestyle polygraph clearances, who directly support and complement CIA's mission support specialists on 26 different programs." The company's clients in the CIA, the pamphlet says, include the Directorates of Intelligence, Operations, and Science and Technology; the chief information officer; the Offices of Facilities Management and Human Resources Management; and the Office of Logistics. General Dynamics contractors offer expertise in a variety of tasks across the agency, including network engineers, project managers, document analysts, logisticians, financial analysts, machinists, and desk officers. While most of the work is done at CIA headquarters, "some programs and personnel support CIA's global mission in the field." The company's "cleared professional personnel" also provide support to mission managers and, in a direct address to government officials, "augmentation to your operational staff. We work with you to identify your specific mission needs and to develop solutions for your success. Our mission support services include analysis support, administrative, logistics, and operations support functions." General Dynamics IT, in other words, is a mini-CIA, offering everything that one of the nation's oldest intelligence agencies needs at a time when its attrition rate is at the highest level in its history and the demands for its services within government are straining its resources (General Dynamics would not comment on its intelligence work).

The two systems integrators most closely identified with the CIA are Booz Allen Hamilton and SAIC, the San Diego–based defense and intelligence contractor. SAIC's private operatives, the company says on its Web site, work with U.S. defense and intelligence agencies to "build an integrated intelligence picture, allowing them to be more agile and dynamic in chaotic environments and produce actionable intelligence." SAIC's largest and most well-known customer in the Intelligence Community is the NSA; so many NSA officials have gone to work at SAIC that intelligence insiders call the company "NSA West."[36] But SAIC also does a significant amount of work for the CIA, where it is among the top five contractors.

Unlike General Dynamics, however, SAIC does not broadcast what it does for the agency. Nothing about the CIA can be found on its Web site or in the few documents the company has filed with the Securities and Exchange Commission since it went public in 2006. And SAIC spokesman Ronald M. Zollars made it clear to me that the company would not comment on its intelligence work ("We will not be participating in an interview," he wrote in a terse e-mail after I sent a series of questions based on comments SAIC executives made at a conference I attended). A 2006 article in SAIC's in-house magazine, however, does mention that the company was part of an NGA team that received a Meritorious Unit Citation in 2004 from CIA director Tenet for its efforts in "developing and deploying a capability making theater airborne imagery available to a wide range of defense and intelligence users."[37] This may have been Tenet's way of recognizing SAIC's role in a famous incident during the early stages of the war against Al Qaeda, when CIA officers, with Tenet in the room, fired a missile from a CIA Predator flying above Yemen, killing a key member of Al Qaeda and one of his American accomplices. According to a recent profile of SAIC in *Vanity Fair*, the CIA relies on SAIC to spy on its own workforce. "If the C.I.A. needs an outside expert to quietly check whether its employees are using their computers for personal business, it calls on SAIC."[38]

SAIC employs large numbers of former CIA officials. Leo Hazlewood, the senior vice president for SAIC's Mission Integration business unit, which works with the NGA, joined the company in 2000 after a twenty-three-year career with the CIA. His positions there included comptroller, director of the National Photographic Interpretation Center (later merged into the NGA), and deputy director for operations. Other former high-level CIA officials working for SAIC include chief technology officer Andy Palowitch, who previously served as director of the CIA's Central Intelligence Systems Engineering Center, and vice president for corporate development Gordon Oehler, who retired from the CIA in 1997 after twenty-five years of service, including a stint as director of the CIA's Nonproliferation Center. That center was also an area where SAIC held contracts. Peter Brookes, a senior fellow for national security affairs at the conservative Heritage Foundation, was detailed to the CIA's NPC to work on issues related to arms control treaties and the proliferation of weapons of mass destruction while working for SAIC.[39] Other former CIA officials who have worked for SAIC in the past include John Deutch, President Clinton's second CIA director, and Bobby Ray Inman, the CIA's former deputy director. Both men served for a time on SAIC's board of directors.[40]

Another large CIA contractor is BAE Systems Information Technology, the North American subsidiary of the British defense giant. BAE Systems has long been known as a CIA contractor but has kept its classified contracts under wraps. Its cover was temporarily blown in July 2006 when BAE fired a CIA software contractor named Christine Axsmith for posting a message on Intelink, the Intelligence Community's classified Intranet system, criticizing the Bush administration's policies on torture. In her work for BAE at the CIA's software development shop, Axsmith told the *Washington Post*, she had conducted "performance and stress training" on computer programs. Earlier, as a BAE employee, she had also worked at the National Counterterrorism Center.[41] BAE is well structured to attract work from the CIA. Among its outside directors are Richard Kerr, the CIA's former deputy director, who spent thirty-two years at the agency and headed a small team of CIA analysts who assessed the intelligence produced prior to the Iraq War; and Kenneth Minihan, the former director of the NSA (both men also sit on the board of intelligence contractor ManTech International). Joanne Isham, the vice president of strategic development for BAE's National Security Solutions business, is a twenty-year CIA veteran and the former deputy director of the CIA's science and technology division.

But the man with the closest ties to the agency is John Gannon, BAE Systems' vice president for global analysis. He joined the CIA in the early 1980s after earning a Ph.D. in Latin American studies, and quickly worked his way up the agency's analytic chain of command, where he served as director of European analysis and deputy director for intelligence. Between 1997 and 2001, he was chairman of the National Intelligence Council, where he was responsible for producing the National Intelligence Estimates that (theoretically) reflect the consensus of the Intelligence Community on key national security issues. After leaving the CIA, he developed the analytic workforce for Intellibridge Corporation, one of the first producers of outsourced analysis for the CIA. Before joining BAE, he worked for the Department of Homeland Security and for Congress as staff director of the Homeland Security Committee of the House of Representatives.

Gannon's Global Analysis unit, which employs a staff of more than eight hundred analysts with security clearances, is a miniature version of the U.S. Intelligence Community. "The demand for experienced, skilled, and cleared analysts—and for the best systems to manage them—has never been greater across the Intelligence and Defense Communities, in the field and among federal, state, and local agencies responsible for national and homeland security," BAE says in a new brochure distributed at a geospatial intelligence conference in San Antonio in October 2007. BAE's mission, therefore, "is to provide policymakers, warfighters, and law enforcement officials with analysts to help them understand the complex intelligence threats they face, and work force management programs to improve the skills and expertise of analysts." At the bottom of the brochure is a series of photographs illustrating BAE's broad reach: a group of analysts monitoring a bank of computers; three employees studying a map of Europe, the Middle East, and the Horn of Africa; the outlines of two related social networks that have been mapped out to show how their members are linked; a bearded man, apparently from the Middle East and presumably a terrorist; the fiery image of a car bomb after it exploded in Iraq; and four white radar domes (known as radomes) of the type used by the NSA to monitor global communications from dozens of bases and facilities around the world.[42]

Gannon is an interesting figure in the world of outsourced intelligence. Unlike many of his colleagues, he is willing to speak to reporters on the record, as we saw earlier in this chapter. And he is not afraid to voice opinions that go against conventional wisdom. In testimony before the Senate Judiciary Committee in 2006, for example, he voiced deep concerns about the expansion of the Pentagon's role in intelligence under Donald Rumsfeld, a subject few contractors are willing to touch ("The DoD turf grab further wounded a weakened CIA and eventually raised concerns about military involvement in domestic intelligence," he told the panel).[43] In written testimony, he told the committee that the "core problem" in U.S. intelligence today "is that there is minimal executive branch supervision . . . and inadequate congressional oversight"—a perspective frequently voiced by liberal critics of U.S. policy.

When I interviewed Gannon in the fall of 2006, I was surprised to hear him say that contracting had probably gone too far in intelligence. When Congress responded to 9/11 by creating new structures, such as the National Counterterrorism Center and the Office of the DNI, "it was inevitable that the Intelligence Community was going to have to fill the seats from some other source other than the inside," he told me. "That is what generated this unprecedented alliance with contractors." Eventually, he said, contracting would have to be "reined in," and when it is, "it will be a much more surgical approach, where it relates to programs that are competently managed by the government and where contractors are not a substitute for management." He also warned me against simplifying the issue, saying that contracting "shouldn't be portrayed as an undifferentiated mass, and particularly as an undifferentiated mass that is a positive force. It is not. A lot of it is bad, and there's a lot of real hucksters out there. It does need greater oversight and more stringent management to be effective and so we can rein in some of the abuses." When it came to saying anything about his company and what it does, for the CIA or anybody else, Gannon was adamant: he is contractually bound not to talk. "I cannot finger particular companies or talk about the inside," he said.

Two of the largest CIA contractors are companies few people have ever heard of: Abraxas and Scitor. Abraxas was founded by a group of former high-ranking CIA officials, led by CEO Richard "Hollis" Helms, a thirty-year veteran of the CIA who retired in 1999. Helms had served the CIA for twelve years overseas, mostly in the Middle East. He was also head of the National Resources division of the Directorate of Operations, which is responsible for the U.S. activities of the directorate. In the months after the 9/11 attacks, he began taking notice of the many retired intelligence officers who were being hired by defense contractors. "Most contractors did not understand the uniqueness of the problems, nor the potential these people represented," he said in a 2005 interview with *Entrepreneur Weekly*. "So I seized the moment, because I could identify extraordinary people who were available."[44]

Out of that grew a $65-million company with over two hundred former intelligence officers on its payroll—"the largest aggregate of analytical counter-terrorism capabilities outside of the US government," according to Helms.[45] Many of them work as contractors in CIA stations overseas and desk positions in Langley.[46] Indeed, so many CIA officers were enticed by Abraxas to leave the agency for better-paying contractor jobs that, in 2005, CIA director Porter Goss had to ask the company, and a few others, to stop recruiting in the CIA's cafeteria on the Langley campus (director Hayden's recent crack about the CIA being a "farm system" for contractors was reportedly directed at Abraxas). With Abraxas's offices in nearby McLean, Virginia, however, all it takes is a short walk for a dissatisfied CIA employee to find a new job. And Helms has tapped into a rich vein of intelligence talent to grow his company.

Abraxas's president is Richard Calder, the CIA's former deputy director for administration. In 1999, Calder set a precedent at the CIA by bringing in PricewaterhouseCoopers, the global accounting firm, to help the CIA adopt "business-like procedures and analyze CIA products and services for potential outsourcing from other intelligence agencies."[47] Other key executives include Barry McManus, Abraxas's vice president of "deception detection services," who was the CIA's chief polygraph examiner for ten years and served in "worldwide operational activities" during his thirty-year career with the agency, and Terry Wachtell, who put in twenty-two years at the CIA "working against narcotic, terrorist and hostile intelligence service targets," according to the company's Web site. Helms also recruited the CIA's former station chief in China to work for Abraxas.[48] In 2005, Abraxas was rated as one of the nation's fastest-growing technology companies by the Deloitte & Touche accounting firm, and in 2006 Helms received the Ernst & Young Entrepreneur of the Year award.

Abraxas was first identified as a CIA contractor by James Bamford, the author of several books about the National Security Agency.[49] In 2004, he reported that Mary Nayak, who formerly ran the Directorate of Intelligence's South Asia Group, was then working for Abraxas, and had been hired as an Abraxas consultant to the CIA group that reviewed pre-9/11 intelligence. Then, in September 2006, the *Los Angeles Times* blew the cover on one of the company's most sensitive projects: crafting covers, or false identities and front companies, for the agency's nonofficial cover (NOC) program. This was a startling development for the CIA: one of its most sensitive and dangerous tasks had been outsourced. Officers in the NOC program—such as Valerie Plame, whose official cover, until she was outed, was as an energy specialist for the fictional law firm Brewster-Jennings & Associates—operate overseas without diplomatic immunity and face possible prosecution and worse if captured by a hostile government. Abraxas had obtained the work, the *L.A. Times* said, as the CIA came under pressure to devise "more imaginative cover arrangements that might give operatives closer access to terrorist networks."[50] It's unclear whether Abraxas still holds that contract.

But the company is still deeply involved in top secret contracts. Abraxas, I was told by sources inside the intelligence contracting industry, is working on a highly classified project in China: securing the building materials for the new U.S. embassy under construction in Beijing. "It's their job to make sure that the new Beijing embassy isn't another Moscow," a source familiar with Abraxas's work told me. She was referring to the fiasco in the mid-1980s, when construction of the U.S. embassy in the Soviet Union was suspended for nearly two years after U.S. officials discovered that Soviet intelligence had installed hundreds of tiny electronic eavesdropping devices in the floor planks and walls.[51] The Abraxas embassy job was described to me as a natural outgrowth of the company's business in China and its latest offerings in counterterrorism software. In 2004, the company opened an office in Shanghai to provide political risk assessments and security services for foreign multinationals in China.[52] And in 2007, the company began marketing a new software product, called TrapWire, which uses complicated mathematical formulas called algorithms that allow digital surveillance systems to detect patterns of suspicious behavior. The software, the company claims, can predict terrorist attacks or other criminal behavior, and is being tested by police departments in New York and Los Angeles as well as by the Department of Energy and the Marine Corps.[53]

Abraxas would not comment about any aspect of its business. "Sir, we don't talk to the media," an executive in its McLean, Virginia, office told me after I'd called numerous times. The new Beijing embassy, slated for completion in 2008, is being built by a joint venture between Zachry Construction of San Antonio and Caddell Construction Company of Montgomery, Alabama. Caddell, the lead contractor, would neither confirm nor deny Abraxas's role in the project. "We have a very strict policy about the job," a company official who would not identify himself told me. "We have a strict protocol with the State Department to remain silent about it. Talking is strictly verboten to the extent that we could be thrown off the job." Virtually all of Caddell's senior management, as well as most of its engineers and operational managers on the site, have obtained top secret security clearances to work on the project.[54]

To help Abraxas market its surveillance software, Helms recently hired John "Jack" Reis, the former president of i2, a software company with extensive contracts with intelligence agencies, as president of a new company division, Abraxas Applications. Helms has also created partnerships with several defense contractors, including Northrop Grumman, to broaden his company's exposure in defense and intelligence. Another Abraxas partner, Sentia Group, developed a political simulation tool called Senturion that has been used by the CIA to predict events in Iraq and other countries. Brian Efird, a Sentia executive associated with the National Defense University, told me that Sentia supplies its modeling software to Abraxas for intelligence use but doesn't itself have contracts with the CIA. The agency seems to be getting a lot of use out of the software, however. In an e-mail posted on a private Listserv on Iraq, Efird wrote that the CIA "has done the most comprehensive external audit of the accuracy of [Sentia's] methodology, and they concluded that its forecasts are accurate in excess of 90 percent of the time."[55]*

As Abraxas has grown, it has started buying up smaller companies developing technology useful to its intelligence and corporate customers. In December 2006, it acquired Dauntless, a McLean, Virginia, company that makes a search engine technology used by intelligence agencies.[56] And with intelligence and homeland security markets booming, the company has followed the example of many other intelligence contractors by creating an advisory board staffed with former high-ranking officials. In March 2007, Abraxas announced that Tom Ridge, George W. Bush's first secretary of homeland security, had joined its advisory board and was already working "behind the scenes" to refine the company's TrapWire software, which is also designed to protect "critical infrastructure" from terrorist attacks. Another key appointment was retired Air Force General John Gordon, who worked in the Bush White House from 2002 to 2004 as the president's top national security adviser on counterterrorism, and from 1997 to 2000 as the CIA's deputy director. A third adviser, retired federal judge Eugene R. Sullivan, once served as the general counsel of the NRO. And the recruiting goes on: in May 2007, Abraxas was looking for analysts with specific expe-

---

* Perhaps the Bush administration should have used Sentia's prediction software. In 2004, based on a simulation model of Iraqi political factions drawn up between October 2002 and April 2004, the Sentia program tested by the CIA predicted, "Things are ugly in Iraq. And the current simulations suggest that the situation will get even worse, from the perspective of the U.S. Without a change in the approach toward different constituencies in Iraq, it will become increasingly difficult for the U.S.-led 'coalition' to consolidate support for a new regime. Terrorist-like activities are likely to continue and escalate." The Sentia report on Iraq was posted on a blog called *Enough, I've Had It,* and can be found at http://blogs.salon.com/0003752/2004/04/14.html. The report was still posted in February 2008.

rience and expertise in counterterrorism, counterproliferation, and other national intelligence issues and disciplines, including signals intelligence, biometrics, and financial networks.

While Abraxas is making a splash with its advisory board and high-profile small business awards, Scitor, a CIA and defense contractor company based in Herndon, Virginia, has become a $300 million company without creating a single ripple in the media. "It's the biggest company you never heard of," said a former NSA officer who knows the company well.

Scitor is a technology company that does extensive work for the U.S. Air Force in aerospace communications and satellite support services. The privately held company is also an important contractor for the CIA's Directorate of Science and Technology, according to industry sources who have knowledge of the company but spoke only on condition of anonymity. Within that directorate, two sources said, it is used primarily by the Office of Technical Services, the secretive unit that develops the gadgets, weapons, and disguises used by spies. That work apparently involves building and maintaining small satellites used in signals and electronic intelligence. An intelligence analyst familiar with Scitor said the company also does "a lot of value-added software packages, taking commercially available packages and configuring them for specific usages." Scitor did not return numerous phone calls to its offices in California and Virginia.

Scitor was founded in 1979, and has been led since 1994 by Jim Hoskins, an Air Force veteran who is the company's CEO and chairman of the board. He came to Scitor after a long career in U.S. intelligence. He first worked at the Air Force Cryptological Depot, a unit of the Air Intelligence Agency, and then the National Security Agency and the CIA.[57] Scitor's Web site says that Scitor (which is derived from a Latin word meaning "to see to know") provides a "diverse range of systems engineering, information technology, and program management expertise" to government and commercial customers. A Scitor contract with the General Services Administration posted on the GSA's Web site lists the CIA among the company's clients. It states that Scitor helps government agencies manage "major acquisitions and cradle-to-grave programs that are vital to national defense." Those agencies include the National Reconnaissance Office, the National Security Agency, the NGA, the CIA, and the Pentagon. Scitor also provides expertise to government agencies "in all aspects of the privatization process," the GSA contract says. In October 2007, in a significant expansion of its defense business, Scitor led a consortium of fourteen companies that was awarded a $250 million contract by the Office of the Undersecretary of Defense for Intelligence to provide technical and analytic support in the areas of intelligence, surveillance, and reconnaissance over the next five years. (That contract came to light only because a Scitor subcontractor, McDonald Bradley, announced it in a press release.)[58]

In addition to its offices in Northern Virginia, Scitor has a sizable presence in Colorado, which is home to the U.S. military's Northern Command, the Air Force Space Command, and several other important national security agencies. In 2005, Scitor invested over $12 million in a new building in Colorado Springs, where such key intelligence contractors as SI International, Boeing, Lockheed Martin, Northrop Grumman, The Aerospace Corporation, SAIC, and Booz Allen Hamilton also have a presence.[59] Financial information about the company is sparse. In 2002, Allied Capital, a Washington, D.C., investment bank, invested $22 million in Scitor's long-term debt to help the company's employees finance an employee stock ownership plan ("We're not sure exactly what they do," Bill Walton, Allied's chairman and CEO, told the *Washington Business Journal*, "but we know it's something important").[60] Under the employee stock ownership plan, Scitor employees bought out Scitor's founders, Roger Meade and Gene Priestman, said Houlihan Lokey Howard & Zukin, the Virginia bank that advised Scitor on the deal.[61] In 2007, Scitor was acquired by Leonard Green and Partners LLP, a Los Angeles private equity fund. As usual, Scitor released no details about the deal, which was reported in a brief story in *Washington Technology*.[62] According to that story, the company employs 1,200 people; other reports indicate that Scitor's revenues rose from $16 million in 1994 to $300 million in 2005.[63]

One area of intelligence where Scitor appears to be a leading contractor is measurement and signatures intelligence, or MASINT, a highly classified form of intelligence that uses infrared heat imaging, acoustic signatures, seismic data, and other information picked up by air and ground sensors to "sniff" for weapons tests and other activities that other countries want to hide from the United States. MASINT collection is managed by the Defense Intelligence Agency and used extensively by the CIA and other agencies as a tool in arms control and in tracking the use of IEDs and other weapons by insurgent groups in Iraq and Afghanistan (by detecting the "signature" of certain explosives used in IEDs, for example, MASINT analysts have developed countermeasures to those explosives). Scitor is a leading member of the MASINT Association,* a group of contractors that specialize in its science, and in 2005 sponsored and provided some of the funding for a national symposium on MASINT signatures technology. The symposium, which was co-sponsored by the MASINT Association and the DIA, was held at the Scitor Conference Center in Chantilly, Virginia, according to information posted on the association's Web site. A summary of the conference papers says that MASINT "is the intelligence discipline specifically focused on combating terrorism in all its forms." Members of the association include all of the major intelligence contractors, from BAE Systems to SAIC. Scitor may be unknown, but it is definitely not a small player.

There is another class of CIA contractors: companies financed and, in some cases, created by In-Q-Tel, the CIA's venture capital fund. In-Q-Tel was formed in 1999 during the Tenet era, and has invested about $300 million in government money in some ninety companies. It was started at a time when intelligence budgets had been substantially re-

---

* In January 2008, the MASINT Association changed its name to the Advanced Technical Intelligence Association (ATIA) to reflect the expanded use of measures and signatures intelligence by homeland security, defense, and other intelligence agencies. See Wilson P. Dizard, "Intell Group renamed to reflect mission changes," *Government Computer News,* January 16, 2008.

duced and CIA directorates were trying to figure out how to cope with fewer material and human resources. The budget crunch had been especially difficult for the Directorate of Science and Technology, where the CIA's top scientists had helped develop the cutting-edge technologies, from the U-2 spy plane to the CORONA satellite, that allowed the United States to become the global leader in surveillance and earned the directorate the nickname "the wizards of Langley."

Yet all around the CIA in the private sector, in places like Silicon Valley and the high-tech industrial zone around Washington, revolutionary developments in information technology, computers, and the Internet were taking place, almost at warp speed. Faced with the political realities of post–Cold War Washington and the rapidity of change in the commercial world, the CIA proposed the creation of In-Q-Tel as a technology incubation center that would fund research and development in innovative IT technologies that held promise for intelligence agencies; in return for direct investments from the CIA and other agencies, high-tech companies would be offered a huge, natural market—the Intelligence Community and the federal government, plus assistance in testing and perfecting their products for use by the private sector. Congress approved the program in 1998.

With an initial investment of $28.5 million, the venture fund set about to provide seed money to small firms that could help the CIA and other government agencies deal with the vast amounts of data they were processing, thus leveraging the private sector to accomplish what the government could no longer do. This was the final frontier of intelligence outsourcing: after years of downsizing, the CIA was now contracting out its core skills in research and development. Rather than have its own scientists, physicists, engineers, and behavioral psychologists find the breakthrough technology that would help the CIA confront the new dangers of the twenty-first century, the agency began turning to the private sector to do it. The need for outsourced R&D grew exponentially after 9/11, when the demand for analysis and technology grew by leaps and bounds, and the CIA, already strapped for staff, was forced to "surge" its resources to areas where they were needed most.

Nine years after the In-Q-Tel project got off the ground, Stephanie

O'Sullivan, the CIA's director for science and technology, would actually use the word "outsource" to describe In-Q-Tel. By tapping into the private sector, the CIA is "incentivizing outsourcing," O'Sullivan said in a rare public speech in 2006.* "We're getting the best minds that we can find out there to think about our problems, to think about our need and the technology curve. It's a human capital investment, and it pays off." The CIA, she continued, faces adversaries who are "adept and agile" and doing things that require an immediate response. "So we need to be leveraged in every way possible. In-Q-Tel was one of our first initiatives to leverage research. We were going after those mosquitoes out there—the small businesses and start-ups where a lot of the innovation of this country resides—to make them part of our team. There is no technology out there that is not relevant to our mission."[64] The fund now makes about ten investments a year from an annual budget of about $30 million.

One of the most valuable technologies funded by In-Q-Tel is now used by virtually anyone who uses a computer: Google Earth. This massive database of 3-D satellite images, which lets a computer user "fly" anywhere in the world and zoom in and out of cities and countries, was first developed as EarthView by a company called Keyhole Inc., based in Mountain View, California. In 2003, seeing value in EarthView for military applications, the CIA fund—in a partnership with the National Geospatial Intelligence Agency—invested an undisclosed amount of money in the company, and within two weeks EarthView was being used by U.S. forces in Iraq.[65] Google bought In-Q-Tel's shares in Keyhole in 2004 and quickly incorporated the program into its widely used search engine. One of In-Q-Tel's most recent investments was in Initiate Systems Inc., a Reston, Virginia, company that got its start in 1995 by matching health care records with huge patient databases. In 2006, the fund invested in the company to adapt its records system to help intelli-

---

* O'Sullivan spoke at a panel on intelligence R&D at the GEOINT 2006 conference in Orlando, sponsored by the United States Geospatial Intelligence Foundation. "I've spent my career in the clandestine and the black world, and I don't often step out of those shadows to speak at events like this except when it's a topic I feel deeply about," she began. "Our reliance and need for research and innovation in order to push intelligence to where it needs to be to serve our policy-makers is one area I care greatly about."

gence and law enforcement agencies track down suspected terrorists across large nationwide databases. Since In-Q-Tel made its investment, Initiate's sales have grown by nearly 70 percent and the company has been hired by Raytheon to refine its database tracking system for the FBI.[66]

Technically, In-Q-Tel claims not to be either a government agency or part of the CIA ("We are an independent, nonprofit, and nongovernmental firm," Donald W. Tighe, In-Q-Tel's vice president of external affairs, told me). Yet every deal it makes must be cleared by the CIA, which appoints its board of trustees and all of its executives. The key players in its formation were George Tenet and his executive director at the CIA, Buzzy Krongard, a former investment banker. To get the fund rolling, they put together an oversight board made up of successful capitalists with strong ties to defense and intelligence. Its chairman, then and now, was Norman R. Augustine, the former CEO of Lockheed Martin. Other current board members include James Barksdale, the former CEO of the computer services firm Netscape Communications and a member of George W. Bush's President's Foreign Intelligence Advisory Board (PFIAB); retired Air Force General Charles G. Boyd, the president and CEO of Business Executives for National Security, which conducted the only outside audit of In-Q-Tel in 2001; David Jeremiah, the former vice chairman of the Joint Chiefs of Staff, who sits with Barksdale on the PFIAB and is a director of ManTech International and several other defense contractors; and Paul G. Kaminski, the former undersecretary of defense for acquisition and technology who, like Jeremiah, is very active in the intelligence business. The fund is run by a management staff led by CEO Chris Darby, a former vice president of computer giant Intel. (In-Q-Tel's name, like the U.K.'s QinetiQ, is derived from the British operative who gives Agent 007 the cuff link cameras, shoe guns, and other gadgets made famous in the James Bond movies.)

In-Q-Tel's focus has changed dramatically during its ten years of existence. When it was first founded during the late 1990s, the fund was primarily interested in technologies that would help the CIA and other government agencies improve the way they managed data. "Originally, we were looking for information management software that addressed the challenges of intelligence," Tighe recalls. "Our challenges were the same as the Fortune 500."[67] As a result, most of what In-Q-Tel invested in was "shrink-wrapped" software products ready to go; in June 2001, the *Washington Post* described In-Q-Tel as simply an innovative way to "link the bureaucratic, buttoned-up CIA with the entrepreneurial, free-flowing private sector."[68] But the mission changed after September 11. By July 2002, the *Post* was describing the fund as "a sort of anti-terrorism matchmaker." Gilman Louie, In-Q-Tel's CEO at the time, couldn't get into specific details of what he was looking for, or why, the *Post* said, because the fund was "focusing much of its energies on tracking terrorists, finding links between criminals and even guessing what they might do next."[69]

Because In-Q-Tel is funded through the classified parts of the intelligence budget, it won't disclose its total funding levels or how much it invests every year. Tighe, the In-Q-Tel vice president, told me in January 2008 that the fund's investments "tend to be in the $1 million to $3 million range," and generally involve twelve to fifteen deals a year. That comes to between $20 million and $30 million a year. The "most important and least well-known" fact about In-Q-Tel, Tighe added, is that the great bulk of its investments—about 80 percent—now go toward funding "specific technology advancement work driven by identified Intelligence Community needs."[70] The remaining 20 percent goes to "simple equity or traditional venture capital–style funding." Companies lucky enough to obtain In-Q-Tel investment raise the rest of their capital from private venture capital firms. According to the In-Q-Tel Web site, the fund has cultivated a network of more than two hundred venture capital firms and leveraged more than $1 billion in private sector funds "to support technology for the CIA and the IC."

Attensity, a CIA and NSA contractor that has developed a method of instantly parsing electronic documents and fitting them into a database, has In-Q-Tel to thank for its business success. In the fall of 2001, it was nearly bankrupt, and the post-9/11 downturn in the stock markets had kept investors away. One day that December, Todd Wakefield, Attensity's co-founder, got a call from In-Q-Tel asking if his company was still around. "Barely," he said, according to an account in *Business-*

Week, "so talk fast."[71] Within a few months, In-Q-Tel was the lead investor in a $3.5 million cash infusion into the company. Now the company's text extraction software—which takes less than ten seconds to analyze and diagram the text in *Moby-Dick*[72]—is a flourishing, multimillion-dollar company with 60 percent of its sales going to the federal government. Company literature lists its customers as the CIA, NSA, DIA, and the FBI.

In-Q-Tel works with companies like Attensity because "we let the Intelligence Community agencies know what's out there, and let the companies know the interests in government," said Tighe. "There's some amazing capabilities out there."[73] In an interview during the GEOINT 2006 symposium, where In-Q-Tel had a booth, he pointed out a few more of his success stories. With seed money from In-Q-Tel, piXlogic of Los Altos, California, has developed a software that quickly searches large files of digital images and video for particular objects, such as cars and street signs, and then alerts an analyst when a match to a known object is found. In-Q-Tel invested in the company, which is now contracted with the CIA and selling its software to other intelligence agencies. Joseph Santucci, the company's president and CEO, underscored that In-Q-Tel sought him out. "We don't go looking for them," he told me. "They come looking for you." Santucci said he couldn't say how his software is used by the CIA or the Intelligence Community. But the In-Q-Tel relationship helps the company find customers it wouldn't attract on its own, he said. "They're very close to the customer and help mediate the process with the agencies."[74]

In 2005, In-Q-Tel invested in a company called SkyBuilt, which has developed a mobile power station that runs on solar and wind power, and can run for months with very little maintenance. That project met an initial demand from U.S. Army units operating in western Iraq, which were having problems keeping electric generators supplied with fuel. "Our investment helped spur their capability," said Tighe. But developing portable power stations is also important for the clandestine world of the CIA, said Stephanie O'Sullivan. "A basic fact of life for us is, we're trying to hide things like sensors and packages," she said. "And sometimes you can't connect to a power source somewhere.

We've had a decades-long leadership role in power sources, and it's something we need to sustain."

Agent Logic, which In-Q-Tel helped finance in 2002, sells software that can track streams of data about individuals and business events—such as the cargo manifest and crew list of a ship in transit to a U.S. port—and alert analysts to any changes as they occur en route. In 2003, In-Q-Tel invested in Language Weaver Inc., which has developed capabilities to translate massive volumes of foreign language information into English in minutes. That has saved the CIA four thousand months of man-hours of work that would have been spent translating using human translators, officials said.[75] Another In-Q-Tel company, Tacit Knowledge Systems Inc., makes collaboration software that allows a customer like the CIA to search computers linked to a network to glean who on that network is an expert on a given subject.

Because of the net of secrecy thrown over CIA contracts, it's extremely difficult to verify claims made by the companies and In-Q-Tel about the reliability or effectiveness of their products for intelligence. Congress, which has oversight authority over the CIA and approved the formation of In-Q-Tel, has not looked into its operations. Its only action was in 2001, when it directed the CIA to arrange for an independent audit of the fund. That was done in 2001 by Business Executives for National Security, the same organization that lobbied in favor of the Clinton administration's outsourcing initiatives in the Department of Defense.

The BENS study found the In-Q-Tel model "impressive," but cautioned that the CIA took too long to insert new technologies into its operations. Since then, the pace of technology funded by In-Q-Tel has risen considerably. But I could find no record of a congressional oversight hearing, either classified or not, into In-Q-Tel's operations since then. Ken Beeks, BENS's vice president for policy, said his organization still keeps tabs on In-Q-Tel. "I think it's worked pretty well," he said. "In-Q-Tel has succeeded in finding new and inventive companies and matching them up with the highly classified requirements of the Intelligence Community."[76] Technology experts seem to agree. "In-Q-Tel is probably not a bad investment for the country," Michael Kleeman, the director of cyber-infrastructure policy research at the University of California, San Diego, told me. "Maybe the government should do more to leverage the market so agencies don't have to do it all." [77]

Still, the In-Q-Tel model raises questions. For one thing, these taxpayer-funded investments serve as a kind of subsidy for corporate expansion. After obtaining its investment from In-Q-Tel, Attensity, the company that can parse *Moby-Dick* in ten seconds, created a government advisory board of former high-ranking officials to help it crack the government contracting market. That board includes Arthur L. Money, the former assistant secretary of defense for command, control, communications, and intelligence, and Neil Birch, a former division chief at the NSA. With Attensity's recent contracts with the Pentagon and the NSA, these appointments have clearly paid off for the company.

Ionatron, a company that was funded by In-Q-Tel to make laser weapons, went even further. In 2003, the same year it won its first government contracts, Ionatron retained the services of the Blank Rome lobby group, which has close ties to former homeland security secretary Tom Ridge, and in recent years has paid Blank Rome thousands of dollars in lobbying fees; a Blank Rome disclosure statement filed in February 2006, for example, shows that the lobbying firm received $120,000 in fees from Ionatron in 2005 for lobbying the House and Senate as well as the Departments of Defense and Homeland Security. Ionatron has also dished out more than $80,000 in campaign contributions to key lawmakers on defense and homeland security committees.[78] Chris Byron, a technology reporter for the *New York Post,* is one of the only reporters who has looked into the underside of In-Q-Tel. In a series of articles he wrote for the *Post* on Ionatron in 2005, he documented how In-Q-Tel employees—who are allowed to hold stock in companies the fund invests in—pocketed thousands of dollars in profits when they sold their holdings in Ionatron that year. That, too, amounted to a government subsidy, Byron told me. "I think In-Q-Tel is a government-owned black box that has no reason for being." [79]

• • •

Getting back to the larger question of outsourcing in general, many former CIA analysts believe that contracting has eroded the CIA's authority. Ray McGovern, who co-founded Veteran Intelligence Professionals for Sanity, a group of former analysts critical of the Bush administration's foreign policy, calls it the "sacrifice of professionalism."[80]

"Maybe I'm sounding sort of archaic now," he told me, "but there used to be an ethos within the CIA that was really, really important. It gave us an esprit de corps that was absent from every other part of the government: we had no agenda to defend, and we could tell it like it is." During McGovern's last couple of years at the CIA, he often went to the White House to brief President George H. W. Bush. McGovern and his fellow analysts, he said, "often took a perverse delight in telling the president that the Soviets weren't twelve feet tall, like the Pentagon said, but were instead five foot nine, and shrinking. That was heady stuff." Some CIA directors actually lost their jobs because they backed up honest assessments like that, he added. "There's an absence of any of that courage now—an absence of the ethos that you really do owe the president the truth, and not something contractors want. I did a little bit of contracting myself, and I know that the contracting officer wants a certain gloss on things and most people are paid to provide that. And that's anathema to intelligence analysis."

But that problem is exacerbated when top CIA officials themselves bend their findings to fit a White House agenda, as many believe George Tenet did during the lead-up to the war in Iraq. "There really was no objectivity in the organization" under Tenet, said Melvin Goodman, the former CIA analyst at the Center for International Policy. "Yes, there were people who challenged them on the issues about the aluminum tubes and the mobile biological labs, but they were given short shrift and given other jobs to do. The people who corrupted the stuff were given cash awards and promotions." Goodman himself resigned from the CIA over what he perceived as the politicization of Soviet analysis during the 1980s. "There's been a real corruption and a real loss of the whole moral compass of the place," he added. "But when you add the contractors, that just makes it worse, because then there is no accountability at all."[81]

Veterans of the CIA's Directorate of Operations see a similar pattern in the area of covert action. Because there was so little growth in the Intelligence Community during the 1990s, "we had no choice but to hire people on contract" after 9/11, said Michael Scheuer, the outspoken former director of the CIA's bin Laden unit. "But the problem was, the pool they drew from did not necessarily produce people familiar with fighting Islamic militancy. So they used them, but they didn't really enhance our capability." To get the IC up to speed, he said, "we need to do a great deal more training, government-wide. Just like we used to train people in Soviet affairs, we need experts in Islamic culture and the religion." [82]

Robert Baer, who worked undercover in Lebanon and Iraq during his years as a covert operator, told me that contractors in the Directorate of Operations are unlikely to take the same risks as a career officer. To truly understand the politics of the Middle East, he said, CIA officers must be able to infiltrate organizations like Hezbollah in Lebanon and recruit spies; being successful in dangerous endeavors like that is also the path to promotion within the agency. "But if you're a contractor, you don't get promoted," he said. "You're not there for a career, you're just coming in and collecting a salary. If there's a risk of getting caught, or even getting executed, what's your incentive if you're a contractor? You have no motivation." Contractors, Baer said, are "inherently risk-averse. Profit is the motive, not intelligence." [83]

Since the CIA wouldn't talk to me, I passed Baer's comments by Timothy Sample, the executive director of the Intelligence and National Security Alliance and a former CIA case officer. He didn't have a simple answer. "I think there may be some concerns about contractors, depending on the type of job that's been asked of them," he told me. "But generally, my experience is that, even for some of the most sensitive and dangerous things, contractors are not coming in [to the IC] just to make a fortune, but because they believe in the importance of it. A lot of the contractors I met when I was on Capitol Hill were all about the mission. There may be some areas where Bob is right, and where there might not be an incentive. But I have to tell you, I haven't experienced much of that." [84]

But Sample's defense of the CIA underscores a key problem with outsourcing. In addition to his job at INSA, Sample is an executive with General Dynamics Information Technology, one of the agency's largest contractors, and therefore has an interest in defending the CIA and its contracting policies. After all, companies that profit from CIA outsourcing can hardly be expected to support the renationalization of intelligence analysis; concomitantly, as long as contractors dominate the halls of the CIA, the public can never be sure that profits haven't trumped principle in the creation of actionable intelligence. Until Congress begins to provide stronger oversight over the contracting process and sets some standards for what work can be outsourced and what should remain in government hands, the issues raised by Baer and other critics will be left unresolved and unanswered, and the American people will be worse off for it.

5

The Role of the Pentagon

"A Kremlin approach to organizational responsibilities."

—Booz Allen Hamilton vice president Joan A. Dempsey, speaking about Donald Rumsfeld's management of defense intelligence in a speech at Harvard University, February 2006

IF THE CIA IS AMERICA'S best-known intelligence agency, the Pentagon should be considered its most powerful. Its significance is due to one simple fact: more than 80 percent of the Intelligence Community's budget falls under the jurisdiction of the Department of Defense, whose control extends to the three most important collection agencies in the U.S. government—the National Security Agency, the National Geospatial-Intelligence Agency, and the National Reconnaissance Office. Like the rest of the IC, these agencies outsource at least 50 percent of their operations to private companies; in the case of the NRO, that figure is an astounding 95 percent. Those numbers in part reflect the historical role played by the private sector in building and maintaining the nation's spy satellites and their ground support system. But over the past seven years, they have stayed high as a result of the technology-intensive military strategies adopted by President George W. Bush and his first Secretary of Defense, Donald Rumsfeld. We begin the narrative in the spring of 2007, when the U.S. Air Force launched the first phase of a new computer network called the Distributed Common Ground System (DCGS).

Designed and built by Raytheon Corporation, the DCGS is slated to become the Pentagon's first Internet-based portal to combine tactical intelligence from military units with signals intelligence and imagery from the national collection agencies. When completed in 2008, it will link fighter pilots with intelligence analysts and commanders on the ground, giving them a common platform from which to read, interpret, and act upon intelligence data. Similar systems are being developed for the Army and Navy by Raytheon and several of its competitors in the defense industry, including Lockheed Martin, Northrop Grumman, General Dynamics, and Science Applications International Corporation.

The idea behind these systems is to give members of the armed forces and their commanders the ability to import raw sensor feeds from military satellites, U-2 spy planes, and unmanned aerial vehicles, and thus see and hear the entire panoply of intelligence, including imagery, signals, streaming video, and radio communications, from a single platform. Eventually, military planners say, the networks will be linked together by a Global Information Grid, which will offer U.S. forces a "seamless, secure, and interconnected information environment, meeting real-time and near real-time needs of both the warfighter and the business user" (that's according to the NSA, which is charged with protecting the grid from outside tampering).[1] Air Force officers involved in the planning describe their prototype as the military's equivalent to Travelocity, the Internet site used by consumers to make airline and hotel reservations. "For the first time, on a simple workstation, we'll be able to guide all our ISR [intelligence, surveillance, and reconnaissance] products," says Steven G. Zenishek, an Air Force lieutenant colonel who is managing the development of the DCGS system for the Air Force. By using the DCGS to create a common "battlespace awareness," he says, war-fighters will be able to find and track enemy soldiers and insurgents, "making sure we target the bad guys and not the good guys." The ultimate object is to "compress the kill chain"—the time it takes from identifying a target to launching a strike—from hours into minutes.[2]

The Distributed Common Ground System is a striking example of how national intelligence collection agencies have been incorporated into military operations during the Bush administration. The Raytheon system was developed under the direct supervision of Stephen Cambone, who served from 2002 to 2007 as the nation's first undersecretary of defense for intelligence and was the top intelligence adviser to Donald Rumsfeld. During that period, the Pentagon emerged as the dominant force in U.S. intelligence, with vast new powers in human intelligence and domestic counterterrorism. Its new powers were partly a reflection of its control over intelligence budgets; but they also flowed from a strong desire by Rumsfeld, Cambone, and their allies in the Bush administration—most notably Vice President Dick Cheney—to place intelligence collection under the Pentagon's command and control system, and to create within the Department of Defense a separate spy network that would provide an alternative source of intelligence to the Central Intelligence Agency, which had been the nation's primary source of human intelligence since its founding in 1947.

Much has changed since Rumsfeld left the Pentagon in the wake of the crushing Republican defeat in the 2006 congressional elections. But despite the efforts of his successor, former CIA director Robert Gates, to rein in the Pentagon's spying units and return the locus of power to the Office of the Director of National Intelligence, most of the systems created during the Rumsfeld era to institutionalize the military's role in intelligence were left intact. Understanding those systems, and how they tie in with the broader spying industry, is essential background to the story of U.S. intelligence, and a prerequisite to our analysis of the role of contractors at the NSA and the NGA, which both play a significant role in military operations as combat support agencies and are the subjects of the next two chapters.

In 2002, the National Commission on Terrorist Attacks Upon the United States, also known as the 9/11 Commission, was given a mandate by Congress to launch an investigation into the U.S. government's actions before and after the attacks. As the commission was beginning its work that autumn, Rumsfeld seized the opportunity to push legislation—backed by Cheney since the 1980s—to create an intelligence "czar" within the Pentagon. It wasn't a hard sell: CIA director George Tenet favored having a central point of contact for intelligence at the Pentagon, and congressional Democrats, who had made a similar proposal for an assistant secretary for intelligence during the Clinton administration, generally favored the idea. As innocuous as the legislation sounded, it would have serious repercussions for the way the government organized and managed its intelligence services.

The bill creating the new position was passed by a lame-duck Congress on November 12, 2002, and signed into law on December 2, 2002. Shortly thereafter, Stephen Cambone was appointed to the undersecretary position. He was a natural candidate: during the first Bush administration, he had worked under Cheney at the Pentagon as director of strategic defense policy and, in the 1990s, had been staff director for the two commissions Rumsfeld ran on missile defense and space weapons. Plus he was a die-hard neoconservative and a charter member of the Project for the New American Century, the group of foreign policy hard-liners that, in a major policy document on "rebuilding America's defenses" issued in 2000, had proposed a greater role for intelligence agencies in war fighting.[3]

The new position provided enormous powers to Cambone. Under the law, the Pentagon's intelligence chief exercises the secretary of defense's "authority, direction and control" over all DoD intelligence, counterintelligence and security policy, plans and programs, and serves as the Pentagon's representative to the DNI. That specifically meant control over the Defense Security Service, which is responsible for all security clearances in the U.S. government, as well as the Counterintelligence Field Activity office, the Defense Intelligence Agency, the National Geospatial-Intelligence Agency, the National Security Agency, and the National Reconnaissance Office. Cambone's power increased even more when President Bush signed an executive order making the undersecretary for intelligence the number three person in the Pentagon's line of succession, after the secretary and his deputy. Previously, the line of succession had run from the deputy secretary to the undersecretary for policy.

Rumsfeld's drive to centralize Pentagon control reached another milestone in 2004 in the legislative battle over intelligence reform, when pro-military lawmakers in the House prevailed in a major fight to maintain the Pentagon's control over the three national collection agencies: the National Security Agency, the National Geospatial-Intelligence Agency, and the National Reconnaissance Office. In its final report issued that year, the 9/11 Commission had argued strongly against the consolidation of intelligence within the Pentagon and recommended the transfer of the three national agencies to a new Office of the Director of National Intelligence (ODNI).* Under its proposal, the assistant secretary of defense for intelligence—Cambone's position—would also report to the DNI as the chief representative of the Pentagon. Budgetary authority over the three "nationals" would thus be passed to the ODNI, while control over tactical intelligence by the four armed services would remain under the domain of the Department of Defense. These proposals were folded into the intelligence reform legislation creating the ODNI that was backed by President Bush. The bills were passed by both the House and Senate.

When the legislation went into conference in December 2004, however, it ran into a storm of opposition. Led by Duncan Hunter, R-California, the chairman of the House Armed Services Committee, pro-military lawmakers argued that the transfer of authority over the

* The 9/11 Commission's findings in this area are as relevant now as they were then. Since the end of the Cold War, the commission argued, the CIA had gradually lost its influence over imagery and signals intelligence, which were now concentrated in the hands of the NGA, the NSA, and the NRO. Meanwhile, following the first Gulf War, the Pentagon had grasped "the value of national intelligence systems (satellites in particular) in precision warfare" and "appropriately drawn these agencies into its transformation of the military." The commission also drew attention to Cambone's new job, saying that an "unintended consequence" of the creation of this position was "far greater demand made by Defense on technical systems, leaving the DCI less able to influence how these technical resources are allocated and used." In short, the commission was saying that the Pentagon had far too much power over intelligence. See *Final Report of the National Commission on Terrorist Attacks Upon the United States,* page 409.

national agencies to the DNI would weaken the power of the Pentagon to wage war. After weeks of stalemate, Cheney stepped in to negotiate a provision that met the demands of the Hunter group by guaranteeing direct access to intelligence for military commanders. Afterward, Hunter explained how the arrangement would work. In a wartime scenario, he told reporters, "it's important for the combatant commanders and their subordinates, whether it's a platoon leader in Fallujah or a Special Forces team leader, to be able to access that information very quickly." That intelligence, he pointed out, included satellite surveillance.[4] Once the compromise was approved, the die was cast: henceforth, the NSA, the NGA, and the NRO would remain under the Pentagon's command and control system.*

Melvin Goodman, the former CIA officer who was one of the most vocal critics of Rumsfeld's tenure at the Pentagon, believes that the Cambone appointment and the congressional battle to keep the national collection agencies inside the Pentagon were turning points in the national desire to reform the Intelligence Community. "That to me pre-empted all reform; that's when the damage was done," he told me. In particular, "the CIA really was savaged by all these reforms, and they were vulnerable because of their own corruption, particularly in the run-up to the war in the use of intelligence," said Goodman. "So the Pentagon has been the big bureaucratic winner in all of this."[5] Goodman has been a lone voice in arguing for the return of the NSA, the NGA, and the NRO to the director of national intelligence. His views, however, were apparently widely shared inside the Intelligence Community.

In 2006, Joan Dempsey, the former number three official at the CIA, delivered a remarkable speech at Harvard University in which she de-

---

* Industry, perhaps reflecting differences within the Intelligence Community itself, never took a formal stand on Hunter's bill. Nevertheless, defense and intelligence contractors have been extremely supportive of Hunter at election time. Between 1989 and 2004, defense contractors donated $1.3 million to the San Diego congressman, three times more than any other industry group. Hunter's top defense contributors over his career, according to the Center for Responsive Politics, are Northrop Grumman, General Dynamics, Lockheed Martin, General Atomics, the Carlyle Group, SAIC, Titan Corp., Raytheon, and BAE Systems. All of them have extensive portfolios in intelligence. The $246,410 Hunter received from the industry in 2006 made him the third largest recipient of defense money in the House behind Jack Murtha, D-Pennsylvania, and Curt Weldon, R-Pennsylvania.

nounced both Cambone's elevation within the Pentagon hierarchy and Rumsfeld's power grab over the national collection agencies. Those "two very arcane and little-understood bureaucratic events sent seismic shudders through the intelligence community," Dempsey said. Placing the undersecretary for intelligence in the line of succession was "pretty extraordinary in my book," she added. It represented "a Kremlin approach to organizational responsibilities." Those were extremely harsh words for someone who had spent her formative years in government working for the Department of Defense.

Dempsey, who had just left her job in government to take a position at Booz Allen Hamilton, argued that Cambone's appointment "signaled to everyone in the national security community" that this was a "key position," and gave the new undersecretary "further clout and influence over his domain." As for the intelligence reform legislation, which Dempsey called "very flawed," she noted that the DNI was now dealing with the Pentagon hierarchy "with no interaction with the secretary of defense, who is the 800-pound gorilla in any conversation about national security. It's a very different environment, and from where I stand it's not a better environment than the one we came from."[6]

Her dissent, in retrospect, was highly significant. At the time of Cambone's appointment in 2002, Dempsey was the deputy director of central intelligence for community management, and had spent the past four years dealing with intense interagency rivalries within the IC. Moreover, since 2003, she'd been the executive director of the President's Foreign Intelligence Advisory Board and, in 2004, had been awarded the Intelligence Community's highest award. If anybody represented the voice of the IC, it was Joan Dempsey. By publicly repudiating Rumsfeld's power grab, she was giving voice to intelligence officials and contractors who believed in civilian control over the national collection agencies. That tension would persist throughout the remaining years of the Bush administration.

For Cheney and Rumsfeld, the "arcane" measures that caused the IC to shudder in despair provided the cover for an extraordinary expansion of power. Even before the ink was dry on the 9/11 reform legislation, Rumsfeld was circulating a directive instructing regional military commanders to create a plan for an expanded Pentagon role in military intelligence.[7] This led to the creation of a new clandestine espionage unit called the Strategic Support Branch, which was designed to end what Rumsfeld called his "near total dependence" on the CIA for human intelligence.

By 2005, the support branch was deploying small, covert teams of case officers, interrogators, and special operations forces to Somalia, Iran, the Philippines, and other places—sometimes without contacting the U.S. ambassador or the local CIA station chief—to launch covert military operations and prepare for future U.S. military action. The Pentagon had moved into the management and deployment of secret intelligence teams both abroad and at home, seizing the initiative from the CIA in every theater of action where the United States was involved. "The Pentagon is now running its own covert operations, and running them in a big way," Philip Giraldi, a former CIA officer who once worked in military intelligence, told me at the time. "The whole playing field has changed."[8]

Soon the capital was abuzz with reports that the CIA had been outmaneuvered and overpowered by the intelligence bosses at the Department of Defense. Rumsfeld had "consolidated control over the military and intelligence communities' strategic analyses and covert operations to a degree unmatched since the rise of the post–Second World War national security-state," Seymour Hersh concluded in January 2005 in a startling report in *The New Yorker*.[9] For contractors, the Pentagon's power grab had immediate, and very lucrative, consequences. The most important were the adoption by the Pentagon of the concepts of network centric warfare (NCW); the expansion of the Defense Intelligence Agency, the primary intelligence collection agency for the Joint Chiefs of Staff and the secretary of defense; and the creation inside the Pentagon of two organizations that would become extremely influential in national intelligence over the next three years, the Joint Intelligence Operations Centers and the Counterintelligence Field Activity office. With the Intelligence Community depending on information technology more than ever before and outsourcing the equivalent of 70 percent of its budget, the programs initiated by Rumsfeld and Cambone became vehicles for an extraordinary expansion of contracting within the Department of Defense representing hundreds of billions of dollars' worth of new business for the Intelligence-Industrial Complex.

Even in the face of his appalling record in Iraq, Donald Rumsfeld will long be remembered, for bad or worse, as the man who forced the armed services to embrace the revolutionary, IT-driven concept of network centric warfare. The road to military domination, he believed, was to create a global, network-based communications system for all information and intelligence on military operations; transformation and "netcentricity" were the keys to future American power.

Boiled down to its essentials, network centric warfare means two things: harnessing information technology to maximize the power and accuracy of weapons; and using computer networks to instantly link ships, planes, satellites, and ground forces into a single, integrated unit connecting every player in the military chain of command, from the highest-ranking general to the lowliest war-fighter on the ground. The idea is to fight wars more "efficiently" by deploying fewer troops armed with lighter, more mobile weapons, utilizing vehicles and vessels that are easier to maneuver in battle, and using the full spectrum of signals intercepts and imagery to see and track the enemy in real time. According to official Pentagon statements, the concept involves "shared awareness, increased speed of command, higher tempo of operations, greater lethality, increased survivability and a degree of self-synchronization."[10]

The national collection agencies play a pivotal role in netcentric warfare. The NSA, in addition to its considerable abilities to intercept enemy communications and weapons signals, is responsible for security assurance at the Department of Defense and providing encryption technologies that keep defense and intelligence networks secure from cyberattacks and hackers (that includes protecting the Global Information Grid, the mother of all computer networks).* The NGA contributes the

* The Global Information Grid, according to the Frost & Sullivan report, is "a Department of Defense communications infrastructure that supports intelligence missions, and enhances information sharing across the DoD from military bases in the United States to tactical mobile platforms." If readers have difficulty understanding what the grid is and how it works,

imagery and mapping critical to real-time action on the battlefield. The NRO controls all military satellites and, by a simple tip of an antenna, can shift the visual "situational awareness" of U.S. war-fighters and fighter pilots in an instant. The DIA integrates all the information available from intelligence units of the unified commands, and is responsible for ensuring its delivery to the war-fighter on the ground (its efforts to provide "dominant battle space awareness" are "essential to the success" of netcentric warfare, the Pentagon said in its 2006 Quadrennial Defense Review). The DIA is also responsible for measurement and signatures intelligence (MASINT).

For defense contractors previously focused on military hardware, the opportunities presented by networking these agencies into the new paradigm of war fighting have expanded their market from tanks, planes, and ships into software and information technology. By 2005, according to a 2006 study conducted by the research firm Frost & Sullivan, the corporations supplying the information technology and integration tools for network centric warfare were a $25 billion industry.[11] The network, it said, "is not an entity in itself" but rather a "compilation of systems . . . built by linking transmitters, receivers, servers, routers, displays, encryption devices, firewalls, satellites, manned and unmanned sensor systems and weapons systems." The top suppliers of these technologies were Northrop Grumman, Lockheed Martin, and Raytheon, which together held a 44 percent share of the netcentric warfare market.

Northrop Grumman was the dominant player with a 20.1 percent share, and was involved, Frost & Sullivan said, "in nearly every major [network centric] program either as a lead systems integrator or as a

---

they are not alone. As I was reporting on this chapter, I asked the intelligence expert John Pike what he knew about it. "I'm having a little difficulty figuring out whether the GIG is a piece of hardware, a program or a slogan," he said. "I keep having to come back on the [GlobalSecurity.org] Web site to rework these C3I programs, because it is often hard to figure out if we're talking about an actual piece of hardware, or whether it is a programmatic collection of only tangentially related pieces of hardware—or whether it's just a slogan or simply an intelligence construct. And there have been times when I was trying to figure out a piece of hardware, and it was not [a piece of hardware], it was just a slogan. This C3I stuff is sometimes difficult to understand." (C3I refers to command, control, communications, and intelligence.)

contributor." Lockheed Martin's market share was 12.4 percent, and Raytheon's was 11.5 percent. Frost & Sullivan predicted that the network centric warfare market would reach a peak of $38 billion to $40 billion a year by 2012. While the military's investments in IT systems and the Global Information Grid will boost total netcentric company revenues to $32 billion by 2012, Frost & Sullivan also expressed concern about the ability of the different military networks to communicate with each other. "Competition between some of the market participants is having the effect of slowing progress on interoperable systems," it concluded.

With the emphasis on computer networking, netcentric warfare has opened markets for companies not ordinarily associated with defense, such as AT&T, Cisco Systems, Sun Microsystems, IBM, Hewlett-Packard, and Dell. For Cisco, which makes networking gear for Air Force Airborne Warning and Control System surveillance planes (AWACS) and many other military missions, network centric warfare is a natural extension of its global business. "Just about everything we make can be adapted in one way, shape or form to the military," says Terence C. Morgan, a retired Marine Corps officer who is director of the defense initiative team for Cisco Systems' Global Defense, Space & Security Group. "If you think of a base, it's a city. If you think of the [Global Information Grid], it's a major telecom service provider." From that perspective, he said, Cisco "is a netcentric company." [12]

In 2004, Cisco and twenty-seven other contractors involved in computerized warfare formed a business association called the Network Centric Operations Industry Consortium (NCOIC). Its purpose, according to the NCOIC Web site, is to "recommend a unified approach that would enable sensors, communications and information systems to interact within a global network centric environment" and enable "continuously increasing levels of interoperability" across government, corporate, and national lines. Corporate members include BAE Systems, Boeing, General Dynamics, IBM, ITT Industries, L-3 Communications, Lockheed Martin, Raytheon, Argon ST, CACI International, Hewlett-Packard, Microsoft, and Sun Microsystems, as well as a handful of companies from the U.K., Sweden, Germany, and Israel.

In 2007, the consortium's day-to-day activities were run by the chairman of its executive council, Harry D. Raduege, a retired Air Force lieutenant general. He came to the NCOIC after serving for five years as the director of the Defense Information Systems Agency, which manages the Pentagon's netcentric operations and oversees the acquisition of all communications networks within the Department of Defense, from the White House to the lowest tactical levels of the military. DISA also oversees the construction of the Global Information Grid.*

As a retired Air Force general and the former director of command and control systems for the North American Aerospace Defense Command, Raduege has had extensive experience in netcentric operations. By using advanced technology and the power of the Internet to increase the accuracy and speed of air strikes, Raduege explains, U.S. forces can gain an edge over an adversary that, he says, doesn't respect international borders and "makes his stand" in the cities and neighborhoods where his own people live. "These hoodlums, these terrorists, hide in the mosques, they hide in the hospitals, they hide in the schools," he said. "So when they move away from the noncombatants—because that's the way we function as a society here—we try to get them when they are by themselves, away from the noncombatants."[13]

Here's where technology—a field that Raduege knows well—comes into play. "We have someone on the ground with night goggles," he continued. "Think of that. See, these guys think under darkness, they can move. So they start moving under darkness, but the guy with the goggles sees them, identifies them, they call this in, or type this in, over a data stream to a command center. And the command center gets an

---

* While at DISA, his official bio states, Raduege led the efforts to restore communications to the Pentagon after the 9/11 attacks and managed the agency's expansion of the Global Information Grid into a "$1 billion transformational communications program." In addition to his job at the NCOIC, Raduege works in the private sector as a consultant on defense and intelligence matters. At present, he is chairman of the Deloitte Center for Network Innovation, a division of the consulting firm Deloitte & Touche that helps corporations and government agencies develop "netcentric solutions" (other Deloitte consultants include Tom Ridge, the former secretary of homeland security, and Mary Corrado, the former financial director of the CIA and the NRO). Before that, Raduege was a member of the Strategic Business Relationships team at IBM, where he focused on "net-centric operations across war-fighting, intelligence and business applications," according to the NCOIC.

aircraft, they go airborne quickly, they fly over, they look down, they use a GPS, making sure they are actually on the right target, another person on the ground puts a laser on it to make the weapon follow the laser to the guy's front-shirt pocket. That's network centric warfare right there." *

Among the key institutions created to expand the reach of intelligence into military operations are the Joint Intelligence Operations Centers, which link the Pentagon's nine Unified Combatant Commands and U.S. Forces in Korea with the Office of the Director of National Intelligence. Known by the acronym JIOCs, these centers were formally established in April 2006 by Stephen Cambone after his office completed a year-long study of the defense intelligence system. They have become the domain—and a major profit center—for SAIC, one of the largest contractors in the Intelligence-Industrial Complex.

The JIOCs are jointly controlled by the Defense Intelligence Agency and the Office of the DNI. They are designed to integrate DoD intelligence with traditional military operations and functions, with the ultimate aim of increasing the speed, power, and combat effectiveness of U.S. military forces. The Department of Defense describes them as the "fulcrum" of a worldwide group of joint intelligence organizations that gather, interpret, and act on information collected by the DIA and its sister agencies, the NSA, the NGA, and the NRO.

During their first eighteen months in operation, the JIOCs were commanded by Lieutenant General William G. Boykin, the deputy undersecretary of defense for intelligence. Boykin is an evangelical Christian who stirred controversy in 2003 for making outlandish, anti-Muslim remarks; he was mildly reprimanded by the White House for referring to the U.S. battles in Afghanistan and Iraq as part of a broader war against "a guy named Satan." Despite his extremist views, he is

* This is not the place for a full-blown analysis of the pros and cons of netcentric warfare. For an excellent overview, I direct readers to the work of the military journalist Noah Sachtman. See, for example, his excellent article, "How Technology Almost Lost the War," in *Wired*, Issue 15–12, November 27, 2007.

highly respected within the Intelligence Community for his long military experience, which has included service in Vietnam, Grenada, Somalia, and Iraq. "What we're trying to do is move towards operationalizing intelligence," he said in a Pentagon press briefing on the JIOCs in April 2006. In a speech later that year to a conference on geospatial intelligence, Boykin described the JIOCs as "coordinated, synergistic efforts" that are "running intelligence as an operation." [14]

Many details of the JIOC system are classified. But the first operational tests of the JIOC concept may have taken place in January 2007, when commandos from the Pentagon's Joint Special Operations Command launched air strikes against Al Qaeda bases and personnel in Somalia, where the U.S.-supported Ethiopian army had routed an Islamist government that had sheltered the terrorist Al Qaeda army. The attacks, carried out by Air Force C-130 gunships, were guided in part with intelligence supplied by the CIA and the NSA, which, if the public descriptions of the joint intelligence system are to be believed, would have flowed out of the JIOCs, the highest level command for sharing military intelligence.[15] The JIOC in Iraq, meanwhile, is serving as a "template" for other new centers around the world and, according to the DNI, is "beginning to benefit operations down to the battalion level." [16]

As the JIOCs become institutionalized within the military, Pentagon documents claim, they will slowly morph into the larger Global Information Grid, which will eventually include the Distributed Common Ground Systems being built for the armed services by Raytheon and other companies, using standards set by both the Department of Defense and the director of national intelligence.[17] Surprisingly, from the beginning, Pentagon officials stressed that the JIOCs would take their orders from the DNI. In his April 2006 briefing, for example, General Boykin explained that the DIA director, Michael Maples, will "take requirements" for the JIOCs directly from Mary Margaret Graham, the deputy director of intelligence for collection, and pass them down to the Combatant Commands, thus creating "an unprecedented level of access to these commands" for the civilian directors of national intelligence.[18] As a result of this direct interface, Boykin explained, analysts working out of the JIOCs will draw from the dozens of databases maintained by the NSA and the NGA without having to go through their respective chains of command. "What we're trying to do is create a situation where the analyst is talking to the collector and there's no filter in the middle," he said at the briefing. That's a perfect job for a contractor, particularly one that is as closely integrated with defense intelligence as SAIC.

In 2005, a few months after the JIOCs were launched by Cambone's office at the Pentagon, SAIC was hired by the U.S. Army to be the operations manager of the JIOC-Iraq under a two-year, $110 million contract.[19] Since then, according to an SAIC briefing for investors in May 2007, the company has signed similar contracts for the JIOCs established at the other major commands (SAIC is also involved as a contractor in the construction of the Global Information Grid, and is "helping achieve the netcentric warfare mission" at the Defense Information Systems Agency, company officials said at the briefing).

An in-house SAIC publication describes the JIOC in Iraq as a "large interactive data repository that allows analysts to pull in information from a wide range of sources," including imagery and visualization tools. SAIC's Intelligence and Security Group, which manages the JIOCs, had roughly three hundred to five hundred people overseas working at the centers in 2007. More details were provided by SAIC in its 2007 annual report to shareholders. The JIOC-Iraq, it says, draws on SAIC's Biometric Automated Toolset, a portable system that records an individual's unique characteristics for iris, fingerprint, and facial recognition; JIOC analysts use the toolset to "break up terrorist cells and track and capture the enemy." SAIC has also worked with the Army to "transition" the JIOC-Iraq capabilities into the Distributed Common Ground System. It's all in a day's work for SAIC, which is one of the most ubiquitous companies in the Intelligence-Industrial Complex.

SAIC was founded by J. Robert "Bob" Brewster, a nuclear physicist who had worked at the Los Alamos National Laboratory in the 1950s. In 1957, Brewster went to work for General Atomics, a nuclear research company that was later sold to Gulf Oil. In 1969, dissatisfied with the oil business and Gulf's plans for its subsidiary, Brewster founded SAIC as a consultant to Los Alamos and other federal labs. From the start, the company's stock was owned and sold by its own employees—a practice that helped motivate workers to increase revenues and profits, but also allowed the company to avoid filing public reports with the SEC (it went public in September 2006). In 1970, SAIC set up a branch office in Washington to solicit work from the government. Twenty years later, on the strength of Pentagon contracts involving submarine warfare and missile defense and work for the Federal Aviation Administration and other agencies, SAIC revenues surpassed the $1 billion mark.

SAIC is deeply entrenched in the intelligence business. Over five thousand of its employees, or about one in every seven, hold security clearances. They offer "domain expertise" across a wide range of intelligence, including counterterrorism, counterproliferation, remote sensing and imaging, intelligence analysis support, signals analysis and processing, signals intelligence systems, surveillance and reconnaissance systems, and unmanned aerial vehicles. "We develop solutions to help the US defense, intelligence and homeland security communities build an integrated intelligence picture, allowing them to be more agile and dynamic in challenging environments and produce actionable intelligence," SAIC says on its Web site, which defines its role as providing "mission-critical intelligence support in the war on terror." Interviewed in an SAIC internal newsletter, Larry Prior, a thirty-year veteran of U.S. intelligence who runs the company's Intelligence and Security Group, explained: "That's where you have anywhere from 10 to 100 employees and, oh, by the way, the future of the nation rests on their backs."[20]

According to a remarkable article by journalist Paul Kaihla in *Business 2.0*, a monthly magazine that covers cutting-edge, high-tech industries, SAIC's data mining and sensor systems provided critical clues to the U.S. intelligence team in Pakistan that captured the alleged mastermind of 9/11, Khalid Sheikh Mohammed. "We are a stealth company," a company official told the magazine. "We're everywhere, but almost never seen."[21] SAIC, normally reticent about press coverage, proudly displayed the article on its Web site. (The company declined to comment for this book.)

SAIC, as we'll see in the next two chapters, is an important contractor at the NSA and the NGA. Its extensive work for intelligence agencies requires the company to be constantly searching for new employees with security clearances. "We really are a hiring machine," CEO Ken Dahlberg told analysts during the earnings conference call quoted earlier. "If you are a cleared polygraph Intel specialist, you command a lot of activity. So we are doing our best to find ways to keep as well as hire these kind of folks."

One of SAIC's largest contracts is with the DIA, which hired the company to manage 2,900 secure rooms known as Sensitive Compartmented Information Facilities, or SCIFs, where DoD employees and contractors handle classified information. SAIC is responsible for designing, constructing, and maintaining security at these facilities, which are located at defense offices around the country. SAIC also provides the DIA with "highly trained and experienced professional security personnel" cleared at the SCI level—the highest possible in the Intelligence Community—to manage the SCIFs.* But that work is merely the tip of the outsourcing iceberg for the DIA, where contractors make up a substantial part of the workforce.

The Defense Intelligence Agency may be the least known of the nation's top spy agencies. It was organized in 1961 to create a unified voice for the intelligence branches within the armed forces, and is the nation's primary producer of foreign military intelligence. The DIA has a budget

---

* There is an intriguing detail about SAIC and its SCIFs buried in George Tenet's Acknowledgments in *At the Center of the Storm*, his book about his experiences with the Bush administration: "Arnold Punaro of SAIC," he wrote, "graciously provided me with a secure workspace to review and work with classified material." Punaro is identified on the SAIC Web site as the company's executive vice president for government affairs, communications, and support operations, as well as general manager of its Washington operations. Getting use of such a secure room is no small feat. To prevent eavesdroppers from picking up top secret conversations, a typical SCIF has film on the windows, walls fitted with soundproof steel plates, and white-noise makers embedded in the ceiling. Punaro must have had approval from SAIC and the CIA to allow Tenet such access. Bill Harlow, Tenet's co-author, told me that Tenet could have used office space at the CIA to work on the book, but that he "believed it would be better not to be producing his memoirs at a government facility." It was "a matter of convenience" to use the room at SAIC, Harlow said.

of about $1 billion and employs more than 11,000 military and civilian personnel, many of whom work overseas as defense attachés at U.S. embassies. Its current director, Army Lieutenant General Michael Maples, previously served as director of management of the Joint Chiefs of Staff. Historically, the DIA director has answered directly to the military brass and then to the secretary of defense.

The DIA describes its primary mission as being to provide "timely, objective, all-source military intelligence to policy makers, war fighters, and force planners to meet a variety of challenges across the spectrum of conflict."[22] One of its most significant assignments is providing centralized management for all national and defense activities related to MASINT, or measurement and signatures intelligence—the sniffing by sensors described earlier that measures, detects, identifies, and tracks what the DIA calls "unique characteristics of fixed and dynamic targets." MASINT is "particularly important for detecting ballistic missiles, directed energy weapons, and weapons of mass destruction," Maples told a defense publication in 2006. "We've got to have the right kinds of signature databases that we can compare against and the right kinds of collection capabilities to look into those three areas."[23]

The DIA was given major new responsibilities under Rumsfeld's reorganization of the Pentagon. The Strategic Support Branch was an arm of the DIA's Defense Human Intelligence Service, and DIA personnel were part of the special operations teams dispatched by Cambone and his deputy, Army General William Boykin, to Somalia, Iran, and other countries to conduct counterterrorism activities. The agency is also responsible for management of the Joint Intelligence Operations Centers.

In Iraq, the DIA led the U.S. hunt for weapons of mass destruction, both before and after the invasion, and placed Ahmad Chalabi, the crafty and controversial leader of the Iraqi National Congress, on contract to find evidence of WMD (the DIA paid the INC $340,000 a month between October 2002 and May 2004, when the DIA cut Chalabi off).[24] Nearly all of Chalabi's sources turned out to be unreliable, including the infamous "Curveball," the defector who concocted a fantastic story about mobile biological labs that appeared in the National Intelligence Estimate that laid the groundwork for the invasion of Iraq.*

The DIA's requirements for information technology and skilled analysts have made the agency a major employer of contractors, who represent at least 35 percent of the DIA workforce.† According to DIA officials who spoke to a May 2007 Defense Intelligence Acquisition Conference in Colorado, DIA contractors are filling a "workforce gap" that exists at DIA and most of the other agencies. During the 1990s, as intelligence budgets contracted, hundreds of career DIA officers retired and left the Intelligence Community. When the DIA began hiring new people after 9/11, the veteran officers who should have been around to train and mentor them were gone. But because it takes five to seven years to train a new officer, there was a "generational hole" that could only be filled by former intelligence officers with security clearances; and most of them were now working in the private sector. To carry the agency through, officials said, contractors were the only solution.[25] "Although we continuously review our mix of government and contractor personnel to ensure we have the right resources to accomplish our missions, contractors are an integral part of our DIA team," Maples, the DIA director, told the *Washington Post* in a letter to the editor in August 2007.[26]

In the spring of 2008, the agency will award the first contracts under a new $1-billion umbrella contract called Solutions for Intelligence Analysis (SIA). According to Donald L. Black, the DIA's Chief of Public Affairs, the SIA contracts will have a maximum value of $1 billion over the next five years and will combine "multiple functions under a single contract vehicle." The purpose of the SIA, he added, "is to provide the defense intelligence community with a responsive, efficient, and reliable means to satisfy requirements for intelligence analysis support and related services. We believe that it encourages competition and team-

---

* George Tenet was quite critical of the DIA in his memoirs. In one section, he chided agency officials for sitting through a review of the NIE "without ever mentioning that possibly bogus information was being cited. . . . Perhaps they didn't recognize their own information when they saw it, but that strains credulity."

† The 35 percent is the official figure, provided to me by Donald L. Black, the DIA's Chief of Public Affairs in January 2008. I have heard reliable estimates that the DIA's contracting level may be as high as 51 percent.

ing."[27] DIA officials also told the *Washington Post* that the SIA contract was the first of its type "specifically intended for the procurement of intelligence analysis and related services," and would ensure adequate outside support for the DIA as well as Army, Navy, Marine, and Air Force intelligence centers and the military's overseas command centers."[28] In his letter to the *Post,* Maples clarified that the DIA "does not outsource analysis . . . Government managers are fully in charge of this process."

The DIA's new contract vehicle is similar to a more secretive series of blanket purchase agreements (BPA) through which the DIA does much of its contracting. A blanket purchase agreement is a simplified acquisition method that allows government agencies to fill anticipated repetitive needs for analytical services and other supplies. According to *FedMarket.com,* an Internet site for government contractors, "BPAs are like 'charge accounts' set up with trusted suppliers. Both agencies and vendors like BPAs because they help trim the red tape associated with repetitive purchasing. Once set up, repeat purchases are easy for both sides."[29] Under the BPA system established by the DIA in 2003, seven teams of vendors were selected to compete against each other for outsourced work with the agency. Each agreement was worth about $300 million to the individual vendor teams, which were led by BAE Systems; Booz Allen Hamilton; Computer Sciences Corporation; Lockheed Martin; Northrop Grumman; SRA International; and Titan Corporation, now a subsidiary of L-3 Communications. Contrary to Maples's assertion to the *Post,* the agreements *do* incorporate analysis: a 2005 DIA report says the BPAs "provide the full spectrum of Information Technology (IT) planning, design, implementation, Intelligence Analysis support services."[30] A similar system of BPAs was established by the ODNI after Michael McConnell was sworn in as DNI in February 2007.

The DIA's blanket purchase agreements are known collectively as DIESCON 3,* and are also open for bidding to other agencies in the Intelligence Community (if the NSA is looking for IT expertise in a certain

* DIESCON 3 stands for "Defense Intelligence Information Systems Integration and Engineering Support Services Contract 3."

area, for example, it can ask for bids from the DIA's bidding consortiums). The DIA would not place a value on them: Terry Sutherland, a DIA press officer, told me that "because of classification, we're not going to be able to get into specific numbers." Instead, he referred me to the DIA contracting Web site, which states that the purpose of the DIESCON 3 contracts is to meet "IT-related program requirements in support of counter-terrorism, homeland defense and intelligence collection, production and dissemination."[31] DIA contractors are required to provide IT support within twenty-four hours of a request from the DIA or any other intelligence agency.

Modern IT skills were badly needed at the DIA after 9/11. Like the rest of the IC, the agency had been very slow in adapting to the rapid changes in the commercial world. To newly hired youth, it also seemed hopelessly behind in technology. Writing in the *New York Times Magazine* in December 2006, journalist Clive Thompson described the scene when Matthew Burton, a twenty-two-year-old "high-tech geek fluent in Web-page engineering," arrived at the DIA in January 2003. For Burton, trained in the rapid-fire world of the Internet, the DIA was a "colossal letdown."

"The spy agencies were saddled with technology that might have seemed cutting edge in 1995," Thompson wrote. "When [Burton] went onto Intelink—the spy agencies' secure internal computer network—the search engines were a pale shadow of Google, flooding him with thousands of useless results. If Burton wanted to find an expert to answer a question, the personnel directories were of no help. Worse, instant messaging with colleagues, his favorite way to hack out a problem, was impossible: every three-letter agency—from the Central Intelligence Agency to the National Security Agency to army commands—used different discussion groups and chat applications that couldn't connect to one another. In a community of secret agents supposedly devoted to quickly amassing information, nobody had even a simple blog—that ubiquitous tool for broadly distributing your thoughts."[32]

The DIA's DIESCON program was designed in part to modernize these antiquated systems. Each team in the DIESCON 3 system has a specific focus. The Booz Allen team, for example, includes ten thousand analysts with Top Secret/Sensitive Compartmented Information (TS/SCI) security clearances, and its consortium includes Accenture, a major outsourcing consultant to government agencies and private corporations, and Attensity, a data analysis company initially funded by In-Q-Tel, the CIA's venture capital firm. The Booz Allen team works closely on issues related to MASINT for the DIA; another important line of work, according to the Booz Allen BPA Web site, is data mining and link analysis for the CIA, the NSA, and the FBI.

BAE Systems, which captured forty-one orders worth $105 million during the first year of its agreement with the DIA, leads an industry team that specializes in analyzing enemy military forces, providing mapping and 3-D imagery to Pentagon intelligence teams, and preparing finished intelligence on paramilitary forces and insurgent and terrorist organizations operating in Iraq and other countries of interest. BAE's BPA team includes SAIC, Booz Allen, Intellibridge Corporation, General Dynamics, Advanced Concepts Inc., SpecTal, and forty-one other companies (the last two were acquired in 2007 by L-1 Identity Solutions, the intelligence conglomerate where George Tenet is a director).[33]

The Lockheed Martin BPA team claims to have the largest cleared workforce in the nation and, according to its DIESCON 3 Web site, provides "exceptional depth to respond to both surge requirements and planned customers tasks." Its forte seems to be providing large, agency-wide IT systems for the DIA and other agencies. The team includes three of the top U.S. IT firms, Hewlett-Packard, Oracle, and Sun Microsystems, as well as the consulting firm BearingPoint, which helped plan the U.S. occupation of Iraq for the Department of Defense. Another member of the team is The Analysis Corporation, the intelligence contractor run by CIA veteran John Brennan. Northrop Grumman, meanwhile, has put together a powerful combination of companies that have made their way up the federal contracting chain by managing the oversight of other contractors. They manage the DIA's system for processing bids and awarding contracts. The team includes CACI International, AT&T, ManTech International, and four small, high-tech companies that provide contract analysts to the CIA. A fifth consortium is managed by

CSC, one of the NSA's most important contractors. It manages global information networks and produces and disseminates intelligence products, including specialized expertise in the area of imagery processing and archiving. The CSC team includes CACI International and L-3 MPRI, a subsidiary of L-3 Communications. The last company is one of the largest private armies in the world, and would have at its disposal hundreds of paramilitary officers who would fit in exceedingly well with the DIA's secret intelligence teams in the Middle East and North Africa.

Contractors are so ubiquitous at the DIA that some employees have dual identifications. At the DIA acquisition conference mentioned earlier, the agency scheduled an afternoon workshop titled Offshore Threats to DoD Networks. It was led by Charles H. Thomas, who was identified as the "Computer Network Operations Program Manager" of the DIA Command and Control Office, Booz Allen Hamilton—as if the DIA and Booz Allen were one and the same.

As they do at the NSA and the CIA, business associations play an important role at the DIA. In mostly classified environments, they sponsor conferences and industry gatherings where green-badgers and agency officials discuss issues like security and future technology. In April 2007, for example, the Armed Forces Communications and Electronics Association sponsored a classified symposium on the DIA called "Intelligence and the Long War." Only those with the highest clearances were allowed to attend. Speakers represented key players in the privatized Intelligence Community, including the NSA, the DNI, the FBI, the National Counterterrorism Center, and CACI, SAIC, and In-Q-Tel. Herbert Browne, the former naval intelligence officer who retired in 2007 after five years at the helm of the AFCEA board, explained that such conferences are designed to keep defense intelligence officials apprised of the latest technology developed by the private sector for the Intelligence Community. "Our board is absolutely convinced that the very best way to look at intelligence is to have it as part of command and control, computers, communications, intelligence, surveillance, and reconnaissance," he told me. "We believe it is important to show how an investment in defense could be used to benefit for the Intelligence Community." He added: "We're convinced that's the right role for us, and we think it is what distinguishes us from the more narrow, pure intelligence associations."[34]

Many of the same companies integrating intelligence for the U.S. military in Iraq and Afghanistan have found work at the Pentagon's controversial Counterintelligence Field Activity office. CIFA was launched in 2002 by Rumsfeld's former deputy, Paul Wolfowitz, to "usher in a revolutionary era of counterintelligence" and "deliver unique, actionable information to DoD decision-makers," according to a pamphlet published by the agency in 2004.[35] Another key official involved in its creation was John Stenbit, a former TRW executive who served under Wolfowitz as assistant secretary of defense for command, control, communications, and intelligence.[36]

CIFA's original purpose, according to a Pentagon brochure, was strictly military, and was to gather information and conduct activities "to protect DoD and the nation against espionage, other intelligence activities, sabotage, assassinations, and terrorist activities."[37] From the beginning of its existence, CIFA had extensive authority to conduct domestic counterintelligence. In 2002, for example, a CIFA official was the deputy director of the FBI's multiagency Foreign Terrorist Tracking Task Force, and other CIFA officials were assigned to more than one hundred regional Joint Terrorism Task Forces, where they served with other personnel from the Pentagon as well as the FBI, state and local police, and the Department of Homeland Security.

CIFA was one part of a series of steps taken by the Pentagon to enhance its domestic spying capabilities after the establishment in 2002 of the Northern Command, or NORTHCOM, in Colorado Springs. NORTHCOM operates major intelligence centers in Colorado and Texas where intelligence from CIFA, the FBI, and other U.S. agencies is "fused" into a larger picture for military and national security officials. By December 2005, NORTHCOM's centers employed about three hundred analysts, making the command's intelligence staff larger than those of the State Department's Bureau of Intelligence and Research and the Department of Homeland Security.[38]

Much of the information collected by CIFA was amassed in a database called Talon, which stands for Threat and Local Observation Notice. Under a classified order dated July 20, 2005, and reported in the *Washington Post* by military affairs blogger William Arkin, CIFA was allowed to collect information about U.S. citizens in Talon if there was reason to believe those citizens were connected to international terrorist activities, narcotics traffic, and foreign intelligence organizations and were a "threat" to DoD installations and personnel ("In other words," Arkin commented, "some military gumshoe or over-zealous commander just has to decide [that] someone is 'a threat to' the military").[39] CIFA also obtained information about U.S. persons from the NSA and the DIA.[40] As it turned out, however, many of these threatening people were antiwar activists, and the information about them came from monitoring meetings held in churches, libraries, college campuses, and other locations.

Eventually, after Congress raised questions in 2003 about CIFA's activities, the Pentagon found that about 260 records out of 13,000, or about 2 percent of the total, improperly contained information related to U.S. persons. "These failures were especially troubling in light of CIFA's important mission to set the standards while protecting the Constitutional rights of American citizens," the House Intelligence Committee said in a bipartisan report issued in February 2006.[41] In 2007, the Privacy and Civil Liberties Oversight Board established under the 2004 intelligence reform legislation faulted the Pentagon for failing to properly manage the TALON database and for its "improper and unauthorized collection and retention of information on U.S. Persons."[42]

Like so many other intelligence programs, CIFA's spying operation was staffed primarily by contractors. By 2006, the agency had spent more than $1 billion on its operations, with most of that going to outsourced services. The first CIFA contract to come to light was a $6.3 million contract to provide "leading edge information technologies and data harvesting," awarded in 2003 to MZM Inc., of San Diego.[43] That same year, MZM won another contract worth $503,144 from CIFA to select software to use in geospatial mapping systems.[44]

CIFA's contracts with MZM only came to public attention because of a federal investigation into the activities of MZM and former congressman Duke Cunningham, a San Diego Republican. In March 2006, he was sentenced to eight years in prison after being convicted of accepting more than $2 million in bribes from executives with MZM. In return for the bribes, Cunningham used his position on the House appropriations and intelligence committees to win tens of millions of dollars' worth of contracts for the company at CIFA as well as at the CIA.

MZM was far from alone at CIFA, where at least 70 percent of the budget has been spent on contracts. I've found at least eleven other companies holding CIFA contracts. They include large prime contractors such as Lockheed Martin and small, high-tech firms such as White Oak Technologies Inc., of Silver Spring, Maryland. Based on public information, such as press releases, SEC filings, intelligence job listings, and the occasional press report, here is what I found:

- Lockheed Martin is contracted to provide counterintelligence analysis for CIFA for jobs that include analyzing data for logical combinations of keywords that might indicate planning for a terrorist attack; estimating current or future threats; and monitoring current intelligence. In 2006, the company was recruiting counterintelligence analysts to work at CIFA to "create and deliver briefings, write reports, and represent Counterintelligence Field Activity," according to a classified ad it posted on the Internet.[45] In a 2004 job posting, Lockheed Martin was seeking "experienced counterintelligence or intelligence analysts" for jobs at CIFA, where they would "conduct research and analysis and draft products; prepare intelligence reports and risk assessments; provide source and operations reviews; and provide CI operations and CI/Antiterrorism investigative support."[46]

- US Investigations Services, a former subsidiary of the Carlyle Group, provides counterintelligence support to CIFA that is "oriented towards supporting counter-terrorism, technology protection and force protection missions."[47]

- Analex Inc., a Virginia intelligence contractor owned by the U.K.'s QinetiQ, provides experienced analysts to CIFA, who sift through information "from traditional to non-traditional providers, ranging from unclassified through top secret classification using sophisticated information technologies and systems specifically designed by CIFA analysts."[48]

- ManTech International provides analytical support to CIFA's Global Watch Center by monitoring and searching intelligence and law enforcement databases and providing "line analysis, data extraction and other analytical methods to formulate and develop" counterintelligence and law enforcement intelligence products "for senior DoD and other agency officials."[49]

- Harris Corp., a Florida contractor, provides IT and professional engineering services to CIFA to "support the protection of critical research assets and technologies" of the DoD "from foreign intelligence services, terrorists and various covert or clandestine threats."[50]

- SRA International Inc., according to its Web site, runs its own service, called the Orion Center for Homeland Security, which provides counterterrorism and counterintelligence "analytical solutions" to CIFA (and the DIA). The center is run by SRA vice president Mike Wagner, a former U.S. Army intelligence officer.[51]

Other CIFA contractors I could confirm were SAIC's Homeland Intelligence Solutions group, CACI International, General Dynamics Information Technology, and Intelligence Software Solutions Inc., a contractor based in Colorado Springs. As of August 2006, CIFA had four hundred full-time employees and eight hundred to nine hundred contractors working for it.[52] By that time, there were reports that CIFA was going to merge with the Defense Security Service. A DSS spokesperson told me in 2007 that that proposal was "still under consideration." By that time, however, the entire concept of CIFA was under review.

• • •

When Robert Gates took over the Pentagon in 2007, he immediately set about to reduce the Pentagon's footprint in the spying business.[53] During his Senate confirmation hearing, he expressed his "deep unhappiness" about the "dominance of the Defense Department in the intelligence arena," and shortly thereafter walked into the Pentagon determined to end that dominance. His first act was to find a replacement for Stephen Cambone, who had been Rumsfeld's undersecretary of defense for intelligence and resigned a few days after his boss and mentor. Cambone's successor, retired Air Force General James Clapper, spent his career in military intelligence and had directed both the National Geospatial-Intelligence Agency and the Defense Intelligence Agency. He also had a reputation for being strong-willed and independent: in 2004, he'd earned Rumsfeld's wrath by telling a Senate committee that the NGA's work would be unaffected if the agency were removed from Pentagon control and placed inside the Office of the Director of National Intelligence. Incensed, Rumsfeld told Clapper that he was "out of line" because the NGA provided "combat support and should be under the Pentagon's control," and made sure that Clapper was let go when his term expired in 2005.[54]* After taking Cambone's job, Clapper moved quickly to dismantle some of Cambone's prized programs. In April 2007, after ordering a review of the Counterintelligence Field Activity office, he terminated CIFA's massive Talon database, which over a period of six years had compiled dossiers on thousands of U.S. citizens (after assessing Talon's results, Clapper said, he no longer believed that the results merited "continuing the program as currently constituted, particularly in light of its image in Congress and the media").[55] In a move that brought the DNI right into the Pentagon, Gates signed an agreement with Mike McConnell at the ODNI designating Clapper as McConnell's chief adviser on military intelligence. Slowly, bureaucratic power began to shift back to the DNI and away from the Pentagon.

---

* Air Force General Michael Hayden, then the director of the NSA, made a similar statement to the Senate and was also reprimanded by Rumsfeld. He was later appointed second in command to the DNI and is now director of the CIA.

Gates showed his cards again in May 2007, when he accepted the retirement of General William Boykin, who had overseen the Pentagon's counterterrorism operations and commanded the Joint Intelligence Operations Centers. Gates replaced him with Major General Richard Zahner, the NSA's director of signals intelligence.[56] This, too, sent a strong message: Boykin had been one of the biggest proponents of dispatching Pentagon intelligence collectors abroad to gather information for future military operations, a practice that Gates and Clapper quietly ended in 2007.[57] Now the military's covert operations would be run by a technocrat skilled in the classified arts of electronic eavesdropping and information sharing. Putting an NSA man loyal to the DNI in Boykin's place meant, first, no ranting about Muslims following "the devil"; and, second, someone whose loyalties were to the national agencies—the NSA, NGA, and NRO—rather than to the Pentagon.

As Gates and McConnell began to mend relations between their two organizations and stop the corrosive rivalry between the Pentagon and the CIA, the Bush administration's intelligence policies, and the relations between key national security agencies, began to return to the "normalcy" of earlier, pre-Rumsfeld years, with the civilians (now ensconced in the new DNI) in charge of the intelligence enterprise. For the contractors, however, nothing changed: Gates and Clapper continued to fund the expensive programs in netcentric warfare and information technology started by their predecessors.

One sign of the continuity was the Pentagon's record spending on secret research and development, which was expected to exceed $17.5 billion in fiscal year 2008—more than the Department of Defense has ever spent on classified R&D, according to the Center for Strategic and Budgetary Assessments, a nonpartisan research group. In the fall of 2007, the military was also seeking nearly $15.5 billion to buy classified weapons and equipment.[58] Meanwhile, in June 2007, Clapper initiated an assessment of the Joint Intelligence Operations Centers to find out what "we can do to make JIOCs better and take them to the next level." The team studying the JIOCs, he said, will also consider whether the centers "need more resources and whether more analysts should be assigned to them."[59] In July, Raytheon participated in Empire Challenge

2007, a joint exercise between the U.S. and British militaries designed in part to test the data sharing capabilities of the Army's Distributed Common Ground System.[60] And in August, the DIA announced its plan, described earlier, to dramatically expand its outsourcing of analysis and collection—a plan the *Washington Post* said would "set a record in the outsourcing of such functions by the Pentagon's top spying agency."[61]

But even longtime critics of Pentagon outsourcing were taken aback in January 2008, when the Counter-Intelligence Field Agency awarded a five-year, $30-million contract to the Missions Solutions Group of QinetiQ North America (QNA), the U.S. subsidiary of the British intelligence contractor QinetiQ Group PLC. Under the contract, the QNA unit, which was formerly known as Analex Corporation and had been working for CIFA since 2003, will provide a range of unspecified "security services" to the controversial agency. The contract was noteworthy because it was awarded just two months after QinetiQ North America hired Stephen Cambone, the former undersecretary of defense for intelligence, as its vice president for strategy. And it came on the heels of a series of QinetiQ deals inked with the Pentagon in the booming business of network centric warfare. That's an area that the British firm specializes in with a line of products that includes military drones and robots, low-flying satellites and sophisticated jamming technologies.*

Cambone is the most senior of a savvy group of former high-ranking Pentagon and intelligence officials hired by QinetiQ to manage its expansion in the U.S. market—a list that includes, as we saw earlier, Duane Andrews, a former top aide to Dick Cheney when he was secretary of defense, and former CIA Director George Tenet. While he was at the Pentagon, Cambone oversaw CIFA and was deeply involved in the promotion of network centric warfare. His appointment, observes intelligence expert Steven Aftergood, reflects the "incestuous" relationships that exist between former officials and private intelligence contractors. "It's unseemly, and what's worse is that it has become normal," he told me. "The problem is not so much a conflict of interest as

* For a detailed account of Cambone's new role at QinetiQ, see my article, "QinetiQ Goes Kinetic: Top Rumsfeld Aide Wins Contract from Office He Set Up," *CorpWatch*, January 15, 2008, available on the web at http://corpwatch.org/article.php?id=14898.

it is a coincidence of interests—the IC and the contractors are so tightly intertwined at the leadership level that their interests, practically speaking, are identical."[62]

For Gates and Clapper, however, managing a privatized enterprise like today's Pentagon was second nature: after all, both men had spent a considerable amount of time working in the defense and intelligence industries. After Gates left the CIA in the early 1990s, he had served as a director for SAIC as well as the intelligence contractor TRW.[63] Clapper, too, was well connected: in between his defense jobs, he was a director of satellite vendor GeoEye, which is largely funded by NGA contracts, and worked as an executive for several other NGA companies.[64] Previously, as NGA director, Clapper had presided over an agency where half the employees were full-time contractors. And just before taking the position of undersecretary of defense, Clapper had served as the chief operating officer of DFI Government Services, which holds IT and consulting contracts with the National Intelligence Council, the Office of the Secretary of Defense, the Department of Homeland Security, and other military and intelligence agencies.[65] As if to underscore Aftergood's point, nine months after Clapper assumed his duties at the Pentagon, DFI—newly merged with the British defense contractor Detica Group PLC and renamed DeticaDFI—signed a contract with Clapper's office to provide analytical services to the Pentagon in collaboration with the CIA contractor Scitor. Under the contract, Detica announced, the DeticaDFI/Scitor team will "improve the client's ability to provide more rapid and effective intelligence aimed at curbing terrorist threats."[66]

Clapper and Gates were thus more than comfortable with the extent of outsourcing in the intelligence business. In that sense, nothing had changed. And if that was true at the Pentagon, it was equally true at the NSA and the NGA, where we now turn our attention.

6

The NSA, 9/11, and the Business of Data Mining

OVER THE PAST THREE YEARS, the American public has learned more about the National Security Agency and its formidable abilities in signals intelligence than it did over the agency's previous sixty-year history. As recently as 1995 it was highly unusual for an NSA director to give a public speech or testify before Congress, and rarer still for a national leader to visit NSA headquarters in Fort Meade, Maryland. Even the vaguest references to the NSA were routinely excised from White House memoirs and congressional reports.[1] But the revelations in December 2005 of the existence of the NSA's warrantless eavesdropping program, and the subsequent debates in Congress about the President's wiretapping powers, completely altered the political landscape for the once-secret agency.

By 2008, the director of the NSA was as ubiquitous in the media and Congress as the secretary of state or the chairman of the Federal Reserve. President George W. Bush had paid three public visits to Fort Meade, more than any president in history. As the debate over the NSA's powers and its ties to the private sector spilled into the federal courts and the media, terms like "intercept," "SIGINT," and "data mining," rarely uttered outside the closed doors of the Intelligence Community before the turn of the century, had become part of the popular vernacular. For people accustomed to keeping every detail about the NSA's technical prowess under wraps, the changes were astonishing.

"NSA used to stand for 'No Such Agency,' and now you have books on it," marveled Peter Swire, an expert on surveillance law at Ohio State University who was the chief counselor for privacy in the Clinton administration. "We've had a national education on this." To industry professionals used to operating under a thick cloak of secrecy, however, the new transparency was alarming, even dangerous. The intelligence business "is conducted in secret for a reason—you compromise sources and methods," Director of National Intelligence Michael McConnell sternly instructed the House Intelligence Committee in September 2007 as it opened yet another hearing on the 1978 Foreign Intelligence Surveillance Act (FISA), which set the rules for domestic wiretapping. The congressional debate about the NSA and FISA has "allowed those who wish us harm"—Al Qaeda and its terrorist allies—to "understand significantly more about how we were targeting their communications," warned McConnell. By merely talking about this subject, he added, Congress could cause Americans to die.[2]

It was a revealing moment for McConnell, the former contractor who had spent the better part of the last ten years working to improve the government's eavesdropping powers, first as NSA director, then as the senior executive for intelligence at Booz Allen Hamilton, and finally at the Office of the DNI. More than anyone else in government, he understood that public deliberations about the NSA's targeting abilities were exposing the Intelligence Community's worst-kept secret: that the NSA, once the nation's leading technology incubator, has developed an overwhelming dependence on the private sector for the very "sources and methods" that make electronic surveillance possible.

Over the last decade, as the NSA's budget doubled from $4 billion a year to over $8 billion, the agency has become the outsourcing vanguard of national intelligence. In 2007, well over half of its budget was spent on contracts, according to industry officials and former intelligence officers who work with the agency. Every time the NSA detects unusual activity at a missile base in North Korea, tracks down a terrorist suspect in Pakistan, or analyzes the content of domestic and international phone calls, you can be certain that a contractor wearing a green badge is involved at every level.

The NSA's classified budget—which probably exceeded $10 billion in 2007—is the largest single appropriation in the Intelligence Community, and has been augmented over the last few years by $2 billion or $3 billion more in funds from the supplemental bills passed by Congress for the wars in Iraq and Afghanistan. Much of that money goes toward information technology projects—data mining, signals analysis, making and breaking codes—that have helped make the NSA the technical leader of the Intelligence Community. At the same time, the NSA is at the forefront of the IC's top priority of integrating information across agencies and getting intelligence directly to the war-fighter involved in combat.

The companies doing this work range in size from huge defense contractors to small, focused companies that provide specialized technology for mining and analyzing data. Science Applications International Corporation, the secretive San Diego company that expects to earn $9 billion in 2008, may be the NSA's largest contractor: more than 75 percent of its revenue flows from national security contracts. Computer Sciences Corporation, a $15 billion IT services company based in El Segundo, California, and the defense giant Northrop Grumman are the prime contractors on Project Groundbreaker, the $5 billion project started in 2001 that outsourced the management and operations of NSA's internal computer and communications networks to private companies. The day Project Groundbreaker began, more than one thousand NSA employees were transferred from the government to the private sector. "They walked out on Friday as NSA employees, and came back Monday as employees of CSC," recalls Frank Blanco, who was the NSA's director of personnel when the transition occurred in December 2001.[3]

Booz Allen Hamilton, McConnell's old company, is a key adviser to the NSA on outsourcing and a prime contractor for some of the agency's most sensitive projects. "While outsourcing information technology has long been common at corporations, it was not typical in the government until Booz Allen helped [the NSA] find advantages in private-sector practices," the company boasted in its 2001 Annual Report about the consulting services it provided on Project Groundbreaker.[4] Among other tasks, Booz Allen helped the NSA select software programs and evaluated vendor proposals. As a result, Booz Allen remains "a key member of the team managing the entire NSA infrastructure," the company says.[5] In 2002, IBM won a major contract to jointly develop a system to mine data and help the NSA "learn about our targets," according to congressional testimony by former NSA director Michael Hayden. Other big contractors, such as Lockheed Martin, Raytheon, and L-3, as well as smaller, more focused firms such as CACI and ManTech, provide extensive IT and technical support to the NSA. Below them are literally dozens of start-ups developing specialized technology for the agency.

Outsourcing extends to every division of the NSA. Inside the agency's Signals Intelligence Directorate, which provides U.S. military leaders and policy-makers with intelligence derived from monitoring global communications, contractors analyze data, write reports, and produce finished intelligence that is passed up the line to high-ranking officials in government. They supply and maintain software programs that manipulate data as well as remote sensing technology, data mining programs, and software that can translate data into visual graphics.

At the NSA's information assurance directorate, which is charged with securing the communications of high-ranking American officials in the national security infrastructure, contractors provide collaboration tools to help the NSA communicate with other intelligence and defense agencies, and supply information security tools to protect the integrity of NSA and other intelligence data. At the management level, the NSA has contracted out background investigations and performance reviews on individuals working for the agency, including both government employees and the contractors themselves.[6] And, as with Booz Allen, many of the agency's contracts are monitored by private sector companies.

According to my best estimates, at least 50 percent and as much as 75 percent of the people at NSA headquarters and its ground stations around the world are contractors working for the private sector. Unfortunately, my figures could not be matched against official numbers because the NSA would not comment on its outsourcing policies or make anyone available for an interview. "After thoughtful review, the NSA respectfully declines the invitation to participate in your book project," Ken White of the NSA's corporate communications and strategy group informed me in an e-mail in the spring of 2007.

The NSA's headquarters is a gleaming black edifice that towers over the landscape of Fort Meade, a sixty-acre military base about fifteen miles due north of Washington, D.C. The monstrous building, designed with specially darkened glass that keeps outsiders from snooping in, dominates a complex of more than sixty office buildings, warehouses, semiconductor chip factories, and laboratories. More than 65,000 people work there as engineers, physicists, mathematicians, linguists, and computer scientists. The machines and computers they use eat up more electric power than the nearby city of Annapolis, and make the NSA the largest customer of Baltimore Gas & Electric, the state's largest utility. Since 2005, the NSA has been headed by Army Lieutenant General Keith Alexander, the former deputy chief of staff of the Army and a one-time director of intelligence for the United States Central Command. His campus is the nucleus of a global network of radar domes, satellites, aircraft, ships, and ground interception stations that provide the most sensitive intelligence available to the U.S. government.

More than 70 percent of the President's Daily Brief, a summary of the key events of the day presented to the White House every morning by the DNI, is said to come from the NSA. The agency, under the direction of the White House and the DNI, collects, decodes, translates, and analyzes all signals intelligence relevant to U.S. foreign policy, including phone calls placed by Al Qaeda, foreign political and military leaders, insurgent groups considered dangerous to America, drug dealers, and trade and arms control negotiators. And as a combat support agency of the Department of Defense, the NSA is charged with transmitting actionable intelligence to military units and war-fighters in places like Iraq and Afghanistan, and using its surveillance and encryption units to detect the make and type of weapons systems the enemy is using. "There is not a single event that the US worries about in a foreign policy or foreign military context that NSA does not make a very direct contribution to," McConnell remarked when he was running the NSA in 1995—a statement as true then as it is now.[7]

Much of the global chatter analyzed by the NSA is captured by its Central Security Service. The CSS is the parent organization for signals and cryptology units of the Army, Navy, and Air Force, and includes the Army's Intelligence and Security Command (INSCOM), the Naval Security Group, and the Air Force Intelligence, Surveillance and Reconnaissance Agency, formerly known as the Air Intelligence Agency (AIA). These units listen in on global communications from NSA posts at home as well as overseas, including from such places as Misawa Air Base in Japan and Menwith Hill in the United Kingdom. CSS units operate the NSA's huge fleet of spy planes and drones that fly along the borders of China, Colombia, and other countries to monitor military and commercial communications traffic and track emissions from radar and missile guidance systems operated by foreign armies.

The NSA's most important partner in the Intelligence Community is the National Reconnaissance Office, which builds and manages the nation's fleet of spy satellites and operates ground stations where signals and imagery from those satellites are downloaded and analyzed. When the NSA needs coverage of a certain area, say the western third of Iraq or a mountain chain in North Korea, it sends a request up to the NRO, which can tip the satellites just a degree or two to sweep a new area (that can still take days and even weeks, I'm told). The same satellites are used by the NGA for its imagery and mapping programs, thus creating a strong, symbiotic relationship between the NSA and its sister national agencies that answer to the Pentagon's chain of command.

The NSA also maintains a close and frequently tense relationship with the CIA. Analysts at Langley use information from the NSA's intercepts of phone calls and e-mails in their intelligence estimates for the White House and Congress, and work closely with the NSA in their collection efforts against Al Qaeda and governments considered hostile to the United States. The cooperation isn't always smooth, however. During the first six months of 2002, according to the 9/11 Commission, which studied the events that led to the September 11 terrorist attacks, the White House issued "no less than seven executive-level memoranda" to delineate the agencies' separate responsibilities in collection and stop their perennial squabbling.[8] The CIA's Office of Inspector General elaborated on the "persistent strain" in relations between NSA and the CIA in a top secret report that was declassified in 2007. It found that, throughout the 1990s and right up to 9/11, the NSA monitored cell phone conversations between top Al Qaeda operatives but refused to share the raw transcripts with the CIA.[9] Indeed, the NSA remains one of the most security-obsessed agencies in the Intelligence Community.

As you approach Fort Meade by car, you're surrounded by electric fences topped with barbed wire, armed security guards in black Humvees, and signs reading "Danger: National Security Zone." Around a curve is National Vigilance Park, where the NSA has on display two reconnaissance aircraft used for its secret missions during the Cold War.* The only building on the campus where the public is allowed is the National Cryptological Museum, which opened in 1993. It is housed in a former motel that the NSA acquired to keep the building out of public hands. The museum holds thousands of artifacts marking the history of electronic surveillance, from its origins during World War II through its many triumphs and tragedies during the Cold War. "It's kind of like the baseball Hall of Fame," a museum staffer told me as I walked through during a recent visit.

Inside, you can see parts of the U-2 that was shot down over Soviet territory in 1960 and tributes to the officers and crewmembers killed on the USS *Liberty,* an NSA spy ship that was attacked by Israeli fighter

* One of them is the RU-8D, a small prop plane used by the Army Airborne Signal Intelligence Corps to fly over battlefields in Vietnam. The other is a much larger C-130 that commemorates an Air Force spy plane shot down over Armenia by a Soviet MiG-17 in 1958, killing all seventeen crewmembers. Altogether, more than forty U.S. spy planes were shot down between 1945 and 1977, according to the NSA, and 156 cryptologists died in action. According to NSA literature, a Cryptologic Memorial Wall inside the walls of the NSA lists the names of these NSA heroes and heroines, ending with the latest victim—a U.S. Navy cryptologist, Petty Officer Steven P. Daugherty, who was killed by an IED while returning from a mission in Iraq on July 6, 2007.

planes and torpedo boats during the 1967 Arab-Israeli War. Other exhibits are dedicated to the USS *Pueblo,* the NSA spy ship captured by North Korea in 1968, and the VENONA program, a World War II surveillance program that intercepted Soviet diplomatic communications and helped identify a handful of Soviet spies in the United States. For computer buffs, the museum houses several models of the first computers used by the NSA to handle the massive amounts of data scooped up by the agency's global network of radars and satellites. Here, a visitor begins to appreciate the important role corporations have played in the history of signals intelligence. Among the machines on display is a 1976 HARVEST data-processor designed for the NSA by a consortium of companies that included IBM, RCA, Sperry Rand, Philco, and General Electric. It sits next to an XMP-24 supercomputer built by Cray Research Inc., which was, according to NSA literature, "arguably the most powerful computer in the world" when it was delivered in 1983. Once installed, the NSA used the Cray computer as its operation center for a global computer network that linked "into a single cyber-web" all of the NSA's listening posts around the world as well as those operated by Britain's Government Communications Headquarters (GCHQ), the NSA's closest ally. Next to the XMP-24 is the SIGSALY, the first secure voice encryption system for telephones, invented and built by Bell Labs.

"NSA has been a silent partner with private industry from the earliest days of postwar computer development," a museum handout says. Indeed, many experts agree that advanced computing owes its very existence to its early funding from the NSA, which bought the first two or three of every computer produced by Control Data, IBM, General Electric, Cray, RCA, and other leading companies.[10]

With the assistance of these companies, by the end of the 1960s the NSA had broken many of the Soviet Union's most sophisticated codes, including diplomatic traffic from Moscow to the Soviet embassy in Washington. By the time Richard Nixon occupied the White House, NSA eavesdroppers were listening to the telephone conversations of Soviet leaders as they drove in limousines to and from the Kremlin.[11] In one celebrated operation during the 1970s, NSA divers placed a tap on a Soviet communications cable on the ocean floor north of Japan; the

NSA used it to listen in on sensitive Soviet military communications until 1981, when the operation was blown by Ronald W. Pelton, an NSA analyst on the payroll of the KGB. In another espionage feat, the NSA secretly rigged encryption machines sold by a Swiss firm, Crypto AG, to more than 120 governments around the world, thus gaining access to secret diplomatic and military communications sent to and from top officials of dozens of countries, including such prime U.S. targets as Iran, Iraq, Libya, and Yugoslavia.[12]

In its heyday, the NSA had close to 100,000 employees monitoring communications from hundreds of sites around the world. But the end of the Cold War brought that era to a close, and new enemies to the fore. After the Soviet Union collapsed in 1991, the NSA's budget was drastically cut back, and the agency shut down twenty of its forty-two radio listening posts around the world.[13] In the intervening years, the agency was forced to reengineer its operations for a new world of espionage in which the primary subjects of U.S. intelligence were no longer the static armies of the Soviet Union and its allies, but a globally dispersed network of terrorist organizations such as Al Qaeda and insurgent groups opposed to U.S. policy in the Middle East, Israel, and Asia.

The contours of the NSA's new world were sketched out in June 2007 by Air Force General Michael Hayden, who led the NSA during the transition out of the Cold War era and is now the director of the CIA. When U.S. intelligence assessed Soviet power during the Cold War, he told the National Guard Association of the United States, "we tracked troop movements, fighter wings, ICBMs, big stuff." In that context, the enemy "was easy to find" but "hard to finish," making firepower more important strategically than intelligence. But in the war on terror, he argued, that equation has been reversed. "Our enemy is easy to finish, he's just very, very hard to find," said Hayden. "Today we're looking for individuals or small groups: groups planning suicide bombings; running violent jihadist websites; sending foreign fighters into Iraq; acting as conduits between al Qaeda and potential nuclear, chemical, or biological weapons experts. We can see why the drive for intelligence is paramount in this post-9/11 world. Our mission as intelligence officers is to locate the threat, identify precisely who it is and what their intentions are so that we can bring the full resources and capabilities of our nation to bear before the enemy strikes."[14]

Thus has the role of intelligence changed, particularly for the NSA and its sister collection agencies. Gail Phipps, a former NSA official who is the executive vice president of CACI International, refers to the new science of espionage as "exquisite intelligence." "We need to be able to pinpoint a person or a cell and be 99 percent confident that we know where they are, and in exact time," she says. "That's very different from the type of analysis systems we put together in the past."[15]

Until 9/11, few Americans were aware that the NSA was the fulcrum of a global system built around the government's relentless drive to intercept virtually every radio signal, telephone conversation, e-mail, and fax transmission on earth. But from time to time there were hints of the agency's enormous powers. During the 1990s, for example, the NSA's global eavesdropping system became a source of a serious political spat with Europe. In 1997, Margaret Newsham, a contract engineer working for Lockheed Space and Missile Corporation at an NSA listening post in the United Kingdom, disclosed to Congress the existence of Echelon, a global surveillance network run by the NSA and its counterparts in Britain, Australia, New Zealand, and Canada. She made the disclosure after hearing NSA intercepts of international calls placed by Senator Strom Thurmond, the conservative Republican from South Carolina. Her revelations sparked a spate of inquiries in Congress about whether the NSA was illegally listening in on domestic conversations. The discussions, led by a Republican civil libertarian, Representative Bob Barr of Georgia, presaged the intense debate that would follow the revelations about President Bush's Terrorist Surveillance Program in 2005.*

In July 1998, a report commissioned by the European Parliament confirmed that, through Echelon, the United States and its closest allies

---

* The story of Echelon and the broader intelligence relationship between the United States and the United Kingdom was told by the journalist Patrick Redden Keefe in his 2005 book, *Chatter: Dispatches from the Secret World of Global Eavesdropping* (New York: Random House, 2005).

had the capability to intercept most European phone calls, e-mails, and data communications, as well as the technology to decode almost any encrypted communication. This sparked deep suspicion in European capitals that Echelon was being used by the NSA to capture European business intelligence and trade secrets and pass them on to U.S. companies. But the issue never captured the attention of the American public, in part because senior intelligence officials, led by Director of Central Intelligence George Tenet, denied the European reports and flatly refused to give credence to the parliamentarians' findings. "The notion that we collect intelligence to promote American business interests is simply wrong," Tenet told Congress in April of 2000 (he went on to say, however, that SIGINT "has provided information about the intentions of foreign businesses, some operated by governments, to violate US laws or sanctions or to deny US businesses a level playing field").[16]*

Another incident involving the NSA three months into President George W. Bush's first term triggered the administration's first foreign policy crisis. In April 2001, a Chinese fighter plane collided with a Lockheed EP-3E signals reconnaisance plane about seventy miles off the Chinese island of Hainan. The collision caused the death of the Chinese pilot, and the U.S. spy plane was forced to make an emergency landing in Hainan. The EP-3E was part of a secret unit, operated by the Navy for the NSA, which monitors the Pacific skies from bases in Japan, Okinawa, and Alaska; but the Chinese government complained that it had flown over its "air territory." The plane and its crew were returned after several weeks of negotiations, and the crisis was defused and

---

* Jim Woolsey, who had left the CIA in 1995, contradicted Tenet's claim of innocence. In an article for the *Wall Street Journal* on March 17, 2000, he exhibited the righteous and indignant anger toward Europe that would so endear him to neoconservatives after 9/11. "Yes, my continental friends, we have spied on you," he wrote derisively of Echelon. "We have spied on you because you bribe. Your companies' products are often more costly, less technically advanced or both, than your American competitors'. As a result, you bribe a lot." The core of Europe's problem, he argued, was the role of the state. "In spite of a few recent reforms, your governments largely still dominate your economies, so you have much greater difficulty than we in innovating, encouraging labor mobility, reducing costs, attracting capital to fast-moving young businesses and adapting quickly to changing economic circumstances." In the end, he added: "Get serious, Europeans. Stop blaming us and reform your own statist economic policies. . . . Then we won't need to spy on you."

quickly forgotten. Still, it served as a reminder of the NSA's global reach and its determination to capture signals everywhere it can.[17]*

The American public's education about the NSA began in earnest in early 2003, when the Bush administration provided an unprecedented display of the NSA's technical capabilities as part of its effort to build international support for its pending invasion of Iraq. On February 5, Secretary of State Colin Powell, with CIA director George Tenet in full view behind him, delivered his infamous presentation to the United Nations Security Council on the evidence the U.S. government had collected on Saddam Hussein's weapons of mass destruction. In an unusual break from NSA secrecy, Powell was given permission to declassify and display three NSA intercepts of Iraqi military communications to buttress his argument that Saddam possessed WMD. One of the calls was between a brigadier general and a colonel of a unit that had been involved with WMD in the past, discussing the removal of their hardware. In another, a member of the elite Republican Guard was heard discussing what he called "forbidden ammo." And in the third, a colonel instructed another officer not to use the term "nerve agents" in his instructions to other soldiers. The calls didn't prove much of anything (General Hayden later said the intercepts were "arguably more ambiguous and open to interpretation" than Powell had suggested).[18] Their lasting impact lay in the stunning display of technical prowess: out of millions of words uttered by Iraqi military officers, the NSA had the capability to pluck three conversations out of thin air that discussed, in great detail, military movements. Two years later, Americans would

* NSA surveillance isn't only directed at hostile governments or organizations; the agency eavesdrops on friend and foe alike. In fact, U.S. surveillance of trade negotiations is so routine that security authorities in South Korea held a special briefing in 2006 for trade negotiators preparing for talks on a proposed free trade agreement between Washington and Seoul. At a two-day workshop in Seoul, according to the conservative daily *Chosun Ilbo*, Korean intelligence officials "revealed the extraordinary inventiveness of the US's intelligence surveillance power" and warned negotiators to be on the watch for a "dragonfly robot that records conversation with microphones concealed in its trunk as it sluggishly drones about the room." One official drew special attention to Echelon, the U.S.-U.K. surveillance net. "There is no telling what lengths the US with its technological might will go if it decides to eavesdrop," the Koreans warned. See "Korean FTA Negotiators Primed on US Bugging Tricks," *Chosun Ilbo*, April 20, 2006, www.chosun.com.

learn that the vast surveillance and eavesdropping powers that Powell displayed at the U.N. were being directed at them.*

In the aftermath of the 9/11 attacks, the Bush administration ordered the NSA to launch a three-pronged offensive to detect and intercept phone calls, e-mails, fax messages, and Internet communications that might be related to terrorism. At first glance, the differences between these three programs might be difficult to grasp. In fact, each one is a separate piece of a broader NSA surveillance system put in place after 9/11, and each one required a separate relationship between the NSA and sectors of the Intelligence-Industrial Complex. In the first program, under what became known as the Terrorist Surveillance Program, the NSA was given the authority to monitor domestic telephone calls and Internet messages in which a suspected terrorist was at one end of the conversation without seeking warrants from the secret FISA court established by Congress in 1978. That program, which involved the close cooperation of the telecommunications industry, lasted until January 2007, when it was brought under the supervision of the FISA system. But during the intervening years, two other projects came to light. One required telecommunications carriers and Internet service providers to grant the NSA direct access to high-speed communications switches that connected U.S. telephone and Internet traffic to the global communications system, thus giving the NSA the ability to monitor domestic communications as well as foreign-to-foreign phone calls routed through the United States.[19] And in a third program, the NSA sought and received permission from the leading telephone service providers, including AT&T, Sprint, and Verizon, to sift through their massive records of telephone calls, e-mails, and Internet messages for possible clues on potential terrorists.

There was also a fourth program: a vast data mining effort on the

---

* Powell's presentation provided a satisfying lift to the NSA workforce. At Fort Meade, thousands of NSA employees and contractors "watched from a packed cafeteria and auditoriums that thundered with applause when Powell played the three intercepts, a rare display of their Top Secret work," Bob Woodward wrote in *Plan of Attack*, his second book on the Bush administration's war policies. See Bob Woodward, *Plan of Attack* (New York: Simon & Schuster, 2004), p. 309.

part of the NSA to sift through the massive amounts of data gathered in the three wiretapping programs. This effort would have involved the NSA's outsourced IT vendors, and has largely been overlooked by the media and Congress. The first hints of such a program first appeared in *State of War,* James Risen's book about U.S. intelligence and the NSA spying program. According to the *New York Times* reporter, President Bush wrote his October 2001 executive orders so the NSA would have "the freedom to employ extremely powerful computerized search programs"—originally designed to scan foreign communications under the Echelon program uncovered in Europe during the 1990s—in order to "scrutinize large volumes of American communications." The names of the companies involved in the data mining operation were a tightly held secret, and "only a very few top executives in each corporation" were aware of the relationships or even knew about the "willingness of the corporations to cooperate on intelligence matters." [20]

During the summer of 2007, the *Times* elaborated further. Quoting "current and former officials" who had been briefed on the NSA program, it reported that a 2004 confrontation between the Justice Department and the White House over the NSA program "involved computer searches through massive electronic databases." The *Times* could not determine precisely why searching the databases raised "such a furious legal debate" and led several top Justice officials to threaten to resign. "But such databases contain records of the phone calls and e-mail messages of millions of Americans, and their examination by the government would raise privacy issues," the paper concluded.[21] If it had chosen to dig further, however, the *Times* could have identified some of the players. The number of companies that could be involved is not large, and can be traced to the NSA's outsourcing of its communications and signals intelligence operations over the past eight years. Once again, we must return to the last years of the Clinton administration.

By the 1990s, the NSA's historical dominance in computers and code breaking had begun to fade. Commercial developments in computing power, cryptology, and high-speed telecommunications surpassed the agency's ability to keep up with the millions of calls it was monitoring every day. And in the course of a few years, the world switched from using telephone lines and calls beamed by radar to using fiber-optic lines, cell phones, and wireless technology. The NSA's eavesdropping skills, in contrast, were in the old telephony infrastructure and electronic signals; the fiber-optic lines increasingly used around the world were almost impossible to monitor from above the ground.

"Wiretapping was physically relatively easy" prior to the 1990s, says Peter Swire, the Ohio State law professor. "If I touch my copper wires to your copper wire, I can listen in. That's the old-fashioned wiretap." But that doesn't work with fiber optics. "If I touch my glass to your piece of glass, it doesn't do anything to conduct."[22] As fiber optics increasingly became the system of choice for communications, intelligence analysts began to say the NSA was "going deaf." As it faced up to the technological challenge, the NSA was also reeling from budget cuts that decreased its workforce by 30 percent over the 1990s. These cuts were part of the peace dividend that Congress had insisted on after the collapse of the Berlin Wall and the end of the Cold War, but their consequences were lethal, Hayden told Congress in 2002. The danger, he said, "was not that SIGINT would go away, but that it would cease to be an industrial strength source of American intelligence."[23]

The NSA's wake-up call came just a few weeks into the new century. On the morning of January 24, 2000, the agency's internal computer systems suffered a catastrophic crash, blacking out the huge agency for three and a half days. "This was not your garden-variety computer crash," former senator Bob Graham, who once chaired the Senate Intelligence Committee, recalled. "It was a full shutdown of the largest computer system in the world. For the next three days, as hundreds of engineers and technicians worked around the clock to restart the complex network, trillions of bytes of data were being collected daily but not analyzed."[24] The NSA would later report that the outage "greatly reduced the signals intelligence information available to national decision makers and military commanders" and cut the President's Daily Brief "to a small portion of its typical size."[25] Graham blamed the outage on the NSA's failure "to keep pace with the rapid change in computer and telecommunications technology, the greater complexity of collecting that information, and the expanded target." Simply put, he said, "the NSA's system was outdated. Given the volume of information it was collecting, it was as if the system were trying to drink from a fire hose; it couldn't keep up."[26] The blackout was the final straw for an agency that now faced becoming a sideshow in a telecommunications and computer revolution that was sweeping through the world. But there was worse to come: just prior to 9/11, NSA eavesdroppers picked up a conversation by Al Qaeda operatives referring to the attack; but its analysts had failed to translate it in time. The NSA director, Mike Hayden, didn't want that ever to happen again.

The challenges facing the NSA were summarized in a secret report presented to President Bush when he came into office. A declassified copy of the report was obtained in 2005 by the National Security Archive at George Washington University and published on its Web site.[27] Throughout the Cold War, the NSA report said, the agency had "operated in a mostly analog world of point-to-point communications carried along discrete, dedicated voice channels. These communications were rarely encrypted, and those that were used mostly indigenous encryption that did not change frequently. Before the arrival of fiber optic technology, most of these communications were in the air and could be accessed using conventional means; the volume was growing but at a rate that could be processed and exploited." But that had all changed, presenting the NSA with an enormous challenge.

> Now, communications are mostly digital, carry billions of bits of data, and contain voice, data and multimedia. They are dynamically routed, globally networked and pass over traditional communications means such as microwave or satellite less and less. Today, there are fiber optic and high-speed wire-line networks and most importantly, an emerging wireless environment that included cellular phones, Personal Digital Assistants and computers. Encryption is commercially available, growing in sophistication, and packaged in off-the-shelf computer software. The volumes and routing of data make finding and processing nuggets

of intelligence information more difficult. To perform both its offensive and defensive missions, NSA must "live on the network."

In practical terms, that meant tearing down the wall that had separated intelligence from the commercial worlds and adapting the same technologies that now dominated the World Wide Web. At his headquarters in Fort Meade, NSA director Hayden began taking measures to reorganize the agency and create a SIGINT system that would work as effectively against cell phones, fiber optics, and other advanced communications as it did against the Soviet military. To accomplish that goal, he and his staff decided to radically expand the agency's dependence on the private sector. After all, the high-tech capitalism churning in the computer industry and the Internet was the source for most of the new technologies coming online; if the NSA couldn't beat them, it would join them.

"The NSA had two choices," recalls Stan Soloway, a Washington lobbyist for contractors who worked as a Pentagon acquisition official during the Clinton administration, when these changes took place. "Let those networks atrophy because they didn't have any money to develop the people, or get the hell out of the business of managing the networks and put resources toward the intelligence side—the core mission that they had. And that's what they've done."[28]

In the mid-1990s, twenty companies accounted for 85 percent of the NSA's contracting. But starting in the last years of the Clinton administration, the NSA began to expand its contractor base and outsource on a massive scale. From 2000 to 2004, the NSA doubled its procurement spending, and increased the number of contractors to more than 2,690. What this would mean for the NSA was spelled out in 2002 by Michael Hayden in a cryptic statement to Congress. In terms of "buy vs. make"—the percentage of the NSA budget spent on buying technology versus making it—"we spent about a third of our SIGINT development money this year making things ourselves," he said. "Next year the number will be 17 percent." In other words, 83 percent of the NSA's signals intelligence development budget was spent on contractors. That was five years ago; as outsourcing has increased, that percentage has probably grown considerably. In any case, the number of NSA suppliers now exceeds 5,400.[29] That marks an astounding shift for an agency that helped bring the modern computer age into being.

To cushion the blow to NSA employees who were being laid off, the NSA created a program called Soft Landing, which helped NSA workers find jobs with the contractors. "The idea was to transfer the employees to jobs within the crypto-industrial complex—jobs with defense firms that had significant contracts with the NSA," James Bamford wrote in *Body of Secrets,* his second book on the agency.[30] Many of these contracts called for the former NSA employees "to remain right at NSA, although in a different job and in a different office." Companies participating in that early program included Allied Signal, TRW, SAIC, and Lockheed Martin. By 1998, the NSA's Soft Landing office had placed more than three hundred retirees at eight contractors, saving the NSA $25 million. In July 2000, hoping to bring "corporate rigor" to the NSA's operations, Hayden hired Harry Gatanas, a former senior Pentagon contracting official, for the new post of senior acquisition executive.[31] Other managers were brought in from Legg Mason, the financial services company, and Walt Disney Corporation.

Gatanas and Hayden also organized a PR campaign to drum up congressional support for their outsourcing plans. In June 2004, Ellen McCarthy, the *Washington Post*'s technology correspondent, took the bait and wrote a flattering profile of Gatanas that captured the spirit of the times. "Sitting in a dark boardroom and flanked by World War II spy posters," she began, "Harry D. Gatanas is blunt about what's happened at the National Security Agency over the past 15 years: The codebreaking organization has lost its technological edge. . . . To keep up with the world around it, the secretive organization based at Fort Meade has been forced to open its doors and do business with the private sector."[32] Later, in a highly unusual step, Gatanas and other acquisition executives held a press conference to explain their buying procedures, and even announced a partnership with the state of Maryland intended to help companies develop ties with the agency. "This revolution in information technology is far more than we can handle,"

Gatanas told the briefing. "We've got to have the support of industry."[33] Eric Haseltine, the Disney executive hired as the NSA's director of research, expounded on this theme. "We in the NSA are encountering problems with the flood of information that people [in the outside world] won't see for a generation or two," he declared. "We can either be drowned by it or we can get on our surfboard and surf it and let it propel us."[34]*

The story of Essex Corporation, an NSA contractor now owned by Northrop Grumman, is emblematic of the outsourcing revolution that transformed the NSA. Earlier, we met Leonard Moodispaw, its CEO, who was one of the founders of the Intelligence and National Security Alliance. Like many of his colleagues in the intelligence industry, he began his career working for the NSA, where he was employed for more than fifteen years as a senior manager in the Signals Intelligence Directorate. In 1978, at a time when NSA was under fire in Congress for monitoring the phone calls and telegrams of American citizens, Moodispaw said goodbye to the agency and set off to use the law degree he had earned in night school. Over time, he built a flourishing practice in Annapolis, where he did some civil liberties work and represented former NSA colleagues in their private legal matters.

Ten years later, a group of NSA scientists Moodispaw had known formed a company called System Engineering & Development Corp. (SEDC). Their goal was to commercialize a new optical technology they had invented while at the NSA, which used light beams to process images from satellites. Moodispaw was invited to join them, and he eventually rose to the position of vice president and general counsel. He was soon recruited away to another company, ManTech International; but he didn't like the hyper-competitive atmosphere there, and within a few years had rejoined his colleagues at SEDC. By that time, the Cold War was over and the defense industry was moribund. SEDC, now owned

---

* Haseltine is now associate director for science and technology with the Office of the Director of National Intelligence.

by an engineering company called Essex Corporation, was floundering. It needed Moodispaw's executive leadership and his experience working in the government.

At the time, Essex was marketing its laser technology primarily to private companies. One of its clients was the electronics giant Motorola, which had launched an ambitious and expensive project—known as the Iridium project—to build a global constellation of satellites for the new mobile phones that were just coming on the market. But the Iridium project was an idea before its time, and eventually floundered. At that point, Moodispaw and his team decided to focus on government markets, which had the potential to provide the R&D money that could turn their optical technology into a commercial success. Their first government customer was the Pentagon's Ballistic Missile Defense Organization, which saw potential in optical technology for missile-detecting radar.

Then, in 1999, the NSA came calling. Under the leadership of Michael Hayden, Moodispaw's old employer was turning to the private sector for new ideas that could help it stay ahead of the technological revolution under way in IT and communications. Optical processing, NSA analysts believed, had the potential to vastly improve NSA's ability to collect and analyze the oceans of signals intelligence it was scooping up from its global network of satellites and listening posts. With seed money from NSA, Essex and its team of scientists, led by NSA veteran Terry Turpin, slowly began to expand. But success was still a long shot. "I just hope they can stay in business long enough so the Defense Department gets to leverage off what they're doing in the commercial world," a U.S. official told the *Baltimore Sun*.[35]

The events of September 11, 2001, erased all doubts about the company's future. The NSA, which had captured but failed to translate several crucial Al Qaeda messages that might have alerted officials to the attacks, came under intense pressure from Congress and the Bush administration to apply its technical skills to find terrorists before they had a chance to strike again. Essex was in the right place at the right time, and the work started pouring in. Shortly after 9/11, for example, the NSA and the Department of Defense became very interested in how

Essex was using optical technology to build three-dimensional images from data transmitted from reconnaissance planes and spy satellites. The projections allowed intelligence analysts to see objects normally blocked by clouds, trees, foliage, and the ground—things like mines, improvised explosive devices, and the insurgents using them—that are often hard to spot from five miles in the air.

Soon the classified contracts were flowing in almost as fast as Essex could sign them. One contract, for a secret project called Thunder, started at $57 million in 2003, and was increased by $225 million in 2004 and by $160 million in 2006 (in the arcane language of NSA contractors, Essex CEO Moodispaw would only say that the rapid expansion "reflects the urgent requirements of our customer").[36] By the end of 2006, Essex's earnings had increased from $2.6 million in 2002 to over $250 million, capping an astounding five-year span of growth in which its revenues increased by *156 percent every year*. Over that time, Essex grew from a staff of fifty to over one thousand. Now it is part of the Mission Systems division of Northrop Grumman, which paid $580 million for the company. (With the acquisition, *Defense News* observed, "Northrop Grumman gains entrée to several key classified programs under the aegis of the NSA, the Missile Defense Agency and other Washington-area government clients.")[37] The NSA is now responsible for 90 percent of its business, and the company's lightning-fast optical processors are now employed throughout the Intelligence Community. But the way Moodispaw tells it, it's in signals intelligence where Essex has made its mark. Essex, he told me shortly before his company was sold, "provides the right tools to use in different signals environments. We put together the teams to work closely with agencies so they can figure out how to intercept calls, analyze things, and locate people. And the more successful we are, the less they want us to talk about it."[38]

Essex was also involved in the NSA's largest outsourcing project to date: Project Groundbreaker, a ten-year, $5 billion project to rebuild and operate the NSA's internal telephone and computer networking systems. The project was managed by a vendor team led by Computer Sciences

Corporation and Logicon, the IT subsidiary of Northrop Grumman, and remains the largest outsourcing project ever attempted by the federal government. The "outsourcing partnership" with CSC and Northrop Grumman, Hayden said in announcing the contract award on July 31, 2001, will allow the NSA to "refocus assets" on its "core missions of providing foreign signals intelligence and protecting U.S. national security-related information systems" by turning over key IT services "for industry's purview."[39] He added: "The ability of NSA to perform its mission depends on an efficient and stable Information Technology Infrastructure, one that is secure, agile, and responsive to evolving mission needs in balance with the requirements to recapitalize and refresh technology."

CSC had been in the government contracting business for nearly half a century when it was selected to manage the Groundbreaker project. It was founded in 1959 to write software for defense manufacturers and in 1963 became the first software company to go public. Over the years, it built a multibillion-dollar business as a systems integrator for companies and government agencies, starting with computer contracts with the National Aeronautics and Space Administration. After 9/11, CSC formed a new business unit to go after homeland security and intelligence work ("One reason we did this was the wealth of discussion about sharing data among the agencies and the first responders, especially when it comes to terrorist threats," said Pat Ways, CSC's vice president for federal sector business development).[40] By 2004, largely as a result of Groundbreaker, CSC had become the nation's third-largest federal contractor, with prime contracts worth more than $4 billion.[41] Northrop Grumman, CSC's partner in the Groundbreaker project, is best known as a designer and manufacturer of military surveillance and combat aircraft, defense electronics and systems, as well as large naval combat ships. It first became an important intelligence contractor in 1999 when it acquired DPC Technologies, a Maryland IT company with close contractual ties to the NSA. It moved deeper into intelligence in 2002 when it acquired TRW, a longtime CIA and NSA contractor. Those acquisitions, plus its recent takeover of Essex Corporation, have greatly expanded Northrop Grumman's presence at Fort Meade.

In managing the project for the NSA, CSC and Logicon drew in practically every major company involved in defense and intelligence outsourcing and called the consortium the Eagle Alliance. Subcontractors included General Dynamics, BAE Systems, Titan Corp., CACI International, TRW, ManTech, Lockheed Martin, and Verizon (one of the companies that allegedly granted the NSA access to its consumer database under the Terrorist Surveillance Program), as well as Dell, Hewlett-Packard, and Nortel Networks. Under the NSA's "employee-friendly approach," contractors received monetary incentives to hire NSA employees.[42] The companies involved were delighted with the project. "This type of outsourcing program hits our sweet spot," boasted Frank Derwin, Logicon's vice president.[43]

Groundbreaker, however, was marred from the start by technical and managerial problems. Moodispaw, whose company was a subcontractor on the project, told me that CSC had badly mismanaged the project from the beginning. "CSC is the absolute worst prime in the world to work for," he said. "They'll screw you right and left. And I'm not asking to be off the record."[44] (CSC would not comment.) In 2006, Siobhan Gorman, the *Baltimore Sun*'s intelligence reporter, interviewed dozens of NSA officials and contractors involved in the project. She found that Groundbreaker's $2-billion price tag had doubled, and that technical problems with the system were legion.

"Computers are integral to everything NSA does, yet it is not uncommon for the agency's unstable computer system to freeze for hours, unlike the previous system, which had a backup mechanism that enabled analysts to continue their work," she wrote. "When the agency's communications lines become overloaded, the Groundbreaker system has been known to deliver garbled intelligence reports." Worse, agency linguists told Gorman that the number of conversation segments they could translate in a day had dropped significantly under Groundbreaker. The NSA, she concluded, "has no mechanism to systematically assess whether it is spending its money effectively and getting what it has paid for."[45]

In June 2007, the NSA exercised its options in the original contract and extended Project Groundbreaker for another three years. The new contract is worth $528 million.[46] The NSA's action "underscores NSA's confidence in the Eagle Alliance's experience and ability to deliver state-of-the-art information technology solutions that result in sound operational performance for the agency," James W. Sheaffer, the president of CSC's North American Public Sector division, announced in a press release. Chuck Taylor, CSC's director of North American communications, said the company would not answer any questions about the Groundbreaker project because its details are classified. "Generally we're not at liberty to discuss this contract at all," he told me.

Project Groundbreaker spawned an industrial renaissance near the NSA, and the results can still be seen today in an innocuous-looking cul-de-sac called National Business Parkway less than a mile from the NSA's headquarters in Fort Meade. Here, you can see the entire panoply of companies involved in the Intelligence-Industrial Complex.

Driving in from the south, one of the first buildings on the parkway is the regional headquarters for Boeing, a key NRO and NSA contractor. Boeing is deeply involved in signals intelligence through its Integrated Defense Systems unit, based in St. Louis. In 2006, it began testing for its defense and intelligence clients a new product that downloads signals and imagery from military satellites and sends it instantly to analysts in ground stations. "For the first time," said Boeing, "signal intelligence receivers proved that they could automatically identify the target—a mock terrorist—and trigger airborne surveillance assets to track the target on the ground, while capturing full-motion imagery and broadcasting it instantly to analysts several hundred miles away." The system will eventually become part of the U.S. Army's array of high-tech weaponry.[47]

Next to the Boeing site is a large building carrying the logo of Lockheed Martin, the nation's largest defense contractor. Lockheed's ties to the NSA go way back: in the mid-1950s it built the U-2, the spy plane that played a key role in the Cold War, and conducted some of the NSA's initial research in signals collection. "Some of our work you will never hear about," the company says on its Web site. "Our classified work has supported the Defense Intelligence Agency (DIA) and National Security Agency (NSA) as they dealt with the most high-visibility situations in recent U.S. history and many others you never saw on the news." Under a contract signed in 2005, Lockheed Martin provides an integrated electronic security system to protect NSA facilities in the Washington area. A similar system is in place at the Pentagon and dozens of U.S. military facilities abroad.

Adjacent to Lockheed Martin sit the Washington offices of Titan Corp., a $2 billion contractor that provides technical support for many of the UAVs deployed by the Intelligence Community over Iraq and Afghanistan. In 2005, L-3 Communications acquired Titan for $2.6 billion, instantly transforming itself into the nation's sixth-largest defense contractor and a major force in intelligence. Titan's office, which includes over 15,000 square meters of floor space, houses six hundred workers and is the headquarters for Titan's National Intelligence Solutions Group, which works closely with the NSA. Titan contracts included a $300 million, five-year contract for program management and planning, and a $36 million, four-year contract for translation and analysis services at Fort Meade and two of the NSA's regional centers.[48] In 2007, after Titan had been absorbed, L-3 began working on a new $35 million, five-year contract to supply online network encryptor cards to national security agencies. The cards allow intelligence and defense agencies to link up with other classified networks.[49]

Across the parkway from L-3 is the Maryland headquarters of Booz Allen Hamilton, the NSA's largest systems integrator and one of its chief advisers on IT and network issues. Further down, you see signs for Applied Signal, one of NSA's leading suppliers of SIGINT processing equipment; Electronic Data Systems (EDS), the Dallas IT firm once owned by Ross Perot that makes the "smart cards" used by the Pentagon to identify its employees in bases around the world; and Omen Inc., an IT subcontractor on the Groundbreaker project. You also pass a smattering of small companies with names like Praxis and Synsys, just waiting for an acquisition deal. Other companies known to work for the NSA include PricewaterhouseCoopers, the financial auditing company; BearingPoint, the Virginia consulting company; and US Investigations Services (USIS), a company owned for most of its existence by the powerful Carlyle Group. It does background checks on NSA employees and contractors.[50]

There's no such thing as a typical NSA contractor. But if you had to pick one, it might be SI International of McLean, Virginia, which runs some of the NSA's support and management functions. SI is one of the fastest-growing IT companies working for the federal government, and in 2006 earned 48 percent of its $462 million in revenue from contracts with intelligence agencies. SI's niche is advising intelligence and defense agencies on their acquisition and outsourcing strategies. It also helps intelligence agencies as they shift from proprietary "stove-pipes" located within one agency to integrating their IT systems with sister agencies and the Pentagon's evolving Global Information Grid, the Internet-like system described earlier that will link military commanders, war-fighters, and national collection agencies into a single classified network.

In 2005, SI signed a three-year contract with the NSA to provide training in financial management, and in 2006 added a five-year $6.9 million task order to run the NSA's human resources welcome center in Fort Meade. SI bought into many of these contracts by acquiring smaller companies holding specialized NSA contracts. Of particular importance was SI's $30 million acquisition in 2004 of Bridge Technology Corporation, which had extensive contracts with defense intelligence agencies. Bridge "really gave us name-brand recognition within the Intelligence Community," S. Bradford "Bud" Antle, SI's president and CEO, told investors during a 2006 Washington conference on defense investing. "The IC wants other players. They get a bit in-bred because they have a set of contractors that are clean with capabilities they've known forever." For that reason, agencies are pleased when they "see an acquisition like us buying Bridge."

Because of its high-visibility role as an adviser for the NSA, SI has filled its management team and board of directors with former high-ranking intelligence officials. Harry Gatanas, SI's executive vice president for strategic programs, oversees the company's business with the Pentagon and its intelligence agencies. He came to SI directly from the

NSA, where, as we just saw, he was the agency's senior acquisition executive and the contracting manager for Project Groundbreaker. Prior to coming to the NSA, Gatanas spent thirty years in military intelligence, where his duties included managing contracts for the Army.

Outside of providing IT support, what contractors actually do for the NSA is shrouded in secrecy. Nearly all NSA contracts are classified, and companies that work for the agency are under strict orders not to divulge details of their operations to the public. Still, the details available in corporate literature and investor presentations can be quite revealing.

ManTech International, for example, claims on its Web site and in SEC filings that it manages "real-time signal processing systems" for the NSA. ManTech's work for the agency is managed by its Security and Mission Assurance division, which encompasses intelligence and operations, counterintelligence, information operations, and cyber-warfare, as well as "sources and methods protection planning." Another ManTech specialty, much in demand at the NSA, is providing security for networks within the IC that are used to transmit and receive intelligence from other agencies. "For highly classified programs, including intelligence operations and military programs, we provide secrecy management and security infrastructure services," ManTech states on the Web site, which features a photograph of a woman with her finger to her lips, presumably whispering "shh." ManTech also assists the NSA in intercepting enemy communications, a job that entails working closely with NSA teams deployed overseas with the U.S. Army. "For example," ManTech explains, "when an adversary of a customer implements a new communication technique or protocol, we provide rapid prototyping and re-engineering services, which enable our customers in the Intelligence Community to decipher and exploit the communications."[51] (This work often places ManTech employees at risk. In 2006, three contractors working for ManTech lost their lives when the Air Afghanistan jet they were taking on their way to a mission crashed in the mountains, killing everyone aboard.)

CACI International has designed an elaborate Web site to explain the services it provides in the area of signals intelligence. On one page,

CACI boasts that it is a "dynamic provider of the nation's SIGINT needs," providing SIGINT services "ranging from concept development to system integration." Most of its NSA work, I was told by industry executives familiar with CACI, is done through a subsidiary called CACI Technologies. In Iraq, units from this division have provided mobile, high-performance computers to support the NSA's interception of signals emanating from enemy weapons systems, CACI officials told a Washington-area military forum in 2004. They also help the NSA download data about insurgent movements picked up by UAVs.[52] That program is "effective, affordable, and deployable" and provides "an incredible amount of power down to the lowest echelon" of the Army, Jeffrey Posdamer, a senior manager at CACI Technologies, told the forum. The system can be used practically anywhere, and apparently has been deployed in Iraq. According to CACI's chairman, Jack London, his company was instrumental in the joint tracking by the NSA and the NGA that resulted in the 2006 capture and execution of Abu Musab al-Zarqawi, the former commander of Al Qaeda in Iraq.

London made that disclosure in a surprisingly informative interview with WMAL radio in Washington. In what may have been an unguarded moment, CACI's CEO boasted of his company's prowess in signals intelligence and explained how CACI helps the NSA and other agencies monitor Internet traffic and terrorist communications. Data mining—an important task for an agency that must sift through millions of bits of data every day—is "one of our specialties," he said. He added that CACI does "forensic-type work" using information from "overhead imagery, communications satellites, and intercepts, pulling all these things together in a forensic way, playing the detective, if you will, and connecting the dots and being able to determine connections among organizations and among cells of people."[53] Under contract to the NSA, CACI appears to be spying on a global scale.

So far, none of the NSA's IT contractors have admitted their involvement in the agency's domestic surveillance program, and for the most part congressional hearings on the NSA have avoided the subject of the NSA's data mining exercises. One lawmaker, however, has pressed the issue: Senator Patrick Leahy, D-Vermont, chairman of the Senate Judiciary Committee, one of the few senators to be briefed on the NSA surveillance program before it became public knowledge. He first noted his concerns in a Washington speech to a conference on computers, freedom, and privacy on May 3, 2006, one week before *USA Today* broke the story that the major telecommunications companies had turned over their massive customer databases to the NSA.

One of the potential dangers facing American democracy, Leahy said, is the "post-9/11 rise of partnerships between government and private data collectors, and the outsourcing of data banking and data mining functions that used to be handled by government agencies. This outsourcing already is blurring the few lines of privacy protection that once protected the public." If these trends continue, he added, "then before too long we will tend to think of privacy as a quaint twentieth-century American value that no longer applies to our everyday lives."[54] In June 2007, Leahy, acting as the chairman of the Judiciary Committee, issued subpoenas to the White House for all documents addressing President Bush's authorization for the warrantless electronic surveillance program. The subpoenas sought virtually all legal documents about the program, including documents describing agreements or understandings between the White House, the Department of Justice, and the NSA and "internet service providers, equipment manufacturers, or data processors regarding criminal or civil liability for assisting with or participating in the warrantless electronic surveillance program."[55] Leahy was one of the few lawmakers who understood the critical role that IT companies play in the analysis of electronic intelligence.*

In my reporting for this book, I broached the subject of NSA data mining to more than a dozen contracting executives. None would comment about Leahy's concerns. But one executive, after making clear we were completely off the record, expressed deep regret about what the NSA's warrantless surveillance program had done to the reputation of the Intelligence Community. Like many of the "seniors" in the industry, he had worked at the NSA and knows how stringent the FISA rules are.

---

* The White House produced some documents on the IT and Internet companies, and Senator Leahy made them available to other lawmakers in a classified briefing.

Since the 1970s, electronic surveillance has only been permissible for the purpose of collecting foreign intelligence on persons who are knowingly acting on behalf of a foreign power. To reinforce this rule, analysts who are listening to the content of telephone calls have always had large signs over their workspaces saying what to do when the subject is a "US Person"—a category that includes American citizens as well as foreigners residing in the United States. "They have it all worked out, and it works very nicely," the contractor recalled, and therefore "there is absolutely no [expletive] need to stretch it as Bush and Cheney wanted to do." If someone on the NSA floor sees something that may require a judgment on FISA, "the system is set up for instant approval virtually, and they never get turned down. So it's just a crock to say that some bad guy is getting away" because of the FISA system. What "Bush did to the intelligence business set it back years in terms of reputation."[56]

If there's one generalization to be made about the NSA's outsourced IT programs, it is this: they haven't worked very well, and some have been spectacular failures. We saw earlier that Project Groundbreaker, which involved the outsourcing of the NSA's internal communications system, encountered mismanagement and cost overruns. But despite its problems, the project was renewed in 2007 for another three years. The NSA's second experiment in outsourcing, Project Trailblazer, managed by SAIC, fared far worse: launched in 2001, it experienced hundreds of millions of dollars in cost overruns, and was canceled in 2005.

In 2001, around the same time that Project Groundbreaker was transferring the first NSA employees to the Eagle Alliance, the NSA launched an extensive collaboration with the private sector to help the agency sift through the oceans of data flowing into headquarters from its SIGINT systems around the world. The idea behind Trailblazer was to replace the NSA's Soviet-era eavesdropping technology, which was oriented around capturing communications beamed by radio waves, with software designed to capture communications traveling on cell phones, fiber optics, and across the Internet. At the time Trailblazer was conceived, the *Baltimore Sun* would report in 2006, the NSA was unable to analyze much of the information it was collecting and using "only blunt tools" based on the origin of a particular message or certain keywords as the basis for keeping or discarding its data.[57] As a result, more than 90 percent of the information it was gathering was being discarded without being translated into a coherent and understandable format; only about 5 percent was translated from its digital form into text and then routed to the right division for analysis.

The NSA wanted a system that would swiftly spot threatening messages amidst the millions of words and phrases flowing through the global communications systems and use computers to sort through the 130 languages used around the world. "How do you find the terrorist ordering a pizza, which is actually a signal for another 9/11?" a former senior intelligence official asked a reporter at the time. "It's a daunting task."[58] The project was awarded in 2002 to SAIC, which led a team that included Northrop Grumman and Booz Allen Hamilton. "The SAIC team will provide and integrate commercial technologies proven to be scalable, agile, robust, secure, and interoperable to produce and deploy state-of-the-art solutions to challenges facing the NSA today and in the future," the agency declared in a press release issued on September 19, 2002. "This contract is a continuation of NSA's effort to transform its national security missions of providing foreign signals intelligence and protecting national security-related information systems using the innovation of industry partners."[59] The initial $300 million Trailblazer contract, said Hayden, the NSA's director at the time, would "revolutionize how we produce SIGINT in a digital age."[60] Duane Andrews, SAIC's corporate executive vice president, declared in a press release that SAIC "will continue to provide NSA with all the technology and systems support needed to help them achieve their goals."[61]

SAIC has somewhat of a symbiotic relationship with the NSA: the agency is the company's largest single customer, and SAIC is the NSA's largest contractor. SAIC's penchant for hiring former intelligence officials played an important role in the company's advancement. As we saw earlier, Andrews, who managed SAIC's NSA programs for many years, had close ties with Vice President Cheney dating back to the first Gulf War, when he was an assistant secretary of defense in Cheney's

Pentagon. The story of William Black is another case in point. In 1997, Black, a forty-year veteran of the NSA, was hired as an SAIC vice president "for the sole purpose of soliciting NSA business," according to a published account.[62] Three years later, after the NSA initially funded Trailblazer, Black went back to the agency to manage the program; within a year, SAIC won the master contract for the program. Other key SAIC hires for its intelligence division include John Thomas, a retired army major general and commander of the U.S. Army Intelligence Center; Larry Cox, an eleven-year NSA veteran and former director of Lockheed Martin's SIGINT division; and John J. Hamre, a former deputy secretary of defense in the Clinton administration.* Two former secretaries of defense, William Perry and Melvin Laird, as well as the current secretary, Bob Gates, have served on its board of directors.

SAIC was chosen in part because, in the years leading up to 9/11, it had developed several key data mining products that were used extensively by the NSA and other agencies. One of them was a powerful program called TeraText, which was first developed in Australia. It supposedly can download millions of pages of texts from books, magazines, Web sites, and intercepted e-mails—in any language—and then sift through them at lightning speeds of *two billion documents every four seconds*—an amazing feat if it is true. According to *Business 2.0* magazine, the program works by identifying patterns and relationships between names, terms, and ideas that "would take the human mind months to collate."[63] SAIC still won't say if or how TeraText is used by U.S. intelligence, but the TeraText Web site claims that its products have been used for applications in military intelligence "with substantial return on investment," and by the U.S. Department of Defense "to manage critical assets related to U.S. National Security."[64]

Another SAIC program, called Latent Semantic Indexing (LSI), was developed by SAIC's Telcordia subsidiary.[65] It uses artificial intelligence tools to search for abstract relationships in intercepted messages and public documents. Using LSI, *Washington Technology* reported in

---

* Hamre was a fortuitous pick for SAIC. In October 2007, he was selected by Secretary of Defense Robert Gates to chair the Pentagon's Defense Policy Board Advisory Committee. His term as an SAIC director expires in 2008.

2006, "intelligence and investigative agencies can discern meaning, pinpoint threats and suspicious activity, and disambiguate aliases, regardless of language." [66] A third program, called Pathfinder, is a Web-based software application used to sort rapidly through structured and unstructured data. According to SAIC's Web site, it is used by the NSA, the Defense Intelligence Agency, the Office of Naval Intelligence, and Joint Task Force 7 and Joint Task Force 180, the unified U.S. military commands in Iraq and Afghanistan. Among its uses, SAIC says, are terrorism link analysis, information warfare, financial investigations, and detection of money laundering, "and a host of other applications [that] make Pathfinder an indispensable part of any indications and warning or predictive intelligence operation." [67]

As envisioned, SAIC and its subcontractors would translate all digitized communications intercepted by the NSA into plain text or voice, and then run the information through the TeraText, LSI, and other data mining programs to search for possible terrorist connections and patterns. That data would then be stored in searchable databases and forwarded to the right desk at the NSA for appropriate analysis. But the program quickly ran into trouble. In December 2002, the House and Senate intelligence committees studying the failures that led up to 9/11 reported that, although Trailblazer was "frequently cited" as the solution to the NSA's data management problems, "implementation of those solutions is three to five years away and confusion still exists as to what will actually be provided by the program." The report was also scathing in its criticism of the NSA itself. The joint inquiry "found a high level of frustration among contractors who do business with the NSA." Common themes included "extremely poor quality of solicitation packages and acquisition expertise and the inability of program managers to speak with consistency and authority on future contract opportunities." [68]

In April 2005, Hayden informed Congress that Trailblazer was several hundred million dollars over budget and months behind schedule. The NSA, Hayden said, had underestimated the costs by a long shot. "It was just far more difficult than anyone anticipated," he told a Senate hearing.[69] In May 2006, *Newsweek*'s investigative team looked into

Trailblazer and concluded that the program "has produced nearly a billion dollars' worth of junk hardware and software."[70] A few days later, Hayden was asked about that article during his confirmation hearing for CIA director. He argued that the NSA had overreached, and should have tried to bite off smaller pieces of the project one at a time. "We were throwing deep and we should have been throwing short passes," he told Senator Ron Wyden. "A lot of the failure was, we were trying to do too much all at once. We should have been less grandiose, not gone for moon shots and been tighter in, more specific, looking at concrete results, closer in rather than overachieving by reaching too far."

The project was formally canceled in 2005 when General Keith Alexander assumed the directorship of NSA. But Congress wasn't pleased and had already taken action. In 2004, in response to the debacle, the Senate took the extraordinary step of taking away the NSA's independent acquisition powers and handed them over to the Department of Defense; they would only be returned when Congress certified that NSA's business practices had "improved substantially."[71] "Congress took this action because of serious deficiencies in NSA's systems acquisition capabilities that prevented the Agency from effectively modernizing signals intelligence capabilities to meet new threats," the Senate Intelligence Committee noted. The suspension was still in effect in 2007.[72] By March of that year, the NSA was still processing much less than one percent of the data it was collecting. The agency has simply "been overwhelmed" by the explosion of information, Senator Jay Rockefeller, the chairman of the Senate Intelligence Committee, concluded.[73]

Despite the project's cancellation, however, SAIC is apparently working on Trailblazer's successor program. In its investor prospectus mentioned earlier, SAIC said it had nine thousand active government contracts as of July 31, 2006. Listed among them was a contract called EXECUTELOCUS, described as the former "Trailblazer Technical Development Program." The customer was listed as "confidential." The NSA, as I said before, would not comment on any matter involving its contractors, and SAIC declined as well. "In a situation like this, we would defer to our government customer and deny comment completely," SAIC spokesperson Ron Zollars told me.

According to industry officials I spoke to, the NSA turned over far too much to the private sector. "SAIC did a terrible job of managing Trailblazer," a contractor who provided data mining technologies for the project told me. "I had people work on it as subs, but they quit and would not work on the program because it was badly managed—badly managed by SAIC and NSA—not because they didn't try, but because they didn't have the ability to manage the program." This contractor, who once worked for the NSA and agreed to speak about Trailblazer only if granted anonymity, also had harsh words for Hayden, the former NSA director. "Trailblazer was his, and he [screwed] it up. He's in my view the worst director NSA ever had. He left after five years still talking about 'them,' not 'us.' He never took responsibility for anything that went bad, including Trailblazer, and this was his thing."

Critics of intelligence contracting see Trailblazer as the ultimate example of what goes wrong when huge projects are handed over to large corporations. "Trailblazer, as executed by SAIC, is one of the lasting disgraces of this era," says Robert David Steele, a former CIA case officer who once chaired an IT steering committee for the Intelligence Community.[74] John Gannon, the former chairman of the CIA's National Intelligence Council and a senior executive with BAE Systems, called Trailblazer a "monumental failure" that "resulted from our expectation that the private sector could do it for us. What we needed to do was to have the contractor do what we couldn't do ourselves." Trailblazer, he added, is a case where "the government let the private sector get ahead of the government. When that happens the private sector doesn't perform competently, and the government loses its ability to manage, with disastrous results. When you look where the numbers of analysts in units are heavily contractor, the government really does lose its ability to maintain quality control. And that is definitely not a good thing in my judgment."[75]

Part of the problem, intelligence expert John Pike told me, may have been differing interpretations between SAIC and the NSA over data mining. "My instinctive gut reaction tells me that's where they got into trouble," says Pike, the director of GlobalSecurity.org. "There was something about the specification process that fouled them up. There was something about the key performance parameters that either SAIC didn't understand, or that all the various little fiefdoms within NSA didn't understand. Or they started out with one set of requirements and then over time the requirements just got out of control on them." In addition, after 9/11, the NSA was processing data "on a scale that was larger than had previously been done. So both the agency and the contractor were outside of their experience base."[76]

McConnell himself may have settled the case in his eye-popping interview with the *El Paso Times* in August 2007. "There's a sense that we're doing massive data mining," he said. "In fact, what we're doing is surgical. A telephone number is surgical. So if you know what number, you can select it out."[77] That seemed to negate almost a decade's worth of work and research on Project Trailblazer, which was probably the mother of massive data mining schemes; but as McConnell knew, it simply hadn't worked. His comments seemed to indicate that the NSA was going back to its traditional role that began with the reading of telegrams—that is, selecting certain people to be targeted based on human intelligence and simple link and relationship analysis.

Even prior to McConnell's remarks, it was clear the NSA's experience with Trailblazer had convinced intelligence officials that large-scale project contracting was eroding the NSA's ability to do its job. In November 2006, Eric Haseltine, who left the NSA in 2005 to become the ODNI's associate director for science and technology, warned contractors at a conference on geospatial intelligence that change was afoot. "We need to have a variety of small, agile, and quick programs because we don't know what the future holds," he said. "We may have to dynamite the huge, decades-long multibillion-dollar programs and run in their place a whole plethora of small, quick programs. If we don't do that, we will become fossils."[78] A few months later, the Defense Information Systems Agency, which buys IT for the Pentagon and works closely with the NSA on protecting the nation's IT infrastructure, announced that agencies under its command—including NSA—would be required to buy "easy-to-implement commercial solutions" that could be subdivided into smaller projects. "The day of the big systems integrator is over," said Brigadier General David Warner, DISA's executive officer for command and control programs.[79]

The NSA's start in small-scale data mining programs may have originated with the Total Information Awareness program started by Navy Rear Admiral John Poindexter and briefly described in chapter 2. In 2001, Poindexter was working as the senior vice president for a Beltway bandit called Syntek Technologies, which had research contracts with the Defense Advanced Research Projects Agency and other government agencies. After the 9/11 attacks, he persuaded DARPA to fund an early-warning system for detecting terrorists and other national security crises.[80] Using data mining techniques culled from years of DARPA research, Poindexter and his colleagues began sifting through huge public databases holding private information where terrorists might leave "footprints"—credit card purchases, rental agreements, medical histories, e-mails, airline reservations, and phone calls. By searching this "total information" using every search engine imaginable, Poindexter believed the government could develop a national surveillance database that would be able to pick up the trail of unknown terrorists and stop the next attack. He called his project a "Manhattan Project for Counter-Terrorism." DARPA was interested, and funded it. Poindexter was soon director of DARPA's Information Awareness Office.

TIA was not a secret program. It received considerable attention in the trade press covering information technology and government research. The scope of its mandate was breathtaking: the Information Awareness Office was instructed to "imagine, develop, apply, integrate, demonstrate and transition" IT systems that would "counter asymmetric threats by achieving total information awareness"—thus the name and acronym.[81] Poindexter himself spoke frequently about his work. In August 2002, he delivered a speech to a DARPA Tech conference in Anaheim, California, and spelled out the aims of his new project. In the new world of terrorism and asymmetric threats, the United States faces an enemy organized in "shadowy networks" that are difficult to identify yet dedicated to the destruction "of our way of life," he said.[82]

He reminded his listeners of the recent Cold War past: tracking the elusive enemy of today, he said, was analogous to the "anti-submarine warfare problem of finding submarines in an ocean of noise." We had to penetrate that "noise" with information technology—finding new sources of data, mining that information and creating actionable intelligence. The key place to look, he argued, was in the "transaction space":

> If terrorist organizations are going to plan and execute attacks against the United States, their people must engage in transactions and they will leave signatures in this information space. . . . Currently, terrorists are able to move freely throughout the world, to hide when necessary, to find sponsorship and support, and to operate in small, independent cells, and to strike infrequently, exploiting weapons of mass effects and media response to influence governments. We are painfully aware of some of the tactics that they employ. This low-intensity/low-density form of warfare has an information signature. We must be able to pick this signal out of the noise. Certain agencies and apologists talk about connecting the dots, but one of the problems is to know which dots to connect. The relevant information extracted from this data must be made available in large-scale repositories with enhanced semantic content for easy analysis to accomplish this task. The transactional data will supplement our more conventional intelligence collection.[83]

Thus was born the TIA, one of the most controversial projects launched by the Bush administration.

Much of the initial work on TIA was handled by SAIC and Booz Allen Hamilton. Hicks & Associates, a consulting firm wholly owned by SAIC, won the $19 million contract to build the prototype system.[84] And, as mentioned earlier, Booz Allen won more than $63 million worth of contracts,[85] and Mike McConnell, who was Booz Allen's executive vice president in 2002 with authority over the company's military intelligence programs, was a key figure in making his company the prime contractor.

During his confirmation hearing as DNI in 2007, McConnell told the Senate Intelligence Committee that DARPA's mining of transactional data from credit card companies and other private entities was an important weapon against terrorists. "What's happening today is the terrorists are using those very systems for their own benefit—think of it as command and control for remote terrorists, who have a particular ideology they're attempting to spread so they can communicate around the globe," he said. DARPA, he added, merely wanted to move data mining "from where it was to where it could be" to keep ahead of the terrorists. Other contractors involved, according to the Electronic Privacy Information Center, included Alphatech, a subsidiary of BAE Systems; SAIC's Telcordia Technologies; Raytheon; Lockheed Martin Information Technology; Veridian Systems; and more than a dozen other smaller companies.[86]

One of the companies funded by TIA was SRD, a company founded by Las Vegas entrepreneur Jeffrey Jonas that is now owned by IBM. During the 1990s, Jonas developed a unique software that allowed casinos to search their internal databases to watch for hidden relationships between casino employees and problem gamblers placed on the state of Nevada's Exclusionary List (which bans those gamblers from doing business in the casinos). The software works differently than most data surveillance programs. It doesn't use information to *predict* the behavior of its subjects; instead, it uses names of known people as starting points to discover relationships and patterns that can reveal people working in cahoots. Second, it is designed to help an organization make use of its own data—such as employee records—and therefore doesn't require access to other databases that could violate a person's privacy. These two functions are perfect for matching people against a static list like the Exclusionary List.

But as casinos like the MGM Mirage began putting the software to work to comply with the law, the software also began identifying insider threats the casinos weren't aware of. There was the accounts payable manager who was also a vendor. There was the high-roller getting free rooms and free meals, who happened to be the roommate of the casino worker entering all his points on the computer. And there was the blackjack dealer who shared an apartment with a gambler who always seemed to win when he played that dealer's table. His software, Jonas told me, doesn't help you find the next criminal. But "if you know a bad guy, then our technology helps you find that bad guy in your data to make sure he's not right under your fingers."[87]

In 2000, Jonas was invited by the NSA to Northern Virginia to attend a national conference on information security. There, he found himself amidst the area's rapidly growing Intelligence-Industrial Complex. Among the many speakers at the conference were executives from Booz Allen Hamilton, AT&T, TRW, IBM, ManTech International, and Lockheed Martin and officials from the NSA, DARPA, and the Department of Justice. Jonas's specialty of tracking "sophisticated scams and collusion-based relationships" was described by the NSA planners on their Web site as "an exciting topic that invariably captures the interest of everyone associated with the field of security." One of the officials watching was Chris Tucker, who was at that time the chief strategist at In-Q-Tel, the CIA investment bank. He thought Jonas's software might have immediate relevance to the government, and began introducing him to people in the Intelligence Community. In January 2001, SRD became only the second company to receive an equity investment from In-Q-Tel. But after the September 11 terrorist attacks, In-Q-Tel began looking at SRD's software—and its ability to find human relationships among various streams of data—in a new light. In the immediate aftermath of the attacks, In-Q-Tel made a second investment in SRD and helped Jonas tweak his software to make it faster (neither SRD nor In-Q-Tel would specify the size of its investments). "We also did a special project to help larger organizations," Jonas said. One of those organizations was the NSA. Jonas wouldn't confirm or deny if SRD has contracts with the NSA. But after the attacks, he said, "a couple of government entities" used SRD's software "to see if there was a bigger plot—was there really twenty planes and all that. But I don't have security clearances, so I can't get that close to that."

Around the same time, Poindexter's TIA project came calling, and contracted with SRD for some of its research. "I'm intimately familiar with [TIA]," said Jonas. At the time of his first contract with TIA, Jonas said, he was enthusiastic about the program because it was spending between 5 and 7 percent of its budget on privacy technology. For the first time in a mass surveillance program, he said, considerable resources were going into software that would protect the rights of U.S. citizens from unwarranted invasions of their privacy. Among the projects, Jonas told me, were immutable audit logs, which recorded everything done by a software program so audit bodies—such as the Pentagon's Office of Inspector General or a congressional committee—could go back in time to see how an intelligence or law enforcement agency used particular programs to monitor people.

After TIA came to light in 2003, Congress defunded the program.[88] But the program lived on at the National Security Agency. In 2006, Shane Harris, a reporter with *National Journal,* discovered that key parts of TIA, including the prototype search program developed by SAIC, had been moved from DARPA to the NSA's research component, the Advanced Research and Development Activity (ARDA) office, located at NSA headquarters in Fort Meade (according to the Congressional Research Service, ARDA spends NSA money on research that can "solve some of the most critical problems facing the US intelligence community"[89]). The NSA had been one of the first users of Poindexter's data after he started the TIA program, and began installing nodes on the TIA's classified network in early 2003, according to Harris.

Another TIA program, designed to build "information technologies to help analysts and policy makers anticipate and pre-empt terrorist attacks," was also moved to ARDA and renamed Topsail; subsequently, SAIC won a $3.7 million contract for that project, according to Harris.[90] In 2006, the DNI took over management of ARDA and renamed it the Research and Development Experimentation Capability, or RDEC. The Armed Forces Communications and Electronics Association, which represents many defense intelligence contractors, describes RDEC as "a virtual network in which new tools (and tool integration) can be tested and evaluated apart from the DoD infrastructure."[91]

To the chagrin of privacy advocates, however, none of the privacy projects initially funded by TIA made the move to the NSA. "The program now has been killed, and all the privacy work is dead," Jonas told me in 2006 (neither the NSA nor the ODNI would comment).

• • •

It's impossible to know if the NSA's TIA programs are still being funded. In any case, the NSA has responded to its IT problems and the new mandate from the Pentagon by funding small-scale data mining projects to troll the Internet and cyberspace for clues to the next terrorist attack. The projects, which come under the name Turbulence, have become the top priority of NSA director Keith Alexander. According to reports in the *Baltimore Sun* and *Washington Technology,* it has cost upward of $500 million, and has concentrated primarily on searching the Internet for networks believed to be used by terrorists and terrorist sympathizers, and targeting those networks for key words that might provide clues to future attacks on U.S. citizens and soldiers. According to the *Baltimore Sun,* Turbulence includes nine core programs designed to map "social networks based on intercepted communications, embedding technology on networks to collect data, and searching for patterns across hundreds of NSA databases."[92]

In 2006, more clues to the NSA's latest program were provided by *New Scientist,* a British magazine. It discovered that the NSA was funding research into the "mass harvesting" of information that people post about themselves on social networks on the Internet, such as *MySpace.* By using the information from these networks, the magazine concluded that the NSA "could harness advances in internet technology" and "combine data from social networking websites with details such as banking, retail and property records, allowing the NSA to build extensive, all-embracing personal profiles of individuals."[93] *New Scientist* discovered the NSA's research quite by accident in a scientific paper entitled "Semantic Analytics on Social Networks," written by a research team at the University of Georgia and the University of Maryland, which focused on how data from online social networks could be combined with other databases to uncover new and unknown facts about people. A footnote in the paper explained that the research was sponsored by ARDA.

One of ARDA's primary aims is to make sense of the massive amounts of data the NSA collects from its eavesdropping and surveillance systems. Given the descriptions of the NSA's Turbulence and the NSA's promise to "live on the network," the ARDA research into social networks and the Internet seems like a logical progression. And even the NSA's staunchest critics say Turbulence is something the NSA should be doing. "I'd be surprised and upset if they weren't doing that," says Jim Dempsey, a FISA expert at the Center for Democracy and Technology.[94] So far, however, the results have not impressed the House and Senate oversight committees with jurisdiction over the NSA. Congress's displeasure was spelled out in March 2007 by the Senate Armed Services Committee when it held a confirmation hearing for Air Force General James Clapper to be the undersecretary of defense for intelligence. In its written questions to Clapper, the committee noted the previous problems with Trailblazer and, for the first time in public, mentioned the new program. "Since Congress first acted to stimulate better executive branch oversight of NSA systems acquisition, NSA's transformation program, Trailblazer, has been terminated because of severe management problems, and its successor, Turbulence, is experiencing the same management deficiencies that have plagued NSA since at least the end of the Cold War," the committee wrote.[95]

I have not been able to confirm any contractor for the Turbulence program. One contractor familiar with NSA operations said the most likely candidates for the Turbulence contracts are the companies affiliated with TIA and Project Groundbreaker, which was renewed, as mentioned earlier, for three more years starting in 2007. A look through the "strategic alliance partners" involved with Groundbreaker reveals many of the companies we have discussed in this book. Among them are BAE Systems, L-3/Titan, CACI, EDS, General Dynamics, ManTech, Lockheed Martin, Microsoft, Nortel, Northrop Grumman/Essex, Raytheon, and NCI. None of these companies would respond to questions about their relationship with the NSA or their possible role in Turbulence.

We will pick up the story of the NSA and its corporate partners in surveillance in chapter 9. Before that, we will visit the geospatial side of intelligence and the companies that have made the merger of signals and imagery into an art form: the pure plays.

7

Intelligence Disneyland

ONE OF THE BIGGEST events of the year for the Intelligence Community is the annual conference and exhibition sponsored by the United States Geospatial Intelligence Foundation. The USGIF is a nonprofit corporation based in Herndon, Virginia, that promotes the interests of the contractors doing business with the National Geospatial-Intelligence Agency. With a classified budget of about $2.5 billion a year, the NGA is responsible for collecting and analyzing imagery downloaded from U.S. surveillance satellites and aircraft and disseminating it to other intelligence and homeland security agencies, domestic law enforcement, and the Pentagon. Geospatial intelligence incorporates a wide variety of disciplines, including mapping, high-resolution photography, three-dimensional and thermal imagery, and live video, and is used in everything from climate studies and human rights reporting to the tracking of enemy soldiers and insurgents in Iraq.

The NGA was formally inaugurated as a combat support agency of the Pentagon in 2003. Initially known as the National Imagery and Mapping Agency, it was cobbled together in the early 1990s from the relevant divisions of more than a dozen intelligence agencies, including the Central Intelligence Agency, the Defense Intelligence Agency, and the National Reconnaissance Office, the super-secret agency responsible for managing and operating the nation's spy satellites. The USGIF was organized in 2004 by executives from two of the NGA's largest contractors, Raytheon and Northrop Grumman, with assistance from Republican lawmakers from the House Intelligence Committee. Since then, its membership has expanded to 115 companies and agencies, and its annual budget exceeds $1 million.

Its leading members, known as strategic partners, pay $50,000 a year to belong. They include most of the NGA's top commercial vendors as well as its biggest user in government, the CIA; the NGA itself is also a member. K. Stuart Shea, the foundation's president and CEO, is the vice president of the space and geospatial intelligence business unit of Science Applications International Corporation, another leading contractor. Other top corporate members of the USGIF include GeoEye and DigitalGlobe, which operate the country's only commercial surveillance satellites and sell the bulk of their imagery to the NGA; Environmental Systems Research Institute and Analytical Graphics Inc., the leading commercial vendors of imagery software; Booz Allen Hamilton, Lockheed Martin, and other big systems integrators; and a handful of companies not normally associated with intelligence, such as Oracle and Microsoft.

The foundation's annual fall conference has become the nation's premier showcase for intelligence contractors and agencies alike, and brings together all the key players in the $50 billion Intelligence-Industrial Complex. They come because the NGA has strong ties throughout the sixteen-member Intelligence Community and offers a neutral ground for the disparate and sometimes warring agencies that dominate the IC. As a result, the USGIF's annual event, dubbed GEOINT, provides one of the few open windows into the thinking at the highest levels of U.S. intelligence, and is both informative and entertaining.

The highlight of the 2004 symposium was a joint appearance by the directors of the CIA, the National Security Agency, and the NGA—the only time during the seven years of the Bush administration that the top officials from those three collection agencies all spoke from the same stage during a public, unclassified event. During that session, outgoing CIA director George Tenet made his first public defense of his stormy tenure at the agency. "If you read everything in the newspapers, you're led to believe that we're about as dumb and stupid as anyone on the face of the earth, and we're not," he said, startling some observers with his vehemence.[1] At GEOINT 2005, Mary Margaret Graham, the deputy director for collection in the Office of the Director of National Intelligence, committed one of the biggest intelligence gaffes in recent history when she accidentally disclosed the nation's intelligence budget for that year—$44 billion. Her blooper, noted by an alert reporter from *U.S. News & World Report,* marked the first time since 1998 that the aggregate figure for U.S. spending on its spy agencies had been revealed, and provided a solid benchmark to gauge intelligence spending into the future.

GEOINT 2006 took place at the swank Gaylord Palms Resort in Orlando, Florida, an eight-hundred-room hotel and convention center about a mile from Disney World. The lineup of government speakers, as in earlier years, came from the highest levels of the IC. John Negroponte, Michael McConnell's predecessor as director of national intelligence, delivered the keynote address on the closing day. In what turned out to be his last public speech as DNI, Negroponte eloquently described the science of geospatial intelligence. GEOINT—geospatial intelligence—is "a window providing undeniable evidence of events taking place on the ground; GEOINT reveals hidden aspects of otherwise poorly understood phenomena," he said, "it brings visual clarity and precision to identifying and locating targets anywhere on the globe; it enables us to search vast expanses of the earth's surface; and it depicts intelligence issues in areas otherwise denied to us." He was preceded to the stage by several of his top aides and more than a dozen high-ranking officials from the CIA, the NSA, and the DIA, as well as the director of the NGA, Navy Admiral Robert Murrett.

GEOINT 2007, held at the spacious Henry B. Gonzalez Convention Center in San Antonio, Texas, offered up an equally stellar lineup of speakers that included Marine Corps General James E. Cartwright, the vice chairman of the Joint Chiefs of Staff; Marine Corps Major General

Michael E. Ennis, the deputy director for community HUMINT at the CIA; and Brian V. Biesecker, the technical director of analysis and production for the National Security Agency. "Today we have the giants of industry and government standing together," Jeffrey Harris, the vice president and managing director for situational awareness for Lockheed Martin and the former director of the National Reconnaissance Office, said in San Antonio as he introduced a panel of speakers from the Intelligence Community and the private sector.

Because the NGA falls under the Pentagon's command and control system, its primary responsibility is to provide imagery and maps for ongoing military operations. "When the fog of war thickens, GEOINT creates a visual picture of the battlespace," says an NGA pamphlet distributed in Orlando. "From the White House to the tip of the spear, GEOINT enables decisions, shortens wars and saves lives." Since 2005, the NGA has been sending special imagery teams to Iraq and Afghanistan to assist U.S. air and ground forces there. By the fall of 2007, the agency had two hundred specialists deployed in thirty-eight locations in six countries, and was also providing close support to U.S. Special Forces teams, NGA officials said.[2] NGA teams, Admiral Murrett disclosed during GEOINT 2006, have been deployed with military units directly engaged in combat and supply computer feeds of urban areas in Iraq "which are most threatening" to the troops. Target areas have included the city of Ramadi, where U.S. troops fought running battles with Sunni insurgents throughout 2006. A "key component" of the NGA's support for the war, Murrett said, is providing streaming video from low-flying Predators and other aircraft. "Video in support of operations is increasing in importance and increasing in complexity, and NGA is very much a part of that in all the places where we are threatened in Central Iraq," he said.[3] In a briefing for reporters, Murrett explained that the NGA's overhead video is enhanced with additional capabilities for data mining, transforming the pictures into "automated tools for detection."

To capture much of its military-related imagery, the NGA relies on a network of highly classified satellites controlled by the National Reconnaissance Office. The same satellites are used by the NSA for its global signals intelligence system, thus creating a strong, symbiotic relationship between the NGA and its sister national collection agencies, including the CIA. "We are the glue that holds together the Intelligence Community," says Murrett.[4] Since 9/11, the NGA's relationship with the NSA and NRO has deepened in significant ways. Information generated by the national agencies, for example, is increasingly collected and analyzed at large ground stations run jointly by the NSA, the NRO, and the NGA. At these centers, analysts and contractors combine imagery and signals intercepts to monitor people and events in real time—a synthesis that intelligence officials like to call the "magic on the ground."

During GEOINT 2006, then–NRO director Donald Kerr disclosed that the NGA, NSA, and the NRO were building a new listening post—at a site he would not identify—that will establish a new model of collaboration in U.S. intelligence. At this "unknown ground station," he said, "we are integrating data that comes from our entire U.S. SIGINT system, from imaging capabilities and other space assets, and doing it to a cell at that ground station, which is empowered to other tasking as well. We're doing real-time collection, fusion, and tasking modifications to get a better intelligence effect."[5] These ground stations are major operations: according to Lance Killoran, the NRO's director for imagery acquisition, the NRO owns the fifth-largest communications network in the United States. At the ground stations, less than 20 percent of the data is from the NRO; "the other 80 percent is from you," he said, meaning the NGA, the NSA, and their contractors.[6]

Imagery and signals intelligence are also collected by the U.S. Navy, whose newest ships and aircraft carriers come equipped with America's most advanced listening and eavesdropping technology. As a result, said Kerr, "our carrier strike groups are going to sea looking more like mobile ground stations than ever before."[7] Submarines, too, are getting in on the action: according to Loren B. Thompson, an analyst at a military think tank called the Lexington Institute, submarines today "are used mainly for conducting clandestine reconnaissance in littoral regions, and there is a surge in demand for their collections from intelligence agencies and combatant commanders."[8]

The ties between the national collection agencies were institutionalized in 2005, when the NSA and the NGA announced a far-reaching agreement to share resources and swap staff. The document announcing the agreement itself is classified. In its only public explanation so far, the NGA said in a press release that the agreement allows "horizontal integration," which it defined as "working together from start to finish, using NGA's 'eyes' and NSA 'ears,' " thus making it possible "to solve intelligence challenges that cannot be resolved through separate application of normal GEOINT or SIGINT methods."[9] The NSA's Biesecker says that, under the agreement, 40 percent of the two agencies' staffs are now "conversational" with both SIGINT and GEOINT.[10]

These collaborative efforts have had a dramatic impact on the war in Iraq. During GEOINT 2006, NGA director Robert Murrett explained how the NGA and the NSA work together on the battlefield. In an unusually detailed briefing, he disclosed that both agencies were deeply involved in the 2006 capture and killing of Abu Zarqawi, the leader of Al Qaeda in Iraq (earlier, remember, we learned that CACI had been involved in this operation). According to Murrett, U.S. forces were tipped off to Zarqawi's location and cell phone number by an unlikely source—Zarqawi's spiritual adviser. With that information, the NSA began monitoring his movements through phone intercepts, while the NGA flew Predators over the area to take live video. All of that data was fed to an F-16, which dropped two bombs on the house, killing everybody inside. "Eventually, it all comes down to physical location," said Murrett. The networking between the two agencies and military forces on the ground, he said, "is absolutely essential. When we have NSA and NGA partnering on combating Al Qaeda, the multiplier effect is dramatic."[11]

The NGA's origins go back to the early 1990s, when Robert Gates was director of central intelligence in the administration of President George H. W. Bush. At the time, U.S. national security officials were just beginning to understand the new world that was presenting itself in the aftermath of the collapse of the Soviet Union and the stunning defeat of

Saddam Hussein's army in Kuwait during the first Gulf War. A commission appointed by Gates to study how intelligence had functioned during Operations Desert Shield and Desert Storm found that updating maps and other visual information was a difficult and tedious exercise for military commanders. For instance, commanders in the field sometimes had to wait up to a week to receive the mapping data they had requested, compared to mere minutes for the transmission of signals and other forms of electronic intelligence. It was a "horror story," recalls retired Air Force Brigadier General Michael G. Lee, who is now a vice president in the global security solutions division of Lockheed Martin. "The imagery couldn't get to the battlefield." [12] Moreover, transmission itself was crude and slow: in the early days, images collected from satellites could only be printed out because the files were too large to be sent electronically from one computer to another. And while it took one call to the NSA to talk to someone about signals intelligence, there was no single point of contact at either the Pentagon or the CIA for imagery.

The imagery community "was a loose association of semi-friends operating in relative independence from one another," says Richard Haver of Northrop Grumman. "And when you asked imagery [officials] for something you had at least five phone calls to make. It was very frustrating." [13] Haver knows the story well: during the administration of the first George Bush, he was the intelligence adviser to Secretary of Defense Cheney, a post he held again during the first two years of Rumsfeld's reign at the Pentagon.

One reason that people like Haver were calling imagery offices was the changing demands on U.S. intelligence. Up to the early 1990s, the fine art of satellite and aerial surveillance, particularly the CIA's high-altitude reconnaissance of Soviet bases and missiles, had been used primarily by national leaders to understand the "strategic balance" with the Soviets. But as Cold War tensions ebbed and new threats began to emerge in the eyes of the nation's military and political elite, it became clear that the wonders of computerized mapping had revolutionary implications in war, particularly in asymmetric warfare—a military buzzword used to describe conflicts between the United States and insurgencies—and counterterrorism. Imagery, according to Haver, became "something that was essential on the battlefield."

Gates's proposals to create a central imagery intelligence office took several years to germinate. The initial idea was nixed by Colin Powell, then head of the Joint Chiefs of Staff, who felt that the military would lose control of a strategic asset if all imagery was controlled by an intelligence agency outside the Pentagon. Finally, in 1996, Congress, the CIA, and the Department of Defense agreed to create the National Imagery and Mapping Agency. As the Department of Homeland Security would do eight years later (with far less success), the new agency combined offices and agencies spread across the government and the military. The largest were the CIA's National Photographic Interpretation Center, which President Eisenhower created in the 1950s to manage the photos taken by U-2 spy planes, and the Defense Mapping Agency, which was formed in 1972 during the Vietnam War. Also folded in were all the imagery-related units of the DIA, the Defense Airborne Reconnaissance Program, and the NRO. In 2003, the NGA was formally brought into the IC as a combat support unit of the Pentagon.

From the start, the new imagery agency was an instrumental part of U.S. foreign policy. During the Balkans wars, satellite photos of destroyed mosques and mass graves in Bosnia helped the State Department make the case that the Serbian government was engaged in ethnic cleansing. The evidence led the Clinton administration, under cover of NATO, to launch air strikes against Serbia. NIMA mapping tools were also used by the administration to help resolve border disputes between Peru and Ecuador and Israel and Lebanon. And under the guidance of Al Gore, NIMA was tapped to provide imagery and intelligence about climate change, and its scientists produced the GPS "safety of navigation" effort that greatly improved aerial data available to airports and air traffic control agencies.

On a strategic level, geospatial intelligence has deepened longstanding ties between U.S. and British intelligence. Booz Allen Hamilton's Joan Dempsey, who managed relationships between the CIA and the rest of the Intelligence Community during the Clinton years, emphasized the importance of these ties in her remarks to GEOINT 2006. NIMA, she said, was "far and away the most aggressive agency in trying to find ways to cooperate with our international coalitions." The current leaders of the NGA "believe very strongly in sharing intelligence, and that we had an obligation if we were going to operate on an international level to find ways to share intelligence." Admiral Murrett exemplifies this trend.

After taking the helm of the NGA in 2005, one of Murrett's first tasks was to meet directly with his counterparts from the British commonwealth countries. "In terms of our future system architecture, we are fully imbedded," he said in a press briefing. In the fall of 2006, the NGA held a series of exercises with its commonwealth allies at the Naval Air Warfare Center in China Lake, California. During the interoperability exercise, which was fittingly dubbed "Empire Challenge," the English-speaking allies shared imagery and simulated battles in a desert environment with American-made UAVs and British-made Tornado jets. Under this multinational effort, the NGA explained, "we can downlink live data from a British aircraft directly to a US ground station, and then send it via satellite to another country to be analyzed. Capabilities like this will enable the US and its allies to share each other's intelligence data, building a timely, more accurate picture on today's battlefield."[14]

Domestically, NGA imagery has become an integral part of a set of tools used by the FBI, the Secret Service, and local police to establish security at National Special Security Events, designated as such because of the large numbers of ordinary people and officials drawn to events like the 2006 Major League All-Star Game in Pittsburgh and the 2002 Winter Olympics in Utah. The events predate 9/11: there have been more than thirty such events since the designation was invented in 1999. "We really do worry about special security events," says Charles Allen, a longtime CIA official who was tapped in 2005 to be assistant secretary of homeland security for intelligence and analysis.[15]

In fact, the NGA has been a steady, unseen presence in American skies since September 11. After the attacks on the Twin Towers, the NGA flew surveillance planes over the World Trade Center site in New

York to survey the extent of the damage. In 2002, when a pair of snipers terrorized Washington by randomly shooting people in parking lots and gas stations, the NGA, at the request of the FBI, monitored nearby highways for signs of the criminals. During Hurricane Katrina, the NGA provided thousands of images that helped the National Guard, FEMA, and state officials in Louisiana and Mississippi determine the depth and extent of the flooding and allowed people who had fled the region to see if their homes had survived. That may have been the first time in U.S. history that a national intelligence agency provided information it had gathered for a domestic crisis (it has also raised significant questions about the use of military spy satellites at home).

The NGA's dual mission was underscored in the GEOINT 2006 exhibition hall by General Dynamics, which ran the largest booth in the conference center.* Most of its space was taken up by a huge van called a Mobile Integrated Geospatial Intelligence System, or MIGS. The NGA first deployed these portable intelligence and communications units with the U.S. Army in Baghdad. The MIGS are now being deployed by the NGA to disaster areas within the United States to download and transmit imagery that might be used by local law enforcement and first-responders—another sign of how intelligence tools developed for the global war on terror have become part of homeland security. "This is a good example of how we can take our Department of Defense experience and apply it to domestic support, and a good use of taxpayer dollars," William Dennis, a General Dynamics staffer, told

---

* It paid for the privilege. At the GEOINT conference, major contractors were offered exclusive rights to sponsorship of key events. For $50,000, General Dynamics won the right for exclusive sponsorship of the exhibit hall itself ("Dominate the landscape! Get attendees to start thinking about your company before they enter"). The welcome reception, including cups and napkins complete with company logos, was snatched up for $40,000 by BAE Systems. For the same price, Boeing and SAIC won the sponsorship rights for the Hall of Fame Dinner on closing night, where Joe Scarborough, an MSNBC talk show host, delivered the keynote address. Other deals included $30,000 for sponsorship rights to the golf tournament (won by SAIC); $20,000 for the Internet Café (Harris Corp.); $30,000 for the conference tote bag (ManTech International); and $10,000 for the shoeshine stand (Lockheed Martin). Everything was for sale, even the hotel door hangers ($5,000)—but these, alas, went unclaimed, along with the $5,000 hotel turn-down service ("Make one last impression before the GEOINT 2006 attendees turn in for the night").

me after showing me through the vehicle. A similar vehicle, painted white so it didn't look like a military vehicle, was deployed to New Orleans during Hurricane Katrina. John Goolgasian, the director of the NGA's Office of the Americas, told me that the imagery captured during Katrina was used to create a database of hospitals and schools in the hurricane zone and analyze industrial sites for potential chemical leaks and other hazards. When used domestically, the vans are called DMIGS, "but the tradecraft and the methodology stays the same," Goolgasian said.

Most of the exhibitors were displaying technologies designed to combat the Iraqi insurgency. Raytheon's Intelligence and Information Systems, based in Falls Church, Virginia, was offering a visualization software called Enterprise Modeling and Simulation that provides three-dimensional views of urban centers loaded with data from airborne sensors. The program, said Raytheon, will "open up substantial new possibilities for mission planning, rehearsal of upcoming battles, and even tactical replanning during actual combat." A U.S. commander will use the simulation software "to roam about and see the precise relationships among the various structures, enemy forces and his own force distribution," allowing him to search for signs of "incipient terrorist activity" and even "look at the world from the perspective of their enemy." The Enterprise software is part of the larger Distributed Common Ground System, described in Chapter 5, which Raytheon has designed to give Air Force commanders and fighter pilots instant access to imagery, signals intelligence, and measurement and signatures intelligence.

At a nearby booth, Northrop Grumman was displaying its new "NGesture" video table. It is a giant plasma screen imbedded into a tabletop and loaded with satellite imagery and other data to create a 3-D view of any city on the planet. What makes it special is the control system: users' hands and fingers manipulate the images. Two fingers in an outward movement, and your perspective shifts skyward; bring them together, and you move down to the ground. With a single finger, you can trace the route of a vehicle driving up a street, or circle a key building. Soon, I'm told, we'll be seeing this device on television news broadcasts; Northrop Grumman, in a joint venture with GeoEye, has sold it to CNN.

The idea for a foundation to promote the interests of the NGA's contractors first emerged in 2003 in discussions between K. Stuart Shea, then a senior executive in Northrop Grumman's intelligence unit; Steven Jacques, a former Air Force officer and a lobbyist for Raytheon; and John Stopher, a former CIA officer who was until January 2007 the budget director of the House Permanent Select Committee on Intelligence. Shea was on friendly terms with the Republican leadership in the House at the time, and had been appointed to a twelve-member national commission studying the research and development programs of U.S. intelligence agencies by House Speaker Dennis Hastert, R-Illinois.

Initially, the three men wanted to replicate the Space Foundation, an organization of NASA and NRO contractors based near the U.S. Space Command in Colorado. "Their purpose in life is to try to bring together the space community, whether it's the national security community, black or white, with the civil and commercial community," Jacques told me. "We thought, we don't have that for the geospatial intelligence community, and maybe that should be our focus, too." [16] In 2004, when I first inquired about the purpose of the organization, Shea told me in an e-mail that the USGIF had no intention of trying to influence policy. "Quite frankly, we are simple in our focus: to build an organization that served the many disparate disciplines involved in the geospatial intelligence community, and to develop a stronger partnership between government, industry, academic and professional organizations and individuals involved in the development and application of geospatial intelligence data and the deployment of geo-processing resources to address national security objectives," he wrote. "We are doing good things for the community at large." [17]

Shea and Jacques's first move was to organize a conference of NGA contractors; that event attracted more than 1,200 people and proved the need for an umbrella organization to represent the industry. So they put together a three-person board—Shea, Jacques, and, initially,

Stopher—and soon more than a dozen companies had signed up. Charter members, who initially ponied up at least $800,000 each for the first year, included their own companies, plus SAIC, Lockheed Martin, Booz Allen Hamilton, the satellite company DigitalGlobe, and other major contractors. The USGIF was born in 2003.

But a month before the foundation was to be formally announced, it ran into its first crisis. *Roll Call,* the newspaper that covers Capitol Hill, reported that Stopher had written a provision into the classified section of an intelligence bill providing $500,000 to establish a new foundation to promote satellite imagery, and had not disclosed his role on the USGIF's board to the House committee. After the story came out, he was asked by the committee to resign from the board, and although the committee's seed money had been dropped from the final bill, the episode proved embarrassing to both the foundation and the staffer. "Stopher's involvement in creating and championing a foundation funded by the very same contractors who support the national security efforts he is supposed to watch over from his position on the oversight committee has alarmed individuals both inside and outside government who view the endeavor as an insurmountable conflict of interest," *Roll Call* wrote.[18]

Jacques, in an interview, dismissed the incident as a partisan political attack. He argued, convincingly, that it had little impact on the foundation, which now has a budget of about $1 million a year and draws more than double that in revenues from membership dues and conference fees.[19] Jacques is now an independent consultant for the USGIF, and Shea, who is now president of SAIC's intelligence, security, and technology group, is chairman of the foundation's board of directors. The rest of the board consists of a combination of the NGA's key partners in the corporate world and the defense community, and includes representatives from Raytheon, the U.S. Air Force, Lockheed Martin, and Boeing. Stopher is still a close friend of the foundation's, and was a featured speaker at GEOINT 2006, where he gave a detailed preview of what the industry should expect from the new Democratic Congress. (He was there again in 2007, but with his party out of power, he sat in the audience as a mere observer.)

• • •

To soldiers who've been around for a while, the advances in geospatial intelligence tools displayed at GEOINT are revolutionary. One of the most informative talks at the Orlando symposium was delivered by General William Boykin, the deputy undersecretary of defense for intelligence (the same general reprimanded in 2003 for publicly expressing his strident views on Islam). During a panel discussion entitled "Warfighters: Saving Lives and Winning Wars," Boykin compared today's geospatial capabilities to what was available during the Cold War, and provided an extraordinary glimpse into how the contemporary sciences of imagery and information technology might have been employed during one of the most disastrous U.S. military expeditions of all time: the 1980 operation to free the fifty-three American hostages held by radical Muslim students in Iran.

Boykin is one of three military men still on active duty who took part in the ill-fated mission, which was known as Operation Eagle Claw. As designed by President Jimmy Carter's National Security Council, the operation involved flying U.S. Special Forces, carried by transport planes and attack helicopters, into Iran from an airbase in Egypt and an aircraft carrier in the Arabian Sea. From those positions, they were to rendezvous at Desert One, a crude airstrip that had been scouted by the CIA, and another site in the mountains near Tehran. After that, the plan was to storm the embassy, grab the hostages, bring them to a nearby Iranian military base, and then fly them out of the country under cover of U.S. fighter jets. But the mission was aborted at Desert One due to mechanical problems that grounded some of the aircraft, and then lurched into tragedy when one of the helicopters crashed into a transport plane, killing eight U.S. soldiers. The disaster caused irreparable political damage to the Carter administration (and sparked the principled resignation of Secretary of State Cyrus Vance, who thought the mission was a mistake). As a result of the fiasco, Congress created the U.S. Special Forces Operating Command to better coordinate secret U.S. military missions.

To Boykin, the failed undertaking underscored the critical importance of geospatial intelligence. Using the capabilities the NGA has today in multiple spectrum imaging, he said, "we would have known a lot more about what was inside that embassy compound than we knew then. We could have seen a lot more. We could have seen changes over a period of time that would have told us a lot about what those radical students were doing to defend that twenty-seven-acre compound that we were going into." Moreover, overhead imagery and multidimensional maps available today would have given his crew much more information about Desert One. "We were on a wing and a prayer," he recalled. "All we were looking at was first-generation imaging, and taking the word of people who'd been hunting up in that area"—presumably the Iranian CIA assets who were later exposed when the fleeing helicopter crews left behind classified documents in their ditched aircraft. The NGA's current capabilities "would have given us a tremendous advantage—and, frankly, we might not have gone into either place," Boykin concluded.

These capabilities are now being enhanced in a new NGA unit called the Advanced Geospatial Intelligence office, which opened in January 2007. It uses commercially available software from ESRI, Intergraph Corporation, and other GEOINT companies to dig into the data behind the pixels imbedded in imagery to extract usable information. Like the operations in Iraq described by Admiral Murrett, the process combines imagery with other intelligence disciplines, including signals intelligence from the NSA and human intelligence from CIA and DIA operatives, to generate a fuller picture on the ground. (Using the techniques of measurement and signatures intelligence, for example, NGA analysts looking down at a truck convoy moving through the desert can analyze sounds from vehicles so precisely that they can actually identify the make and engine of the truck.)[20] To speed these technologies to the warfighters, the NGA signed a memorandum of understanding with the U.S. Joint Forces Command in December 2005. Under the agreement, they will jointly develop common procedures to help soldiers at the joint task level and below use geospatial intelligence.[21] Donald Kerr, who is now the deputy director of national intelligence, told the GEOINT 2006 audience that the joint operations launched by the

NRO, NGA, and NSA are creating a capability "that will provide the United States with an integrated and automated, worldwide tripwire capability to detect anything of intelligence or operational interest."

During the first stage of the U.S. invasion of Iraq, the NGA won the support of U.S. troops when it distributed 250 megabyte hard drives loaded with maps and pictures of the region. That was easily downloaded onto laptops, and gave soldiers instant access to the NGA's massive collection of imagery. "This was truly a defining moment" for the agency, said Lockheed Martin's Lee. In just one quarter of 2004, according to Robert W. Burkhardt, the director of the U.S. Army Corps of Engineers' Topographic Center, the Corps and the NGA transmitted over 3.5 million maps and seventy thousand images to the U.S. military, primarily to the Marines. "This is big business," he says. "We have all the ISR [intelligence, surveillance, and reconnaissance] in the world today."

But commanders have discovered a downside to the new imagery technology. As more and more data are transmitted to the front lines, soldiers are suffering information overload. Brigadier General John M. Custer, the director of intelligence for the U.S. Central Command (CENTCOM), explained. Just before U.S. troops crossed into Iraq from Kuwait, he said, a contractor showed up with several boxes "full of the most gee-whiz stuff that would supposedly revolutionize what we needed to do." Custer looked it over and told the contractor it would do more harm than good on the eve of combat. "I can't tell you how many people deliver what I would tell you are science-fair projects," he complained. "There are some great tools you are producing—analytical processing and GEOINT tools which we need to embrace. But we want to be sure we don't break the ability of our guys out there in the field to actually use it." Custer also noted that, despite the advances in GEOINT, "we're still issuing thousands and thousands of hard-copy maps." They're easier to use and, in many cases, far more reliable than electronic maps sent by computer, he said.

Retired Marine Corps General Anthony Zinni, the former commander of CENTCOM, also cautioned the tech-oriented crowd at GEOINT on the limitations of technology. He spoke at GEOINT 2006 about how CENTCOM used intelligence during the period that followed the first Gulf War. While satellite imagery and intercepts helped his command locate Iraqi tanks and track the departures of Iranian submarines from their bases, he said, the technology couldn't tell him what a particular group or organization was planning to do. "What I couldn't get was intention," he stressed. In other words, an army can buy all the fancy technology it wants, but it still takes people on the ground—human intelligence—to truly understand an adversary.

The NGA is by far the most open of the national intelligence agencies. At one point during the GEOINT 2006 conference, I asked David H. Burpee, the NGA's easygoing director of public affairs, if he could give me a breakdown of the agency's workforce. I was expecting the answer I'd gotten at the CIA and the NSA: sorry, classified. But to my utter surprise, Burpee provided the exact figure: half of its 14,000-person workforce are government employees, and the other 7,000 are "full-time equivalent contractors," he said. Burpee's willingness to answer questions and provide as much detail as he could was a pleasant change from the rest of the Intelligence Community.

That openness is primarily due to the NGA's relationship with commercial industry and technology, and the peculiar timing of the NGA's emergence as a major discipline in intelligence. In the NGA's earliest incarnation, when it was known as NIMA, the agency designed most of its software by itself or in cooperation with the CIA's Directorate of Science and Technology. In 1994, NIMA, using government-developed software, released a Joint Mapping Toolkit that was used by other intelligence agencies and the Department of Defense for visualizing geospatial data. Within a few years, however, commercial companies like ESRI and AGI were selling off-the-shelf mapping and integration software that was much faster and far more user-friendly than NIMA's toolkit, which kept failing. To some observers, the developments in private industry made NIMA's products look like a Model T.

"Except for some really high-end stuff, like radiation-hardened circuits," the government was no longer on the leading edge of imagery technology, says John Pike, the executive director of GlobalSecurity.org and a longtime user of imagery software, of the late 1990s. "For a lot of just plain vanilla IT stuff, they understood they were in danger of becoming a Mac in a Windows world. If they did not keep up with the commercial sector, they would get left behind irretrievably. And it turns out the commercial sector had a lot to offer in terms of hardware and software and imagery exploitation."[22]

Private sector vendors of satellites and imagery software also got a major boost from the Clinton administration. As we saw earlier, President Clinton and Vice President Gore came into office determined to use government incentives to boost U.S. industrial competitiveness in cutting-edge technologies. One of the most promising areas for commercial innovation was overhead imagery from satellites and aircraft. According to people in the industry, Clinton's interest in promoting commercial imagery was communicated early in his administration by Secretary of Commerce Ron Brown and Director of Central Intelligence Jim Woolsey. Brown and Woolsey "explained to us this was the course of action they wanted to take," Northrop Grumman's Richard Haver recalled in 2007.[23] "It was our job [as a corporation] to figure out how to do it and drum up an industrial base for this." (At the time, Haver was a senior executive with TRW, which was deeply involved in classified reconnaissance operations.) In 1994, the administration followed up with a presidential directive that granted operating licenses to U.S. companies to build high-resolution imaging satellites for both domestic and foreign sales.[24] The administration's commitment to the commercialization of space imagery was further spelled out in a 1996 memorandum announcing the establishment of the National Imagery and Mapping Agency. In the pro-business language of Clinton and Gore, it noted that one of NIMA's key thrusts would be "to promote the use of commercial solutions."[25]

As a result of these directives, NIMA stopped trying to develop software in-house and simply turned to the commercial market. For Pike, who was just starting to post satellite images on his popular Web site, the NGA's selections helped him decide what to buy himself. "When I started to do imagery exploitation a decade ago, what did I do? I just identified which commercial products the agency had specified, and I went out and bought them," he said. "I used the same imagery exploitation software that the NGA uses. And when I went out to get trained on the software, I had a dozen people in the class—me and eleven people from the agency."

In 2002, NIMA awarded one of its first commercial contracts for software when it hired AGI and the IT division of Northrop Grumman to redesign its toolkit with the latest commercial technologies. That product, now called Commercial Joint Mapping Toolkit, is used throughout the Department of Defense to transmit geospatial intelligence and data to commanders and soldiers on the ground in Iraq and other battlegrounds. After NIMA was rechristened as the NGA in 2003, CIA director George Tenet ordered the agency to use commercial imagery as its primary source for map-related products.[26] Partly on the strength of its government contracts, privately held ESRI has grown into a $600 million corporation, and has sold its mapping software to more than 300,000 organizations worldwide.[27] AGI, the leading maker of three-dimensional animation software that helps users visualize geospatial data, is a $46-million company that claims the NGA, the CIA, and the NSA among its customers. It, too, is privately held.

The names of both companies are unlikely to be recognized by most readers. But their products are. ESRI's mapping software is employed in GM's OnStar location devices installed in the company's latest vehicle models. And AGI's software was used to create the digital imagery that appeared on the computer monitors at the IMF, the fictional intelligence agency in the Tom Cruise thriller *Mission: Impossible III*. In the movie's climactic scene, a computer geek at IMF headquarters in Washington monitors Cruise through his cell phone signal as he races through the streets of Shanghai, and tracks the hero's moves with overhead mapping and images of the city. According to one of the film's producers, the "animated intelligence scenarios" created by AGI for the movie are "used by real-world intelligence professionals for the exact purpose we wanted to depict in the film—it seemed like a natural fit." In fact, AGI has considerable experience in this area: in addition to the NGA, it holds contracts with both the CIA and the NSA, which operate war rooms that probably look a lot like that of the fictional IMF.

Not surprisingly, the satellite industry receives a big chunk of the NGA's investments. Eighty percent of the NGA's imagery is purchased from DigitalGlobe and GeoEye, the only two U.S. commercial imagery satellite operators. "We're committed to a long-term engagement with the commercial industry," Murrett declared at GEOINT 2007. DigitalGlobe, founded in 1992, is owned by an international consortium that includes Ball Aerospace & Technologies Corporation, Japan's Hitachi, and the investment bank Morgan Stanley. Its QuickBird satellite, said to be the world's highest-resolution commercial imaging satellite, was launched in 2001. In September 2007, DigitalGlobe successfully launched a new satellite called WorldView-1 capable of collecting nearly 300,000 square miles of imagery a day at a half-meter resolution and spotting objects as small as a footstool or a license plate—four to five times the capacity of QuickBird. It also has more onboard storage and greater agility than the older model.

"With this satellite, you'll be able to map out a city much quicker than you could before," says Chuck Herring, DigitalGlobe's director of marketing communications. In an interview, he said WorldView-1 was partially funded by the NGA through its NextView satellite program under a contract with a total value of $500 million. "There is a lot of privatization of what used to be government functions," Herring pointed out. But that's not the case with commercial imaging satellites, he said, because "the government is not replacing anything. The things our satellites do are better filled by the private sector." WorldView-1 was built by Ball Aerospace and ITT Corporation, an important intelligence contractor that built the sensors for CORONA, the CIA's first spy satellites, and was launched at Vandenberg Air Force Base in California.

GeoEye, DigitalGlobe's only U.S. competitor, is the world's largest commercial satellite operator, and earns over 40 percent of its revenue selling to the NGA, according to company officials. It was formed in January 2006, when a company called Orbimage acquired Space Imaging, a satellite operator that had recently gone bankrupt after losing a major NGA contract. Under its new name, GeoEye operates a constellation of four earth-imaging satellites, including the IKONOS, which provides high-resolution images from its orbit five hundred miles above the earth. Sometime in 2008, GeoEye is scheduled to launch GeoEye-1, which will be able to locate an object to within three meters of its actual location on earth. The NGA financed half the cost of the new satellite and will use the same contract to buy imagery, NGA spokesman Dave Burpee told me. "That way, we get a terrific cut-rate price," he said.

Mark E. Brender, GeoEye's vice president for corporate communications and marketing, told me that his company's future is based largely on the expectation of NGA contracts, which now provide 40 percent of its revenues. "NGA is going to be a big customer for a long time," he said. GeoEye's satellites are built by General Dynamics, and use cameras designed and built by ITT. The total cost for GeoEye-1 will be $490 million. "That's why two guys in a garage can't do this," said Brender. Just before the GEOINT conference, GeoEye scored a major coup by signing up retired Air Force General James Clapper, the first director of the NGA, for its board of directors ("It's like hiring Colonel Sanders if you're selling fried chicken," Brender told me). But Clapper's service for GeoEye was short-lived. In a sign of the fluidity of the intelligence industry, Clapper resigned in January 2007 to take the job as assistant secretary for intelligence for Secretary of Defense Robert Gates.

Two of the biggest buyers of satellite imagery outside the government are Google and Microsoft. As mentioned earlier, Google Earth, the popular imagery product used by millions around the world, was first developed by a company funded by In-Q-Tel, the CIA's venture capital fund, and acquired by Google in 2004. Over the last three years, Google has moved heavily into the U.S. defense market, selling enhanced products such as Google Earth Fusion, which allows the NGA and other agencies to manipulate and integrate their own images with the company's software. During that time, its government business increased from $73,000 to $312,000.[28] Google Earth is now the standard mapping software used in geospatial intelligence.

Google, however, has run into controversy: the detail in the high-resolution photographs that Google distributes to the public has alarmed governments in India, Russia, and South Korea, which have made their complaints known to the company.* The wide availability of its imagery has also raised concerns in the U.S. military, which believes that terrorists and insurgents in Iraq are using Google Earth as a tool for targeting attacks on U.S. soldiers. In 2007, British intelligence officials claimed to have found printouts of Google Earth images when they searched homes in Basra, the southern Iraq city occupied by British forces. ("The insurgencies in Iraq and Afghanistan are definitely using Google Earth," warns Army Colonel Bill Harman, the chief of the NGA support team to the U.S. Central Command.) Speaking at a GEOINT 2006 panel on future challenges for the industry, Michael T. Jones, the chief technology officer for Google Earth, admitted that it would be easy for enemy soldiers to use Google. "Unfriendlies can use our commercial data because the barrier of entry is so low," he said. But Jones, who stood out from the suited crowd with a stylish, high-collared Nehru jacket that he wore without a tie, argued that such incidents reflected the wide diffusion of modern technology. "As long as cell phones are on, Google Earth should be on," he said.

The GEOINT crowd also got to hear from musician Jeffrey "Skunk" Baxter. The former lead guitarist for the Doobie Brothers and Steely Dan, Baxter now works as an independent technology consultant for the Intelligence Community, the Missile Defense Agency, and the U.S. Air Force, and apparently makes a decent living advising several defense contractors (according to a biography posted on the Web site of the Potomac Institute, a military think tank he works with, he has also participated "in numerous wargames for the Pentagon" and advised leading Republican lawmakers on the issue of missile defense).[29] Responding to Jones's remarks on cell phones, Baxter argued that U.S. forces are "playing catch-up all the time" because "the enemy has outfoxed us." But he cautioned the audience that he doesn't "think like my colleagues in Hollywood" on issues of national security. Pointing to the

* Due to those complaints, Google has hired former Secretary of State Colin Powell as an adviser.

NSA's domestic surveillance program as an example, he argued that "if you have nothing to hide, you have nothing to worry about." Offstage, however, he was uncomfortable with reporters. One afternoon, I asked Baxter, who looked quite dapper in a tailored suit and a long gray ponytail tied neatly behind, what he actually did for the intelligence industry. "Can't really talk about it," he replied, adding without irony, "I'm into open source." The next time I saw him, he was happily signing autographs in front of the Raytheon booth in the exhibition hall.

Above all, GEOINT is a showcase for contractors. Every session at the symposiums is chaired by a master of ceremonies representing a major corporation doing business with the NGA. The opening session in 2006 was chaired by Keith Hall, the former director of the NRO, who played a key role in the formation of the NGA during the 1990s. As a senior vice president of Booz Allen Hamilton, he leads a "strategic intelligence initiative" that integrates activities across the firm's intelligence community clients. His opening speech to the conference was a tribute to the contractors in the room. Imagery, he said, was essential in every U.S. military campaign of the last ten years, particularly in Kosovo, Iraq, and the global war on terror. "We can all be proud of the role the government-industry team has played in the advancement of a discipline so important to our national security," he said, referring to the nearly seven thousand private contractors who work at the agency. "Those who wear the green badges play a critical role at the NGA."

Hall was followed as emcee by a parade of former officials who've gone through the government-industry revolving door—some of them two or three times. They included the aforementioned Joan Dempsey, one of Hall's colleagues at Booz Allen; Richard Haver, of Northrop Grumman; and retired General Patrick Hughes, the former director of the DIA and recently designated as corporate vice president–intelligence and counterterrorism for L-3 Communications. Hughes, who retired from the U.S. Army in October 1999 after more than thirty-five years of military service, described the current outsourcing regime as the final step of a process that began during the 1960s. "We now have seen come to fruition a phenomenon that many of us saw developing in the Vietnam conflict forty-plus years ago," he said. "That is, the government cannot act, especially overseas, without the involvement of American industry. And that industrial involvement now is so pervasive—you may call it invasive—that we are now speaking to each other about the employees of American companies who have died in combat." Therefore, he continued, "American industry is no longer detached from the government in any of the endeavors of government, in my view."

The climax of the conference was a huge bash one evening at Universal City in downtown Orlando, where the NGA's largest contractors had each rented one of six themed nightclubs lining a section of the amusement park called CityWalk. Everyone, from the highest-ranking former official to the lowest office flunky, drank, danced, and traded corporate pins late into the night. This was definitely not the CIA, I thought to myself as I nursed a beer outside one of the pavilions and tinkered with the General Dynamics pin someone had given me.

The NGA operates at two levels—classified and unclassified. The imagery that the NGA buys from the GeoEye and DigitalGlobe satellites is all unclassified, and can therefore be widely distributed within government—to local, state, and federal agencies—as well as with the general public.* Most of the software is unclassified, too; as we've seen, the same software programs that the agency uses to analyze and manipulate imagery is commonly used by consumers and can be seen in everything from GM cars to motion pictures. But the NGA is, first and foremost, an intelligence agency focused on military operations. Admiral Murrett, NGA's director, recently described the agency's mission in the context of the Bush administration's war on terror: "to provide the intelligence necessary to help predict, penetrate and pre-empt threats to our national security."[30] While much of the intelligence for this broad military mission may be acquired from the private sector, the NGA

* That doesn't mean it can't be used for intelligence. In July 2007, for example, a DigitalGlobe satellite took detailed photos of two roads leading to a construction area near Iran's nuclear sites. The photos were clear enough to show rocks and debris in large piles, leading U.S. analysts to conclude that a major tunnel complex was being built. See Joby Warrick, "Tunneling near Iranian Nuclear Site Stirs Worry," *Washington Post*, July 9, 2007.

overlays it with data from spy satellites and sensors controlled by the NRO, the DIA, and other parts of the Intelligence Community. Here, the NGA's imagery and its output enter the realm of classified, or black, information.

According to the agency, imagery transmitted by U.S. military satellites is far more detailed than what is available from the commercial satellite vendors and therefore highly classified. "What's classified is the detail," Dave Burpee, the NGA spokesman, told me. But John Pike, who closely follows what satellites are launched and when, disputes that. Military satellites *do* provide higher-resolution photographs than what is available from companies like GeoEye, he told me.* But that's not why they're classified, he explained. The secrecy has to do with the flexibility of NRO satellites—that is, how quickly an agency like the NGA can get the image it's looking for, and how quickly the NRO can respond to a request.

"Most of these satellites are the size of a city bus," says Pike. "You can go out in your backyard and watch them fly overhead at sunup and sundown. Any country that wanted to hide something from one of these satellites by running something indoors to hide it, is doing it."[31] Therefore, intelligence officials classify the information about the origin of certain images so the targets of U.S. surveillance don't know they're being watched. From studying the details of recent satellite launches, Pike claims that "there's at least one spacecraft up there that is stealthy and not observable optically or by radar." That's kept secret for an obvious reason. "If somehow or another it got out that the Americans had an image of a particular place or time when none of the known spacecraft were in the sky, it would become apparent by deduction that they have a stealth satellite, and that's where they got the image." ("And now," he said with a laugh, "I've come pretty close to the fun facts that can be acknowledged about these things.") Information about military satellites, however, is

---

* The satellites with the highest possible resolution are no longer flying, according to Pike. Current satellites have a resolution of about six inches or so. The KH-8, which flew during the Cold War and was used to photograph Soviet military installations, had a resolution of *three* inches. The NRO stopped flying KH-8s in the 1980s.

not the only data that are classified. MASINT, the discipline of "sniffing" the air, picking up subtle changes in vegetation, and other forms of measurement, is one of the most classified areas of national intelligence. The overall picture obtained by merging imagery with SIGINT, MASINT, and HUMINT is where the real secrets of NGA are found.

This classified zone is where the major intelligence contractors, specifically the systems integrators, come into play. To transmit classified NGA imagery and data to other agencies as well as military consumers, the NGA relies on IT contractors with large numbers of employees with security clearances. In 2001, the NGA awarded a $17 million contract to Booz Allen Hamilton to build one of the Intelligence Community's first multiagency databases for the imagery agency. The first stage of the Future Intelligence Requirements Environment, known by the acronym FIRE, was completed in 2006, and has been demonstrated to other potential customers in the military and the IC over the last eighteen months. The system is designed to help intelligence agencies cut across their own stovepiped systems and share information widely across the IC.[32]

According to *Defense News,* the database collects information from multiple agencies and provides a "suite" of analysis and simulation tools that allows analysts to decide how to use imagery. "FIRE can play out all the possibilities and options based on stacks of accumulated data being collected from sensors, and from known data about friends and enemy platforms and systems," the newspaper said. "Armed with that vast amount of multi-intelligence information, its modeling and simulation tools can play out the 'what-ifs.' "[33] Booz Allen wouldn't comment on any aspect of its work for the Intelligence Community. But its Web site provides some details of its offerings to the NGA, including expertise in a "wide range of imagery formats, commercial remote sensing systems and information systems." Judging by the prominent role played at GEOINT by Booz Allen executives such as Keith Hall and Joan Dempsey, the NGA is one of the company's most important customers.[34]

SAIC has a major contract with the NGA (the agency won't put a value on it) to produce geospatial information transmitted to U.S. troops and intelligence staff around the world. In 2004, as mentioned earlier, the company received a Meritorious Unit Citation from CIA director George Tenet for developing the imagery systems used by the Predators, U-2s, and Global Hawk surveillance aircraft deployed by the CIA and the NGA over Iraq.[35] SAIC also plays a key role in NGA activities as a result of its work as the principal contractor for the Joint Intelligence Operations Capability-Iraq, the Pentagon unit that transmits classified intelligence to U.S. military forces engaged in battle. Managing SAIC's work for the NGA is Leo Hazlewood, a twenty-three-year veteran of the CIA who served as the NGA's first deputy director.

Lockheed Martin is responsible for what may be the NGA's most sweeping project. It is developing for the NGA a "ground-based infrastructure" designed to help users of the NGA's satellite and imagery data to improve their ability to distribute, share, and exploit the information. The contract, called GeoScout, was awarded in 2003 for an unspecified amount, and is proceeding in four "blocks" that could take up to ten years to complete. The ultimate goal, Lockheed Martin executives say, is to create a system that seamlessly blends data from unclassified commercial and classified military satellites. "GEOSCOUT allows the foundation for connectivity," says Jeffrey Harris of Lockheed Martin. The project, now in Block Two, is managed by Michael Thomas, a Lockheed Martin vice president in its Integrated Systems & Solutions unit and a member of the USGIF board of directors. Its future, however, is uncertain: GeoScout is frequently cited by intelligence analysts, along with the NSA's Trailblazer, as an expensive project in which too much power was ceded by government managers to the contractor.[36]

Some of the NGA's smaller software vendors operate on a classified level as well. AGI, the company that produced the imagery for *Mission: Impossible III,* operates as a subcontractor to SAIC and Booz Allen's classified integration programs, and offers workshops (called "agi-classified") to intelligence agencies. A brochure distributed at the GEOINT conference advertised a series of workshops in 2007 in El Segundo, California; Colorado Springs, Colorado; and Chantilly, Virginia; where AGI said experts from key U.S. defense and intelligence organizations and AGI engineers would explain how AGI technology could be used for intelligence applications. Similarly, the USGIF and the

NGA co-sponsored a series of technology workshops in May 2007 for private companies and government agencies to learn about the latest offerings in geospatial technology. The first day's session was a classified event, open only to officials and contractors holding SI/TK clearances. Those designations are part of a broader clearance called SCI, or "sensitive compartmented information," which must be obtained before working on intelligence collection systems. SI refers to special intelligence, and TK to talent keyhole; both are common security clearances for professionals working with signals and geospatial intelligence. (The second day of the conference was unclassified and open to everyone.)

In addition to being classified, the integration and analytical services provided by SAIC, Booz Allen, and other companies are proprietary. That is, they are produced by those companies with the understanding that the key technology won't be disclosed to their competitors. It's kind of a private form of classification—a fact that General Clapper, when he was still director of the NGA, alluded to in a 2004 interview with *Directions*, the NGA's in-house magazine. Asked if the NGA is working to declassify and commercialize its leading technologies, he replied that "the reverse of what you describe is the norm." The NGA, he said, "works closely with industry to take its unclassified technology and use it as a platform upon which we add classified data." But there is a "crucial difference" between the industry's technology and the NGA's classified data, he explained: the former is "protected because it is proprietary in nature," while the NGA data is protected "because it is classified."[37] In both cases, however, the information is kept secret from the general public. At the same time, the issue of proprietary systems and their inability to communicate with each other has become one of the biggest weaknesses in the Intelligence Community.

It was no accident, therefore, that the theme of the GEOINT 2006 conference was "interoperability." Every speech seemed calibrated to emphasize the need to fuse intelligence across agencies, the military, and domestic law enforcement. John Negroponte laid out the broad strokes of the policy in his closing speech. But he left the details up to his aides, who were in Orlando to lay down the law on intelligence sharing. Mary Margaret Graham, the same DNI official who had spilled the beans on the intelligence budget two years before, issued a not-so-veiled warning to intelligence agencies and their contractors that the days of proprietary systems and endless budgets for satellites were over. From here on out, she said, the DNI was going to stress interoperability. "The shining spacecraft, crucial though it may be, is not the whole story," she said. "Today we must ensure that the ground architecture—the magic on the ground—receives as much if not more attention to ensure we take full advantage of the finely tuned and highly capable sensors that we operate." That is beginning to happen with the "public-private partnership between NGA and the commercial imagery industry," she concluded.

Graham and other officials were careful to define information sharing as a government mandate. But they knew, as did every attendee at the GEOINT conference, that the actual work of integrating intelligence is being done by the private sector information technology companies that now dominate the intelligence contracting industry. "There is a real need inside the IC to share information and domains," John F. Olesak, the vice president of Northrop Grumman's Intelligence Group, explained to me during a break in the proceedings. "The idea is to move away from stovepipes, whether derived from imagery, signals intelligence, or human intelligence, to be shared across multi-disciplines and multi-organizations to get more synergy and make it more available to people who might not have it." Northrop Grumman's "response as a corporation," he said, "is to look to develop tools, techniques, and technologies to help get us to the point where customers share information. Information sharing is a very important part of our entire portfolio."

To drive this point home, Northrop Grumman and about a dozen other companies at the conference joined forces to produce an "interoperability technology event" that would show agency officials in the audience that many companies already have the capabilities demanded by the nation's intelligence leaders. The demonstration, the highlight of the symposium's second day, was narrated on the GEOINT 2006 stage by Chris Tucker, the president and CEO of IONIC Enterprise Inc., a supplier of communications software used by the NGA and its contractors.

He described a complex scenario involving a high-level mission to Greece and Turkey by Secretary of State Condoleezza Rice, complicated by political turmoil and a disastrous earthquake. The scenes played out against a percussion-laden soundtrack that sounded suspiciously like the theme to *The Exorcist,* and a raft of high-tech graphics reminiscent of *24,* the popular Fox counterterrorism show.

Under the scenario, Rice's first stop was Athens for a meeting of the G8. From there, she was to fly to a gathering of NATO ministers in Istanbul, where Eric S. Edelman, the undersecretary of defense for policy (and the former U.S. ambassador to Turkey) was to join her. The big headache in Greece was a series of protests by "potentially conflicting groups" determined to "air their grievances." Among them were Muslim groups "protesting the latest Middle East conflicts." But of greatest concern—and here the drumbeat intensified—was the Greek nationalist group November 17th, which, according to the narrator, had a long "record of international terrorism."

The interoperability phase of the scenario began with the Greek police transmitting, via e-mail, topographical maps of Athens, along with Rice's planned route to the airport, to a multinational operations center where U.S. intelligence officers were monitoring the protests. One officer checked open source reporting from the news media to get a handle on emerging threats, and then ran the names of some of the groups identified in news reports through a Web-based data mining service he had handily loaded onto a laptop. Instantly, the screen showed several "Salafist detainees," presumably Sunni extremists imprisoned by the Greek government. The agent put these names through a link analysis program that searched for hidden relationships, and came up with a "host of specific individuals known to be in Athens." More information was added to the link analysis results, including NSA intercepts of the Salafist cell phone calls overlaid with NGA imagery of the area. Seeing this, the U.S. intelligence agents on the scene reported that the detainees had gathered "at construction sites in and around Athens." At that point someone on Rice's security detail piped up: "This is a bad scene. How did we miss this on the security prep?"

The next sounds were a British reporter describing mayhem at the construction sites, including percussion grenades exploding among the crowds. U.S. officials asked for the latest from the Greek police: they reported major fires and explosions, and urged a rerouting of Rice's motorcade to the airport. The new map was then "pushed out" to the Secret Service and the Greeks, and Rice arrived safely at the airport to catch her flight. As her plane lifted off, she issued a press statement decrying the "loss of civility in this seat of civilization." (Take that, you Greek militants.)

In-flight to Turkey, things took a turn for the worse. The pilots on Rice's plane, dubbed Air Force Two, radioed ahead to Turkish Air Traffic Control, which suddenly went silent. So they checked in with their counterparts at CENTCOM headquarters in Doha, Qatar, and were told that a big earthquake had just rocked Turkey. Rice decided to land at a U.S. airbase in Turkey where she could "personally assist in the relief." Then she heard that her colleague Edelman couldn't be located; he'd been speaking about U.S. foreign policy at the country's largest university, the epicenter of the quake. He was now somewhere in the rubble. U.S. intelligence analysts started looking for imagery that might help in Edelman's rescue, and transmitted it directly to the computers used by their colleagues in the U.S. and Turkish militaries.

But the destruction at the university, as bad as it was, was suddenly overshadowed by a shadowy organization called Black Friday, which warned the Turkish government not to use "infidels" to look for Muslims in the rubble. To counter this threat, U.S. intelligence brought in two UAVs to fly over the area—one to establish a wireless communications network, and the other to monitor the security situation at the university "as the crowd grows larger and expresses its discontent." By now there were fifty thousand dead, and gunfire could be heard in the streets: the "unintended result" of the U.S. rescue mission had been "heightened unrest amongst Turkish workers who now think the U.S. forces are taking over Istanbul." After another sweep by one of the UAVs, the security team was given new rules of engagement in case they came under attack. Hours later, the U.S. official was found alive in the rubble and flown to Germany. The crisis was over, and "the good guys made it out alive."

"What we have just witnessed," Tucker said as the lights went back on, was twenty applications from sixteen different vendors, "all working seamlessly together with each application knowing nothing about the other vendor's platforms, their operating systems, or the code base on the other side of that request." Michele Weslender, one of Negroponte's top deputies at the DNI, took the stage next. The demonstration, she said, was an example of what American companies and U.S. intelligence were now capable of. "We planned ahead, we adapted open international standards across the board for the government, military, and industry, and we were able to seamlessly on the fly take data from multiple sources and fuse it so we have shared situational awareness." Later, I was told, representatives from several U.S. agencies asked the foundation to make the same demonstration available to them.

It's not at all clear how easily the big contractors will be able to make their systems interact with each other. After the GEOINT conference, I spoke to retired Admiral Herbert Browne, who was about to retire after five years as the executive director of the Armed Forces Communications Electronics Association. AFCEA is the largest organization for intelligence contractors, and represents companies involved primarily in military intelligence. The message from the Intelligence Community and the Pentagon about integration, Browne told me, has been heard "loud and clear. They are saying to us, 'make sure it can interconnect, or we don't intend to spend any of the taxpayer money on it.' " But the problem for contractors and agencies alike, he said, is that most of the systems "were built in a stovepiped environment, and it's going to take a while to make the transition." It's a lot like cars and houses today, he said—each has its internal computers that control the temperature, but neither system is linked to the other; starting over would mean burning down your house and buying a new car. "Well, we're just not ready to burn down the intelligence houses and buy brand-new cars," he said. "We're ready to do what we can to progressively increase the amount of info exchanged between the intelligence communities, and that's the direction we're headed." [38]

Some outside critics of the Intelligence Community are wary of such claims. One of the most skeptical is Robert David Steele, a twenty-five-year veteran of national security who served in the CIA, worked on classified programs involving both imagery and signals intelligence, and founded the Marine Corps Intelligence Center. As an advocate of open source intelligence that uses publicly available information, such as foreign language newspapers and journals, to build U.S. knowledge about the world, Steele is particularly scornful of the classified work done for intelligence agencies by contractors, which he sees as wasteful and of little value. When I described the USGIF interoperability event to him, his voice seemed to leap at me out of the telephone.

"One of the huge problems that we have in intelligence is that every agency and every division has a whole range of sweetheart deals with contractors built up over the years to the point where there is never really true and proper competition," he said. At one point in his career, when he was part of a steering group that studied the use of IT across the Intelligence Community, "we found twenty different contracts across the agencies for advanced analytic workstations, and every single one of them was with a different contractor." Steele added that this was true across the board in the IC, and makes the idea of linking disparate systems a pipe dream. "When a contractor talks to you about interoperability, that is code for wrapping a huge blanket around its proprietary system and putting together a very ugly bridge to everything else. It won't work, it's not affordable, it's not scalable, it's idiocy. It's a huge waste of money and time."[39]

Clearly, the information sharing scenario so dramatically portrayed at the GEOINT conference is a long way off. As a high-level study group convened by the NGA concluded in July 2007, "the DOD continues to be frustrated by the inability to get direct theater downlinks to the regional combatant commanders who view current unclassified imagery information and products as critical to mission execution."[40] But for every skeptic like Steele, there are five companies ready to prove him wrong. The most eager to jump into intelligence projects, no matter which agency funds them, are a group of contractors that depend almost entirely on spying for their revenue and trade their shares on the stock market. This shrinking breed, known as the "pure plays," is where we turn next.

8

The Pure Plays

"We are a national security pure play."

—George J. Pedersen, chairman and CEO of ManTech International, at the Friedman, Billings, Ramsey Group defense investors conference in Washington, D.C., February, 28, 2006

ON A SWEET springlike night in 2006, a group of investors and entrepreneurs gathered in the Living Room Bar at the swank Mandarin Oriental Hotel in downtown Washington. They were there for a conference on defense and homeland security, where top executives from twenty-one companies would present their investment and acquisition strategies to a parade of securities companies, investment banks, and private equity funds. Over sushi and Chinese hors d'oeuvres, they networked, shared industry gossip, and talked about the growing business of intelligence contracting. The evening's affair was off the record, which was fine by me; I was here to learn what was happening in U.S. intelligence from the perspective of the capitalists making money from it, and this was the perfect setting for that. The importance of the event was magnified by the presence at the conference of former CIA director George Tenet, who was scheduled to deliver the keynote address the next morning. Tenet had been deeply involved in Bush's war on terror, and I was interested in what he had to say to the intelligence contractors who were here.

After making my way to the elegant bar, I found myself standing next to a sharply dressed man in his early thirties. He was from India and had recently become an American citizen. "I'm here to invest," he told me, whipping out a business card listing a high-tech investment firm in Silicon Valley. A thirtyish entrepreneur standing nearby joined our conversation and informed us that he was working for his mother, a physicist from Tennessee who had spun her company out of a university laboratory with the help of a private equity fund. They were now making "very decent money" selling specialty software to the Department of Homeland Security. Over by the window, which framed a lovely view of the Jefferson Memorial and the Tidal Basin, a gray-haired man leaned comfortably on a radiator, sipping cognac and greeting everyone walking past with a friendly nod and handshake. He turned out to be one of the senior partners of Friedman, Billings, Ramsey, the Washington, D.C., investment firm that had organized the conference. This event was only in its second year, he told me, and he was delighted by the turnout. "The industry's on a roll," he said.

But the exuberance seemed oddly misplaced given the news of the past few days. Iraq was on the verge of civil war, and the number of U.S. military deaths there had just hit 2,300. The lead story in the morning papers painted a grim picture: grisly attacks and other sectarian violence unleashed by the recent bombing of a Shiite Muslim shrine had killed 1,300 Iraqis, making the past week one of the deadliest of the war. The next day, General Michael Maples, the director of the Defense Intelligence Agency, told Congress that the insurgency in Afghanistan was growing almost as fast as Iraq's, "presenting a greater threat to the central government's expansion of authority than at any point since late 2001."[1] Things in the Middle East seemed to be going downhill, and fast; as it turned out, these events were precursors to a tumultuous year in the Middle East that would take 1,500 more American lives and cost the Republican Party control of both houses of Congress in the midterm elections that fall.

At the plenary session and the corporate presentations that followed the next day, the human dimensions of the war were far away. Instead, the talk focused on the business opportunities presented by the war and how the Bush administration's military and intelligence strategies in Iraq and Afghanistan could open markets for companies specializing in information technology and intelligence, surveillance, and reconnaissance (ISR). The talk was of money and profits, "market drivers," being "in sync with our customers," and providing "soup-to-nuts support" to the U.S. military.

George Tenet set the tone in his keynote address. In an hour-long speech closed to reporters (and summarized to me later by some of the executives in the audience), the former CIA director explained that the chief priority of the Intelligence Community was getting timely intelligence onto the battlefields in Iraq and Afghanistan to support U.S. ground forces and fighter pilots. Over the last few years, he said, the Department of Defense had made a major effort to push information out "to the soldier at the pointed end of the spear," and allow that soldier to download data, imagery, and intelligence from computer databases located in nearby command posts or from spy planes flying overhead. Done properly, soldiers would gain "situational awareness," understand the scenario unfolding before them, and gain a decisive edge over Iraqi insurgents, Afghan fighters, and Al Qaeda foot soldiers.

In a nutshell, Tenet had laid out the basic precepts of network centric warfare. It was a subject he knew well: under Tenet's command, the CIA had been the first agency to put these theories into action in Afghanistan, where, as we saw earlier, CIA paramilitary teams armed with mobile phones and laptops had directed air strikes at Al Qaeda and the Taliban. But looking back at his speech two years later, it's also clear that Tenet was making the case for his own career moves. Within three months of his talk, Tenet would join, either as a director or an adviser, four companies that were directly involved with the high-tech military strategies he was endorsing: L-1 Identity Solutions; The Analysis Corporation; Guidance Software; and QinetiQ. None of this was known at the time, of course. But to the companies in the audience, Tenet's remarks were an affirmation of their own commitment to defense and intelligence.

Netcentric warfare is "right in the sweet spot we provide for our customers," exulted Robert Coleman, the chief operating officer of ManTech International, during his company's presentation to investors. He described a spiraling effect: as the NSA and other agencies pushed information "out to the ultimate point of consumption," the military was seeking "timely, accessible, and actual intelligence," requiring more complex systems and increasing demand for "more contractors to support those systems." Steven Waechter, the executive vice president of CACI International, noted that the Pentagon's needs for intelligence on the battlefield had driven CACI's intelligence business up by 26 percent over the past year; intelligence contracts, he said, now accounted for more than a third of CACI's revenue stream. Over the next eighteen months, CACI would see a 63 percent increase in national security contracts, including a $300 million hike in classified work. Intelligence, Waechter concluded, "is a very attractive place to invest."

ManTech and CACI are the largest companies in an elite group of six intelligence contractors known on Wall Street as "pure plays." That term refers to companies focused on a single market and earning most of their revenue from that market. In the world of food products, for example, the Coca-Cola Company is a pure play because it only makes soft drinks and related products; but PepsiCo, which is a conglomerate that makes everything from Lay's potato chips to Quaker Oats cereal, is not. SAIC, which depends on federal contracts for more than 90 percent of its revenue, considers itself a *government* pure play. But in the intelligence markets we're concerned with, pure plays are companies focused almost entirely on spying, earning up to 90 percent of their revenue from contracts with the Pentagon, the CIA, and the national collection agencies. In addition to ManTech and CACI, they include Applied Signal Technology, one of the NSA's leading providers of digital signal processing equipment and outsourced signals analysis services; Argon ST, a company created by former executives of Raytheon, which provides much of the NSA's supply of sensors and is the dominant supplier of communications intelligence (COMINT) to the U.S. Navy; MTC Technologies, which operates the Intelligence Community's fleet of U-2 spy planes so important to the NSA and the National Geospatial-Intelligence Agency; and SI International, the NSA's leading adviser on outsourcing.*

The pure plays are riding an enormous wave of Pentagon spending on secret intelligence programs for the wars in Iraq and Afghanistan, funded in large part by supplemental bills. In 2006, on the eve of the Friedman, Billings, Ramsey conference, Congress passed an $80 billion supplemental that included $4 billion in classified spending for "operational intelligence activities" in the military and five key agencies controlled by the Pentagon: the Defense Intelligence Agency, the National Geospatial-Intelligence Agency, the National Security Agency, the National Reconnaissance Office, and the Counterintelligence Field Activity office. That money, the Pentagon informed Congress, would enable U.S. intelligence agencies to field "new tools and methods for collection, for processing, and for detecting high value targets."[2] A few months after the supplemental was approved, Donald Rumsfeld told a Senate committee how it was being used. U.S. forces, he said, "are bringing intelligence to battalions and brigades that before terminated at corps level." That included "HUMINT, counterintelligence, analysis, UAVs; reconnaissance, surveillance and target acquisition capability into these formations." Troops on the ground "now have the connectivity to the joint force that will make the difference," he said.[3]

A year later, with Rumsfeld gone from the Pentagon and U.S. policy in Iraq in shambles, the Department of Defense asked for another major

---

* Three other companies qualify for the list because they are focused almost entirely on providing intelligence for one or more of the armed services. But they will receive only a mention because they are more narrowly focused on defense. They are NCI Information Systems Inc., a major Army contractor that provides information assurance services for the NSA and the NRO; DRS Technologies Inc., which supplies signals intelligence equipment and defense electronics to the NSA and the Department of Defense; and Dynamic Research Corp., a major supplier of information technology to the U.S. Air Force and Army, with a sizable presence in the NSA. In addition, two important intelligence contractors, SAIC and SRA International Inc., have diversified clients within the federal government, and (as mentioned above) are more rightly known as federal government pure plays. SAIC earns 90 percent of its revenue, and SRA 99 percent of its revenue, from federal contracts.

increase in intelligence spending. Essentially, this request funded a massive counterintelligence effort in Iraq and the Middle East designed to (1) stop attacks from improvised explosive devices, IEDs; (2) determine the source of weapons being fired at U.S. troops and the origin of the attacks on U.S. helicopters; and (3) expand the fight against an organized Islamic resistance that appears to have spread widely throughout the Middle East and the Horn of Africa since Bush invaded Iraq in 2003. The $94 billion supplemental included $2.4 billion for IED Defeat, $2.7 billion for Military Intelligence, and $3.6 billion for Non-DoD Classified, which refers to the agencies outside the tactical chain of command—that is, the NSA and the NGA. Specific projects destined for contractors included "identity management for access control and persistent surveillance capabilities" (a capability offered by L-1 Identity Solutions) and "contract linguists and cultural advisers," a contract awarded in 2006 to a joint venture of DynCorp and McNeil Technologies. In counterintelligence, there were requests for "contracted analytic efforts and related operations to enable these efforts to function 24/7 in support of operations around the world" as well as "contract support in the development and revision" of counterintelligence and human intelligence doctrine—quite a task for a private company. For signals intelligence, the supplemental requested "contracted support and personnel-related costs to ensure our forces are trained in the latest equipment and tactics, techniques and procedures." Without those funds, "essential surveillance against the Iraq insurgency will not be as thorough or as effective," the Pentagon said.

In the last two chapters, we saw that much of the "connectivity" referred to by Rumsfeld is provided by the large systems integrators—SAIC, Booz Allen Hamilton, Raytheon, Lockheed Martin, and Northrop Grumman. But it's the pure plays that do the heavy lifting. They employ small armies of analysts with top secret clearances who can move in and out of war zones quickly; they supply what they call "mission-critical" technology that can detect, identify, and locate signals coming from enemy weapons and eavesdrop on communications between insurgent units; they have the technical ability to link all this collection and dissemination through mobile radios and computers down to the war-fighter on the ground. Pure plays also supply the means to counter IEDs. They make and service the sensor systems that detect enemy weapons systems. The pure plays are the shock troops of the Intelligence Community. And for the last six years, theirs has been a dizzy ride.

In Chapter 6, we met Essex Corporation, a Maryland contractor specializing in optical technology that was earning nearly 90 percent of its revenues from the NSA when it was acquired, in 2007, by Northrop Grumman. Essex is one in a long line of pure plays that have been (and will continue to be) acquired by larger companies.

In 2002, just before a major wave of mergers and acquisitions swept through the industry in the wake of 9/11, there were at least two dozen companies that fit the criteria of an intelligence pure play. The two with the brightest future were Veridian Corp. and Anteon International Corp., both of which were later acquired by General Dynamics. When it was sold in 2004, Veridian, which specialized in developing sensors and secure networks for the NRO, the Defense Advanced Research Project Agency, and other agencies, had 7,300 employees and sales of $1.2 billion a year.[4] Anteon, with $715 million in revenue in 2001, was big in IT, systems engineering, and technical management, and employed 5,300 people, 85 percent of whom held security clearances. When General Dynamics bought it in 2005 for $2.1 billion, it was one of Washington's best-known technology firms, with a star-studded board of directors that included former defense secretary William Perry and retired Army General H. Hugh Shelton, the former commander of U.S. Special Forces and chairman of the Joint Chiefs of Staff from 1997 to 2001.[5] One of Anteon's largest contracts was with the U.S. Army Intelligence Center in Fort Huachuca, Arizona, to train army interrogators.[6]

Another pure play that disappeared into a larger company is Titan Corp., which was acquired in 2005 for $2.6 billion by L-3 Communications, bringing with it several important NSA contracts and nine thousand employees, including 5,000 with top secret clearances.[7] Lockheed Martin and other large defense contractors have snatched up the rest. In 2004 and 2005, Lockheed Martin acquired the government IT unit of Affiliated Computer Services Inc., inheriting several contracts with defense intelligence agencies, and Sytex, a $425 million company based in Philadelphia that held contracts with the Pentagon's Northern Command and the NSA/Army Intelligence and Security Command.* By 2007, the company employed 52,000 IT specialists with security clearances, and intelligence made up nearly 40 percent of its annual business, company executives said.[8]

The remaining pure plays are often the subject of acquisition rumors. In 2006, for example, several British publications reported that CACI International was about to be acquired by BAE Systems; both companies denied the reports, and the rumors quickly died down. Still, the churning in the industry never stops: by the end of 2007, L-1 Solutions, one of the companies Tenet works for, had joined the ranks of the pure plays and announced plans to expand further through acquisitions. Robert LaPenta, L-1's CEO, told investors that his company was buying companies "in the high-end government services arena" to challenge the large IT and systems engineering firms for intelligence contracts. Among the companies on his hit list were CACI and ManTech.[9]

It's easy to see why investors would be attracted to the pure plays. They are highly profitable, and individuals and investment funds that have risked their capital in them have seen the value of their stock skyrocket. In 2006, A. G. Edwards's Defense Banking Group, a Boston fund that invests in intelligence, traced the growth of nine pure plays—CACI, ManTech, SI International, Dynamic Research, SRA, Essex, NCI, MTC, and Anteon—by tracking their public market capitalization (this was before Essex and Anteon were sold, of course). That capitalization figure, derived from a company's stock price per share multiplied by the total number of shares outstanding, is generally a good indication of investor interest in a specific industry. Collectively, the value of the intelligence pure plays exploded in the first five years of

* Through Sytex, Lockheed Martin has become a major force in military interrogations. Throughout 2006 and 2007, Lockheed Martin was recruiting counterterrorism analysts and linguists for Guantanamo Bay, Cuba. The positions require top security clearances. One such job listed on www.intelligencecareers.com in April 2007 stated that "regional and cultural knowledge of various entities associated with known terrorist groups being targeted in the Global War on Terrorism are a plus."

the war on terror, from $980.5 million in 2001 to $8.3 billion in 2006. Imagine a bar graph showing the capitalization of these companies. In May 2001, the companies stood at 100 percent. Two years later, just before President Bush sent U.S. troops into Iraq, they had risen to nearly 300 percent of their pre-9/11 value. On election day in 2004, when President Bush won his second term in office, they peaked at nearly 900 percent. By May 2006, they had settled down—to 543 percent of their value in the months before 9/11. Over that time, by comparison, the S&P 500 rose by a factor of 4 percent and the top defense stocks increased by 56 percent.

Much of this capital flow was the direct result of a string of initial public offerings that reverberated through the defense industry in the wake of 9/11. The first defense-related IPO after the attacks took place in December 2001, when the Carlyle Group sold off its shares in United Defense Industries, the maker of the Bradley Fighting Vehicle and other weapons systems widely used by the Army. The timing of the IPO drew sharp criticism from some analysts, who accused the well-connected private equity fund of capitalizing on the terrorist attacks and the Bush administration's first strikes in Afghanistan to push its stock. William Conway, one of Carlyle's founders, told me at the time that the IPO had been planned for many months before the attacks. "No one wants to be a beneficiary of September 11," he said.[10] That may have been true, but Carlyle's willingness to tap the capital markets at this sensitive moment in the nation's history inspired other companies to do the same.

When ManTech launched its IPO, it had just emerged from a reevaluation of its business strategy with a plan to focus exclusively on its military and intelligence contracts. To obtain the cash it needed for expansion and acquisitions, it went public in June 2002. In its pitch to investors filed with the Securities and Exchange Commission, ManTech explicitly linked its future with the war on terror. "Our solutions enable our customers in the intelligence community and Department of Defense to identify evolving foreign and domestic threats, including terrorism; to quantify exposure to these threats, and to implement prudent physical and cyber countermeasures," ManTech said. It made note of its large number of cleared employees, "including over 1,000 with access to Top Secret Sensitive Compartmented Information, allowing us to work with our customers in highly classified environments and at front-line deployments." And it predicted, accurately it turned out, "strong growth opportunities" for IT and technical service providers and increased defense spending on "C4I (command, control, communications, computers and intelligence), homeland security and intelligence activities."[11]

ManTech's IPO was a huge success. Originally, the company had planned to raise $90 million by selling six million shares to the public. But sensing strong demand, particularly from large institutional investors, ManTech's underwriter increased the size of the deal, and raised more than $115 million.[12] (CEO George Pedersen, however, continued to control the company by virtue of his command of over 90 percent of ManTech's stock.) With its newly raised cash, ManTech went on an acquisition spree, buying seven companies over the next five years and raising its ranking to twenty-first among the top one hundred federal contractors by 2006. ManTech's success set off a stream of IPOs by many of the companies we have classified as pure plays, including SI International (November 2002), MTC Technologies (June 2002), Veridian Corp. (June 2002), and Anteon International (March 2002). These same companies have consolidated the industry and are now at the core of a broad defense-intelligence industry. Here are their stories, starting with the largest of the pure plays, CACI International.

CACI: Preemption and Counterterrorism

In 2006, *Iraq for Sale: The War Profiteers,* a film made by Hollywood producer Robert Greenwald, began circulating around the country in DVD form. Financed with over $350,000 in donations from liberal activists, it portrayed four U.S. military contractors in Iraq—Halliburton, Blackwater, CACI International, and Titan—as greedy, opportunistic corporations oblivious to the human suffering caused by their actions. One of the film's most devastating segments used footage from former military interrogators and Iraqi prisoners to detail what Greenwald called one of his "most shocking and troubling discoveries"—how CACI "profiteered" by torturing Iraqis at the notorious Abu Ghraib prison.

Jack London, CACI's CEO, personally pocketed "over $22 million" from the Abu Ghraib contract, the film claimed. London, who had refused numerous requests from Greenwald for an interview, lashed out after the film was released, calling Greenwald's accusations "maliciously false" and labeling the film "a classic example of the 'big lie' propaganda technique." The company also challenged the idea that its growth came solely from its business in Iraq, saying that its Abu Ghraib contracts were less than one percent of total worldwide revenue.[13]* In fact, CACI's contracts for its work at Abu Ghraib were worth about $40 million to the company, which in 2004 earned $1.1 billion from dozens of government contracts, ranging from signals intelligence work for the NSA to managing documents for the Department of Justice.

In that narrow context, therefore, the company was right: antiwar activists, journalists, and filmmakers critical of CACI have vastly *underestimated* its role in U.S. foreign policy and the war on terror. By focusing exclusively on CACI's role at Abu Ghraib—abysmal as it was—journalists and antiwar activists have obscured a much larger picture: CACI is one of the world's largest private intelligence services providers and deeply involved in classified black operations everywhere on the globe where U.S. military forces are active.

The best way to describe CACI is as a private supplier of signals intelligence, human intelligence, imagery, and black ops, all rolled into one enterprise. "We support all four of the intelligence community's priority focus areas: analysis, collection, user outcomes, and management," CACI stated in its 2006 annual report. CACI's intelligence contracts now make up 35 percent of the company's revenues, 95 percent of which is earned from the federal government. London rattled off the company's clients in a conference call with analysts in February 2007: "the Department of Defense, all the military services, the intelligence community at the strategic level. That'd be your CIA, your NRO, your

---

* CACI posted a lengthy rebuttal to the film on its Web site, with a ponderous title that sounded like something out of Borat's Kazakhstan: "CACI Corrects False Information About Its Former Business in Iraq 2003–2004." That posting is no longer on its Web site, but has been substituted with a section listing questions and answers about CACI's role in Iraq. See: http://www.caci.com/iraq_faqs.shtml.

NSA, DIA, and NGA." CACI's primary intelligence customer, he said, is the Army. "We know what's happening out there in terms of the global war on terrorism threat," he said. "And that is primarily being supported in the military from the United States Army's perspective as well as the United States Marine Corps."[14]

CACI's services, London constantly reminds investors, are perfectly aligned with the Pentagon's. "As the fight against terrorism and the Islamofascists continues, technologies will keep evolving to collect, analyze and disseminate vital intelligence to support the war fighter and the national security authorities," he said in 2006. "Information and intelligence is where the growth is likely to be for the simple reason that, in the final analysis, accurate information from quality sources, communicated through secure channels to the right people, will trump all other weapons of war. In this environment, CACI is at the forefront."[15]

CACI's most important asset is its ten-thousand-person workforce, two-thirds of whom hold security clearances. Of those ten thousand, CACI's Web site says, "about 2,000 have top-secret sensitive compartmented information clearances," one of the highest possible clearances attainable in the Intelligence Community. CACI's employees are stationed throughout the world, including Iraq and Afghanistan, Kosovo, Bahrain, Kuwait, Belgium, Bosnia, Hungary, Germany, Italy, the U.K., and Japan.[16] Recent job postings also show that CACI performs classified work in South Korea and Colombia, where U.S. intelligence agencies have extensive electronic warfare and eavesdropping operations.

CACI views itself as a virtual extension of the Bush administration's foreign policy and the global war on terror. "CACI supplies one of the most vital weapons in the war on terrorism: cleared, qualified experts in intelligence gathering, analysis, operations and support," the company declared in its 2004 annual report. "Working with the intelligence community in its mission to preempt, disrupt, and defeat terrorism worldwide"—notice the careful placement of that word *preempt,* lifted directly from the Bush lexicon—"our people provide counter-terrorism intelligence analysis and terrorist targeting support. They assist with intelligence collection. And their unique skills help thwart terrorist attacks against the United States."

From the first days of the invasion of Iraq, CACI positioned itself as utility player for the Department of Defense, which provides the company with more than 70 percent of its revenue. Days before U.S. troops rolled into Iraq in 2003, London boasted to the *Washington Post* that CACI is "playing a role in a large choreography to make sure the president and Rumsfeld have the right information at the right time and can disseminate their decisions back to the battlefield. We'll be ahead of the enemy's ability to outmaneuver us." [17] This included "enemies" at home as well. One of CACI's key Pentagon clients is the Counterintelligence Field Activity office, which uses CACI's HighView document and records management software to "help combat the growing foreign adversary intelligence collection threat," according to CACI's Web site. In 2005, Rumsfeld's office rewarded CACI for its contribution to the war effort with two contracts worth nearly $20 million to streamline its IT operations. The two one-year projects supported the Pentagon's transformation initiatives and allowed Rumsfeld's staff to manage its classified and unclassified computer networks supporting homeland security and the war on terror.[18]

London's political philosophy closely matched the imperial visions of Rumsfeld and the neocons he brought into the Pentagon. His world is a Manichaean one, divided between the United States and the forces of evil. He stands out among his peers in the business of intelligence for his almost religious allegiance to the Bush-Cheney agenda of preemptive war and global military dominance. Like George Bush, he sees evil lurking throughout the developing world, where he points to a "rising environment" of extremist individuals and organizations. "It seems that nobody [in the Middle East] has organizational self-control; everything flips into an aggressive violent reaction," he told Washington's WMAL radio in 2006.[19]

In 2002, London came up with a "simpler way" to define the asymmetric warfare practiced by the Palestinians and other Arab groups in their resistance to the United States and Israel: "Not fighting fair." He added: "Precisely, asymmetric warfare means facing a cunning and conniving adversary of inferior strength, who finds ways to exploit vulnerabilities to radical extreme, and frequently with frightening psychological effect."[20] In a speech to the Northern Virginia Technology Council, which has honored him twice for his contributions to IT, London laid out his analysis of the war on terror. Today, he said, "instead of warring against a single empire, we're facing" not only Al Qaeda but "groups like the Islamic Resistance Group, or Hamas; the Islamic Jihad; Hizbullah; the Liberation Tigers of Sri Lanka"—as if they were all connected. He informed his audience that "some of the Al Qaeda leadership is now believed to be in Lebanon with the Hizbullah."[21] If so, that would be news to U.S. intelligence, which has never mentioned any such connection.

London traces the origins of today's troubles to the Iranian revolution of 1979, and argues that the current confrontation between the United States and Islamic groups in the Middle East is "not only a global war but a culture clashing kind of situation." He seems easily frightened by the prospect of even peaceable protest. In 2006, alerted by a friend, he watched a Web site broadcast from London of a demonstration by Muslims carrying "incredible placards and posters" about "what Islam meant and how it was going to resist Western culture, and 'don't pick on us.' It was a very scary kind of thing. That's a small group of people, but it's an idea that is taking hold and getting some traction and is a serious concern for us going forward." CACI's position as a contractor in the Intelligence Community, he went on, is to "provide solutions that the politicians and military organizations can use to either suppress or redirect some of those aggressive energies."[22]

One of the "solutions" embraced by London is Social Network Analysis, which the company describes as "an increasingly crucial aspect of counterintelligence and counterterrorism."[23] This school of analysis was first developed by Israel's military intelligence services in their efforts to defeat the Palestinian intifada in the West Bank and Gaza, and was recently employed by the Israeli Defense Forces in Lebanon and the U.S. military in Iraq. It involves tracking the relationships between resistance fighters and their family and community network, and—in Israel's case—destroying the social infrastructure that supports both.

Toward that end, CACI claims that its "intelligence experts" have developed a modeling program that "maps relationships among members of highly complex human networks—like terrorist cells or extremist groups—and analyzes how the network might behave when faced with various changes."[24] One such program, advertised on CACI's Web site, is called URWARS, for Urban Warfare Simulation. It was built by CACI for the U.S. Marine Corps to prepare soldiers for urban warfare, and helps them locate buildings, highways, roads, sewers, and "subterranean entries, subways and tunnels and waterways" used by insurgents. The Marine Corps would not say how the program was used, but it is likely that URWARS saw action when CACI intelligence specialists were deployed with the Marines at Fallujah, as several CACI employees have attested.

London has integrated Israel's experience into CACI's operations. In 2004, at a time when CACI interrogators at Abu Ghraib were trying to break the anti–United States resistance in Iraq, London traveled to Israel as part of the first annual Defense Aerospace Homeland Security Mission of Peace to Israel and Jordan. His visit was sponsored by the Jerusalem Fund of Aish HaTorah, a pro-Israel lobbying and funding group, and Greenberg Traurig LLP, a powerful Washington lobby group. While in Tel Aviv, London accepted an award on behalf of CACI "as a provider of information technologies for helping fight the war on terrorism and transform the Middle East from a source of global instability into a peaceful, stable region," according to a CACI press release.[25] The award was presented by Israel's defense minister at the time, Shaul Mofaz, a hard-liner who had quit the Likud Party to join the right-wing government of Ariel Sharon.*

According to CACI's Web site, a secondary purpose of London's visit was to promote opportunities for strategic partnerships between U.S. and Israeli defense and homeland security firms and to attend "high-level briefings and demonstrations on innovative technologies and their application to homeland security, counter-terrorism and national defense." While in Israel, according to an itinerary obtained by

* Given London's own extremist views, Mofaz was an interesting choice. For the last two years, Mofaz had been in charge of fighting the Palestinian intifada, and under his command the Israel Defense Forces had stepped up the demolitions of the homes of suicide bombers, blockaded Palestinian towns, and carried out the assassination of key Palestinian militants. Mofaz had even compared the uprising to the 9/11 attacks on the United States and branded the Palestinian Authority as a "terrorist entity."

Lebanon's *Daily Star* newspaper, London visited the Beit Horon military base, which the *Daily Star* described as "the central training camp for the anti-terrorist forces of the Israeli police." There, London was briefed by top counterterrorism experts and witnessed exercises "related to anti-terror warfare."[26]

CACI didn't start out as an intelligence company. From the time of its founding in 1962 until the late 1990s, CACI grew primarily by selling proprietary software, including an optical scanning technology it developed for the Navy, to various agencies of the federal government, including the Departments of Justice, Commerce, and Transportation. In 1972, the company transferred its headquarters from California to Washington, D.C., and hired London, a former Navy pilot, as a program manager. A year later, it shortened its name from California Analysis Center Inc. to CACI International. London headed steadily up the company's ranks and was named president and CEO in 1984. He moved methodically to capture software markets in the areas of law enforcement and the military. He also gave the company its motto: "Ever Vigilant."

CACI's optical scanning technology has been a particularly profitable niche. Used extensively by the Justice Department and the FBI, it can scan up to 26 million documents a month, transform the data into digitized information, translate foreign text into English, and then search for concepts and ideas within the data. "What it does is eliminate the need for a person to actually look at the stuff and try to interpret it," says Dave Dragics, CACI's vice president for investor relations. "So they can do analysis a lot quicker than they did before."[27]* After U.S. forces invaded Afghanistan in 2001, CACI's technology was used to read and analyze the thousands of Al Qaeda documents found in caves and other hiding places, CACI has said.[28]

* The technology was employed by the Department of Justice during the discovery part of the trial of two Libyan intelligence agents charged with masterminding the bombing of Pan Am Flight 103 over Lockerbie, Scotland, on December 21, 1988. Before the trial began, CACI built a special facility in New Jersey to scan and search the thousands of documents collected by the Justice Department, which helped draw up the Lockerbie indictments. The eighty-four-day trial in the Netherlands ended on January 31, 2001, with the conviction of one of the agents, Ali Mohmed Al Megrahi, who was sentenced to life in prison; the second defendant was acquitted. Two hundred seventy people died in the incident.

London first began eyeing the intelligence market in the late 1990s, when his company identified defense outsourcing as a "business opportunity trend line" and made a specific decision to move into the area of classified intelligence contracts.[29] His first major acquisition in the intelligence sphere took place in 1998, when CACI paid $42 million to buy a company called QuesTech Inc., which was involved in "very important information warfare and intelligence markets," according to the *Washington Post*.[30] Another acquisition, worth $415 million, was the defense intelligence business of AMS, a major IT contractor whose customers included all the major defense intelligence agencies as well as the Air Force, Army, and Navy. When that sale went through in 2004, CACI added several thousand employees with security clearances to its roster, increasing the company's cleared workforce to 9,400. Altogether, CACI made nearly three dozen acquisitions between the late 1990s and 2007, pushing its cleared workforce to more than ten thousand.

As he bought into the intelligence market, London began hiring as advisers people with extensive experience in defense and covert operations. His first big catch was Richard Armitage, who served on CACI's board of directors from 1999 to 2001. At the time, Armitage was a member of the Pentagon's Defense Policy Board and, as described earlier, had recently joined the private sector after a long career in defense, intelligence, and covert operations. Price Floyd, who was Armitage's press officer when he was in the State Department under George W. Bush, told me that Armitage played only a minor role at CACI and "didn't consult with CACI on its contracts." But the company itself has indicated otherwise. After Armitage joined the Bush administration as deputy secretary of state in 2001, CACI proudly described Armitage's role as providing "valuable guidance on CACI's strategic growth plans and the federal government and Defense Department markets."[31]

Once CACI was committed to defense, it changed the makeup of its board of directors. London's board recruits included retired Navy Admiral Gregory G. Johnson, the former commander-in-chief of NATO forces in southern Europe; Arthur Money, a former assistant secretary of defense for command, control, communications, and intelligence; Larry Welch, the former chief of staff of the Air Force and former commander-in-chief of the Strategic Air Command; former NSA deputy director Barbara McNamara; and retired Army General Hugh Shelton, the former chairman of the Joint Chiefs of Staff. (Shelton's "unsurpassed knowledge of our military markets and clients will be extremely valuable as an asset to CACI," London told investors after his appointment in 2007. Shelton was also a director of Anteon before it was sold to General Dynamics.)

Meanwhile, as the Defense Intelligence Agency expanded its outsourced activities during the Rumsfeld years, CACI concentrated heavily on building relationships with that agency. In January 2006, CACI appointed Lowell "Jake" Jacoby, a former Navy admiral and former DIA director, to be executive vice president for strategic intelligence opportunities. A year later, CACI hired Louis Andre, Jacoby's chief of staff at the DIA, to be Jacoby's deputy—in effect, transferring the former top two officials at the DIA to CACI (Andre's official title is senior vice president of intelligence business strategy). Jacoby was a valuable asset: as DIA director under Stephen Cambone, Rumsfeld's assistant secretary for intelligence, he was in charge of managing all HUMINT within the Department of Defense and played a key role in managing the Pentagon's intelligence reporting for the war in Iraq, including the DIA's assessment that Iraq possessed weapons of mass destruction. Jacoby also played an instrumental role at DIA in establishing the Joint Intelligence Task Force—Combating Terrorism (JITF-CT), a special interagency unit that consolidates terrorism-related intelligence at the national level.*

Both Jacoby and Andre had intimate knowledge of the Pentagon's strategic plans for years into the future, and their CACI appointments have paid off in significant ways. In the spring of 2007, CACI obtained a contract from the DIA to build a "terrorist screening database," and was recruiting for analysts to work with the Joint Intelligence Task Force to search data sets for information on known or suspected terror-

* The task force provides daily assessments of potential terrorist threats to U.S. military personnel and facilities around the world, and played a significant role in the tracking and eventual arrest of Jose Padilla, a U.S. citizen held for a time as an enemy combatant who was accused by U.S. authorities of conspiring with two Muslim men to create a North American terror cell that allegedly provided money, recruits, and other support for anti–United States terrorist activities.[32] Padilla was convicted on these charges in 2007.

ists and "warn of pending attacks" on U.S. forces, according to job advertisements placed in *IntelligenceCareers.com.* In June 2007, CACI won a $75-million task order from the U.S. Army to manage the development and maintenance of the DIA's "knowledge management and visualization efforts."[33] Around the same time, CACI was awarded a two-year, $33-million contract to furnish geographic information system technology to the DIA.[34]

CACI's largest single contract, worth $450 million, is with the U.S. Army's electronics communication command, which is responsible for electronic warfare—command, control, communications, computers, intelligence, surveillance, and reconnaissance, also known as C4ISR.[35] Other customers include the U.S. Navy's littoral and mine warfare program, the Air Force's Pacific Command and Control unit, and the Defense Information Systems Agency, the Pentagon unit responsible for network centric warfare. Elsewhere in the IC, CACI holds major contracts with the Department of Homeland Security and its Customs and Border Protection agency. But the one contract that CACI will always be known for is the one to provide interrogators at Abu Ghraib. How a request for information technology services became a cover for the brutal treatment of Iraqis remains one of the strangest episodes of the history of outsourcing.

As mentioned earlier, CACI got involved in Abu Ghraib through an IT contract it obtained when it acquired a company called Premier Technology Group in 2003. PTG was formed in the late 1990s by a group of former Army intelligence officers who had worked in Bosnia. By acquiring PTG, CACI told investors, it expanded its activities "to a whole host of tactical units in country and in other theaters of operations" around the world.[36] Best of all for CACI, PTG had existing contracts with the Pentagon for intelligence analysis and security services, IT, training, program management, and logistics, and 360 employees with high-level security clearances.

At the time of CACI's acquisition, all of PTG's contracts were being administered by the Department of the Interior. Two of the contracts, one worth $19.9 million, the other $21.8 million, required CACI to supply "screening, interrogation and support functions" and "human intelligence" at an unspecified site in Iraq. Because CACI was also being asked to screen Iraqis captured by U.S. forces, the contracts also called for biometric software that could identify suspects through facial characteristics and fingerprints. According to Frank Quimby, a Department of the Interior press officer, the Army justified these IT requests because "enormous amounts of information had to be integrated in order to prepare for interrogations and make maximum use of the information gathered."[37] It was through this convoluted—and virtually untraceable—route that CACI ended up at Abu Ghraib prison. Altogether, CACI hired thirty-one interrogators under its two IT contracts.

The interrogators arrived at the prison at a critical time. For the first few months after U.S. forces took control of the prison, the interrogations were conducted by U.S. military intelligence officers. But their efforts didn't yield the kind of information on the insurgency sought by Rumsfeld and Cambone. Their solution, Seymour Hersh reported in *The New Yorker,* "was to get tough with those Iraqis in the Army prison system who were suspected of being insurgents." Cambone ordered Major General Geoffrey Miller, the commander of the detention center at Guantánamo, to visit Baghdad to review interrogation procedures. His solution "was to 'Gitmoize' the prison system in Iraq—to make it more focused on interrogation"—by using techniques of sleep deprivation, exposure to extreme temperatures, and placing prisoners in stress positions for lengthy periods of time. Miller and his new recruits, Hersh wrote, brought "unconventional methods to Abu Ghraib."[38] CACI was brought in precisely at the time that Miller's "unconventional methods" were being introduced.*

In 2004, after the desperate conditions at the prison were reported to Army criminal investigators by a brave MP, Specialist Joseph M. Darby,

---

* In February 2006, Samuel Provance, an Army soldier who had been penalized by the military for blowing the whistle on detainee abuse at Abu Ghraib, testified before the House Government Reform Committee. Provance, who was stationed with the Army's V Corps, was in charge of information systems at the prison. He arrived at Abu Ghraib in September 2003. At first, he told Congress, "there were only a couple companies of military intelligence soldiers and a handful of computers, but then a group came from Guantánamo Bay (GTMO), Cuba, to 'make the place better run' (as we were told). There was a conflict between the GTMO soldiers and those who were already at Abu Ghraib, having to do with the way interrogations were being conducted and reported." In general, he said, "our people wanted to use the tech-

ay one, London, CACI's CEO, has treated Abu Ghraib as a ations problem. Over the past four years, CACI has sued or l to sue more than a dozen journalists because of their cover- u Ghraib. In September 2004, for example, Peter Singer, a Institution scholar and the author of *Corporate Warriors,* assic book about private military companies, penned a rather on piece for the *Washington Post* in which he criticized the corporations involved in Abu Ghraib have escaped federal n response, Singer told me, London wrote several letters to nding a retraction. When Singer refused to respond, London ante by threatening to sue Brookings for libel. Brookings's who received the letters, called London's bluff by ignoring don finally gave up. London also threatened to sue Rob- wald, the producer of *Iraq for Sale,* unless he corrected his ny opinion, CACI's people are classic and complete bullies," d told me during a 2007 media conference in Memphis we aded.

ler coda was offered up that year by General Taguba, who was retire from the Army in January 2007 after more than thirty service. During an appearance before San Francisco's Com- h Club on June 25, Taguba was asked what he thought about nce of private contractors at Abu Ghraib. The "private out- was "rather interesting," he replied, but wasn't by itself sig- What was more important was the way contractors and fficials "pointed fingers at each other" and refused to accept ility. "No one but one"—Specialist Darby—"would account elves," he said.[40] Like a good soldier, he left unsaid the fact wn commanders, including Donald Rumsfeld and the other ning the Pentagon, refused to accept responsibility for them- at it was very clear, from his tone and body language, that was deeply troubled about the lack of accountability.

seemed to lose some of its swagger after Rumsfeld left the Pen- arting in January 2007, CACI's stock began a rapid plunge in king from a high of about $60 at the end of 2006 to a low of gust 2007, where it stayed for most of the year. The reason for

the military launched several investigati
General Antonio Taguba, found numer
tant, and wanton criminal abuse" at tl
CACI employee, Steven Stefanowicz, as
directly or indirectly responsible" for the
he be fired and have his security clearanc
tion, led by Army Major General George
tary and the contractors. Fay looked into
at Abu Ghraib and expanded Taguba's cri
report detailed serious misconduct "rangi
on the part of twenty-three military inte
civilian contractors from CACI.[39] Many
and Fay investigations were corroborated
at the prison. Altogether, nine low-level A
for their abuse at Abu Ghraib and given
months to ten years in prison. But despite t
tions found that CACI interrogators direct
Abu Ghraib, they and their employer escap

niques we were trained to use at Ft. Huachuca, and t
ideas. After this period, the number of civilian contra
cantly. Those contractors were principally from CACI
from other MI units then came, as well as even more civ
pared statement for the House Government Reform C
available by the National Security Whistleblowers Coal
Oversight. Provance added more detail in an hour-long
Goodman on January 25, 2008. See www.democracyno

* In 2006, *Salon* reporters Mark Benjamin and Michael
closures about CACI's interrogators. In one story, they
the prison guards convicted for his role in the abuse, told
Stefanowicz had given orders to him and other guards to
of sleep, put them in stress positions, and humiliate tl
of Graner's testimony obtained by *Salon*, "Graner told A
Stefanowicz's orders because Stefanowicz worked with
charge of prisoners." Later, Benjamin obtained a previou
ing a CACI contractor, Daniel Johnson, interrogating an
Fay, in his report, had called "an unauthorized stress posi
Ivan Frederick, another low-level soldier convicted of abu
vestigators that Johnson directed him to abuse the Iraqi
port, including putting "his hand over his mouth" to stop
Files," *Salon*, March 14, 2006; and " 'Big Steve' and Abu

Since
public re
threatene
age of A
Brooking
the now
mild opi
fact tha
scrutiny.
him den
upped t
presider
him. Lo
ert Gre
film. "I
Greenw
both at

A sa
forced
years c
monw
the pr
sourci
nificar
milita
respo
for th
that h
men r
selves
Tagu

C
tagor
value
$42 i

the sell-off was CACI's decision to lower its revenue predictions for 2007 from $2 billion to $1.8 billion and cut its earnings estimates about 50 cents per share (in the end, CACI's 2007 revenues hit $1.9 billion, a 10 percent increase over 2006). The news came "as a shock to Wall Street, whose analysts [had] been overwhelmingly upbeat on the stock," *MarketWatch* reported.[41] The drop apparently forced the company to seek the resignation of its chief financial officer, Steven Waechter, who left the company in January.[42]* The company attributed its revised numbers to "unexpected reductions in demand on contracts supporting certain operations and maintenance activities in the Department of Defense."[43] But it was hard not to conclude that CACI's star had dimmed at the Pentagon.

Despite the slide in CACI's stock price, by the end of 2007 CACI's intelligence business was growing at a rate of nearly 20 percent a year. In September, CACI continued its buying binge by acquiring Athena Innovative Solutions, an intelligence analysis firm owned by Veritas Capital, the private equity fund where Richard Armitage, CACI's former board member, was a senior adviser from 2005 to 2007. The $200 million deal had an interesting backstory: Athena, once known as MZM, was the company at the center of the bribery scandal of former congressman Duke Cunningham. He is serving eight years in prison for receiving financial favors from MZM founder Mitchell J. Wade, who left the company as a result of the scandal. Despite its taint, Athena had something CACI wanted: six hundred professionals, over 95 percent of whom possessed security clearances at the top secret level or above. "You can't duplicate the type of people that Athena has and the clearances it has," Veritas president Robert B. McKeon told the *Washington Post*. "In one fell swoop to be able to buy a company with 600 of them is quite an achievement."[44]

In June 2007, London announced that he would relinquish his day-to-day control as CEO and pass those duties to Paul Cofoni, an intelligence industry veteran who came to CACI after working at CSC and General Dynamics. London continued to serve as chairman of the

* Waechter is now a director of NSA contractor NCI Information Systems.

board, a position he had held since 1990. His transition marked the end of an era of meteoric growth in intelligence spending and outsourcing. Still, it was clear the company's tradition as a shadow intelligence agency would be carried on by CACI's senior executive team, which, as we saw earlier, expanded in the fall of 2007 to include retired Admiral Albert Calland, the former deputy director of the National Counterterrorism Center. Over his long intelligence career, Calland had been a Navy SEAL, a special operations commander, and deputy director of the CIA. Since the Iranian hostage crisis in 1980, he told *Defense News*, his focus has been on counterterrorism operations. "What I want to do [now] is to continue to serve in that capacity in a supporting role," he said. "The terrorism problem can be divided up into three major muscle groups: the defensive piece, which is defending the homeland; then there are two pieces to the offensive, one being capturing and killing bad guys, the other being what's been termed the war of ideas, but it is really a battle over the image of our country." He concluded: "The threat posed by terrorism, and the threat to people, really has become more of an information battle."[45] Jack London could retire in peace: his company was in good hands.

ManTech: On the Battlefield

CACI's primary competitor in the world of the pure plays is ManTech International. ManTech, based in Fairfax, Virginia, defines itself as providing "mission-critical national security programs" for the Intelligence Community and the Departments of Defense, State, Homeland Security, and Justice. Since 9/11, its fastest-growing business has been providing communications software and network services to the National Security Agency, the Defense Intelligence Agency, and other military units directly involved in the war in Iraq. Pentagon and intelligence contracts account for 95 percent of its revenues.

"We are on the battlefield," proclaimed George J. Pedersen, ManTech chairman and CEO, at the 2006 Friedman, Billings, Ramsey investors conference where Tenet spoke. ManTech, he promised investors, is a "national security pure-play" operating "at the convergence of national security and technology" and "driven by expansion into concentrated intelligence, defense and homeland security." Among its many services in what executives call its "global war on terror business" is intelligence analysis, data mining, and producing finished intelligence reports.

ManTech's hottest markets include Iraq and Kuwait, where the company employs more than seventy consultants working to maintain and repair electronic equipment for the U.S. military. It sells and operates signals intelligence systems to U.S. Army units in the Middle East, Germany, Korea, and Bosnia, and has personnel deployed in Afghanistan, Uzbekistan, and Kyrgyzstan to support U.S. Air Force operations. It provides "cyber and physical security" for U.S. embassies and consulates around the world, and in 2005 signed a $10.5-million contract with the Transportation Security Administration to provide intelligence analysis services for the TSA's Alien Flight School Program. As a result of that contract, one of the nation's most important intelligence tasks—monitoring the schools where the 9/11 hijacker pilots received their training—has been outsourced.

Pedersen is a short, no-nonsense Navy veteran with a shock of red hair. He founded ManTech in 1968 in New York and initially focused on technical projects for the Navy. In the 1980s, he moved his headquarters to Washington and began a slow drive to capture markets in defense and intelligence. In 1988, the *Washington Post* called ManTech "something of a mystery," and described Pedersen as a man who shunned the limelight and kept "an unusually low profile."[46] But that's no longer the case: since the early 1990s, Pedersen has expanded ManTech by hiring as advisers and directors some of the most well-connected figures in U.S. defense and intelligence, and then pushing his way to the top through an aggressive PR and lobbying campaign.

In 1999, Pedersen hired Richard Armitage to serve on the company's advisory board (this was at the same time that Armitage was on CACI's board of directors). After Armitage left the State Department in 2005, Pedersen brought him in again to serve as a ManTech director. Armitage brings "enormous insight into our corporation's capabilities and operations, and he will be a tremendous strategic asset as we grow the company," the company said upon his appointment.[47]

ManTech's board also includes three former high-ranking intelligence officials with strong ties to the national security superstructure. Richard Kerr, who was appointed in 2002, is a thirty-two-year veteran of the Central Intelligence Agency, where he served from 1989 to 1993 as deputy director and in 2004 led an internal review of the CIA's performance prior to the Iraq War. During his career, he also served on a scientific advisory board for the NSA and as president of the Security Affairs Support Association, the predecessor to INSA, the association of CIA and NSA contractors. In 2004, ManTech brought onto its board retired Admiral David Jeremiah, the former vice chairman of the Joint Chiefs of Staff who now sits on President Bush's Foreign Intelligence Advisory Board and is a paid adviser to the NRO (Jeremiah, readers might remember, also wrote an influential report for the CIA after the agency failed to predict India's nuclear tests). Kenneth Minihan, the former director of the NSA, was elected to ManTech's board in 2006. ManTech's board members, Pedersen explained, are "very knowledgeable people. They are not salesmen for us. They are basically individuals we go to when we look at new markets or develop new technology."[48] These appointments have paid off, in dividends.

Today, more than 95 percent of ManTech's revenues come from customers in the Intelligence Community and the Department of Defense, including the NSA, the NRO, the Office of the Secretary of Defense, the U.S. Army's Intelligence and Security Command, and various intelligence units in the Departments of Energy and State as well as the Air Force and Marine Corps.[49] (In 2000, ManTech even bid, in a consortium led by OAO Corp., later acquired by Lockheed Martin, for the NSA's Groundbreaker project, one of the largest federal outsourcing projects in U.S. history.) Since going public in 2002, ManTech's revenues have grown substantially, from $701 million in 2003 to $1.1 billion in 2006. Its executives believe that the Pentagon's need for intelligence in Iraq and other hot spots, along with the organizational shifts in the military that are breaking down barriers between the armed services, means that ManTech's growth rates can continue almost indefinitely. "DoD funding is not going to change, certainly not during the Bush administration," Pedersen said at the FBR investors conference. "We believe the war on terror is a long war."

ManTech has six thousand employees, 45 percent of whom hold top secret security clearances or higher. According to company literature, ManTech's intelligence work includes policy development, planning, and program implementation; information collection, intelligence analysis, and linguistic services; and special mission support. Most of its acquisitions are geared toward expanding its workforce, as ManTech did when it acquired Aegis Research Corporation and its five hundred cleared analysts in 2003 and McDonald Bradley and its two hundred cleared employees in 2007. In contrast to many of its competitors, which place their employees in agency offices in the Washington area, ManTech deploys many operatives in Iraq and Afghanistan, where they support U.S. military operations. "The folks they recruit for these positions aren't what you would call Boy Scouts," says Thomas Meagher, who follows the intelligence industry for Friedman, Billings, Ramsey. "They're typically ex–special operations people, having in a lot of cases geographical familiarity, usually some IT capability, and, most important these days, language capabilities as well. A ManTech person might be running an intelligence collection system in Iraq, for example."[50]

ManTech doesn't shy away from talking about its role as an outsourcing agent for the government. In 2006, it paid $100 million to acquire Gray Hawk Systems, a privately held intelligence contractor with $70 million in revenue and 450 employees holding top secret security clearances, and an undisclosed amount to buy GRS Solutions, a company ManTech says is engaged in "counterterrorism/counter intelligence missions around the world."[51] Robert Coleman, ManTech's president and chief operating officer, explained the acquisitions to analysts in a conference call. "One of the fastest-growing outsourcing opportunities in the intelligence community is in the field of intelligence analysis," he said, adding that the Gray Hawk and GRS acquisitions extended ManTech's growth "into a new and highly classified area" of the Intelligence Community. Later on in the call there was an illuminating exchange between Meagher, the FBR analyst, and Coleman and Pedersen about the IC's personnel policies:

Meagher: The Directorate of National Intelligence has published their Strategic Human Capital Plan. And obviously they are trying to increase the number of in-house intelligence analysts. I was just wondering how you see that playing out within the context of what you and other people are doing on an outsourcing basis?

Coleman: Yes, it's too early to tell, but I think that's a longer-term issue, Tom. And the fact is also that as these government folks with this highly specialized training reach the retirement level, they come to contractors. And I don't think the government is going to want to lose that domain knowledge and talent. But in terms of the impact, I think that's a longer-term issue.

Pedersen: May I make a comment? I sat on a committee with one of the intelligence agencies two years ago, and the committee tried to raise the salary structure for the intelligence community because we recognized that it would be very difficult for the government itself to hire the kind of talent they need at the current salary structure. Unfortunately, the committee and those engaged were not successful in raising those salaries. So despite the desire, and I think it would be a damn good thing if they could hire people in-house, I'm not sure they can get their total needs as they anticipate by hiring inside. . . . I just don't see the demand from the professional contracting side really going down.[52]

The exchange was interesting on a couple of accounts. First, it underscores ManTech's strategy of leveraging its six-thousand-strong army of cleared analysts and technical specialists to obtain work that used to be performed by government employees, and its certainty that the trend will continue into the indefinite future. Second, it illustrates how closely the industry and the intelligence agencies work. Pedersen, the CEO of one of the largest outsourcing companies in government, was invited to sit *as an adviser* on personnel issues to an intelligence agency that his company works for. That is a major conflict of interest that underscores the serious need for greater oversight of the Intelligence-Industrial Complex.

Another distinctive feature of ManTech's outsourcing business is its global nature. At the FBR conference in 2006, Coleman presented the company's strategy against a map of the world showing the forty-one countries where ManTech's operatives work. They included Haiti, Turkey, South Korea, Japan, Guatemala, Nicaragua, and about a dozen more in South America and Europe.

"This is a road map of where US forces are engaged throughout the world," explained Coleman, who was trained to give presentations like this when he worked for the White House National Security Council's Crisis Management Center during the administrations of Ronald Reagan and George H. W. Bush. Pointing to Europe, he added: "As NATO expands its role, our local presence in these areas positions us to take advantage of those opportunities and continue to grow our business. And as information flows to the ultimate point of consumption" on the ground, he went on, "the military will need timely, accessible and actual intelligence that will require more complex systems." That, in turn, "will require more contractors to support those systems."

ManTech won't place a number on the percentage of its employees working overseas, but it's substantial. And such work is dangerous. As mentioned earlier, two ManTech contractors deployed in Afghanistan in support of U.S. military operations there were killed in 2005 when an Afghanistan Kam Air Boeing 737 crashed while traveling between the cities of Herat and Kabul.[53]

One element of government contracting that ManTech has excelled in involves intellectual property. Contractors are paid a premium when they develop, from scratch, a computer program that is unique for the agency they work for. But there is nothing to stop the same contractor from selling the same software to the government again and again, for the same premium price. This is essentially a form of subsidy, and ManTech has perfected it. "We use IP as a discriminator to open new markets and to continue penetrating our existing markets for the purpose of driving additional contacts," Coleman explained to investors.

A notable example is the Joint Regional Information Exchange System (JRIES), which was developed by ManTech in 2002. It allows intelligence agencies operating at the highest levels of security to share information and intelligence with agencies and government employees (and contractors) not cleared to work with classified documents. JRIES was first used by the Defense Intelligence Agency to link its counterterrorism centers with police intelligence units nationwide to share sensitive information about investigations. In 2004, it was adapted for use by the Department of Homeland Security, which called it the Homeland Security Information Network (HSIN). It allows Homeland Security to collect threat information from different parts of the government and share it with its own agents and analysts wherever they are stationed, in both classified and unclassified formats. HSIN is now deployed by police intelligence units in all fifty states.

The JRIES software was first developed by ManTech for the National Security Agency. After the software was successfully launched at the NSA, ManTech turned around and sold the same program to the DIA and, later, to the DHS. Until the Friedman, Billings, Ramsey conference, ManTech had not disclosed the identity of the intelligence agency that first bought the software. But during his presentation at FBR, Coleman got carried away, perhaps by bravado, which is not uncommon in these road shows for investors. JRIES, he confided, is "an example of how we were able to take intellectual property development, and a contract to the NSA"—and here he chuckled nervously, probably realizing he had let slip classified information—"and develop a security assessment tool that's one of the mainstream tools of the industry right now."

ManTech's HSIN contract with DHS is worth $7.1 million.[54] So far, it has been a mixed success. In 2006, the DHS Office of Inspector General found that HSIN had been implemented so rapidly that Homeland Security officials could not clearly define what the network's role would be, or how it might work with other systems. Moreover, only about 2 to 6 percent of the potential users were signing on. Those that did use it were frustrated and confused by the system, and didn't trust it to keep sensitive information secure.

"Although users generally like the web portal technology because of its user-friendliness and flexibility, those we interviewed said they are not committed to the system approach," the inspector general said. "Because some lack trust in the system's ability to safeguard sensitive information, and because the system does not provide them with useful situational awareness and classified information, users do not regularly use HSIN. Instead, users resort to pre-existing means such as related systems and telephone calls to share information, which only perpetuates the ad hoc, stove-piped information-sharing environment that HSIN was intended to correct."[55]

In May 2007, a House homeland security subcommittee held a hearing on the system and found that the problems had persisted. "HSIN was supposed to be the department's main pipeline for sharing unclassified information with state, local and tribal partners," said California Democrat Jane Harman. "What we have instead is kind of a mess."[56] Charles Allen, a former CIA official who is now assistant secretary of homeland security for information analysis, agreed with Harman. "HSIN was not a good system," he said. Allen also disclosed that contractors made up 60 percent of the workforce in his office, which is the intelligence arm of DHS. "I won't be comfortable until we reverse the ratio" from 60–40 to 40–60, he said.[57]

ManTech, with its red corporate insignia, is ubiquitous at industry gatherings, and the company runs large, colorful ads in industry publications such as *Government Computer News* and *Signal* magazine ("To deliver highly sensitive information securely, the military and intelligence communities turn to ManTech"). It sponsors a daily intelligence report on WTOP, Washington's all-news radio station. ManTech is also a major lobbyist, having spent at least $208,000 to influence the U.S. Congress during an eighteen-month period in 2005 and 2006, according to company filings with Congress. More than half of that money—$108,000—went to the defense lobbyist (and earmark specialist) John G. Campbell to influence the House and Senate on defense appropriations issues. Another $80,000 went to Grizzle & Company to lobby Congress on Department of State IT security initiatives. In January 2006, ManTech's vice president, Robert D. Knight, registered as a company lobbyist. His focus is privatization and "private sector vs. public sector research"—an indication that the company takes seriously the plans by intelligence officials to reduce the community's reliance on contractors. Meanwhile, to get its way on Capitol Hill, Pedersen runs a political action committee that has become one of the largest donors in the defense industry. In the 2004 and 2006 election cycles, ManTech donated a total of $328,601 to candidates for federal office, equally divided between Republicans and Democrats, according to the Center for Responsive Politics.

During that time, one of ManTech's biggest donations, $21,000, went to Harold Rogers, R-Kentucky, the former chairman of the House Homeland Security Appropriations Subcommittee, which has jurisdiction over spending on such items as ManTech's HSIN system. Overall, the largest recipient of ManTech PAC money is Steny Hoyer, D-Maryland, who is now the House majority leader and represents a district where ManTech has a major facility. Between 2001 and 2006, ManTech donated $49,000 to his campaigns and leadership funds (in a 2006 defense appropriations bill, Hoyer managed to secure $2.8 million in earmarked contracts for ManTech).[58] Those donations, ManTech says, reflect the company's desire to participate in the political process. "We support a broad base of officials with the overall objective of contributing to those officials who support the nation's efforts to fight terrorism, both at home and abroad—and are committed to protecting our country's national security."[59]

But ManTech's contributions to a lawmaker from Arizona with close ties to the company has drawn the attention of federal investigators. That story revolves around former Army Major General Eugene Renzi of Arizona, and his son, the former Republican congressman Rick Renzi. Their actions help us understand how ManTech became a major player in the intelligence outsourcing industry.

The elder Renzi, who was with ManTech from 1993 until his death in February 2008, was ManTech's senior executive vice president and president of ManTech Defense Systems Group, the company's largest unit. He was responsible for management of the company's extensive command, control, communications, computers, and intelligence (C4I) contracts in support of the Department of Defense and the national intelligence agencies. Renzi also represented ManTech in several contractor organizations, including the Armed Forces Communications and Electronics Association, where he served from 2003 to 2007 as chairman of the board of directors. Before joining ManTech, Renzi spent thirty years in the Army, where he worked at the highest levels of military intelligence. At his retirement, he was director of command and control networks for the U.S. Pacific Command. Before that, he commanded several signals intelligence battalions that are part of the NSA, including the USA Communications Command at Fort Huachuca, Arizona, which is also headquarters for the U.S. Army's intelligence school. Renzi served twice in senior command posts at Fort Huachuca, where ManTech has held several multimillion-dollar, multiyear contracts.

Renzi was one of the first Army commanders to outsource military intelligence services. During his years at Fort Huachuca, he developed close ties with Betac, a leading intelligence contractor that we met in chapter 3. During the 1980s, Betac won millions of dollars' worth of contracts for the continuity of government project created by the Reagan administration to prepare a shadow government in the event of a nuclear war. To build the system, readers will recall, FEMA hired the Harris Corporation, the CIA hired McDonnell Douglas, and the Pentagon hired TRW. Most of the military's contracting tasks were assigned to the Army's Information Systems Command in Fort Huachuca. There, the outsourcing orders were handled by Renzi, who was the deputy chief for operations at the base and the senior official for the COG project. Between 1983 and 1985, under Renzi's watch, Betac's contract expanded from $316,000 to nearly $3 million; and by 1988, the journalist Steven Emerson reported in *U.S. News & World Report,* Betac had obtained "multiple COG contracts worth $22 million."[60]

Around this time, W. Thomas Golden, a civilian intelligence officer working for Renzi, began to question the huge contracts flowing to Betac. Specifically, Emerson reported, "he became curious after learning that a number of Army officials who had worked with Betac at Fort Huachuca and elsewhere were retiring from the Army and being hired back, under the auspices of Betac. As paid consultants to the Army, some were earning up to $400 a day. Seldom had the Pentagon's revolving door spun more quickly." Golden also discovered that Renzi "had been the key player" in the Betac award, and that one of his sons, most likely the future congressman Rick Renzi, was working for Betac. Golden took his findings to the Army's inspector general, which launched an investigation. What the IG found was appalling.

At the base, Army investigators discovered that many contract documents had been destroyed. COG contractors had billed more than one agency for the same work. Contracts were increased by as much as 50 percent without any input from oversight officials. Communications vital to the project didn't work properly, and were costing hundreds of millions of dollars in overruns. Despite the massive spending on communications, the agencies involved in the COG network couldn't communicate with each other. Moreover, after Golden spoke to investigators under an offer of confidentiality, his comments were leaked to General Renzi, who let it be known that Golden was not welcome on his base. But the harassment didn't stop there. Golden was investigated by four different agencies (he was eventually cleared). Others who testified had their careers ruined, according to several press reports. "It cost myself and my family three years of living in absolute hell," Golden told CNN in 1991. "My family paid a high price." [61]

The Army inspector general concluded that General Renzi had indeed retaliated against Golden, and reported that because of Renzi's actions, Golden's effectiveness "was diminished" and he "could not do his job." [62] The House Armed Services Committee investigated the COG contracts and agreed with the assessment. In the end, some illegal COG contracts were canceled and Renzi was reprimanded by the Army for retaliating against Golden. But he was soon promoted to the rank of major general and stationed in Hawaii, where he finished his Army career at the Pacific Command.

Renzi's contacts at Fort Huachuca proved to be invaluable for ManTech. The company's first contracts at the intelligence base—testing command and communications networks for the Joint Interoperability Test Command—were awarded in 1983, when Renzi was the commandant. Within a few years of Renzi's hiring at ManTech, the company won several more contracts at the base, including a lucrative $163 million a year contract signed in 2001 to provide IT support through the U.S. Army's 5th Signal Command; it is still in effect.[63] Altogether, ManTech holds $467 million in contracts at Fort Huachuca, with options for an additional $1.1 billion through 2008. The company maintains an office in nearby Sierra Vista, and as of July 2007, was recruiting for at least a dozen jobs at the base.

Rick Renzi now appears to be carrying on his father's tradition of helping intelligence contractors. The junior Renzi grew up in Buena Vista, near Fort Huachuca. After apparently working for Betac during the late 1980s, Renzi went to law school and then parlayed his contacts in Arizona to start a lucrative career in insurance and real estate. In 2002, running as a Republican, he was elected to Congress to represent Arizona's First District during a hotly disputed contest in which both President Bush and Vice President Cheney made personal appearances on his behalf. Once in the House, he quickly earned a seat on the Intelligence Committee, where one of his key issues was integrating information across agency lines—precisely what ManTech does. "Having worked in the intelligence field, and as a member of the House Permanent Select Committee on Intelligence, I know first hand that we must continue to rebuild our intelligence community to guarantee better communication among the various intelligence agencies," Renzi stated on his official Web site. (I interpreted Renzi's "work in the intelligence field" as a reference to his years at Betac, but his staff did not respond to my requests to confirm this.)

In 2003, Renzi apparently carried his loyalty to ManTech too far. During his first year in office, Renzi added a provision to a defense authorization bill that exempted Fort Huachuca from tight federal restrictions on water use. The amendment reversed a 2002 agreement that required the fort to pay half the costs of mitigating the area's water use, including use by private contractors, and saved the fort and its contractors hundreds of millions of dollars. Environmentalists who had fought for the initial agreement charged that Representative Renzi's actions amounted to "a disturbing conflict of interest" because one of the chief contractors at the fort is ManTech, Renzi's father's company.[64] In 2006, the Justice Department opened an investigation of the younger Renzi, including his ties to ManTech, and later expanded the probe into allegations involving real estate deals. The case quickly became embroiled in the scandal over the Justice Department's firing of eight U.S. attorneys (one of those fired, Arizona's Paul Charlton, had opened the Renzi investigation). In April 2007, Renzi resigned from his seat on the Intelligence Committee, and in August announced that he would not seek reelection. (In February 2008, Renzi was indicted on charges of extortion and fraud related to his real estate deals.) Over his career in Congress, no company donated more to his campaigns than ManTech International. Since 2002, ManTech donated a total of $37,200 to the junior Renzi, according to the Center for Responsive Politics.

SI International

Like ManTech, SI International Inc. of McLean, Virginia, took advantage of the post-9/11 rise in military and intelligence spending to go public in 2002. Since then, its revenues have more than tripled, from $150 million to $462 million in 2006. Just a little less than half of SI's revenue, 48 percent, comes from intelligence work, and the number of its classified contracts has seen "double-digit growth" since 2002, according to CEO Brad Antle. That should solidify the company's solid record with intelligence, he says. "If we keep that up over five years, that will double our sales," Antle predicted at the FBR Washington conference.

SI's top executives are all veterans of the intelligence contracting industry. Ray Oleson, executive chairman, and Walter Culver, vice chairman, previously worked in senior positions at CACI International and Computer Sciences Corporation, one of the NSA's premier contractors. SI "defines, designs, develops, deploys, trains, operates and maintains information technology and network solutions for the Department of Defense and federal civilian agencies," Antle told the *Wall Street Transcript* in 2006.[65] It prides itself on its ability to bring "rapid solutions" into its customers' hands, particularly in the area of defense transformation, where SI analysts "support the shift to net-centric warfare so our military can respond more quickly to threats across the globe."[66] Key customers include the National Security Agency, the U.S. Air Force, the Department of Homeland Security, and the Missile Defense Agency.

Because of its high-visibility role as an adviser for the NSA, SI has filled its management team and board of directors with former high-ranking intelligence officials. Among them, as we have seen, is the NSA's former top acquisition executive, Harry Gatanas. John Stenbit, one of SI's directors, was appointed in 2004 after working in the Pentagon as chief information officer and assistant secretary of defense for command, control, communications, and intelligence. In those positions, Stenbit managed the Pentagon's netcentric warfare systems used in the initial stage of the wars in Afghanistan and Iraq. He was also one of the founders of the Counterintelligence Field Activity, the controversial Pentagon intelligence unit; according to an SI press release, Stenbit played an instrumental role in linking CIFA with other intelligence agencies to "share information needed to pursue terrorists in the United States and abroad."[67] Before coming to the Pentagon, Stenbit spent thirty years at TRW, the intelligence contractor now owned by Northrop Grumman.

Other SI directors include Maureen Baginski, the former director of SIGINT at the NSA and a twenty-five-year veteran of that agency (she's also on the board of INSA, the intelligence association), and retired Army General R. Thomas Marsh, the former chairman of President Clinton's Commission on Critical Infrastructure Protection and commander of the electronics division at Hanscom Air Force Base in Massachusetts, where many of the Air Force's networking systems were first developed.

MTC Technologies Inc.

MTC is headquartered in Dayton, Ohio, home of the sprawling Wright-Patterson Air Force Base, one of the most important research centers in the black world of military intelligence. The company was created by a group of former Air Force officers specifically to take certain Air Force operations private. Ninety-six percent of its revenues comes from contracts with the Department of Defense and the Intelligence Community, 77 percent of those as a prime contractor. According to material distributed at the FBR investors conference, MTC commands a staff of 2,900, including more than three hundred with the highest security clearances necessary "to work on the federal government's most sensitive projects." Its revenues rose significantly after the U.S. invasion of Iraq, from $189 million in 2003 to $415 million in 2006.

One of MTC's most lucrative contracts is with Beale Air Force Base in California, where MTC technicians and analysts schedule the flights of America's fleet of U-2s, the surveillance warhorse known as the Dragon Lady. That is a major enterprise—MTC also trains U-2 pilots and maintains the aircraft. That takes its personnel all over the world, including Iraq, where the U-2s provide "around the clock support to warfighters in Afghanistan and Iraq." U-2s also fly sorties out of Osan Air Base in South Korea and Taif Air Base in Saudi Arabia. The U-2 project is probably the "one US Air Force contract" that MTC executives said was responsible for 26 percent of its revenue, which rose significantly in 2005 to $373 million.

MTC describes itself as a disciple of the Rumsfeldian techno-vision of warfare. "Today, the task of defending our Nation against war, terrorism and tyranny has changed dramatically," it states on its Web site. "With the nature of warfighting changing, the face of battle has evolved into urban warfare against a phantom enemy." As a result, it says, U.S. military forces in Iraq and Afghanistan have an "increasing need for real-time" intelligence, surveillance, and reconnaissance (ISR) and "joint-force sharing" of information technology. Those areas "will be beneficiaries of continued, and perhaps increased, government spending to outsource its needs."

Among the contracts listed in MTC's 2004 annual report were projects to maintain and modify aircraft for the Pentagon's Special Operations Forces as well as other specialized surveillance and attack aircraft, such as the B-2 Stealth bomber and the B-52. MTC analysts also support the White House Communications Agency in providing secure communications for President Bush when he flies on Air Force One. But MTC's purview goes way beyond tactical intelligence; it is also deeply involved in what it calls the "strategic" agencies doing intelligence collection and analysis—the CIA, the NGA, the NRO, and the NSA.

At Fort Meade, it provides "technical development" support for signals intelligence and helps collect and analyze the highly classified measurement and signatures intelligence known as MASINT. Its contractors serve as liaison officers from the Defense Intelligence Agency (which has jurisdiction over MASINT) to the offices of the Joint Chiefs of Staff, each Combatant Command, and the State Department. Among the "tasks and capabilities" it specializes in are psychological operations (PSYOPS), electronic warfare, imagery analyst training, and R&D coordination and execution. At the FBR investors conference, it listed growth areas as providing sensors and sensor analysis for the Predator and Global Hawk UAVs, intelligence training, and "all aspects of the Global War on Terror."

Unusual for an intelligence contractor, MTC was founded by a foreign-born entrepreneur. Raj Soin, a mechanical engineer raised and educated in India, moved to the United States in 1969 and founded MTC in 1984 with only $1,700.[68] Its key staffers are former Air Force intelligence officers. They include retired Brigadier General Billy J. Bingham, who runs the company's National Security Group responsible for MTC's intelligence contracts. Bingham capped his thirty-year career in the Air Force as deputy chief of the Central Security Service of the NSA and later served SAIC as director of its SIGINT program. The ubiquitous Ken Minihan, another retired Air Force general who was NSA director for four years, also sits on MTC's board of directors.*

Applied Signal Technology Inc. (AST)

One of the NSA's leading providers of digital signal processing products is Applied Signal Technology. Gary L. Yancey, its co-founder and CEO, spent his entire career in intelligence as a contractor, starting with the

* MTC's status as a pure play is about to end. In December 2007, BAE Systems agreed to acquire the company for $450 million. When the sale is completed in the first half of 2008, MTC and its 2,900 employees will be folded into BAE's Customer Solutions Operating Group, which is based in Rosslyn, Virginia. According to the BAE Web site, the group "provides the full-spectrum of support and service solutions for current and future defense, intelligence, and civilian systems, driven by its customers' needs to ensure their front end operational requirements are supported and maintained." See David Hubler, "BAE Acquires MTC Technologies," *Washington Technology,* December 26, 2007.

defense division of GTE Sylvania. At the FBR investors conference, he described AST as a provider of solutions for intelligence, surveillance and reconnaissance and "global security," with a special focus on "high-tech eavesdropping." AST is one of the purest of the pure plays: a full 84 percent of its work is with intelligence agencies, and about 90 percent of it is through sole-source contracts awarded without competition. Most of those appear to be with the NSA.

Like the other pure plays, AST has experienced dizzying growth over the past five years. Between 2002 and 2006, its revenues more than doubled, from $76 million to $162 million. The company doesn't lobby, but claims on its Web site to devote "significant resources" toward understanding the SIGINT needs of the Intelligence Community through "frequent marketing contact" with government contracting officials. John P. Devine, who has been an AST director since 1995, is the NSA's former deputy director for technology and systems and, before that, was its chief of staff.

AST's specialty is communications intelligence, or COMINT. That is the science of collecting foreign intelligence from global telecommunications systems. The NSA and other agencies use AST equipment to scan through millions of cell phone, microwave, ship-to-shore, and military transmissions. "We select signals for further analysis," said Yancey. This area of AST's business is driven primarily by the global war on terror. "The political instability in certain regions such as the Middle East, Eastern Europe, Africa, and Central and South America and the ongoing counterterrorism campaign have heightened the United States Government's need to be able to monitor activities in foreign countries," AST explained in its 2005 annual report.

Another area of expertise is electronic intelligence, or ELINT, which are signals emanating from enemy weapons systems. This is an important piece of military counterintelligence carried out by NSA teams on the ground in places like Iraq and Afghanistan. U.S. agencies are turning to AST, its annual report said, because "the same countries that have political instability and terrorist activities are modifying older Soviet-deployed weapon systems as well as developing new weapons systems." Under its government contracts, AST is investing in ELINT processors that can locate and characterize these systems. According to Yancey, the company teamed with Northrop Grumman and Lockheed Martin to place the equipment on high-altitude UAVs, which the company believes will be "the platform of choice for future ELINT missions."

The company also invests heavily in sensors that process imagery, heat, acoustics, and magnetic effects to help the U.S. military and the IC find and pursue terrorists. "As the counterterrorism campaign is focused on individuals and groups of individuals worldwide," AST says on its Web site, "ISR requires 'tip-off' information from physical phenomena that can indicate regions where the U.S. government should concentrate its SIGINT and human intelligence (HUMINT) resources for more effective ISR."

Argon ST Inc.

Argon is the successor to Raytheon's E-Systems Inc., long considered one of the crown jewels of the intelligence industry for its production of electronic spying technologies for the CIA and the NSA. Under the leadership of CEO Terry Collins, Argon has emerged as one of the leading developers of command, control, communications, intelligence surveillance, and reconnaissance (C4ISR) for the military. "This is the fastest growing part of the Defense Department's budget," notes Collins, who estimates the C4ISR business as a $40 billion plus market.[69] Argon has seven hundred employees, a majority of whom hold Top Secret/Sensitive Compartmented Information (TS/SCI) clearances, one of the highest available.[70]

Argon had over $400 million in revenue in 2006, up from $80 million in 2003. It provides sensors and security equipment for NSA signals intelligence operations and is the dominant supplier of communications intelligence to the U.S. Navy, which accounts for 69 percent of Argon's revenues. The COMINT equipment it deploys in submarines is used by the Navy to "prosecute and exploit adversary electronic transmissions," the company says on its Web site. Argon also sells C4ISR equipment to the CIA, the DIA, and the National Reconnaissance Office, and in 2006 began testing equipment designed to counter IEDs in the battle-torn Iraq city of Fallujah. Its technology, Argon says, is deployed on "a broad range of military and strategic platforms," including surface ships, unmanned underwater vehicles, UAVs, and land mobile vehicles. Its largest overseas market is the United Kingdom, where it provides "highly interoperable systems" between U.K. and U.S. naval forces.

Argon has gone against the general trend of industry consolidation in intelligence. The origins of the company date back to the 1980s, when Collins, Argon's CEO and chairman of its board, was an engineer with a defense contractor called Engineering Research Associates, later called E-Systems. It was a dominant supplier of electronic surveillance and warfare systems to the CIA and the DIA, working on such classified projects as upgrading the P-3C antisubmarine patrol plane. E-Systems was acquired in 1996 by defense giant Raytheon, which "imposed a steely corporate environment" on the unit, according to an account in *Washington Technology*.[71] That didn't sit well with Collins and several other associates at the company, so they struck out on their own in 1997 to form Argon Engineering. In 2004, the company merged with a smaller company that developed SIGINT systems and sensors for the intelligence community and was renamed Argon ST. (It seems just a matter of time until Argon and the other pure plays are snatched up by one of the big defense contractors; as we've seen time and time again, small- to medium-sized companies that know how to make money in this business have a limited life as independent entities.)[72]

Most of Argon's board members are former executives with Raytheon E-Systems. But in recent years, Collins has brought in two prominent intelligence veterans to serve as directors. One of them, Peter Marino, is the chairman of the NGA's National Advisory Board and worked previously at E-Systems and the CIA, where he was director of the Office of Technical Services. Marino also sits on an intelligence task force of the Defense Science Board, a group of experts who provide technical advice to the Pentagon, and is co-chairman of the CIA's Senior Advisory Group. Another new Argon director, Maureen Baginski, worked twenty-six years for the NSA, where her jobs included lead analyst for the Soviet Union and SIGINT director. As we saw earlier, she is also affiliated with SI International and INSA.

As a result of appointments like these, Argon and its fellow pure plays are well placed to expand their business in the Intelligence Community. One area where their technology has been particularly useful is the analysis and interpretation by the NSA of the millions of telephone calls, e-mails, and Internet messages traveling through the U.S. communications system. That new form of communications intelligence and its close alliance with private sector telecommunications and IT providers is the subject of the next chapter.

9

The Rise of the National Surveillance State

TEN DAYS BEFORE Christmas in 2005, the *New York Times* ignited a political firestorm. In a front-page story that had been over fifteen months in the making, it revealed that the National Security Agency, under a secret directive signed by President Bush in October 2001, was monitoring thousands of international phone calls, e-mails, and fax messages involving U.S. persons without obtaining warrants from the secret foreign intelligence court established by Congress in 1978 to protect Americans from abuse by the Intelligence Community. Within twenty-four hours, President Bush confirmed the story, which up to that point was known only to a few administration officials and a handful of lawmakers allowed to share the nation's most secretive operations. In a live radio address from the White House, Bush explained that, in the aftermath of September 11, he had authorized the NSA to "intercept the international communications of people with known links to Al Qaeda and related terrorist organizations." He argued that the NSA's actions were legal under the considerable powers granted to him under the Constitution and the congressional resolution approving the use of force in Afghanistan and authorizing the president to take military action against the perpetrators of the 9/11 attacks.

Air Force General Michael Hayden, the deputy director of national intelligence and the former director of the NSA, made a highly unusual appearance at the National Press Club a few weeks later to reassure the public that the program was lawful and narrowly focused. "This is hot pursuit of communications entering or leaving America involving someone we believe is associated with Al Qaeda," he said, delivering a line that the NSA and the Bush administration stuck to with almost religious conviction for the next two years.[1] By January 2006, the program had been given a name: the Terrorist Surveillance Program. Between 2001 and 2007, Bush reauthorized the warrantless program more than thirty times, and finally ended it in January 2007, when U.S. Attorney General Alberto Gonzales announced that NSA surveillance would henceforth be returned to the supervision of the court established by the 1978 Foreign Intelligence Surveillance Act. The surveillance program, a Department of Justice lawyer disclosed during a 2007 court hearing on a privacy lawsuit against AT&T, remained classified at "the top secret/SCI level beyond those of top secret."[2]

Aside from the intrusive nature of the NSA's eavesdropping and wiretapping programs, the primary reason for the secrecy was the critical role played in NSA surveillance by the nation's largest telecommunications companies. Since the moment the NSA began listening in to telephone calls in which one party, whether in the United States or overseas, was suspected to be associated with Al Qaeda, carriers including AT&T and Verizon reportedly granted to the NSA complete access to their powerful switching systems that connect international telephone and Internet networks to the U.S. domestic communications system. This allowed the NSA to tap "directly into some of the American telecommunications systems' main arteries" carrying telephone conversations, e-mail communications, and Internet postings, *New York Times* reporters Eric Lichtblau and James Risen concluded in one of their lead stories on the NSA's intelligence-gathering program.[3] Thanks to Director of National Intelligence Mike McConnell, we now know this for a fact. In August 2007, McConnell disclosed what the administration and the industry had been trying to hide for seven years: that the private sector was deeply involved in the NSA's monitoring of domestic and international phone and Internet traffic. "Under the president's program, the terrorist surveillance program, the private sector has assisted us," McConnell declared in an interview with the *El Paso Times* during an intelligence conference in that city.[4] "Because if you're going to get access, you've got to have a partner."

McConnell's apparent motivation for breaching what had until then been considered a state secret was to make the case for giving the companies that assisted the NSA immunity from the more than two dozen lawsuits they faced for violating privacy laws and FISA. "Now if you play out the suits at the value they've claimed, it would bankrupt those companies," McConnell said. "So my position was we have to provide liability protection to these private sector entities." As this book was going to press, Congress was still debating McConnell's—and the Bush administration's—audacious request to grant after-the-fact immunity to the telecom giants. "Those in the private sector who stand by us in times of national security emergencies deserve thanks, not lawsuits," McConnell pleaded in December 2007 in an article strategically placed in the opinion section of the *New York Times*. He approvingly quoted the Senate Intelligence Committee, which had endorsed his proposal, and declared that the "possible reduction in intelligence that might result" from a delay in granting immunity "is simply unacceptable for the safety of our nation."[5] The nation's very security was at risk, he was saying. A month later, Vice President Cheney laid out the stakes for the administration. Without liability protection for the telecommunications companies, he told the Heritage Foundation, "our ability to monitor Al Qaeda terrorists will begin to degrade, and that we simply cannot tolerate."

But as Cheney, McConnell, and other top officials knew, the private sector's partnership with the NSA extended far beyond providing the government with access to their switches to the global communications system. For instance, some telecom companies also took a *proactive* role in the NSA's intelligence-gathering mission by expanding the universe of telephone calls and Internet traffic available to the agency. As mentioned earlier, one of the *Times*'s most important disclosures in 2005 was its discovery that the Bush administration, in order to "fully exploit" the technological capabilities of U.S. companies, had been quietly encouraging the telecommunications industry to increase the amount of international traffic it routed through American-based switches.[6] This single action brought many more international calls under NSA scrutiny and made it possible for the agency to monitor thousands of cell phone and Internet exchanges it might have otherwise missed. In September 2007, in fact, Admiral McConnell told Congress that the routing switches controlled by U.S. companies were carrying more than half of the global communications scooped up by the NSA's signals collection efforts. As a result, he argued, the NSA needed new FISA language lifting the requirement for FISA warrants on such traffic even when an American was at one end of the conversation. Without a change to FISA, the Intelligence Community would lose "50 percent of our ability to track, understand and know about these terrorists," he warned.[7] The Democratic-controlled Congress, concerned about its national security image, went along and, as we will see shortly, passed a temporary bill giving legal cover to the NSA's new ability to listen in on foreign-to-foreign communications passing through the United States.

A second form of cooperation that few Americans are aware of concerns the role of the telecom giants as *contractors* for the Intelligence Community. As commercial communications and encryption technologies advanced in the years leading up to 2001, AT&T, Verizon, and the other major carriers were hired by the government to build classified communications networks for the NSA and the Pentagon. That alliance spawned new institutions where the government could carry out a dialogue with these companies. Many industry executives, for example, hold leading positions in a secretive agency called the National Security Telecommunications Advisory Committee, a group of business leaders who meet regularly with President Bush, Vice President Cheney, and senior officials in the Intelligence Community to discuss critical issues affecting the national telecommunications system.

Finally, underneath the NSA-telco partnership are dozens of intelligence contractors, including most of the companies identified so far in this book, that provide outsourced information technology and analytical services to the NSA to help the agency analyze the calls and e-mails scooped up by its global surveillance network and sift through telephone data and calling patterns for clues to terrorist plots and other threats to national security. In the preceding chapter we saw what a handful of intelligence pure plays are capable of doing for the NSA; add the large systems integrators such as SAIC and Booz Allen Hamilton to the mix, and the result is a surveillance and eavesdropping system without peer in the world today. That broad alliance between the NSA and the government on one hand and the telecommunications and IT industries on the other is the fundamental issue at stake in the national debate that erupted around FISA in 2007 and 2008. That debate was about far more than a few telecom companies cooperating with the government. As the *Times* concluded in December 2007, almost two years to the day after they broke the story about the NSA's surveillance program, "At stake is the federal government's extensive but uneasy partnership with industry to conduct a wide range of secret surveillance operations in fighting terrorism and crime."[8] That "uneasy partnership and its implications for civil liberties" is the focus of this chapter.

The U.S. telecommunications industry is the world's largest and most advanced. It includes dozens of companies that compete with AT&T and Verizon for telephone and mobile services, as well as scores of Internet service providers such as Google, Yahoo!, and AOL that provide e-mail and Internet connections to customers around the world. Beneath them are the multinational conglomerates like Apollo, Flag Atlantic, and Global Crossing, which own and operate the global system of undersea fiber-optic cables that link the United States to the rest of the world. Any one of those companies and their U.S. subsidiaries could have been among the firms asked to cooperate with the NSA when President Bush issued his executive order authorizing surveillance without the FISA court's approval in 2001.* The potential liability, in other words, is huge.

---

* In searching through corporate statements on file with the Securities and Exchange Commission, for example, I found an intriguing notice from Viper Networks Inc., a California firm that allows subscribers to use its Internet service for what is called voice-over-Internet-protocol, or VOIP: "As a provider of telephone services, our company may be asked to provide information regarding our customer telephone records to the National Security Agency

"There's a pretty broad-based group of companies that take communications from overseas and transit them back," Albert Gidari, a partner in the Seattle law firm of Perkins Coie, whose clients include Google, Nextel Communications, and T-Mobile, told me. Although one company—Qwest Communications International—has admitted that it refused to go along with the NSA's request, Gidari said it did not act alone. "The list of those who said no is much longer than most people think," said Gidari, who was unwilling to provide further details.[9]

With the cooperation of a U.S. telecom provider, U.S. intelligence operatives could easily secure access to global transit traffic, Alan Mauldin, a senior research analyst with TeleGeography Research, a Washington firm that follows the global telecom industry, told me. "You could be inland, at an important city like New York or Washington, D.C., where networks interconnect, and you could have the ability to tap into the whole network for not only that city but between that city and the rest of the world," he said.[10] In addition, foreign-owned cable operators are required by U.S. law to maintain security offices manned by U.S. citizens at the landing sites in Oregon, Florida, New Jersey, and other states where fiber-optic cables come ashore.*

The NSA program that the *Times* unearthed in December 2005,

(NSA) and governmental agencies in connection with efforts taken by these agencies to fight the war against terror. In the event that we assist the NSA and other agencies in providing such information, we may be exposed to potential liability in violating the privacy rights of our customers. We may also face the loss of revenues and customer good will." See Section 10, Matter of National Security Agency and Potential Liability, FORM 10-KSB/A, Amendment No. 1, Viper Networks Inc. Annual Report for the fiscal year ending December 31, 2005, Commission File Number 0032939.

* That's because most of the world's cable operators are controlled by foreign corporations. Apollo, for example, is owned by Britain's Cable & Wireless, while Flag Atlantic is owned by the Reliance Group of India. Much of the international "transit traffic" carried by the cable companies flows through the United States (this is particularly true of communications emanating from South America and moving between Asia and Europe). In the old days of copper wires, the NSA could get access to this traffic by sending a submarine team to splice the cables in international waters, as it once did to the Soviet Union's undersea military cables. But that is an extremely expensive and difficult proposition with fiber optics, and politically dicey to boot—which is where the U.S. telecoms come in. "Cooperation with the telcos doesn't make NSA surveillance possible, but it does make it cheaper," Bruce Schneier, the founder and chief technology officer of Counterpane Internet Security, a California consulting firm, told me in a 2006 interview.

however, was a small piece of a massive program by the NSA and the Intelligence Community. During the two years that followed the *Times*'s initial revelations, two more programs came to light, one involving telephone databanks, and the other a direct link between the NSA and private Internet communications. Together, these three programs would provide the NSA with enough data to track the calling and messaging patterns of virtually every American with access to a telephone and a modem. We outlined those programs in chapter 6. Let's now study them in detail.

The databank program was disclosed by *USA Today* on May 11, 2006. It reported that the three largest U.S. telecommunications companies, AT&T, Verizon, and BellSouth (which has since merged with AT&T), turned over their vast customer call records to the NSA, allowing the agency to secretly collect information about "tens of millions of Americans" and store it for future analysis. That program reached "into homes and businesses across the nation by amassing information about the calls of ordinary Americans—most of whom aren't suspected of any crime," the newspaper said. *USA Today* concluded, based on interviews with industry officials, that the NSA's goal was "to create a database of every call ever made" within the nation's borders.[11] Although customer names, street addresses, and other personal information were not handed over, its sources said, the phone numbers could "easily be cross-checked with other databases to obtain that information."* After that story came out, I was told by a prominent industry consultant who founded one of the companies suspected of cooperating with the NSA that the NSA's ability to tap into these databases was the

* Seymour Hersh added more detail to the *USA Today* story in an article for *The New Yorker*. He was told by a security consultant that one carrier set up a "top-secret high-speed circuit between its main computer complex and Quantico, Virginia, the site of a government-intelligence computer center." The telecom companies, the consultant told Hersh, are "providing total access to all the data," allowing the NSA to get "real-time actionable intelligence." See Seymour M. Hersh, "The Talk of the Town: Listening In," *The New Yorker*, May 29, 2006. A 2006 lawsuit filed by public interest lawyers in New Jersey claims that the Quantico circuit was set up by Verizon. See Eric Lichtblau, James Risen, and Scott Shane, "Wider Spying Fuels Aid Plan for Telecom Industry," *New York Times*, December 16, 2007.

most significant part of the NSA's surveillance program. "These are the big market research databases," said the consultant, who asked not to be identified. "It's the scale and scope of this they don't want to disclose. They're looking at every single phone call record they can get their hands on for historical perspective, and looking for patterns and also in real time for intercepts." [12]

Most of what we know about the NSA's third program involving communications surveillance comes from Mark Klein, a former AT&T technician.[13] In 2006, he filed a detailed affidavit to support a lawsuit filed against AT&T by the Electronic Frontier Foundation, a privacy and civil rights organization based in San Francisco. At the time of 9/11, Klein was working in AT&T's Internet operations center in downtown San Francisco, which was an important hub for the World Wide Web in the Bay Area. "My job required me to enable the physical connections between AT&T customers' Internet communications and the National Security Agency's illegal, wholesale copying machine for domestic emails, Internet phone conversations, web surfing and all other Internet traffic," Klein told reporters during a press conference called by the foundation in November 2007 to oppose a bill before Congress backing retroactive immunity to the companies that cooperated with the NSA. "I have first-hand knowledge of the clandestine collaboration between one giant telecommunications company, AT&T, and the NSA to facilitate the most comprehensive illegal domestic spying program in history." [14] The NSA, Klein charged, "committed a massive violation not only of the law but of the Constitution. That's not the way the Fourth Amendment is supposed to work." [15]

Klein's first inkling of NSA activity came during the summer of 2002, about nine months after the surveillance program began, when an NSA official visited AT&T's offices in San Francisco. "What the heck is the NSA doing here?" Klein asked himself.[16] Over the next month, he and other employees learned that AT&T had built a secure office for the NSA in Room 641A at 611 Folsom Street, the site of a key AT&T facility. At first, Klein thought the NSA's secret room was linked to the Total Information Awareness project, the massive data mining effort started by the Pentagon shortly after 9/11. But he soon found out that the NSA project was much larger than even John Poindexter might have imagined.

In October 2002, Klein was shifted over to AT&T's Folsom Street facility, where the NSA's secret room was located. Klein assumed the agency was working out of the sixth floor, next to the telephone switching rooms where AT&T calls flowed through. To his surprise, the NSA operatives were on the seventh floor—right next to his Internet room. There, high-speed fiber-optic circuits were connected to AT&T's WorldNet Internet service, part of the company's common backbone network. From documents that had been left in the room, Klein told *Frontline,* the investigative news show produced by the Public Broadcasting System, he learned that AT&T had allowed NSA to connect a splitter cable from those circuits and divert a duplicate stream of AT&T's global Internet traffic to the secret room.

Klein also learned that the NSA analysts staffing the room were searching through the traffic with a Narus STA 6400, the most powerful piece of telecom and Internet monitoring equipment available on the world market. The Narus product can be programmed to identify and intercept voice or data communications between e-mail, telephone, or Internet addresses, and can track a communication's origin and destination as well as its content.[17] It is renowned in the industry for inspecting individual messages at extremely high rates of speed.[18] By 2002, many telecom companies had chosen the equipment to comply with court-ordered surveillance orders from domestic law enforcement. "The kind of systems we have give you a global view of what's happening on the Internet," Ori Cohen, Narus's founder and CEO, explained to *Fortune.* "They tell you who's logging in, at what time, and what they're doing online."[19]*

Upon learning about the NSA's use of the Narus equipment, Klein ex-

---

* Narus has close intelligence connections: one of its top executives is William Crowell, the former deputy director of the NSA under Mike McConnell. Ori Cohen, the Israeli technology entrepreneur who founded Narus, volunteered Narus's services to U.S. intelligence shortly after 9/11. According to *Fortune,* Cohen had several conversations with intelligence officials interested in using his products in the first month after the attacks. See Melanie Warner, "Web Warriors," *Fortune,* October 15, 2001.

perienced a sudden flash of insight. The NSA, he realized, had managed to download massive numbers of e-mails, financial transactions, and other communications flowing around the world on the global telecom system. "It dawned on me sort of all at once, and I almost fell out of my chair," he told *Frontline*. "My reaction was that from all the connections I saw, they were basically sweeping up, vacuum-cleaning the Internet through all the data, sweeping it all into this secret room. It was a government, many-tentacled operation to gather daily information on what everybody in the country is doing," including Web surfing, e-mail, and bank transactions. Peering into that traffic, he said, "sort of opens a window into your entire private life."[20] In his November 2007 press conference, he released documents showing other companies whose traffic AT&T carried; among them were Global Crossing and UUNet, an Internet provider in Virginia now owned by Verizon. When he saw that list, said Klein, he "flipped out. They're copying the whole Internet. There's no selection going on here. Maybe they select out later, but at the point of handoff to the government, they get everything."[21] (AT&T never flatly denied Klein's charges. In an appearance before the Ninth Circuit appeals court in San Francisco, however, AT&T attorney Michael Kellogg did his best to downplay the significance of Klein's documents. "At best what those materials do is, they speculate about what a certain configuration of equipment would be capable of doing," he said. "But they provide no indication of what is actually happening in the sealed room and what information is being turned over to the NSA as part of the alleged program." The arguments in the Electronic Frontier Foundation's case against AT&T were heard on August 15, 2007.)

Because the NSA programs are so highly classified, it's impossible to know how the agency used the data it obtained from the wiretaps, telephone databases, and Internet surveillance. Close observers of the intelligence business, however, believe that the NSA did in fact gain access to huge streams of domestic telephone calls and Internet traffic and used that data as the starting point for a massive data mining operation. "If there's one thing that Americans should know about this program, it's how extensive it was," says John Pike, who is one of the nation's foremost experts on intelligence. "What is stated publicly is that they are only listening to phone conversations where there is a known or suspected terrorist at the other end of the conversation. That's just not true. I think they're listening to everybody." By doing so, Pike says, the NSA and other counterterrorism agencies "are trying to detect thought crime; they are trying to detect pre-crime. They are attempting to disrupt. They're taking all of this call data and combining it with discount cards and every damn thing under the sun to try to winnow it to see if they can detect evildoers."[22]

The Bush administration has never admitted to such a broad policy. But former administration officials with close knowledge of intelligence operations in the aftermath of 9/11 have provided important clues about what the NSA was up to. In 2007, for example, John Yoo, one of the Department of Justice lawyers called upon by the White House to write the legal justifications for the Bush administration's war policies, told *Frontline* that the guidelines for NSA surveillance were written in a way to gain access to the entire stream of telecommunications moving through the United States, as opposed to individual snippets of conversation. That "entire stream" was then analyzed for patterns and relationships that might indicate a terrorist plot in the making.

In the war on terror, "the hard thing for our side is to identify where in that stream of civilian, innocent communications Al Qaeda members are disguising their messages to one another, trying to intercept those and find out what they mean," Yoo told *Frontline* interviewer Hedrick Smith.[23] "And so the government had to figure out how to tap into Al Qaeda's communications networks. We can't say, well, that line is the devoted line for Osama bin Laden to talk to his lieutenants, or we know they use that frequency, because they use the Internet, and they use cell phones and telephone calls just like you and I do." At that point, Smith, a former reporter with the *New York Times*, paused to ask: So does that mean that the government can "pull out the communications it wants, or does it have to have access to the entire flow?" Yoo was unequivocal: the government needed the entire flow.

"I think the government needs to have at least access to the flow;

even if it was going to enforce a warrant, it has to [have] access to the flow," he said. "There's not like a single wire you could get a warrant for and tap. In order to get Internet messages, you have to be able to dip into the flow of communications, because Internet communications are broken up." The same holds true for phone conversations. "What I think the government needs [is] to have access to international communication so it can try to find communications that are coming into the country where Al Qaeda is trying to send messages to the cell members in the country. In order to do this, it does have to have access to communication networks." And here, Yoo said, is where the number crunching comes in. Humans can't do the sifting alone: we "need to have computers to do it, where we have computers that are able to search through communications and are able to pluck out e-mails, phone calls that have a high likelihood of being terrorists' communications." What he was referring to were the dozens of companies that have been employed by the NSA and other government agencies to sift through the data collected from wiretaps and Internet surveillance.[24]

The NSA's interest in such data was first disclosed in February 2006 when *New York Times* technology reporter John Markoff reported that a small group of NSA officials had "slipped into Silicon Valley" that winter to meet with various companies and venture capital funds. They carried with them a "wish list" of technologies they hoped to obtain, including "computerized systems that reveal connections between seemingly innocuous and related pieces of information."[25] A year and a half later, the *Times* reported that the now famous 2003 confrontation between the White House and John Ashcroft's Justice Department over NSA operations involved the agency's use of "computer searches through massive electronic databases" that contained the records of tens of thousands of domestic phone calls and e-mails.*

We also know from press reports that the NSA passed on the in-

---

* Details about the dispute emerged in 2007 when Congress began to investigate the role of the Justice Department in the NSA surveillance program. One of the most dramatic confrontations was described to the Senate Judiciary Committee by John Ashcroft's former deputy James B. Comey. One night, as Ashcroft lay ill in an intensive care unit in George Washington University Hospital in Washington, D.C., Comey received word that Alberto

formation it gathered from its secret eavesdropping to the Defense Intelligence Agency, the FBI, the CIA, and the Department of Homeland Security.[26] These agencies, according to the *Washington Post,* then "cross-checked" the NSA information "with tips and information collected in other databases." Much of the DIA information, for example, was processed by the U.S. Northern Command, the domestic military command established in 2002. In some cases, DIA personnel inside the United States conducted physical surveillance of people or vehicles identified from NSA intercepts.[27]

That sharing would have greatly expanded the number of contractors with access to NSA data beyond the many companies—IBM, SAIC, CACI, and others—that were identified earlier as managing data for the NSA and the Intelligence Community. Consider, for example, the DIA bidding consortiums (also known as blanket purchase agreements) described in chapter 5. These consortiums, led by Booz Allen, CSC, Lockheed Martin, and other companies, are actually small armies of intelligence analysts that bid for work from the DIA, the NSA, and other intelligence agencies. The Booz Allen team was one of the largest, with ten thousand analysts holding top secret clearances, and was hired to conduct data mining and link analysis for both the NSA and the CIA, according to Booz Allen contract documents. It provides one example of how NSA data might have been used.

One member of the Booz Allen team, Attensity, was initially financed by In-Q-Tel. Its programs were particularly useful in analyzing

---

Gonzales and Andrew Card, President Bush's chief of staff, were on their way to the hospital to get Ashcroft's signature on a paper reauthorizing the NSA surveillance program. Comey was alarmed because he and Ashcroft had rejected the reauthorization; so he rushed over to the hospital, where he asked FBI director Robert Mueller to meet him. The four men all arrived at Ashcroft's bed at the same time. But when Gonzales asked Ashcroft to sign the document, he refused. According to Comey, Ashcroft "lifted his head off the pillow and in very strong terms expressed his view of the matter, rich in both substance and fact, which stunned me." The paper wasn't signed, and the program continued for several weeks without Department of Justice approval. President Bush finally intervened, and agreed to some changes suggested by Comey. Later, Ashcroft himself confirmed to the House Intelligence Committee that he had objected to certain aspects of the eavesdropping program. "It is very apparent to us that there was robust and enormous debate within the administration about the legal basis for the president's surveillance program," Silvestre Reyes, D-Texas, the committee's chairman, told reporters after the closed-door meeting with the former attorney general.

text traffic for suspicious patterns, Attensity CEO Craig Norris told a reporter in 2006. For example, "if a terrorist is planning a bombing, they might say, 'let's have a barbecue,' " said Norris. "The software can detect if the word 'barbecue' is being used more than usual."[28] (In 2006, Attensity formed a partnership with IBM, an important NSA contractor, to "help mutual customers derive more value from the complex, heterogeneous information spread across their IT systems.")[29] Another company on the Booz Allen team, Visual Analytics Inc., provides a specialized program that searches telephone call and video records to expose "underlying patterns and behaviors pertaining to security-related areas," according to its Web site. By obtaining this kind of intelligence, agencies can ensure that "decisive and pre-emptive actions can take place," the company claims.[30]

Meanwhile, Northrop Grumman's bidding consortium includes AT&T, ManTech International, and Cipher, which holds analysis contracts for the CIA's Directorate of Operations. Computer Sciences Corporation, the prime contractor for the NSA's Groundbreaker project to modernize the agency's internal communications system, manages a consortium that includes NSA contractors CACI and L-3 Communications. Any one of these companies would have been well equipped to analyze NSA signals, domestic or international.

The relationship between the NSA and the telecom industry dates back to World War II, during a time when global communications was in its infancy. This was when "surveillance, conducted under the auspices of national security, became an instrument of political power," Laura K. Donohue, a specialist on privacy laws at Stanford University, wrote in a 2006 study on government secrecy published by Northwestern University School of Law.[31] One such program was Operation Shamrock, a domestic surveillance program that was first uncovered in 1975 by the Senate Select Committee to Study Governmental Operations with Respect to Intelligence Activities, chaired by Idaho Democrat Frank Church. Shamrock was put in place by the predecessor to the NSA, the U.S. Army Signal Security Agency. In 1945, with the assistance of Secretary of Defense James Forrestal and the blessing of President Harry Truman, the agency persuaded three companies—RCA Communications, Western Union, and ITT World Communications—to hand over to the government information on all incoming and outgoing international telephone calls and telegrams. After some initial reluctance by their chief executives, all of them agreed to participate in the program after receiving assurances they would be exempt from criminal liability or public exposure. At RCA, which provided the "most complete cooperation,"[32] according to NSA historian James Bamford, the deal was simplified by the presence in the company's management team of Sydney Sparks, a former director of the War Department's Signal Center—an early example of the close ties that still exist between intelligence contractors, the telecommunications industry, and the government.[33]

By the 1970s, the NSA—which took over the spying operation in 1952—was selecting over 150,000 messages a month for its analysts to read.[34] In the 1960s, the communications companies had begun storing their cable traffic on magnetic tapes instead of hard copies. This development, said Bamford, allowed the NSA to make a "quantum leap forward in its ability to snoop."[35] Undeterred by the switch in technology, NSA couriers simply began picking up ten to twelve disks every morning in New York and transporting them by train or airplane to Fort Meade. There, the first Harvest computer so proudly displayed now at the NSA museum began what may have been the first use of data mining by the intelligence community.

"Once copied," Bamford wrote in *The Puzzle Palace,* "the tapes would be run through Harvest, which could be programmed to 'kick out' any telegram containing a certain word, phrase, name, location, sender or addressee, or any combination. It might be a name from a watch list, any message containing the word *demonstration,* or any cable to or from the Israeli UN delegation. In microseconds the full text of any telegram containing selected material could be reproduced. America's Black Chamber had suddenly gone from [Herbert O.] Yardley"—the U.S. spymaster who famously warned after World War I that "gentlemen don't read other people's mail"—"to [George] Orwell."[36]

The NSA quickly put these early data mining skills to use in another top secret program, called Minaret. In this operation, the FBI submitted names of U.S. citizens it viewed as security risks to the NSA, which provided the FBI with intelligence gleaned from its Shamrock program. This, too, was an early example of the information sharing between intelligence and law enforcement that has become routine since 9/11. The lists began with leftists and businessmen who had dealings with Cuba, but over time snowballed into a massive surveillance program of antiwar and civil rights activists. Among those on the FBI/NSA watch lists at the time were Dr. Martin Luther King, Jr., Jane Fonda, Joan Baez, Dr. Benjamin Spock, and the Reverend Ralph Abernathy.

Minaret was first exposed by the Church Committee. A few weeks after the initial revelation, CIA director William Colby appeared before a House committee chaired by Otis Pike, D-New York, that was working in tandem with Senator Church. At this hearing, according to Bamford, Colby "let slip the first public acknowledgement of the NSA's eavesdropping on international communications."[37] Minaret was subsequently killed by President Gerald R. Ford; but the companies that cooperated with the NSA weren't identified until Representative Bella Abzug, the pugnacious feminist from New York, stepped into the picture. As the Democratic chairman of the House subcommittee on government information, she decided to do what her fellow Democrats later tried, unsuccessfully, in 2006—call the companies to hearings. In what Bamford called "an extraordinary and unprecedented expansion of the doctrine of executive privilege," President Ford, under the advice of chief of staff Dick Cheney and Secretary of Defense Donald Rumsfeld, instructed the companies not to appear. But Abzug persevered, and the companies, starting with Western Union, made their way to Washington and the klieg lights of a House committee room. The vice president of Western Union turned over a list of NSA surveillance targets from the past eight years. The president of ITT World Communications testified in detail about how Shamrock worked. The corporate cat was finally out of the bag.

In 1976, Ford issued an executive order banning the NSA from intercepting domestic telephone calls and telegrams. Two years later, Congress passed FISA, the Foreign Intelligence Surveillance Act, limiting NSA to spying only on foreign powers or their agents, including groups "engaged in international terrorism or activities in preparation therefor." To begin surveillance on a "U.S. Person," as American citizens and foreigners living in the United States are called by the Intelligence Community, the government is supposed to apply to the FISA court for approval. In 1994, Congress amended the FISA statute to allow for warrantless physical searches, not just electronic intercepts, if the government is targeting premises, information, material, or property "used exclusively by or under the open and exclusive control of, a foreign power or powers."[38] That same year, Congress passed the Communications Assistance for Law Enforcement Act, known as CALEA, which requires telecom companies to grant the government special access to their communications systems for legal surveillance. As with FISA, warrants are required.

The history of telecom cooperation with the NSA is a guide to how the NSA went about winning cooperation from the industry in 2001. During the 1940s, when telephone and telegraph companies began turning over their call and telegram records to the NSA, only one or two executives at each firm were in on the secret. Essentially, the government raised the issue of patriotism with them, and the companies went along. That kind of arrangement continued into the 1970s, and is likely how cooperation with the NSA works today. "Once the CEO approved, all the contacts" with the intelligence agencies "would be worked at a lower level," Kenneth Bass, a former Justice Department official with the Carter administration, told me. "The telcos have been participating in surveillance activities for decades—pre-FISA, post-FISA—so it's nothing new to them." Bass, who helped craft the FISA law and worked with the NSA to implement it, added that he "would not be surprised at all" if cooperating executives received from the Bush administration "the same sort of briefing, but much more detailed and specific, that the FISA court got when [the surveillance] was first approved."[39]

The Bush administration's promises to the telcos were finally spelled out during a hearing on FISA before the Senate Judiciary Committee on

October 31, 2007. Kenneth L. Wainstein, an assistant attorney general testifying in favor of legislation to grant immunity to the industry, told the committee that "there were letters that went out to these companies that said very forcefully this is being directed, this is directed by the president, and this has been deemed lawful at the very highest levels of the government."[40] Three months later, as the Senate was debating a new FISA bill, Senator Jay Rockefeller, the chairman of the Senate Intelligence Community, declared that the telecom companies deserved immunity because they had received explicit orders from the NSA to cooperate with the warrantless surveillance program. The companies, he told *Politico,* were "pushed by the government, compelled by the government, required by the government to do this."[41] (That prompted Glenn Greenwald, a prominent critic of the NSA spying program and the administration's immunity bill, to respond in disgust. "Can someone please tell Jay Rockefeller that we don't actually live in a country where the President has the definitively dictatorial power to 'compel' and 'require' private actors to break the law by 'ordering' them to do so?" he wrote in his column for *Salon.* "Like all other lawbreakers, telecoms broke the law because they chose to, and profited greatly as a result.")[42]

In any case, AT&T and Verizon (which acquired telecom giant MCI in 2005) have a lot to offer U.S. intelligence officials looking for cooperation. In 2001, when the NSA domestic spying program began, AT&T's CEO was C. Michael Armstrong, the former CEO of Hughes Electronics Corporation, a major defense contractor. At the time, Armstrong was chairman of the Business Roundtable's Security Task Force, where he was instrumental in creating CEO COM LINK, a secure telecommunications system that linked the chief executives of major U.S. corporations with the Department of Homeland Security and the White House.*

* CEO COM LINK was first activated in 2002. It was part of a larger homeland security initiative involving the Business Roundtable and Booz Allen Hamilton that called for "public-private partnerships to play a major role in the overall defense against, and in response to, terrorism," according to documents I obtained from the Department of Homeland Security under the Freedom of Information Act. In 2003, the hotline was tested during a classified war

AT&T makes no bones about its national security work. When SBC was preparing to acquire the company in 2005, the two companies underscored their ties with U.S. intelligence in joint comments to the Federal Communications Commission. "AT&T's support of the intelligence and defense communities includes the performance of various classified contracts," the companies said, pointing out that AT&T "maintains special secure facilities for the performance of classified work and the safeguarding of classified information."[43] In another intelligence connection, David W. Dornan, who was AT&T's chairman and CEO at the time of the SBC merger, once sat on SAIC's board of directors, according to his official biography. Further signs of its role in U.S. intelligence are underscored by job placement ads placed by AT&T. In 2006, for example, AT&T was recruiting for "signals intelligence subject matter experts" with top secret clearances to work for the National Reconnaissance Office's support team at the U.S. Central Command.

At the same time, AT&T is part of a Northrop Grumman team that bids for classified work with the Defense Intelligence Agency, the NSA, and other intelligence agencies. The company also has extensive contracts on its own with the DIA, including experience in something called Intelligence Campaign Planning. A DIA publication explains that discipline as developing the "synchronization and integration of all sources of intelligence and information to include those from DoD and non-DoD agencies, law enforcement and multinational partners."[44] AT&T, in other words, is playing a key role in managing the sharing of intelligence across agencies, a key focus for U.S. intelligence policy in the aftermath of 9/11. In 2005, AT&T's Government Solutions unit an-

---

game in Washington attended by about seventy people from the top levels of government and business. The war game simulated a simultaneous terrorist attack on New York City and Chicago involving biological weapons. James Woolsey played a key role in the exercise as a "subject-matter expert" on terrorism, according to Booz Allen spokesman George Farrar. Afterward, Michael Armstrong of AT&T and the Business Roundtable crowed that the war game had established the "critical importance of rapidly linking the public and private sectors during a national crisis" and underscored CEO COM LINK's "value in enabling collaboration." If the exercise had been real, he said, it would have "saved hundreds of thousands of lives." No such system was ever built for first-responders or civilian aid organizations.

nounced that it had won a $14-million contract to provide engineering and installation work for the Pentagon's Global Information Grid, the cornerstone of the military's network centric warfare program; AT&T was a subcontractor to SAIC on the project.[45]

Verizon's MCI unit is a major government contractor and was highly valued by Verizon in part because of its work in defense and intelligence. Nicholas Katzenbach, the former U.S. attorney general who was appointed chairman of MCI's board after the spectacular collapse of its previous owner, WorldCom, reiterated MCI's intelligence connections in a 2003 statement to the Senate Judiciary Committee. "We are especially proud," he said, "of our role in supporting our national-security agencies infrastructure, and we are gratified by the many positive comments about our service from officials at the US Department of Defense and other national-security agencies."[46]

Verizon's general counsel—who would presumably have had a say in the company's decision to cooperate with the NSA—is William Barr. He is a former assistant general counsel at the Central Intelligence Agency, and served as attorney general during the administration of former President George H. W. Bush. In 2007, he was the leading figure in a telecommunications industry lobbying campaign to persuade Congress to grant immunity to the companies that cooperated with the NSA (another key figure in the campaign was AT&T senior executive vice president James Cicconi, who was the deputy chief of staff for George H. W. Bush).[47]

Verizon is the only one of the major telecommunications companies to admit that it provided customer call records to the federal government. In October 2007, three Democratic lawmakers on the House Energy and Commerce Committee, led by their chairman, John Dingell, D-Michigan, asked the telecom providers for records on their compliance with emergency orders issued by the Bush administration. Two companies, AT&T and Qwest, refused to provide any records. "If such information were to exist," Wayne Watts, AT&T's senior executive vice president and general counsel, wrote, AT&T could not lawfully provide it because the federal government "has formally invoked the state secrets privilege to prevent AT&T from either confirming or denying certain facts about alleged intelligence operations and activities that are central to your inquiries."[48]

But Verizon disclosed that it had responded 720 times between January 2005 and September 2007 to requests from the federal government for both phone data and Internet protocol records. Over that time, Verizon said it received 94,000 "lawful requests and demands for customer information" from federal, state, and local officials, including about 36,000 from the federal government.[49] The most detailed requests, Verizon said, came from the FBI, which used administrative subpoenas and National Security Letters—which are controversial because they require no probable cause and little judicial oversight—to seek private information from the company.

Some of the FBI's subpoenas and letters, Verizon said, contained "boilerplate" language directing the company to identify "calling circles" linked to certain telephone numbers "based on a two-generation community of interest" that would have given the FBI access to lists of Verizon customers and all the people they called. Those requests underscored the broad reach of telephone information that the government has been seeking since 9/11. This "community-of-interest data" is seen by the NSA and other agencies as critical to predicting and preventing terrorist attacks and is the first step in a key data mining technique known as link analysis. It can include analyses of which people suspects call most frequently, the time and length of their calls, and the geographic locations of the calling community.[50] As we have seen, the NSA, through its Advanced Research and Development Activity, has been funding research into social network and link analyses for some time.

Like AT&T, Verizon refused to comment about its involvement in the NSA's programs, telling the lawmakers that it had been informed by the Department of Justice that it "cannot confirm or deny Verizon's role (if any)" in the "classified counter-terrorism programs allegedly instituted in the wake of the September 11 attacks." But it explained that federal and state laws recognize that "criminals and terrorists may use our networks to discuss or implement their schemes and explicitly authorize Verizon"—through FISA and other statutory provisions—"to provide assistance to government entities in their law enforcement and counter-terrorism efforts." Moreover, Verizon's "business records may be of vital importance in investigations and in emergency situations to protect lives," the company said. FISA orders seeking such records, it added, "are classified documents and as such would be delivered by the government to Verizon personnel holding appropriate security clearances," and would contain "detailed and specific directions relating to the actions sought and their duration. Given their critical importance to national security, we would comply with such orders as expeditiously as possible."[51*]

As mentioned earlier, one of the most important national security tasks carried out by the telecommunications industry involves building classified computer and communications networks for the Pentagon and the Intelligence Community. These networks are discussed in a little-known institution in Washington called the National Security Telecommunications Advisory Committee (NSTAC). It is a group of executives from the communications and defense industries, all of whom hold security clearances, who advise the White House and senior government officials on security issues related to telecommunications. They meet at the White House once a year and hold quarterly meetings and conference calls with the Department of Homeland Security, the Office of the Director of National Intelligence, and other government agencies.

Prominent members of the committee, as of 2007, included Randall Stephenson, AT&T's chairman and CEO, who is the vice chairman of the committee; Ivan G. Seidenberg, the chairman and CEO of Verizon; and Stanley Sigman, the president and CEO of AT&T subsidiary Cin-

---

* Comcast, one of the nation's largest Internet service providers, provided further clues about how telecommunications companies comply with FISA in a company handbook published in September 2007. Comcast charges the government $1,000 for an "initial start-up fee" and the first month of intercept service for any FISA surveillance "requiring deployment of an intercept device," the handbook states. After the first month, the fee drops to $750 per month "for each subsequent month in which the original [FISA] order or any extensions of the original order are active." The handbook also says that Comcast complies with disclosure demands presented in the form of National Security Letters. The handbook was obtained by *Secrecy News* and posted on its Web site at www.fas.org/blog/secrecy/docs/handbook.pdf.

gular Wireless. In addition, four of the NSA's most important contractors were also represented on the board: Ken Dahlberg, the chairman and CEO of SAIC, a former top executive at General Dynamics and Hughes Aircraft, Van B. Honeycutt, the chairman of Computer Sciences Corporation, which in 2007 won a three-year extension to its Groundbreaker contract with the NSA; Daniel J. Carroll, the president and CEO of Telecordia Technologies, an SAIC subsidiary that developed key data mining technologies for the NSA; and Arthur E. Johnson, the senior vice president of strategic development for Lockheed Martin, the world's largest defense and intelligence contractor.

In 2006 and 2007, the NSTAC was addressed by both President Bush and Vice President Cheney. Asked if the NSA surveillance was ever discussed at these sessions, spokesman Stephen Barrett told me in an e-mail: "we do not participate in intelligence gathering." Nevertheless, high-level intelligence officials are often in attendance at these meetings and are frequently asked to address the group. An NSTAC meeting on April 26, 2007, at the Washington headquarters of the U.S. Chamber of Commerce, for example, was addressed by DNI Mike McConnell as well as Air Force Lieutenant General Charles Croom, the director of the Defense Information Systems Agency, and Prescott Winter, the NSA's chief technology officer, according to minutes posted on the NSTAC Web site.

Other meetings of the NSTAC in recent years were addressed by John Negroponte, McConnell's predecessor as DNI; Dale Meyerrose, the associate director of national intelligence; and Brian Shaw, the National Intelligence Council's deputy national intelligence officer for science and technology. The committee's first meeting after 9/11, which took place on March 12 and 13, 2002, was addressed by three of the Bush administration's top security officials: Deputy Secretary of Defense Paul Wolfowitz, Secretary of State Colin Powell, and National Security Adviser Condoleezza Rice. The session included a discussion titled "September 11 Lessons Learned," led by Joseph DeMauro, Verizon's vice president for the state of New York, and Kevin Lynch, vice president, AT&T Network Services. Although the details of these meetings are classified, the existence of the committee and the frequency of its interactions with senior intelligence officials illustrate the web of secret relationships between government and industry behind the U.S. telecommunications system. And according to the former chairman of the committee, former Qwest CEO Joseph P. Nacchio, telecom executives involved at that level of national security are often asked to participate in highly classified activities, including the NSA's surveillance programs.

At the time of 9/11, Nacchio was the chairman of the NSTAC. Shortly after the attacks, he was asked, along with other telecom companies, to provide the NSA with access to the private telephone records of his customers with the aim of locating and tracking terrorist suspects and preventing future attacks. But Nacchio, in contrast to executives from AT&T and Verizon, refused; according to a statement released by company lawyers in 2006, when Nacchio learned that no legal authority for the request had been granted "and that there was a disinclination on the part of the authorities to use any legal process, including the Special [FISA] Court which had been established to handle such matters." Nacchio concluded that "these requests violated the privacy requirements of the Telecommunications Act."[52] Nacchio left Qwest in 2006 after being charged with nineteen counts of insider trading on Qwest stock that took place in the spring of 2001. In the fall of 2007, while appealing his April 2007 conviction on those charges, Nacchio and his attorneys released further details of his relationship with the NSA. The documents, which were heavily redacted by the appeals court, were made public in October 2007 at the request of the *Denver Post* and have added significant new details to the story of the NSA's ties with the telecom industry, both prior to and after 9/11.*

Qwest's ties with U.S. intelligence apparently date back to 1997, when Nacchio and Dean Wandry, his director for government sales, were asked to meet with a "three-star lieutenant general" working for

* I attempted to interview Nacchio in January 2008. My request was turned down by his appeals attorney, Maureen Mahoney.

an unnamed government agency that was running "the largest telecom operation in the world." Although that general is not identified in the redacted documents, a contextual analysis tells us he was probably the director of the NSA, who at the time was retired Air Force General Kenneth Minihan* (by law, the NSA director must be a three-star general or a vice admiral; at the same time, the NSA's global communications network is known to be the largest one in the U.S. government and one of the largest in the world). After hearing from Nacchio about the capabilities of Qwest's commercial networks, "the general" told the Qwest executives that he wanted to use their networks "for government purposes." He later informed Nacchio that "there was a big opportunity" for Qwest and asked Nacchio to obtain a security clearance, which he did. Qwest was subsequently awarded a major contract to build a government communications system in 1999.[53]

By early 2001, the NSA (now identified in the document by name) had a project it wanted to discuss with Qwest—Project Groundbreaker, that massive project described earlier that involved the outsourcing of the NSA's internal, non-mission-critical communications systems. Qwest's proposed portion of Groundbreaker apparently consisted of a $50-million to $100-million opportunity to construct a fiber-optic network for the agency. "The contemplated work was similar to what Qwest had already done for" the U.S. government, Nacchio's attorney wrote in his brief. By this time, Qwest was a member of the Computer Sciences Corporation team that eventually won the prime contract for Groundbreaker. As a member of the CSC team, according to the affidavit, Nacchio met with NSA officials at Fort Meade on February 27, 2001, to discuss Qwest's role as a subcontractor.

Nacchio now claims that he was asked at that meeting to provide to the NSA information about Qwest customers and the traffic moving across his network. That is a significant admission: it indicates that, only a month into the Bush administration, U.S. intelligence officials were making inquiries to the industry about their possible participation

* Minihan, who is a partner with the Paladin Capital Group, did not respond to several requests to be interviewed for this book.

in eavesdropping operations. Shane Harris, who covers the NSA for the *National Journal,* partially confirmed Nacchio's account in November 2007. According to a former White House intelligence official quoted by Harris, the NSA wanted Qwest to build a "private version of Echelon," the signals intelligence system developed in the 1990s by the NSA and its counterparts in the U.K., Canada, Australia, and New Zealand. Such a system, the former official said, would have allowed the agency to use Qwest's network to "watch for computer hackers and foreign-government forces trying to penetrate and compromise US government information systems." The NSA "in effect wanted Qwest to be the agency's online eyes and ears," Harris concluded.[54] But Nacchio rejected the request, citing the same privacy concerns that he offered after 9/11.*

At the time of his meetings with the NSA, Nacchio was optimistic about his company's prospects. According to his affidavit, he walked out of the meeting with NSA "thinking that the NSA $50–$100 million opportunity [in Groundbreaker] remained viable."[55] But that optimism—along with Qwest's stock—sank in 2002 when the NSA awarded the contract to another unnamed company, according to Nacchio's documents. (By disclosing that information to the court, the *Denver Post* concluded, "Nacchio wanted to show that he didn't sell Qwest stock illegally in early 2001 and that he was upbeat about Qwest's stock because he had top-secret information that the company would win lucrative government contracts.")[56] Nacchio never got the chance to air his claims in open court, however. In December 2006, U.S. District Judge Edward Nottingham ruled that the "inference of a causal connection be-

---

* The *New York Times* added a few new details to the Qwest story in December 2007. According to reporters Eric Lichtblau, James Risen, and Scott Shane, the NSA informed Qwest in early 2001 that it wanted to install monitoring equipment on Qwest's "most localized communications switches," which carried primarily domestic calls but also offered access to "limited international traffic." The NSA, the *Times* said, "intended to single out only foreigners on Qwest's network." But Nacchio, believing that the arrangement "could have permitted neighborhood-by-neighborhood surveillance of phone traffic without a court order," rejected the request. The NSA concluded that Nacchio and other company officials misunderstood its proposals. See Eric Lichtblau, James Risen, and Scott Shane, "Wider Spying Fuels Aid Plan for Telecom Industry," *New York Times,* December 16, 2007.

tween Mr. Nacchio's refusal [to cooperate with the NSA] and the fact that Qwest didn't end up with the [Groundbreaker] contract is extremely weak" and therefore inadmissible.[57] After Nacchio's documents were unsealed by the court in October 2007, government attorneys further undercut Nacchio's arguments by filing their own papers. According to their affidavit, Qwest "was not 'left off' the list of subcontractors for the Groundbreaker project" and was one of dozens of contractors included in the Eagle Alliance, the contractor coalition put together by CSC.[58] Their finding "only strengthens the court's conclusion" that Nacchio's arguments lacked merit, the prosecutors said.[59] But it left many journalists and observers convinced that the close ties between the NSA and the telecommunications industry were forged long before the events of September 11, 2001.

The CSC/Qwest team, which also included General Dynamics, Verizon, TRW, and Northrop Grumman, was one of three consortiums that bid for Project Groundbreaker. The others were led by AT&T, which was allied with IBM, Lockheed Martin, and SAIC, and OAO Corporation, an intelligence contractor acquired in December 2001 by Lockheed Martin, which was allied with Raytheon, WorldCom (later acquired by MCI), ManTech, and Electronic Data Systems. As part of the bidding process, which lasted more than two years, all of these companies would have met, as Qwest did, with the NSA and been provided with classified contract information available to every other executive on a bidding team with a security clearance. And once the contract was awarded, CSC, Qwest, and their partners in the Eagle Alliance would have had access to classified information about the NSA's signals intelligence programs.*

* The extent of the information provided to the Groundbreaker bidders was revealed in 2005 by Wayne Madsen, a Washington-based investigative journalist who once worked for the NSA. That May, Madsen reported in his newsletter, he obtained a copy of an NSA contract document from 2002 that showed how Groundbreaker "allowed the Eagle Alliance and other contractors to gain access to and even virtual control over some of the most sensitive systems within the U.S. intelligence community." According to Madsen, the document showed that some ten thousand Windows NT and Unix workstations and servers that handled the NSA's highly classified SIGINT and electronic intelligence applications, including databases that contained communications intercepts, were "firmly in the grasp of the Eagle

• • •

Nacchio's documents about Qwest's ties with the NSA, and the fact of the existence of the bidding consortiums themselves, illustrate the depth of the NSA's ties with industry. They also help explain how discussions of classified communications systems prior to 9/11 could have led, almost seamlessly, to administration requests for cooperation on secret programs such as the Terrorist Surveillance Program. But most importantly, they provide the context in which the Bush administration and the Intelligence Community began their legislative offensive to rewrite the Foreign Intelligence Surveillance Act to make domestic spying easier and provide retroactive immunity to the corporations who aided in their wiretapping efforts.

The president's bill, which he called the Protect America Act (PAA), was introduced shortly after the FISA court made its first-ever ruling against the NSA. After Bush returned his initial surveillance program back to the jurisdiction of the FISA court in January 2007, the NSA reportedly began asking for "basket warrants" that encompassed multiple targets, as opposed to FISA warrants on individuals that were issued on a case-by-case basis. Some of these warrants were approved; but at some point in the spring of 2007, a judge on the FISA court ruled that the practice violated FISA and was therefore illegal. House Minority Leader John A. Boehner, R-Ohio, disclosed the secret ruling in an interview with *Fox News,* saying that the decision prohibited "the ability of our intelligence services and our counterintelligence people from listening in to two terrorists in other parts of the world where the communication could come through the United States."[60] Despite the security breach, the administration leaped at the chance to use the ruling to its advantage. As long as the FISA ruling stood, McConnell warned, U.S. spy agencies were miss-

---

Alliance." The document, Madsen said, called for the consortium to establish a SIGINT Applications Office to "provide and maintain Information Technology services, tools, and capabilities for all SIGINT mission applications at the NSA." Those details, he concluded, were "a far cry from the non-operational administrative support functions originally specified in the Groundbreaker contract." See Wayne Madsen, "The Neocon Power Grab at NSA and an Attempt to Stifle the Press," *OnLineJournal.com,* May 24, 2005, at http://cryptome.org/nsa-stifle.htm.

ing "a significant portion of what we should be getting." That included, he said (erroneously as it turned out), cell-phone communications between Iraqi insurgents that happened to cross the U.S. phone system.

Faced with the possibility of being labeled "soft on terrorism," congressional Democrats agreed in August 2007 to temporarily expand the ability of the NSA to eavesdrop, without warrants, on telephone calls, e-mail and faxes passing through telecommunications hubs in the United States. They also provided legal cover to the pipelines to the Internet and the global phone system made available to the NSA by the telecom industry. As James Risen explained in the *New York Times,* the new law allowed the NSA to eavesdrop without warrants "by latching on to" giant telecommunications switches located in the United States "as long as the target is 'reasonably believed' to be overseas. For example, if a person in Indianapolis calls someone in London, the [NSA] can eavesdrop on that conversation without a warrant, as long as the NSA's target is the person in London."[61]* In addition, Congress approved an amendment that cut the secretive FISA court out of decisions involving the NSA's monitoring of communications entering the United States but involving foreigners subject to national security investigations. That power was transferred from the court to the Director of National Intelligence and the Attorney General.†

---

* The key provision, Section 105A, reads as follows: "Notwithstanding any other provision of this Act, a court order is not required for the acquisition of the contents of any communication between persons that are not located within the United States for the purpose of collecting foreign intelligence information, without respect to whether the communications passes through the United States or the surveillance device is located within the United States."

† As the bill was being debated, Jim Dempsey of the Center for Democracy and Technology told me that most civil libertarians, including himself, supported legislation to allow the NSA to intercept foreign-to-foreign communications traveling through the United States without a warrant. "In my reading of FISA, I don't see how that is covered by FISA," he said. "That issue is off the table." But the problem came when the administration insisted on language that excluded warrants for calls that were foreign to domestic. "They want to eliminate the warrant requirement for listening to the communications of U.S. citizens with parties overseas," said Dempsey. "That fact that they aren't targeting me is small consolation when they're listening to my communications and falsely believe I'm a terrorist. So they claim to be targeting a foreigner and they are genuinely targeting the foreigner, but they will use the information against an American. So an American's rights are in jeopardy." I interviewed Dempsey in August 2007.

The FISA bill drew sharp criticism from legal scholars. Martin S. Lederman, a former attorney in the Department of Justice's Office of Legal Counsel from 1994 to 2002 and a professor of law at the University of Michigan, blasted the legislation for deleting a key provision in FISA—that foreign intelligence could only be gathered in the United States against agents of a foreign power and suspected terrorists. Under the FISA exemptions approved by Congress, he wrote shortly after the bill was passed, "there is no requirement that [surveillance] be conducted outside the U.S.; no requirement that the person at whom it is 'directed' be an agent of a foreign power or in any way connected to terrorism or other wrongdoing." If the law was read literally, he added, "it would exclude from FISA any surveillance that is in some sense 'directed' *both* at persons overseas *and* at persons in the U.S." [62] In other words, United States persons could easily get caught in the NSA dragnet.

As this book neared completion, the Bush administration, led by Vice President Cheney and Admiral McConnell, were pressing Congress to make the Protect America Act permanent (it was set to expire on February 1, 2008) with two additional measures: a ban on lawsuits against telecommunications and other companies for giving the government access to information, including customer phone records, in connection with the NSA's surveillance program, and immunity from civil and criminal liability for any persons and companies "alleged to have cooperated" with the program. They also asked that all legal cases regarding NSA surveillance—including lawsuits—be removed from the federal court system and heard only in the secret FISA court. If enacted, the proposals would represent "the most significant change to the (FISA) statute since its enactment in 1978," Senator Rockefeller declared when the package was proposed (he ended up supporting the immunity request and, after his committee approved it by a slim majority, introduced the president's bill on the Senate floor).[63]

From the moment the immunity measure was debated on Capitol Hill, the industry, which had kept a low profile during earlier debates about FISA, began a furious, behind the scenes lobbying campaign. Without retroactive protection, AT&T, Verizon, and other companies feared they would be forced to terminate their partnership with the Intelligence Community, losing millions of dollars in revenue (the partnerships aren't free, after all) and millions more in fines for violating FISA and privacy laws if the courts found the program was illegal—a distinct possibility. "It's not an exaggeration to say the U.S. intelligence community is in a near-panic about this," an industry lawyer told *Newsweek*, which broke the story of the lobbying initiative.[64]* But due to strong opposition from a handful of Democrats, including Senators Christopher Dodd of Connecticut and Russ Feingold of Wisconsin, neither the industry nor the administration was able to convince a majority of the Senate to vote their way. If that stalemate continues past mid-February, when the Protect America Act (under a fifteen-day extension passed by Congress on January 31) expires, the NSA and its industry allies will have to revert back to FISA as it existed before October 2001, when Bush and Cheney decided to circumvent the law and proceed with electronic surveillance without warrants. To many observers, that was a much safer alternative than the new bill.

The bitter debate about FISA badly damaged Admiral McConnell's reputation in Congress. Lawmakers who negotiated with the former admiral accused him of exaggerating the amount of actionable intelligence that was being missed without the new law and of withdrawing, with-

---

* Telecom companies also began directing campaign money to key lawmakers, such as Senator Rockefeller of the Intelligence Committee. Starting in the spring of 2007, executives at AT&T and Verizon contributed more than $42,000 in political donations to the West Virginia Democrat, according to a report that first appeared in *Wired* magazine. Most of the money was raised at a Verizon fund-raiser in New York and an AT&T fund-raiser in San Antonio. Although it represented a fraction of the $3.1 million the senator raised in total during the year, it marked a significant break from the past for the telecom providers: prior to 2007, *Wired* pointed out, "contributions to Rockefeller from company executives at AT&T and Verizon were mostly non-existent." By the end of October, after reading the administration's secret legal documents about the NSA program, Rockefeller decided to back the White House and the industry, and agreed to the immunity provision (his aides scoffed at the idea that the senator from one of the wealthiest families in America "would make policy decisions based on campaign contributions"). See Ryan Singel, "Democratic Lawmaker Pushing Immunity Is Newly Flush with Telco Cash," *Wired*, October 18, 2007, http://blog.wired.com/27bstroke6/2007/10/dem-pushing-spy.html; and Eric Lichtblau and Scott Shane, "Companies Seeking Immunity Donate to Senator," *New York Times,* October 23, 2007.

out explanation, administration offers that the Democrats thought they had agreed to. They also came to believe that McConnell was purposely exaggerating the potential dangers of keeping FISA as it was ("You won. But you did so at a substantial price, one that will be paid in rancor, suspicion, and distrust," Senator Sheldon Whitehouse of Rhode Island wrote him during the summer recess in 2007, after Congress passed the president's bill.[65]) But throughout the discussions, McConnell insisted that the NSA's surveillance programs had been instrumental in preventing further terrorist attacks. During one hearing early in his tenure, McConnell was asked by Christopher "Kit" Bond, R-Missouri, the vice chairman of the Senate Intelligence Committee, to delineate the importance of FISA. McConnell replied by looking back over his past eleven years in the intelligence industry. When he left the NSA in 1996 for Booz Allen Hamilton, he said, FISA surveillance was "almost insignificant." But after only ten weeks on the job as director of national intelligence, he could "immediately see the results of FISA-authorized collection activity," he said. "I cannot overstate how instrumental FISA has been in helping the intelligence community protect the nation."[66]

Months later, with the Senate deadlocked on the immunity bill, McConnell wrote a letter to Bond describing how the changes to FISA over the summer had helped the Intelligence Community. According to the DNI, "PAA collection activities" had provided the NSA and other agencies with a plethora of information about terrorist activities, including planned attacks, efforts by individuals to become suicide bombers, instructions about illegally entering the United States, plans to travel to Europe and disguise their appearances, as well as attempted money transfers and "movements of key extremists to evade arrest." "The IC must continue to collect information of this nature if we are to stay ahead of terrorist and other threats to the United States," McConnell concluded.[67]*

But over the course of the year, McConnell began adding a new wrinkle to the Bush administration's proposals to expand FISA. The old

---

* McConnell knew as well as anyone that the NSA surveillance had roped in quite a few innocent Americans. In a stunning 2008 revelation in *The New Yorker,* journalist Lawrence Wright confronted the DNI with evidence that his phones had been tapped in the course of writing his popular history of Al Qaeda, *The Looming Tower.* The FBI, he told McConnell,

law, he explained in May 2007, had mechanisms so the NSA could obtain a court order directing a communications carrier to assist the government in electronic surveillance. But it didn't provide "a comparable mechanism with respect to authorized communications intelligence activity." And here he made an interesting statement. The new legislation, he said, should provide the government with means to obtain the aid of a court "to ensure private-sector cooperation with lawful intelligence activities and ensure protection of the private sector."

What McConnell, the Intelligence Community, and the Bush administration seemed to be proposing was a new system that would allow the government *to use the telecommunications system itself for intelligence and surveillance.* They wanted a permanent alliance between the most powerful elements of the state—the U.S. intelligence enterprise—and all U.S. companies with the means to tap the world phone and Internet system. The full implications were finally spelled out by Vice President Cheney in his speech to the Heritage Foundation on the eve of a 2008 congressional vote on the FISA bill. "We're dealing here with matters of the utmost sensitivity," Cheney said in the slow, chilling cadence that has become his trademark. "It's not even proper to confirm whether any given company provided assistance. But we can speak in general terms. The fact is, the Intelligence Community doesn't have the

---

had come to his house in Austin, Texas, to ask about some of his calls. And he knew he'd been monitored because a source in the Intelligence Community had read him "a summary of a telephone conversation that I had from my home with a source in Egypt." When McConnell countered that Wright may have been bugged because he got a call from a number "associated with some known outfit," Wright shot back: "Actually I had made that call." A similar experience happened to Wendell Belew, a Washington, D.C., attorney for the Al-Haramain Islamic Foundation, an Islamic charity based in Saudi Arabia. In 2003, Belew learned from an NSA document obtained by his lawyers as part of a lawsuit that he had been subject to NSA surveillance sometime after 2001. The document, according to the lawsuit Belew and others filed against the NSA, "represented an account of a conversation between myself and other attorneys and clients in Saudi Arabia," he told me. Al-Haramain was apparently targeted in connection with the Treasury Department's designation of the charity as an Al Qaeda sympathizer (which the charity denies); but Belew, the former Democratic counsel to the House Budget Committee, hardly fits McConnell's definition of a national security threat. Al-Haramain's lawsuit against the NSA is the one case that may lead the courts to declare the warrantless program illegal; as of this writing, the case was still very much alive. For Wright's disclosure, see his article, "The Spymaster," *The New Yorker,* January 21, 2008. I interviewed Belew in 2007.

facilities to carry out the kind of international surveillance needed to defend this country since 9/11. In some situations, there is no alternative to seeking assistance from the private sector. This is entirely appropriate." This way of thinking marked a qualitative change from the old regime, which respected the Constitution and merely asked private companies for technical assistance in the legal monitoring of telephone calls and e-mails. The system envisioned by McConnell and Cheney is a new kind of private-public partnership, operating in secret and beyond the reach of the law—and has laid the groundwork for what has become a massive system of domestic surveillance.

On October 23, 2007, a U-2 photoreconnaissance aircraft lifted off the runway at Beale Air Force Base in California, the home of the U.S. Air Force 9th Reconnaissance Wing and one of the most important outposts in the U.S. Intelligence Community. Known as the Dragon Lady, the U-2 was originally built in secret by Lockheed Corporation for the Central Intelligence Agency. It has provided some of the most sensitive intelligence available to the U.S. government, including thousands of photographs of Soviet and Chinese military bases, North Korean nuclear sites, and war zones from Southeast Asia to the Middle East. Hours later, a second aircraft—the unmanned drone known as the Global Hawk—was launched from the same base. Developed by the Defense Advanced Research Projects Agency during the 1990s, the U.S. fleet of Global Hawks was built for the Air Force by Northrop Grumman and has been deployed in foreign skies almost continuously since September 11, 2001. Currently, Global Hawks are used extensively for combat and surveillance missions in Iraq and Afghanistan.

But the U-2 and Global Hawk that went airborne that day weren't headed overseas to collect foreign intelligence or to spy on Al Qaeda and its affiliated fighting units in the Middle East and South Asia. Instead, their destination was the skies over Southern California, which had been filled for the last two days with smoke and ash from one of the worst forest fires to hit the state in its history. The U-2 recorded high-resolution photographs of the damage, and the Global Hawk, which was on its first-ever domestic mission, captured infrared images to give state and federal emergency crews the ability to predict the direction of the fires and determine where the calamity was most intense.[68] The next day, as the photos and images were processed, they were compared to commercial imagery produced by the National Geospatial-Intelligence Agency, which had been working with the Federal Emergency Management Agency on recovery efforts since President Bush declared the fires a major disaster and named FEMA the lead federal agency for the government's response. The NGA, the nation's newest intelligence agency, also had analysts working around the clock deployed to FEMA's Joint Field Office in Pasadena, California, and could draw on its domestic imagery teams permanently assigned to the Department of Homeland Security and the U.S. Northern Command in Colorado.[69]

The role of one of the nation's most powerful intelligence agencies in the California fires received little attention outside of a few military and space publications. On one level, the engagement of the agency, as well as the U-2 and Global Hawk flights over U.S. territory, were commendable efforts to use America's vast surveillance powers for the safety and security of its citizens. But at the same time, the incident symbolized a new period in American history when U.S. intelligence agencies created to spy on foreign countries are being deployed to collect information on the United States homeland during domestic crises. It comes on top of a series of intelligence operations mounted within the continental United States since September 11, 2001. Those operations, as we've seen in this book, include the NSA wiretapping programs and the construction of its cyber-pipeline into telephone customer databases and the Internet; the Pentagon's extensive monitoring of domestic threats through the Counterintelligence Field Activity office and NORTHCOM; and the employment of companies such as IBM, SAIC, CACI, and ManTech to apply data mining techniques to the vast collection of information on U.S. and foreign citizens compiled by the NSA, CIFA, the Defense Intelligence Agency, and other sectors of the Intelligence Community. Taken collectively, these efforts have created a national surveillance net that has fostered a deep unease in the body politic about the new domestic powers of U.S. intelligence.

Sometime in 2008, the relationship between the Intelligence Community and homeland security will take a critical leap forward when the Bush administration puts in place a plan to allow the NSA, the NGA, the DIA, and the National Reconnaissance Office to share classified signals intelligence, imagery, and measurement and signatures intelligence from military spy satellites with federal and local law enforcement agencies. Under a program that was approved in May 2007 by the Office of the DNI and the Department of Homeland Security, a new office called the National Applications Office (NAO) will be established within DHS as a buffer between the spy agencies and the domestic security apparatus. Admiral McConnell has been involved in the program since its inception: while he was still working for Booz Allen Hamilton in the spring of 2005, his company contracted with the ODNI to manage a study about how foreign and domestic intelligence could be better integrated. The study team concluded that there was "an urgent need for action because opportunities to better protect the homeland are being missed." It was directed by Keith Hall, a vice president of Booz Allen who once directed the NRO.[70]

According to a Homeland Security fact sheet, the NAO will provide to federal and local agencies "more robust access" to "remote sensing information" as well as "the collection, analysis, and production skills and capabilities of the intelligence community."[71] Charles Allen, the veteran intelligence officer at DHS who was designated to run the office, explained to reporters that the NAO was a natural response to the terrorist attacks of 2001. "The view after September 11 was that we ought to move this to Homeland Security and broaden the domain," he said. "These systems are already used to help us respond to crises. We anticipate that we can also use it to protect Americans by preventing the entry of dangerous people and goods into the country, and by helping us examine critical infrastructure for vulnerabilities."[72]

Many lawmakers and civil liberties advocates are leery about the new office and the growing integration of foreign and domestic intelligence. "It will terrify you if you really understand the capabilities of satellites," Jane Harman, a leading figure on the House Intelligence Committee, said in September 2007, after word of the McConnell plan was leaked to the *Wall Street Journal*. Harman represents a coastal area of Los Angeles where many of the nation's satellites are built (she once referred to her California district as "the intelligence satellite capital of the universe"[73]) and is acutely aware of the power of classified military spy satellites, which are far more flexible, offer greater resolution, and have considerably more power to observe human activity than commercial satellites operated by the U.S. companies GeoEye and DigitalGlobe. Even if the Bush administration could set up a program with the proper legal framework, she warned in a House hearing on the McConnell plan, the possibility exists for serious misuse. "Even if this program is well-designed and executed someone somewhere else could hijack it," she said.[74] Kate Martin, the director of the Center for National Security Studies, a nonprofit advocacy organization, has likened the plan to "Big Brother in the Sky." The Bush administration, she said, is "laying the bricks one at a time for a police state."[75] We'll return to the NAO and its corporate promoters later. For now, let's consider some of the political implications for what legal scholars are now calling a national surveillance state.

That ominous-sounding term was coined by two law professors, Jack M. Balkin and Sanford V. Levinson, who teach at Yale Law School and the University of Texas School of Law respectively and contribute to *Balkinization* (balkin.blogspot.com), the blog edited by Balkin that follows the twists and turns of constitutional law under the Bush administration. In October 2006, they co-wrote a lengthy piece on their theories for the *Fordham Law Review*.[76] The national surveillance state, they said, is "characterized by a significant increase in government investments in technology and government bureaucracies devoted to promoting domestic security and (as its name implies) gathering intelligence and surveillance using all of the devices that the digital revolution allows."

Among the developments that have made such data collection and data mining possible, Balkin and Levinson wrote, are "high-speed computers, lower costs of telecommunication and computer storage, and complex mathematical algorithms [that] allow computers to 'recognize' patterns in speech, telephone contact information, e-mail messages, and Internet traffic that might indicate possible terrorist or criminal activity." And with the United States a likely target for future terrorist attacks, electronic surveillance, data mining, and the construction of what they call "digital dossiers" have become increasingly common in America.

Balkin and Levinson caution that the national surveillance state is "not simply a product of the September 11 attacks" or necessarily a "product of war." What has become known as the war on terror, they argue, is actually a "sustained set of interlocking strategies for dealing with new forms of global threats and new technologies of attack by a host of different organizations, some sponsored by nation-states, and others acting more or less on their own." And they contend that the technologies of surveillance would have been produced whether or not the United States was attacked in 2001: "As soon as these technologies became widely available, it was inevitable that governments would seek to employ them, both to enjoy their advantages and to counter the dangers of the same tools in private hands"; the digital age, therefore, "has altered the technologies of crime and, concomitantly, the way that the state can respond to crime."

Most important to our inquiry, they argue that focusing on war as the primary cause of the surveillance state "overlooks the fact that surveillance technologies that help the state track down terrorists can also be used to track and prevent domestic crime." And because the surveillance state is not "subject to the oversight and restrictions of the criminal justice system, the government may be increasingly tempted to use this parallel system for more and more things. It may argue that the criminal justice system is outmoded and insufficiently flexible to deal with the types of security problem it now faces."

Once databases of all phone calls have been compiled—as we've just seen—they can be combined with consumer data available from any number of private sector organizations. "This allows governments to produce rich digital dossiers that might be employed either by the nation's national security agencies or its criminal law enforcement divisions," Balkin and Levinson conclude. "The information that is useful to the one will increasingly be useful to the other." Finally, "the government will be tempted to move increasingly from investigation and arrest after crimes occur to surveillance, prevention and interception before crimes occur." That brief analysis captures the significance of the privatization of our intelligence system: all that technology funded by the government to promote security and build digital dossiers on suspected terrorists is supplied by SAIC, IBM, CACI, ManTech, and the other members of the Intelligence-Industrial Complex. Let us now review how the public-private intelligence apparatus that has been built over the past decade came to be directed at the American homeland.

The logical starting place for this history is Dick Cheney's infamous One Percent Doctrine and the Bush administration's policies of preemption. Under these theories, even if there is only one chance in a hundred that a certain scenario threatening U.S. security might happen—a terrorist attack, for example, or a launch of a missile by an unfriendly government—the United States has the obligation to go on the attack and prevent that scenario from taking place. That has shifted the paradigm for domestic law enforcement by making it the duty of the government to use its intelligence resources to help law enforcement agencies preempt attacks before they happen, beyond the traditional practice of gathering evidence to prove a crime that took place in the past. According to former Attorney General John Ashcroft, who was part of the inner circle of officials who set the initial policies for the global war on terror, that shift from solving crimes to detecting pre-crime took place almost immediately after 9/11.

In the days after the September 11 attacks, he told a 2006 conference on network centric warfare, President Bush and Vice President Cheney made it clear to their war cabinet that their primary mission was preventing another attack. Ashcroft, despite his apparent opposition to parts of the NSA surveillance program, understood that the Bush-Cheney directive, and its evolving theories on preemption, required sifting through enormous amounts of data to find the patterns that might lead investigators to a plot. "The amount of information you have to have in order to anticipate the future is exponentially greater if your job is to disrupt, interrupt, displace and otherwise make impossible something that is going to happen unless you intervene," he said. The "mandate to prevent is a very significant mandate, and requires significantly more resources, sophistication and capacity to understand what's going on." But the volume of information out there, he added, "is so great that we must be able to process information basically in ways that human minds are incapable of doing. So I encourage you to utilize the capacities that exist in data processing and make sure we have our data and intelligence formatted properly."[77]

(Ashcroft's speech was self-serving. In 2006, after leaving the Department of Justice, he formed a consulting company, the Ashcroft Group LLC, which represents about thirty clients, many of which make products or technology designed to help the government conduct surveillance and counterterrorism investigations. One of his biggest clients is AT&T; another is ChoicePoint Inc., the Atlanta data aggregation company and the nation's leading supplier of identification services. It holds some 17 billion records of individuals and businesses, which it sells to private sector companies as well as the U.S. government and the Intelligence Community. ChoicePoint also owns i2, a British company that has become one of the leading providers of visual investigative analysis software for U.S. intelligence.)[78]*

---

* When Ashcroft formed his lobbying firm in 2006, he told the *Washington Post* it was "a continuation of the aspiration I have that our nation have access to the best possible resources to fight terror, whether domestic or international." During his tenure at the Justice Department, the *Post* pointed out, Ashcroft championed expanded federal powers to conduct surveillance; now, he "wants intelligence and law enforcement agencies to be aided by the tech world's 'best of breed.' " In 2007, as an AT&T lobbyist, Ashcroft signed a letter to the Senate Judiciary Committee supporting legislation to provide immunity to telecom providers that cooperated with the NSA. Immunity, he said, "provides a just and fair protection for companies that allegedly responded to a call for assistance from the president in a time of national crisis." Other companies represented by Ashcroft include Nanodetex Corp., which detects airborne pathogens such as anthrax; Innova Holdings Inc., which makes software to control drones and UAVs; and Dulles Research LLC, which claims to detect "illicit networks" by analyzing the actions of people. See Ellen Nakashima, "Ashcroft Finds Private-Sector Niche," *Washington Post*, August 13, 2006; and Eric Lichtblau, "Key Senators Raise Doubts on Eavesdropping Immunity," *New York Times*, November 1, 2007.

Another great shift involved the idea that the U.S. homeland itself was now a battleground. That concept first took hold in 2002, when the Pentagon established NORTHCOM in Colorado to provide command and control of military efforts within U.S. borders. NORTHCOM was given two primary responsibilities: providing military security during national emergencies, including terrorist attacks and natural disasters; and protecting important U.S. military bases in the fifty states. As part of the Pentagon's domestic security mission, former Secretary of Defense Donald Rumsfeld created the Counterintelligence Field Activity office in 2002 and filled its staff with contractors from Booz Allen, BAE Systems, SAIC, and other suppliers of cleared personnel. CIFA, as we've seen, was used as a weapon against people suspected of harboring ill will against the Bush administration and its policies. Yet even though retired Air Force General James Clapper, the undersecretary of defense for intelligence, has expressed concerns about CIFA's domestic reach, the agency remains an integral part of the Pentagon's counterterrorism efforts.*

In recent years, military, intelligence, and police work have been combined in "fusion centers" being built around the country in a little-known program of the Departments of Justice and Homeland Security. At present, there are forty-three current and planned fusion centers in the United States where data from intelligence agencies, the FBI, local police, private sector databases, and anonymous tipsters are combined and analyzed by counterterrorism analysts. DHS hopes to create a national network of such centers that would be tied into the agency's day-to-day activities. According to the Electronic Privacy Information Center, the project "inculcates DHS with enormous domestic surveillance powers and evokes comparisons with the publicly condemned domestic surveillance program of COINTELPRO," the 1960s program by the FBI to destroy the left. Still, none of these programs can compare to the incredible power of the spy satellites controlled by the NRO on behalf of U.S. imagery and signals intelligence agencies.

---

* In April 2007, Clapper said that he had assessed the results of CIFA's data gathering program called Talon and "does not believe they merit continuing the program as currently constituted, particularly in light of its image in Congress and the media." See Walter Pincus, "Pentagon to End Talon Data-Gathering Program," *Washington Post*, April 25, 2007.

• • •

The groundwork for linking those agencies with homeland security was first laid in 2005, when Hurricane Katrina ravaged the Gulf Coast in the worst natural disaster in U.S. history. Prior to Katrina, the NGA had been used sporadically during domestic crises. Its first baptism of fire came after the 9/11 terrorist attacks, when the agency collected imagery to help in the recovery efforts at the World Trade Center and the Pentagon. A year later, during a two-week killing spree in the Washington, D.C., area by a pair of demented snipers, the CIA and the FBI used images provided by the NGA to search for places near highways where the two men might be hiding. But the storm of 2005 triggered NGA activity on a scale never before seen inside the borders of the United States. "Hurricane Katrina changed everything with what we do with disasters," John Goolgasian, the director of the NGA's Office of Americas, told me in a 2006 interview. In New York after 9/11, the NGA only had a handful of people on the ground, but "with Katrina, we put a lot of people down in the theater," he said, using a term usually reserved for military battlegrounds overseas. The NGA's sophisticated surveillance tools, which can create three-dimensional maps, helped first-responders identify hospitals, schools, and areas where hazardous materials were stored in the Gulf Coast region. And in an unprecedented move, the NGA distributed thousands of unclassified images of stricken areas, via the Internet, to the public.

"People could actually see their houses," General Clapper, who was the NGA director at the time of Katrina, told me a few months before his 2007 appointment as the chief intelligence adviser to Secretary of Defense Robert Gates. The NGA's work during the hurricane was "the most graphic example in my forty years of intelligence of coming to the direct aid of people in extreme circumstances," Clapper, a former director of both the DIA and NGA, added. David Burpee, the NGA's director of public affairs, said the NGA operates under strict oversight rules that ban the agency from collecting imagery over the United States without a formal request from a "lead" domestic agency coordinating efforts during a disaster. In the case of the California fires and Hurricane Katrina, that assistance was requested by FEMA.

The Katrina effort also involved the first known domestic operations of a U-2, which was deployed to the Gulf Coast region in the days before the storm. The link between Pentagon-driven intelligence operations and the homeland was underscored by the NGA's deployment to New Orleans of a special vehicle called a Mobile Integrated Geospatial-Intelligence System, which is loaded with equipment that allows NGA analysts to download intelligence from U-2s and U.S. military satellites. The vehicles, known as MIGS and manufactured by General Dynamics, were first deployed by the NGA to Iraq and Afghanistan, and later to the Gulf Coast. "They're pretty much the NGA in a Humvee—very military," said the NGA's John Goolgasian. "But it kind of sticks out like a sore thumb if you're driving into an urban area" in the United States (as a result, the NGA has painted the domestic vehicles blue, and renamed them Domestic MIGS, or DMIGS).

The purpose and utility of such intelligence tools in a disaster area or in a war zone are clear. But it doesn't take much imagination to see how powerful technologies, when combined with secretive, growing interagency collaboration, can be misused in a domestic context. In recent years many U.S. cities have deployed sophisticated video cameras throughout their downtown areas that track activity twenty-four hours a day. And U.S. intelligence and law enforcement agencies now have at their disposal facial recognition software that can identify one person among thousands in a large crowd. Moreover, as we've seen in previous chapters, the NSA has tremendous power at its disposal to listen in on the conversations of millions of Americans, both at home and abroad. But when collection agencies combine their technologies, as the NGA and the NSA have been doing for the past three years, the effect of such surveillance is increased exponentially.

In 2004, as we have seen, the NSA and the NGA signed an agreement to share resources and staff and link their information infrastructure and exploitation techniques, thus allowing the two agencies to work together "using NGA's 'eyes' and NSA's 'ears.' " The collaboration—which includes permanently stationing analysts at each other's headquarters as well as in war zones in Iraq and Afghanistan—has made it possible for the two agencies to create hybrid intelligence tools that combine intercepts of cell phone calls with overhead imagery gathered by unmanned aerial vehicles to significantly enhance the ability of U.S. forces in combat. In 2006, such tools allowed the U.S. military to locate and kill Abu Zarqawi, the leader of Al Qaeda in Iraq.

Since then, according to the NGA's director, Admiral Robert Murrett, the NGA's collaboration with the NSA has deepened significantly, creating an "absolutely vital" partnership that is "making a big difference" in U.S. contingencies around the world. "When the NSA and NGA work together, one plus one equals five," he told reporters at GEOINT 2007 in San Antonio. When I asked him for examples, Murrett told me that recent developments in full motion video and NSA/NGA collaboration have created "lots of successes" for U.S. forces in combat in Iraq and Afghanistan as well as the Horn of Africa and the Philippines.

Transfer that to a domestic context, and the possibilities are ominous. Using the same technologies the NGA and NSA have deployed in Iraq and in the global war on terror, the government could conceivably follow the movements of certain individuals minute by minute. It could watch a person depart from a mosque in, say, Lodi, California, drive a car from Chicago to Detroit, or move around through a city like New York and Los Angeles. And as the intelligence infrastructure, including the kinds of local camera surveillance systems that proved so useful in identifying the perpetrators of the London subway bombings, expands in the United States, it raises the specter of a nationwide surveillance web. "These networks are going to get denser and going to cover more area over time," says John Pike. "At some point in time somebody's going to drop in an automated face-print recognizer, and then they're off to the races. Anybody who is currently wanted by the authorities, well, there's just going to be parts of the country where such a person could not enter."[79] Those scenarios, under proposals currently under discussion in Congress, are now becoming reality.

• • •

The Bush administration's intelligence sharing plan originally called for the National Applications Office to be set up by October 1, 2007.[80] But after reports of the plan leaked to the press, Congress demanded and received a promise to delay the opening of the office until further studies were conducted on its legal basis and questions about civil liberties were answered. "The enormity of the NAO's capabilities and the intended use of the imagery received through these satellites for domestic homeland security purposes, and the unintended consequences that may arise, have heightened concerns among the general public, including reputable civil rights and civil liberties organizations," Mississippi Democrat Bennie G. Thompson, the chairman of the House Homeland Security Committee, wrote in an August 22, 2007, letter to Homeland Security Secretary Michael Chertoff.* Thompson demanded biweekly updates on the activities and progress of the new organization.

During a Homeland Security hearing in September 2007 called by Thompson, Charles Allen of DHS said the civil liberties concerns were misplaced. "We are not going to be penetrating buildings, bunkers or people's homes with this," he said. "I view that as absurd. My view is that no American should be concerned."[81] But his comments did little to mollify critics and civil libertarians. The formation of the NAO "potentially marks a transformation of American political culture toward a surveillance state in which the entire public domain is subject to official monitoring," said Steven Aftergood of the Federation of American Scientists.[82] In the debate that followed, few observers noted that the plan to expand the reach of spy satellites into the homeland had been drafted

---

* Scientists, too, are concerned about the NAO. It will replace the Civil Applications Committee, which has reviewed civilian requests for classified reconnaissance information for the past thirty years. By placing that authority in the Department of Homeland Security, scientists, including those working for such government agencies as the U.S. Forest Service, worry that their requests for such data could be vetoed or delayed for security reasons. "The scientists say this information is very valuable to them, and they are concerned that this new office will be looking more at homeland security and law enforcement," Representative Norm Dicks, a Democratic member of the House Homeland Security Committee, told a reporter from McClatchy News Service. In a letter to the Bush administration, Dicks said the NAO "represents a potentially serious harm over the longer term to the constitutional protections U.S. citizens expect and deserve." See Les Blumenthal, "Scientists oppose move to restrict satellite data," McClatchy News Service, *Tacoma News Tribune,* January 13, 2008.

by a company that had much to gain from its implementation: Booz Allen Hamilton.

The domestic intelligence study group was commissioned in May 2005 by the Office of the DNI and the director of the U.S. Geological Survey (USGS). Specifically, they asked Booz Allen to analyze how satellite sensing data could be used for applications "that are civil and/or domestic in nature and involve the use of Intelligence Community capabilities and products." In addition to Booz Allen's Hall and seven other Booz Allen employees, the Independent Study Group included retired Army Lieutenant General Patrick M. Hughes, the former director of the DIA and vice president of homeland security for L-3 Communications; Thomas W. Conroy, the vice president of national security programs for Northrop Grumman; Jeff "Skunk" Baxter, the independent consultant for Northrop Grumman, SAIC, and several government agencies; three other former officials employed by private sector companies, law firms, and research institutes; and one official from the ODNI and two from the U.S. Geological Survey.

From the beginning, therefore, the group was heavily weighted toward people and companies with a major stake in the intelligence business. We've seen throughout this book how extensively Booz Allen is involved in both intelligence and homeland security; so, too, are Northrop Grumman and L-3. It's difficult to believe that Hall's group, dominated by companies prominent in the area of integrating classified and unclassified intelligence networks, would have reached any other conclusion than it did: that the rapid merging of foreign and domestic intelligence was desirable and necessary.

The original purpose of the study group was to recommend ways to update regulations that had been in place since the 1970s governing the domestic use of satellite signals and imagery. Previously, the use of such data had been governed by the Civil Applications Committee, chartered in 1975 and managed by the USGS, which, with the National Aeronautics and Space Administration (NASA), was one of a handful of agencies cleared to use spy satellites for civil and domestic purposes. But in the intervening years and particularly after 9/11, the Booz Allen study team said, the "threats to the nation have changed and there is a growing interest in making available the special capabilities of the Intelligence Community to all parts of the government, to include homeland security and law enforcement entities and on a higher priority basis." The capabilities studied by the team encompassed practically every collection vehicle, including satellite and airborne sensors, "NSA worldwide assets," military and other MASINT sensors that can detect traces left behind by chemical weapons or heat emanating from people inside a building, and "sophisticated exploitation/analytic capabilities."

The unclassified Booz Allen report was released in September 2005.[83] It recommended the establishment of a Domestic Applications Program to be funded by the DNI and run jointly by the ODNI and the DHS. The program would house a Domestic Applications Office "to provide a focal point and act as a facilitator to the IC on behalf of civil, homeland security and law enforcement users." It also recommended that domestic users of intelligence be given a "seat at the table" to "influence policy, R&D and acquisition decisions." In addition, the report criticized the legal infrastructure guiding intelligence activities today as "risk-averse." The effect of this approach, the study group said, "causes delay, uncertainty and may result in missed opportunities to collect, exploit and disseminate information critical to the anti-terrorism, homeland security and law enforcement missions."

In one of its most significant passages, the study group zeroed in on what it called the "strong, and often uninformed public reaction" to the Intelligence Community's misdeeds during the 1970s and the homeland security initiatives, such as the Patriot Act, put in place by the government after 9/11. These events, it said, have sparked a backlash in the public and created a narrow, "hyper-conservative view of what can be done" in the domestic arena. The debate that has taken place, the group argued, "often appears to be a debate with only one voice, often ill-informed and sometimes completely uninformed."

In response to this public reaction, the Booz Allen group urged the Bush administration, Congress, and the Intelligence Community to "inform this debate, credibly, on the challenges of intelligence support in the war on terror, and especially on the methods taken to protect the legitimate rights of American citizens." To "optimize support" among the public and ease fears about the "perceived impact" of its actions "on the legitimate rights of American citizens," the group urged the IC to gradually introduce the idea of using SIGINT, GEOINT, and MASINT for domestic security with "a period of considerable experimentation and discovery." That language closely matched what McConnell would propose for the study of domestic intelligence while he was the president of the Intelligence and National Security Alliance and, later, when he testified to the Senate during his confirmation hearings as director of national intelligence. Foreign and domestic intelligence have now merged into a single discipline—the ultimate aim of Booz Allen and its fellow intelligence contractors after September 11.

Despite the complaints from Congress and civil libertarians, the integration of foreign intelligence with homeland security is moving ahead at full steam. The DHS's Allen, who will manage the new National Applications Office, told a conference of geospatial intelligence contractors in October 2007 that the ODNI is working with DHS and the Departments of Justice and the Interior to draft the charter for the organization, which he said will face "layers of review" once it is established by the beginning of 2008.

As he did before Congress, Allen cautioned that public concerns about civil liberties are off the mark. There has "never been one case where the NGA was used domestically" for espionage purposes, he said. The fruits of the IC's collaboration with homeland security agencies, he argued, were exemplified by the NGA's sharing of imagery about the California wildfires: "We're saving lives." Other officials downplayed the dangers as well. What the NGA is doing domestically "is really benign," says NGA director Murrett. "The aspects dealing with rights are transparent."[84]

Congress, however, wasn't buying it. In December 2007, the House and Senate passed an amendment to a defense spending bill that prohibited funding for the new program until Michael Chertoff, the Secretary of Homeland Security, can show the NAO will adhere to civil liberties and the Government Accountability Office, the investigative arm of Congress, has certified the program as constitutional. "We still haven't seen the legal framework we requested or the standard operation procedures on how the NAO will actually be run," Representative Thompson told the *Wall Street Journal.*[85] But the nation's intelligence leadership seemed nonplussed.

In October 2007, after delivering his first public speech as principal deputy director of national intelligence, Donald Kerr, the former director of the NRO, was asked about the DNI's plans to share remote-sensing imagery with homeland security and law enforcement. Did the plan reflect the dangers about state intrusion in private lives as depicted in *Enemy of the State*? (that 1998 film tells the story of a lawyer hounded by the NSA after he learns the details of a crime committed by a politician with close ties to the surveillance agency). Absolutely not, replied Kerr. "The point that everybody should take away is that the rules under which GEOINT is used domestically will not change," he said. "They are still in place. Admiral Murrett will continue to be the release authority under appropriate legislation for all such data acquired domestically. And this proposal does not change that in any way." As far as the movies go, Kerr blasted Hollywood for producing films like *Enemy of the State* and 2007's *The Good Shepherd,* about the CIA. Those films, he said, "have poisoned the well of public opinion in some ways, and make people think we focus on safety mainly for governmental activities to the exclusion of all else." But that's untrue, he claimed: "We have always been a free people who can defend ourselves without giving up the liberties that animate us to action."[86]

That, of course, remains to be seen. But there is no doubt about who will benefit from the new policy: intelligence contractors. As a result of the commercialization and privatization of intelligence operations, particularly in geospatial intelligence, the tools that allow agencies to share information between themselves and with domestic intelligence and law enforcement agencies are owned and operated by private sector companies. As we've seen, three of the leading NGA and NSA contractors—Booz Allen Hamilton, Northrop Grumman, and L-3 Communications—were the primary authors of the "independent" study. ChoicePoint and other companies represented by former attorney general John Ashcroft provide much of the financial and personal data on U.S. citizens used by the government to identify and analyze "communities of interest" for intelligence agencies.

Other key industry players in geospatial intelligence were identified in an interoperability demonstration that took place during the GEOINT 2007 symposium in San Antonio sponsored by the U.S. Geospatial Intelligence Foundation. The demonstration was similar in scope to the one that took place in 2006 and described in chapter 7. But the latest scenario was domestic in nature and involved the tracking by U.S. intelligence of a Cuban ship carrying spent nuclear fuel heading for the U.S. Gulf Coast. Among the many corporations offering analytical, imagery, and signals intelligence tools for the demonstration were both the giants and the lesser-knowns of the Intelligence-Industrial Complex.

They included ESRI, whose popular mapping software is used extensively by the NGA to collect, analyze, distribute, and search its extensive imagery collection. SRA International is an important supplier of intelligence, surveillance, and reconnaissance programs to the National Security Agency and defense intelligence agencies. PCI Geomatics is a Canadian company that sells software to the NGA and other defense and intelligence agencies that allows them to quickly process and interpret geospatial imagery. MetaCarta of Cambridge, Massachusetts, makes software for counterterrorism and homeland security use that allows analysts to search lines of unstructured text for geographic references, which are then viewed as icons on a map; one use, according to the company, is to search news accounts of, say, a shipment of nuclear fuel, and "pinpoint the concentration and visualize patterns" of the incident "within seconds versus minutes or hours."[87]

Lockheed Martin, meanwhile, produces the GeoScout software that allows the NGA to blend its classified data from spy satellites with systems operated by the NSA and other intelligence agencies. ITT Industries makes ISR and "persistent surveillance" software used in unmanned aerial vehicles to collect and transmit imagery, and developed and built the sensor system for WorldView-1, the commercial satellite launched in 2007 by DigitalGlobe (with the financial support of the NGA) that can collect up to 290,000 square miles of images every day. AGI, of Exton, Pennsylvania, produces much of the mapping and imagery software used on the Global Hawk and Predator UAVs, and creates three-dimensional mapping files from Google Earth imagery that allow intelligence analysts to visualize terrain and combine SIGINT, MASINT, and imagery intelligence into a single platform. BAE Systems, an important contractor for the NGA and the CIA, has developed a new electronic system called Geospatial Operation for a Secure Homeland that helps intelligence and domestic security agencies acquire and combine geospatial data from satellites, sensors, and terrestrial sensors to create "situational awareness" and speed recovery from natural disasters and "terrorist or criminal incidents." Intergraph Corporation, of Huntsville, Alabama, produces geospatial information software used by the NGA and other intelligence agencies to share and combine classified data from different sources and to mix data from sensors and video so "complex security problems can be visualized and managed swiftly," according to its Web site. LPA Systems of Fairport, New York, formed a Geospatial Intelligence Group in 2006 following years of research for the Air Force, and now offers a suite of software tools to the Intelligence Community that can, among other things, combine imagery from infrared sensors with high-resolution satellite photographs to monitor conditions on the ground for both homeland security and military situations.

In the demonstration at the GEOINT symposium, all of these companies displayed their software products and explained how they and agencies such as the NGA, NSA, the Office of Naval Intelligence, and the Marine Corps would use them to monitor the Cuban terrorists responsible for diverting the radioactive fuel from a nuclear facility in northern Cuba and then—with the help of a Predator launched from MacDill Air Force Base in Florida—track and intercept the cargo as it departed from Cuba on a ship and moved across the Caribbean to Corpus Christi, Texas, a major port on the Gulf Coast. The exercise illustrated how sophisticated the U.S. domestic surveillance system has become in the six years since the 9/11 attacks, and how it can be used to find and track almost anybody considered suspicious by national security authorities. In the right hands, those tools can do enormous good; but in the wrong ones, America could take on the trappings of a police state. In the end, these companies, and dozens of other firms that work for the CIA, the NSA, and the rest of the Intelligence Community, may be the only winners in America's national surveillance state.

10

Conclusion: Ideology, Oversight, and the Costs of Secrecy

"There are two ways to look at this activity: as a grim attempt to turn public anxiety into a business opportunity or—the viewpoint naturally favored by those in the industry—as a chance to fight the good fight while upholding sound capitalist principles."

—*Los Angeles Times* columnist Michael Hiltzik, writing about the Paladin Capital Group, a private equity fund created after 9/11 to focus exclusively on the homeland security and intelligence markets

INTELLIGENCE CONTRACTING is a lucrative business: it's hard to argue with revenue growth of 15 to 20 percent year after year—or, in the case of Essex Corporation, 156 percent for five years straight. But as we've seen, money and profits are not the sole motivators for the corporations and executives who populate the Intelligence-Industrial Complex. Because so many top executives are former intelligence officers themselves, many of their companies are motivated by politics as well. For CACI's CEO, Jack London, that translates into a desire to "disseminate vital intelligence" for the fight against "the Islamofascists." For ManTech CEO George Pedersen, it's a yearning for his company to be "on the battlefield," whether in Iraq, South Korea, or the Philippines. For the senior vice presidents of the big prime contractors, Booz Allen Hamilton and Science Applications International Corporation, it involves power, either as a way to influence future policy or make changes in the way the Intelligence Community is organized. And for many contractors at the Pentagon and the National Geospatial-Intelligence Agency, it's helping rank-and-file war-fighters in Iraq and Afghanistan get access to the same intelligence being analyzed by men in suits and uniforms in Washington.

These motivations point to something we have yet to broach in our analysis of intelligence contracting: the role of ideology in the business. To get there, we must return to the months after the terrorist attacks on New York and Washington on September 11, 2001, and to how the interpretation of those attacks and the U.S. response that followed created a new ideology that transformed relations between state and capital in the national security arena. Out of those events came an ideological stew that blended patriotism, national chauvinism, fear of the unknown, and old-fashioned war profiteering, all of which have played into the corporate demand for new markets and fresh sources of capital and profits. Thus was born the ideology of the Intelligence-Industrial Complex.

In 2002, as the nation braced for the next move in what President George W. Bush had dubbed the "global war on terror," the Bush administration and its corporate allies began talking of a common ideological framework for the long struggle ahead. America, they said, needed a new form of governance to respond to terrorism—a "partnership" between the private and public sectors that would come together to pursue and defeat the common enemy. That alliance was based on a simple proposition: that the private sector, as the owner of 90 percent of the nation's communications, energy, and transportation networks, must play a central role in the fight against terrorism and for the "homeland." Government, it was said repeatedly, couldn't protect the American people without industry; homeland security, we were told again and again, "was too important to be left to the government alone." Mike McConnell, then the senior vice president of Booz Allen Hamilton, summed up the corporate thinking in a 2002 speech to a group of financial executives. Because "all of the critical infrastructure we're dependent on" is privately owned, he said, "our moral responsibility is to understand the change and have firms engaged in a public-private partnership to protect their businesses and the citizens of this country."[1]

The implications of the new ideology for the private sector were captured in 2003 by the nation's most powerful corporate lobby, the Business Roundtable, which represents the CEOs of America's 150 largest corporations. "Many old paradigms that dominated the American psyche before 9/11 have been set aside since the events of the tragic day," the Roundtable boldly proclaimed in a special report that called for an "anti-terror joint venture" between business and the Bush administration. "So also must the historic government-business relationships of the past be redefined in a new era of cooperation and collaboration." Specifically, the CEOs said, that meant setting aside old conflicts that, in the era before 9/11, had disrupted the ability of corporations to support the government. "Historical suspicions and adversarial relationships between government-as-regulator and business-as-regulated have traditionally made cooperation difficult," the Roundtable argued. "In the current security climate, this could prove disastrous to the common objective of enhancing homeland security."[2]

When that report was released, American corporate executives were still reeling from the stunning collapse of Enron, the Houston energy giant whose meteoric rise in the 1990s was accomplished largely by systematic accounting fraud, and a dozen other scandals that shook Wall Street between 2001 and 2003. The Business Roundtable's new rhetoric blew in like a refreshing breeze: "Nine-eleven changed everything," we were told again and again; conflict between government and business simply would not do in an age when national unity was a matter of survival. From now on, the business of Booz Allen Hamilton, or Halliburton, or ManTech, or CACI, or Blackwater, was the business of America.

Companies benefiting from the enormous expansion of contracting for domestic security, military operations overseas, and intelligence projects began to justify their profits as an incidental benefit for their dedication to the nation's security interests, and executives began to portray themselves as not merely businessmen but as patriots. In the heated atmosphere in Washington after 9/11 and in the months preceding the invasion of Iraq, conferences on defense and homeland security began taking on the trappings of nationalistic pep rallies.

One of the earliest displays of the businessman-as-patriot phenomenon came during a 2003 conference on homeland security financing at the National Press Club. It was organized by Equity International, a public relations company that would go on to sponsor several major conferences on doing business in Iraq, and was attended by a wide range of companies involved in the intelligence contracting industry, including Booz Allen Hamilton, BearingPoint, QinetiQ, Northrop Grumman, Boeing, Lockheed Martin, and Harris Corporation. Throughout the two-day symposium, corporations were told repeatedly that their business plans were akin to military operations. "Clearly this war can only be won if the public and private sectors join together hand in hand," declared John Elstner, the CEO of the Chesapeake Innovation Center, a business incubator funded by the National Security Agency, in his opening speech. During the plenary session, Darryl B. Moody, the vice president of the homeland security and intelligence sector of BearingPoint and one of the first private sector individuals assigned to a Transportation Security Administration task force on terrorism, was introduced as "a soldier in the homeland security war." Moody, whose company also helped plan the U.S. occupation of Iraq and is a prime contractor for the NSA, thanked the organizers for "bringing together industry and government to exchange information and collaborate on what I believe is one of the most noble causes of our time, that is, defending our homeland." William S. Loiry, Equity's president, urged the corporations in the room to prepare for a protracted battle: "The constant dark clouds of further terrorism suggest that we are in for a long, expensive and complicated fight."[3]

That rhetoric smothered the fact that the "noble cause" of homeland security would, over time, yield enormous profits for a host of government contractors. Within three years, the Department of Homeland Security would be spending nearly $16 billion a year on goods and services from the private sector, making it the third-largest employer of contractors in the federal government. Among the beneficiaries of DHS's spending in 2006 were Booz Allen Hamilton, which was awarded $43 million to provide services to the DHS intelligence unit, and BearingPoint, which was paid $8 million to provide strategic planning and legislative support to the Transportation Security Administration (which Moody, BearingPoint's vice president, was advising). Upon reading the $16 billion DHS figures in a government report in the fall of 2007, Senator Joseph Lieberman, I-Connecticut, angrily commented: "Plainly put, we need to know who is in charge at DHS—its managers and workers, or the contractors."[4] To the companies involved, however, the confusion was a small price to pay for their new "partnership" with the federal government.

The new ideology of partnership is evoked just as fervently in the intelligence contracting industry, which is still riding high on a surge of Intelligence Community contracts with the private sector that topped $42 billion in 2006. Its most forceful and eloquent champion is retired Air Force General Kenneth Minihan, who preceded McConnell as NSA director and served before that as commander of the Air Intelligence Agency, and director of the Defense Intelligence Agency. Throughout his career, Minihan has been a strong proponent of using information technology as a weapon of war. "Information dominance is a mindset," he said in 1994. "It is the attitude needed to make ourselves a powerful weapon on the battlefields of the 21st century."[5]

After retiring from active duty in 1999, Minihan became a director of several companies trying to exploit the burgeoning intelligence market of the late 1990s. In 1999, in recognition of his emerging role as a private sector intelligence operative, Minihan was elected president of the Security Affairs Support Association, the predecessor to the Intelligence and National Security Alliance and the primary association for CIA and NSA contractors. But it was the events of 9/11 that really jump-started Minihan's business career and transformed the retired Air

Force general into a strong advocate for public-private cooperation in the arena of intelligence.

In 2002, Minihan joined forces with two former intelligence colleagues—Jim Woolsey, the former director of the CIA, and Alf Andreassen, a former naval intelligence officer who had worked at senior levels for the intelligence research firms Bell Labs and AT&T Government Solutions—to form the Paladin Capital Group. It was the nation's first private equity fund to invest exclusively in companies making products for the homeland security and intelligence markets. (Paladin's goal, Minihan once said, "is to toughen our critical infrastructure so that we can compete in the 21st century with the same success that we had in the 20th century. We also want to make a profit.")[6]* By 2006, Minihan had been elected to the board of directors of four Paladin companies and no fewer than six intelligence contractors, including ManTech International, BAE Systems, MTC Technologies Inc., and Verint Systems Inc., an Israeli-owned company that makes a key wiretapping software used by the FBI and the Intelligence Community.

Those companies hired Minihan for his uncanny ability to understand what technologies are best deployed by an intelligence agency. "During his long and distinguished career of supporting national defense and military information services, Lt. Gen. Minihan focused on defining and selecting technology solutions to solve the most difficult challenges in the Intelligence Community," Robert A. Coleman, ManTech's president and chief operating officer, explained when his

* When Paladin's homeland security fund was announced in 2003, the press immediately seized on the connection with 9/11. "Fight Terror, Make a Buck," was the headline of a *BusinessWeek* story that began by asking: "Does the war on terror have a silver—or even a golden—lining? A couple of onetime intelligence chiefs think so." *Buyside*, a newsletter for mergers and acquisitions specialists, dubbed its Paladin story "Patriotic Profits." Between 2002 and 2006, Paladin raised over $500 million, primarily from the pension funds of large labor unions and industrial corporations, and invested the money in twenty-five companies. The four Paladin companies where Minihan is a director include Nexidia Inc., which develops software sold to intelligence agencies that can phonetically search texts and audiotapes in dozens of languages at speeds 100,000 times faster than traditional techniques, and Arxan Technologies Inc., which develops anti-tampering software used by the U.S. military and defense contractors to protect critical technologies on weapons they sell overseas. See "Fight Terror, Make a Buck," *BusinessWeek*, January 27, 2003; and "Patriotic Profits," *Buyside*, May 1, 2003.

company elected Minihan to its board in 2006.[7] A high-ranking executive at one company told me that he once brought Minihan with him to a meeting with Jim Clapper when the latter was director of the National Geospatial-Intelligence Agency. "Ken was able to describe, general to general, what we had to offer, and it was much better than I could have done," the executive said. "I get him down here when we have a particular problem, and he looks at it from his perspective, based on his service. He's a very visionary kind of guy." George Tenet shares in that admiration. In his Acknowledgments in *At the Center of the Storm,* the former CIA director placed Minihan at the top of a list of twelve intelligence officers and contractors who "understand the strength" of the broader intelligence community and "its unity of purpose."[8]

Minihan's intense interactions with intelligence officials and contractors have made him the de facto ideologist for the Intelligence-Industrial Complex. His basic argument, repeated frequently at intelligence industry meetings, is that economic globalization and the diffusion of computer and communications technologies have shattered the barriers that once allowed agencies like the NSA or the CIA to operate in a vacuum. The Intelligence Community, he argues, cannot ignore the technical innovations taking place in the commercial world. And with America's economic and military superiority under constant attack, his thinking goes, government and business must join together as a matter of survival to confront the common evil. That means erasing the lines that once separated industry and government and joining forces, as the Business Roundtable suggested, to defeat America's adversaries.

During the Cold War, Minihan told a 2005 conference of intelligence professionals, the leading edge of American technology was in government agencies such as the NSA and the Defense Advanced Research Projects Agency. But now, due to the global dissemination of information and communication technologies, "we're all enmeshed together" in a global infrastructure that has become critical to the U.S. "intelligence apparatus." In the past, Minihan said, contractors "used to support military operations; now we participate [in them]. We're inextricably tied to the success of their operations." This new situation, he argued, presents corporations with "interesting opportunities" to create technologies that governments can take advantage of, "with all the complexities that exist in merging the interests of the private and public sector in the intelligence apparatus."[9]

Merging the interests of the private and public sector. That astonishing phrase, which is now the mantra of the intelligence contracting industry, suggests the creation of a new mode of capitalism that specifically serves the needs of government and its "intelligence apparatus." The implications are staggering: once private and public interests are merged, then the need for oversight disappears, along with regulation and other institutions designed to act as a brake on unbridled capitalist development or as watchdogs against corruption. Indeed, with 70 percent of the U.S. intelligence budget now going to private sector contractors, we may have already reached the point of no return. We've seen the manifestations of this merger of private and public throughout this book, as intelligence industry executives seek to convince investors that their interests, and those of the Pentagon and the IC, are one and the same. ManTech is "*on the battlefield*." CACI is "*working with the intelligence community in its mission to preeempt, disrupt, and defeat terrorism worldwide*." SAIC "*is a stealth company; we're everywhere but almost never seen*."[10]

If Minihan is the personification of the new ideology, Booz Allen Hamilton—"the shadow IC," as Joan Dempsey once called it—is its corporate embodiment. We've seen how Booz Allen and its one-thousand-plus former intelligence officials have played a central role in virtually every front in the war on terror, from Total Information Awareness to Iraq, and from the NSA to domestic surveillance. Since 2001, Booz Allen has defined the creation of "partnerships" between government and business as one of its strategic corporate goals. Just weeks after the 9/11 attacks, the company organized a CEO Summit that "explored public-private partnerships for national security" and attracted dozens of senior executives from Fortune 500 companies, according to Booz Allen CEO Ralph Shrader's personal account in his company's 2002 annual report. At the summit, participants agreed that the government needed to create "new types" of partnerships as well as "new types of market incentives" for companies engaged in homeland security. Most critically, Shrader pointed out, using the now familiar refrain, the executives agreed that "business leaders cannot opt out of geopolitics and leave the job of security solely to government and the military."

In 2003, Booz Allen launched an initiative to "shape and implement public-private partnerships" and chose Jim Woolsey to lead it as vice president of its newly created Global Strategic Security unit. It was a fortuitous moment for Woolsey: since 9/11, he'd been working feverishly on behalf of the neoconservatives inside the Bush administration to promote the idea that Saddam Hussein's Iraq was responsible for the September 11 attacks.* His new job, according to the company, was to help CEOs of major corporations integrate security into their strategic business planning and lead an initiative to shape and implement public-private partnerships "to reduce risk and help ensure resilience in corporations, government agencies and critical infrastructures." [11] It allowed Woolsey to seamlessly mesh his obsession with Islamic terrorism and Iraq with his new interest in homeland security.

Woolsey's speeches soon began to reflect his dual interests, and were peppered with references to potential threats to America's privately owned oil and gas, food distribution, electricity, and communications networks. Since 9/11, he told the Northern Virginia Business Council in 2004, "evil men" have figured out how to exploit the weaknesses in our networks. "That's war," he said. "And to fight that you have to think like a warrior, look at the vulnerabilities in your networks that can be intentionally exploited, make them more resilient, and fight back." [12] By pushing the idea that protecting the homeland was the equivalent of armed struggle, Woolsey and his corporate allies helped to expand the defense and intelligence markets into domestic security, thus broaden-

---

* In October 2001, for example, Donald Rumsfeld's Defense Policy Board dispatched Woolsey to Europe to try to confirm reports that Mohamed Atta, one of the 9/11 hijackers, had met in Prague with Iraqi intelligence; later, Woolsey was responsible for bringing several Iraqi dissidents, along with their concocted stories about weapons of mass destruction, to the attention of the Pentagon and the Defense Intelligence Agency. As we know now, none of this information was true; but it helped lay the groundwork for the 2003 invasion of Iraq, which Woolsey, as a longtime member of the Project for the New American Century, had been advocating for nearly ten years.

ing the scope of firms like Booz Allen, SAIC, and other large government contractors. The ultimate outcome of that dual mission is the use by domestic security agencies of imagery and signals intelligence from military spy satellites and surveillance aircraft—a plan drafted by Booz Allen and implemented at the Office of the Director of National Intelligence by Mike McConnell, a former Booz Allen vice president.

The key phrase in the new counterterrorism lexicon is "public-private partnership."[13] Once reserved for partial privatizations in which private capital was mobilized to support public utilities such as subways and roads, that term has been subverted in post-9/11 America to mean something very specific to national security: defense, homeland security, and intelligence contracts and practically any government decision that favors business interests. In reality, "partnerships" are a convenient cover for the perpetuation of corporate interests.* Examples abound. During his tenure as CEO of In-Q-Tel, Gilman Louie referred to the CIA's venture capital firm as a "private-public partnership" between the agency and the information technology industry, masking the fact that the CIA's investments amounted to a hefty government subsidy that allowed companies to do things like hire lobbyists to expand their market share.[14] In 2007, J. Michael Hickey, the vice president of government and national security affairs for Verizon, told a House subcommittee that, as a member of the U.S. Chamber of Commerce Homeland Security Task Force, he had organized a "public-private partnership

---

* For example, "public-private partnerships" could be used as a cover for undermining environmental regulations. In 2004, Booz Allen Hamilton's Jim Woolsey argued that attempts by public interest groups to obtain environmental data about corporations through the Freedom of Information Act were "not a sensible way to behave with respect to vulnerabilities." What the country needed, he explained, "are public-private partnerships that work together so that industry can feel confident that when it discloses something it's not disclosing something in such a way it can be used in litigation against it or more disasters that terrorists could find out about." Following this logic, the American Chemistry Council opposed a Senate bill that would have given the Environmental Protection Agency the power to assess the vulnerability of chemical plants and oil refineries to terrorist attack. A better idea, the council suggested, was to consolidate those responsibilities under the Department of Homeland Security and "continue the public-private partnerships that have advanced our critical infrastructure security since 11 September." Woolsey made his remarks at a speech I attended on March 19, 2004, in Tysons Corner, Virginia. See also "Industry Boosts Attack on Corzine's US Chem Security Bill," *Chemical News & Intelligence*, September 4, 2002.

with the Intelligence Community," an endeavor that involved scheduling briefings with the Office of the Director of National Intelligence on "issues of mutual, long-term strategic interest," including "insider threats from terrorism." [15] There, too, the term masked the fact that Verizon and other large corporations, through the National Security Telecommunications Advisory Committee and the NSA's alliance with industry, have a special relationship with top intelligence officials that no other segment of society can claim.

The most pertinent example of the term came in an amicus curiae brief filed during the summer of 2007 by the Chamber of Commerce to help AT&T defend itself in the lawsuit filed against the telecommunications company for cooperating with the NSA in its warrantless domestic surveillance program. "Homeland security, especially the protection of our nation's critical infrastructure (85% of which is under private control), continues to be one of the Chamber's top policy priorities," the nation's largest business lobby wrote. "To achieve this vital objective, maintaining an effective 'public-private partnership,' particularly between key industrial sectors and the national intelligence community, is essential." [16] There you have it: a secret alliance between business and government that may be one of the most egregious examples of a corporation skirting U.S. privacy and foreign intelligence laws described as a friendly "partnership." That is the ultimate result of the privatization of intelligence activities.

But those partnerships may have reached their limit. By the fall of 2007, it was increasingly evident that the age of unbridled contracting and outsourcing was coming to an end. For that story, we turn to Congress, which has finally found a way to exercise its oversight responsibilities over the Intelligence Community and its corporate shadow.

In May 2007, the House Permanent Select Committee on Intelligence published a report to accompany its budget authorization bill for 2008, which provided a record $48 billion to fund the activities of the U.S. Intelligence Community for the next year.[17] The budget, which included the IC's annual appropriation as well as supplemental funding for the wars in Iraq and Afghanistan, provided the first real oversight over intelligence contracting since outsourcing emerged as a public policy issue in the first years of the Bush administration. It was therefore somewhat of a triumph for Silvestre Reyes, the Texas Democrat who was the surprise choice of House Speaker Nancy Pelosi of California to head the committee after the Democrats took control of Congress in the winter of 2007. The legislation was approved by the full House on May 11, and then sent to the Senate, which passed it in October. After a House-Senate conference in which some of the House language was watered down, the final bill was passed on December 13, 2007.

Under the conference language, the Office of the Director of National Intelligence is now required to provide, on an annual basis, detailed reports to the congressional intelligence committees on the Intelligence Community's use of contractors, including—for the first time ever—an assessment of what intelligence activities should be considered inappropriate and off-limits to private contractors. The DNI must also report on its accountability mechanisms governing the performance of contractors in all sixteen agencies of the IC and submit a list of all contractors that have been the subject of audits by an inspector general or have been investigated for criminal violations, fraud, financial waste, and other actions that could affect their ability to deliver services. And to encourage the hiring of agency employees, McConnell was given authority to convert positions held by contractors into full-time government jobs by allowing him to increase personnel levels by 10 percent. The DNI must also identify agencies where a contractor is performing a "substantially similar function" to that of a government employee and compare the compensation of contract employees and government workers performing the same service. Unfortunately, the Senate deleted a House provision that would have provided much greater transparency on what contractors are actually doing. That provision would have required the DNI to estimate the number of contractors working in the most sensitive areas of intelligence, including collection and analysis; covert action; interrogation of enemy prisoners; the detention and transportation of prisoners; and the "conduct of electronic or physical surveillance or monitoring of United States citizens in the United States"—a reference to the private sector support for NSA domestic spying operations. That amendment would have to wait for a new administration and a new Congress.*

Still, the 2007 intelligence oversight bill, which was the first passed by Congress in three years, was an important document. No longer will the ODNI be allowed to hand over tens of billions of dollars in classified work to the private sector without providing solid and measurable explanations to Congress. At the same time, if the ODNI follows the letter of the law, Congress and the American public will finally have a chance to see how extensive contracting has spread into classified intelligence operations and to understand the standards used by intelligence agencies to determine which jobs can be contracted out and which jobs should be retained as government functions.

Even though it was left out of the final legislation, one section of the House bill was particularly significant. Using unusually strong language, the House committee bluntly declared that U.S. intelligence officials did not "have an adequate understanding of the size and composition of the contractor workforce, a consistent and well-articulated method for assessing contractor performance, or strategies for managing a combined staff-contractor workforce." Worse, the IC lacked a "clear definition of what functions are 'inherently governmental' and, as a result, whether there are contractors performing inherently governmental functions." Those were stunning accusations: after nearly ten years of unprecedented growth, the government was spending more than $40 billion a year on intelligence contracts, yet at no point had the government stopped to consider which one of these services could be safely performed by private companies and which ones should be han-

* As of March 1, 2008, President Bush had not signed the bill. In December 2007, the White House informed Congress that if the conference bill was presented to the president as passed by the House and Senate, "the president's senior advisers would recommend that he veto the bill." The administration opposed several provisions, including a requirement limiting interrogation techniques and the requirement for a cost-benefit analysis on contractors. With or without the bill, however, Congress had established new policies on outsourcing. See "Statement of Administration Policy, H.R. 2082—Intelligence Authorization Act for Fiscal Year 2008," Executive Office of the President, December 11, 2007.

dled only by government employees.* If they follow the letter of the 2007 law, Admiral McConnell and his organization will be forced to come to grips with the dilemma voiced by John Humphrey of CACI International, who warned in 2006 that the Intelligence Community faced "blowback" as a result of the "blurring of lines" in Iraq between private contractors and government intelligence operatives.

The outsourcing amendment to the intelligence bill was largely the work of one congressman who has been diligently pursuing the issue of contractor accountability since 2003: David Price, D-North Carolina. Price, a former professor of political science at Duke University, represents North Carolina's Fourth Congressional District, which encompasses the area known as the Research Triangle and includes Raleigh,

* Even in those limited venues in Congress where contracting has been openly discussed, it was clear that Admiral McConnell and the other people running the Intelligence Community couldn't even decide among themselves what was proper, and what was improper, to outsource. The state of confusion was underscored during two Senate confirmation hearings in 2007. In the first one, which took place in January 2007, McConnell appeared and was politely questioned by Ron Wyden about where he would draw the line on outsourcing. "You wouldn't be likely to want contractors to be interrogators, for example?" Wyden asked. Without hesitation, McConnell answered: "I can't imagine using contractors for anything like that." Given what happened at Abu Ghraib prison in Iraq, where contract interrogators from CACI International were implicated in some of the worst abuses identified by Army investigators, that was a remarkable response. A decision to classify interrogation as inherently governmental would have indicated a major change in administration and military thinking, and a new direction for the Intelligence Community and its partners in the contract interrogation business. Yet less than two months later retired Air Force General James Clapper gave a very different answer when he was asked by another Senate committee to submit written answers to questions about his pending nomination as undersecretary of defense for intelligence. One question asked him to explain the "proper role" of contractors in intelligence interrogation operations. "I believe it is permissible for contractors to participate in detainee interrogation, as long as they comply with the policies and guidance which govern DOD military and civilian interrogators," Clapper replied. "As I understand it, DOD contractors who conduct government-approved interrogations must be properly supervised and closely monitored throughout the interrogation process, and may not themselves, approve, supervise, or monitor interrogations." That was certainly an improvement over what had occurred under Donald Rumsfeld and Stephen Cambone. But it was exactly the opposite of what McConnell, Clapper's boss at the DNI, had said in his confirmation hearing. When the nation's two most senior intelligence officials aren't on the same page on a subject as sensitive as the outsourcing of interrogations, it's hard to believe they could be in sync on anything else.

Durham, and Chapel Hill. Like many citizens, he was alerted to the issue of contracting by two seminal events: the torture scandal at Abu Ghraib and the horrific incident in 2004 in Fallujah, Iraq, when four security guards working for Blackwater, which is based in North Carolina, were killed and mutilated, and their bodies strung up on a bridge over the Euphrates River by Iraqi insurgents and fighters.

In the wake of those incidents, Price began to look into what contractors were doing in Iraq and elsewhere in the war on terror, and discovered that the field was a murky one that offered few answers. "Once you get into outsourcing, you find layers upon layers," Price told me in an interview for this book. "My primary concern was that private security contracting has become so widespread and unaccountable that Congress needed to assert some legal authority." He was certain of one thing: "Interrogations are not what should be in the hands of private companies."[18] In 2004, Price started a small study group within the Democratic Caucus to educate himself and others about contracting. One of the people he sought out was Peter Singer, the military outsourcing expert at the Brookings Institution and the author of *Corporate Warriors: The Rise of the Privatized Military Industry,* the first book to call public attention to the military outsourcing phenomenon. I interviewed Singer around the same time he was meeting with Price's study group.

Singer was especially critical of the government's oversight of military and intelligence contractors. By 2006, after four years of war involving at least 25,000 intelligence and private military contractors in Iraq and Afghanistan, only one private sector intelligence operative, a CIA contractor named David Passaro, had been investigated and charged for a crime—the beating death of a prisoner held in a CIA detention center in Afghanistan. To Singer, that was proof that the government had deliberately turned a blind eye toward contractors. "Your conclusion has to be one of two things: we've either found 25,000 perfect angels—the Stepford Village of Iraq—or we have found the town of 25,000 where no crimes happen," he told me. "It's a statistical impossibility."[19] Singer was further disturbed by a decision, apparently made sometime in 2004 by federal attorneys in Virginia, not to prosecute any of the CACI and Titan contractors referred to their office for criminal investigation by U.S. Army investigators for their role at Abu Ghraib. CACI's response to the decision not to prosecute, Singer told me, was "that 'nobody's done anything, so everything's OK.' I would say no, it doesn't prove that; it actually shows we have major problems." *

Representative Price began his quest for accountability in 2006 by drafting an amendment to an intelligence spending bill that asked the Bush administration to disclose the types of activities that were appropriate for contractors and show how their hiring saved money for American taxpayers; it also asked the ODNI to make public all intelligence contracts worth more than $1 million. As the bill was being debated in the House, I sought out the contractors' view on the legislation from Tim Sample, the former CIA officer and General Dynamics executive who runs the Intelligence and National Security Alliance. INSA never took a formal position on the legislation. But Sample's contempt for the amendment—and for Price's attempt to create a modicum of transparency for intelligence contractors—was all too clear.

As a former House intelligence committee staffer, Sample told me, he had "very little sympathy personally" for the idea that contracting information should be made public. "The public, quite frankly, doesn't know what to do with it. And number two, I've met more people across the United States more surprised by what the Intelligence Community *isn't* doing as opposed to what it *is* doing. If you are legislating things to get information that you're going to utilize in some practical and meaningful way, then that's great. But if it's just that we're going to [do this]

* In a major development in the Abu Ghraib scandal in November 2007, a federal judge in Washington ruled that a civil lawsuit alleging abuse and torture by CACI interrogators at Abu Ghraib can go forward. The ruling means that CACI will face a civil trial where the allegations against the company can finally be placed before a jury. The lawsuit was filed on behalf of more than two hundred former Iraqi prisoners by the Center for Constitutional Rights. CACI officials once again denied any wrongdoing and predicted they would be vindicated at trial. In the same ruling, the judge ended a similar lawsuit filed against Titan Corp., a unit of L-3 Communications that supplied contract translators to military interrogators at Abu Ghraib. See Josh White, "Judge Allows Abu Ghraib Lawsuit Against Contractor," *Washington Post,* November 7, 2007.

because we want everybody to know how many contractors there are, we're going to have people spending endless man-hours compiling lists."[20] For someone who'd been feeding at the government trough for his entire career, Sample's response seemed remarkably obtuse.

Steve Jacques, a former Raytheon executive and a consultant to the U.S. Geospatial Intelligence Foundation, was less hostile to Price's bill but questioned the logic of making certain contracts public. "The devil's in the details," he told me. "I don't think it's a big deal to say that Lockheed Martin just got a $500 million contract with the IC. But if it's a $500 million contract with the NSA to do X, that starts to be a security problem; it's de-layering the onion skin. I honestly cannot imagine [the Price] amendment surviving."[21] He was right about that. After winning approval by a substantial majority in the Republican-controlled House, the Price amendment was added to the Senate's version of the intelligence bill. But in 2006, the Senate never got around to passing an intelligence spending bill, and the Price amendment died with it. But with the Democrats in control in 2007, the provision finally made it through Congress and is now the law of the land.*

Price and his congressional allies were less successful in an attempt to make intelligence contractors operating overseas subject to U.S. criminal law. On October 4, 2007, the House, by a lopsided margin of 389 to 30, passed a bill, partially drafted by Price, designed to bring all military and intelligence contractors under U.S. law. The legislation extended the jurisdiction of the Military Extraterritorial Jurisdiction Act to cover all contractors working for the government in a war zone; previously, contractors working for the State Department and other agencies were not held liable for criminal activity. Before the final vote, however, the Bush administration successfully lobbied to ensure that

* In a statement on the House floor on May 10, 2007, Price explained the intent of his bill. Intelligence officials, he said, must start asking basic questions: "Should [contractors] be involved in intelligence collection? Should they be involved in analysis? What about interrogations or covert operations? Are there some activities that are so sensitive they should only be performed by highly trained Intelligence Community professionals?" Such transparency is absolutely critical as contracting continues to expand, Paul Cox, Price's press secretary, told me. "As a nation, we really need to take a look and decide what's appropriate to contract and what's inherently governmental," he said.

the bill did not cover intelligence contractors, such as companies working for the CIA and engaged in covert activities. The bill, as written, "would have unintended and intolerable consequences for crucial and necessary national security activities and operations," the White House declared. J. Randy Forbes, R-Virginia, explained the implications for U.S. intelligence in a speech on the House floor. If the legislation passed and a "clandestine asset" was implicated in a crime, he said, "investigating and arresting that asset under traditional criminal procedures could expose other assets and compromise critical intelligence activities." As a result, the bill could "implicate the authorized business of the intelligence community employees and contractors." With Bush's backing, he successfully introduced a motion exempting the Intelligence Community and its contractors from possible criminal liability. "Nothing in this Act shall be construed to affect intelligence activities that are otherwise permissible prior to the enactment of this Act," it read.

Price wasn't happy. The Forbes amendment "raises serious questions about the activities its proponents may be seeking to protect," he said during the House debate. "Given that my bill only targets activities that are unlawful, why do my colleagues feel the need to clarify that it does not affect activities that are permissible? What activities are contractors carrying out that are permissible but not lawful? If there are private, for-profit contractors tasked with duties that require them to commit felony offenses, Congress needs to know about it. Such a revelation would point to a need for a serious debate about whether we are using contractors appropriately."[22]

R. J. Hillhouse, blogging at her site *The Spy Who Billed Me,* described the types of illegal activities that contractors in Iraq and Afghanistan might be involved in: "Paramilitary operations—covert actions that involve contract soldiers in offensive combat—are the first things that come to mind," she wrote. "Then, of course, there would be issues of illegal detainment of civilians as well as the problems with the use of 'special interrogation methods' by individuals directly contracted to the Agency (as in non-industrial green badgers)." The White House provision, Hillhouse continued, raised a critical question: "Has intelligence outsourcing gone too far when we start to outsource activities that would be criminal under US law? Did anyone in Congress ask what the hell corporations are doing on the US Government's behalf if intelligence contractors need to be exempt from US criminal laws in war zones?" *

Steven Aftergood offered a more disturbing explanation. "The awkward fact is that intelligence collection operations are routinely conducted in violation of established laws, including international legal norms to which the United States Government is formally committed," he wrote in *Secrecy News*.[23] Aftergood quoted from a 1996 House Intelligence Committee staff report that contained revelations about the CIA that are still amazing to read twelve years later. The CIA's clandestine service, the committee wrote, "is the only part of the IC, indeed of the government, where hundreds of employees on a daily basis are directed to break extremely serious laws in countries around the world in the face of frequently sophisticated efforts by foreign governments to catch them." According to that report, CIA operatives working for the Directorate of Operations engaged in "highly illegal" activities "several hundred times every day (easily 100,000 times a year)." Those activities, the House committee said, "not only risk political embarrassment to the U.S. but also endanger the freedom if not lives of the participating foreign nationals and, more than occasionally, of the clandestine officer himself."

Given the huge increase in contracting since those words were written and the widespread use of outsourcing in the CIA's clandestine service, it's a near-certainty that contractors today are also breaking foreign laws hundreds of times a day. If that's true, Congress has a right to know what outsourced jobs involve illegal acts and a duty to limit contracting to tasks that are both legal and subject to congressional oversight. Classified contracts should not provide cover for corporations to break the law.

• • •

* As of March 2008, Price's bill had yet to be considered by the Senate Judiciary Committee. The Senate version of the bill does not exclude intelligence contractors.

Secrecy has come at a high political cost. As we've seen throughout this book, the lack of transparency and the classified nature of most intelligence contracts makes Congress's oversight job over contractors almost impossible. Only a select few on the House and Senate committees with oversight jurisdiction over intelligence spending have access to specific projects, and that doesn't even apply to the most classified ones. It took nearly two years, for example, for the Bush administration to hand over to Congress the legal documents justifying the NSA's reliance on the telecommunications industry. Yet, as we've also seen, the companies themselves—at least their employees who hold top secret security clearances—have full knowledge of the details of secret contracts, from the bidding stage to the award. That leaves only a handful of people with knowledge of these programs, which allows only for internal debates between people holding such clearances. The public, and most of Congress, is completely left out, and have no real way of knowing how their money is being spent, let alone if it is being spent wisely. As Aftergood remarked in the opening chapter to this book, it's not like a debate when one side loses: "there *is* no debate." As a result, there is corruption in both contracting and the political process. We see it in "earmarking," a process that allows lawmakers to secretly add to legislation spending provisions that benefit a company or project in their district.*

As mentioned earlier, the most notorious case of earmark corruption involved the former Republican congressman Duke Cunningham, who was convicted in 2006 of accepting $2.4 million in bribes from executives with MZM Inc., a San Diego intelligence contractor. In return for

* "Under the earmark process, basically, you hire a lobbyist to get you a pot of money from Congress," says Peter Swire, a professor of communications law at Ohio State University I quoted earlier who directed a Clinton-era White House task force that examined how U.S. surveillance laws should apply to the Internet. "And if you're doing earmarks in order to protect America, that's patriotic, you know everyone can be proud to do that; and if you're doing earmarks to protect America with top secret systems, then everybody understands why it stays in the shadows. But that raises the risk of corruption. Earmarks have low transparency. Top secret projects have even lower transparency. So it becomes almost impossible from the outside to judge between two choices. Choice One is, it's a valuable project that's protecting America. Choice Two is, that powerful figures are lining their pockets. And when you go outside the normal procurement process and you go straight to Congress, the risk of corruption increases."

the bribes, Cunningham used his position on the House appropriations and intelligence committees to earmark tens of millions of dollars' worth of contracts for MZM at the Pentagon's Counterintelligence Field Activity office and the CIA. Marcus Stern, a reporter with the *San Diego Union-Tribune* who broke the MZM story, described the relationship between Cunningham and MZM CEO Mitchell Wade in an interview with Ken Silverstein, the Washington editor of *Harper's*. One day, Cunningham and Wade held a luncheon meeting at the Daily Grill, a fancy restaurant in the Georgetown section of Washington. According to Stern:*

> As they were talking about the future, Cunningham pulled out a piece of his own congressional stationery. He made a line of numbers down the left hand side of the stationery in which he wrote out the millions of dollars in contracts that he could provide to Wade, up to $25 million. He put corresponding numbers down the right hand side, in the tens of thousands of dollars, which was what he expected to get in the form of kickbacks or bribes—or what he would call gifts—from Wade. In exchange for the first $16 million in contracts he delivered to Wade, Cunningham was given possession of a yacht called the Buoy Toy, which he eventually renamed the Duke-Stir. Wade had purchased it for Cunningham with a cashier's check for $140,000. According to the bribe menu, Cunningham would get another $50,000 for every additional $1 million he got Wade in contracts. But after getting to $20 million, there was a discounted rate by which he would get $25,000 per million in contracts. That's why Cunningham was so intense about winning con-

---

* Mitchell Wade, MZM's CEO, pled guilty in 2006 to giving Cunningham more than $1 million in bribes, including a payment of $700,000 over market value for one of Cunningham's homes. Thomas Kontogiannis, another MZM executive, pled guilty in February 2007 to illegally financing Cunningham's purchase of a $2.5 million mansion. In November 2007, former MZM executive Brent Wilkes was convicted of giving Cunningham more than $700,000 in bribes (pleading not guilty, he testified in court that "he felt that giving gifts to powerful members of Congress was an accepted practice among firms trying to get military contracts"). Wilkes faces separate charges of bribing Kyle "Dusty" Foggo, once the CIA's third in command and a childhood friend of Mitchell Wade. Foggo faces charges of bribery in connection with the case, and has pled not guilty. See Tony Perry, "Ex-Contractor Convicted of Bribing Cunningham," *Los Angeles Times*, November 5, 2007.

> tracts through federal earmarks—he'd bully his own staff and staffers on the Appropriations Committee to make sure he got the earmarks he wanted.[24]

But the corruption went far beyond Cunningham's committee. In October 2006, Jane Harman, then the ranking Democrat on the House Intelligence Committee, released an internal congressional investigation into Cunningham's activities that uncovered "major breakdowns" in the oversight process.[25] "To ensure that MZM received government contracts worth tens of millions of dollars," the report said, Cunningham and Wade needed the cooperation of dozens of people. Among them were "the appropriators and authorizers in Congress, who carried Cunningham's funding requests (or 'adds') and wrote the language directing how they were to be used; the various Department of Defense ('DOD') officials responsible for execution of the money, awarding contracts and preparing the Statements of Work; and officials of the agencies for which the contracts were to be performed. This was a lot of people to persuade, cajole, deceive, pressure, intimidate, bribe or otherwise influence to do what they wanted."[26] The intelligence committee's ability to conduct appropriate oversight over CIFA and other agencies "appears to have been seriously impeded by the corrupt conspiracy between Cunningham and Wade," the House report concluded.

Despite the Democratic majority's pledge in January 2007 to cut back on such earmarks, the practice continues unabated. In its voluminous report accompanying the 2007 intelligence budget, the House Intelligence Committee for the first time released a list of earmarked intelligence projects, their cost, and their congressional sponsors. They added up to $95 million, and went to twenty-six projects earmarked by eleven lawmakers from both sides of the political aisle.* And according

* Although the committee didn't name any of the contractors involved, some companies could be identified by the project. Representative Ralph Hall, R-Texas, for example, inserted a $6.2-million earmark to upgrade the RC-135 surveillance aircraft known as the Rivet Joint, which collects signals and communications intelligence for military and other collection agencies; that work is being done by L-3 Communications, an important NSA contractor. Five

to an analysis of earmarks published in the fall of 2007 by Taxpayers for Common Sense, a Washington-based watchdog group, the House version of a $460 billion defense bill included 1,337 earmarks totaling $3 billion, with slightly more than half of that, $1.8 billion, going to projects the Pentagon did not request.[27] Only time will tell how many other Duke Cunninghams and MZMs are waiting to happen in the House and Senate. Given the wall of secrecy that shrouds intelligence contracts, the opportunities for corruption are extensive.

In conclusion, it's not just the secrecy, or the corruption, or the cronyism, or the lack of oversight that's wrong with intelligence contracting: it's also the extent of outsourcing itself, and the way it's carried out. The government, as we just saw, has yet to spell out what intelligence functions are safe to outsource and which ones are not; in the language of the House Intelligence Committee, there is no clear definition of what is "inherently governmental." As a result, decisions about contracting are still being made on the fly, with little regard for their short- and long-term consequences. We first saw that in Abu Ghraib, where contractors were responsible for some of the abuse at the Iraqi prison, and we saw it in the failure of the justice system to properly investigate the companies involved. We saw it in the vast swathes of the CIA's work that is being handled by companies such as BAE Systems, General Dynamics, Scitor, and Abraxas, and in the millions of dollars worth of contracts being

---

separate earmarks worth a total of $15 million were inserted by Representative Bud Cramer, D-Alabama, who represents the area around Huntsville, which is home to the Defense Intelligence Agency's Missile and Space Intelligence Center. The earmarks will benefit four contractors at the center: Sparta Inc. and Intergraph Corporation, which are both based in Huntsville, and Lockheed Martin and Boeing, two of the missile center's prime contractors (those four companies are also among Cramer's top corporate contributors, and together have contributed $268 million to Cramer since 1989, according to the Center for Responsive Politics). The largest single earmark on the House list, for $23 million, was inserted by Representative Jack Murtha, D-Pennsylvania, who is well-known as a master at providing money to companies in his district in Johnstown. It will fund the National Drug Intelligence Center in Johnstown, an arm of the Justice Department providing intelligence and analysis to counter drug traffickers. Since it opened in 1993, Murtha has siphoned more than $500 million to the center, which has remained open despite several attempts by the Bush administration and the Pentagon, which consider the center wasteful and duplicative, to shut it down.

awarded for intelligence analysis. We saw it at the NSA, where the cooperation of the private sector—including telecom providers and IT companies—is so critical that, according to Dick Cheney, a failure by Congress to grant immunity to those companies that assisted the government in the warrantless surveillance program would put the nation in grave danger. When a Vice President of the United States has to stoop to fear-mongering to protect corporations that may have broken the law, it's time to pull the plug on privatization.

Clearly the government will continue to rely, as it has for decades, on the private sector for key technologies, such as spy satellites, sensors, computers, and IT systems. But as the Intelligence Community flounders in its attempt to define which other tasks are inherently governmental, the American public is making up its own mind.

There is widespread agreement, for example, that military and CIA interrogations should only be carried out by government employees answering to a defined chain of command. An interrogation, after all, is where the conqueror meets the conquered, where the invader meets the insurgent, where the American meets the face of his or her enemy. Most of the people I interviewed for this book agreed with the sentiments expressed by Eugene Fidell, the military lawyer I quoted in chapter 1, that outsourcing interrogations is "playing with fire." Even Mike McConnell, the Director of National Intelligence, seems to have reached this conclusion: "I can't imagine using contractors for anything like that," he told Senator Ron Wyden in 2007, when he was asked during his confirmation hearing whether he would approve the hiring of private sector interrogators.*

There also seems to be a consensus about limiting outsourcing in the area of analysis. As we've seen, the vast majority of intelligence spending is not going into building a cadre of experts within government but is instead creating a secret army of analysts and action officers inside the private sector. As a result, large portions of the government's most important documents, such as the President's Daily Brief, are being written by private contractors from companies such as Booz Allen Hamilton,

* See the footnote on page 369.

SAIC, and CACI International. That needs to be reversed, radically and swiftly, so the U.S. government can once again have its own professional ranks of analysts who can inform policy-makers without worrying whether their products will meet the terms of their contracts or enhance their employers' bottom line and future earning capabilities.

As with interrogations, there are signs that the IC itself is moving in this direction with regard to analysis. At the CIA, as we saw in chapter 4, director Michael Hayden ordered a 10 percent cut in the contractor force by the end of 2008. Moreover, some agencies now insist that analysis is out of bounds for contractors. "One point I should emphasize is that we are not outsourcing intelligence analysis," Donald L. Black, the Chief of Public Affairs for the Defense Intelligence Agency, e-mailed me in January 2008. While the DIA does "augment our force with contractors, some of whom have unique expertise," DIA officials are in charge of the final outcome, Black assured me. "A full-time government employee maintains authority, direction, and control over the process, and a senior analyst/leader reviews all analytic products." That's an important step; but it's in our national interest to bring the entire analysis operation back into government so that Congress can have full oversight over what goes into intelligence reports. That doesn't preclude interaction between the IC and the commercial world, academia, or even the general public; it just means interaction as equals, and with a clear demarcation between public and private.

Americans have also spoken loud and clear in the area of NSA surveillance—"communications intelligence," as Admiral McConnell calls it. As this is being written in the winter of 2008, a fierce debate is shaking Washington over the Bush administration's push to win retroactive immunity for the companies that helped the government spy on domestic telecommunications and Internet traffic. Despite making extreme claims in that debate that American lives were at stake, Admiral McConnell and his superiors in the Bush administration found it difficult to overcome the resistance in Congress to blanket amnesty for the companies involved in the secret and possibly illegal partnership with the Intelligence Community. This was largely due to a grassroots campaign by a determined group of citizen-bloggers who spread the word among the voting public and Congress about the issues at stake. At the same time, the popular revolt against unwarranted government and corporate intrusion into privacy encompasses a wide range of political opinion, from liberals like Senators Christopher Dodd and Russell Feingold to conservatives like Bob Barr, a former Republican lawmaker, and Bruce Fein, a former Justice Department official in the Reagan administration. It is a bipartisan consensus: national security should not trump accountability for corporations that may have broken the law.

The looming end of the Bush administration will by no means stop these debates. The national dialogue on contracting and outsourcing that began with Abu Ghraib and continues with Blackwater and the telecom amnesty will be played out through 2008 and well into the next administration. It's going to take years, decades maybe, to get that 70 percent of the intelligence budget spent on contractors down to a tolerable and more controllable level; that will mean constant focus on the issues of accountability, transparency, and oversight. The current proposals for the Orwellian-sounding National Administration Office discussed in chapter 9 will almost certainly be left to the next president and Congress to implement or reject, meaning that discussions about expanding access of domestic security agencies to intelligence from satellites and sensors in the sky—and the role that private contractors play in that enterprise—will remain at the top of the national security agenda long after January 2009. In short, spying for hire is not going away anytime soon.

In the end, if America is to reform its intelligence apparatus, decisions about resources and structure must be made by its citizens through the government they elected—not by private sector contractors like Booz Allen Hamilton or SAIC, who are paid to determine a certain outcome. The spies for hire may not like the idea of subjecting the intelligence process to more stringent oversight, but they're not the ones paying the bill. It's high time that we returned intelligence to its rightful owners: the American public and its representatives in Congress.

Acknowledgments

THIS BOOK would never have seen the light of day without the support and perseverance of my agent, the incomparable John Ware. Since we first became acquainted in 2002, he has been a constant source of encouragement for my work, and his enthusiasm for this book and my writing never flagged. Thank you, John, for a job well done. Roger Labrie, my editor at Simon & Schuster, helped me refine my arguments at key points and fine-tuned my manuscript by eliminating material that was fascinating to me but not always germane to my focus. The book you read now was vastly improved by his editorial stewardship. Sarah Bershtel of Metropolitan Books planted the first seeds for this book when she called me after reading my 2002 take in *The Nation* on the Carlyle Group and the new blend of national security capitalism emerging during the first years of the Bush administration. Knowing the fine quality of books Sarah has published, I am proud to be on her list of interesting writers.

Chalmers Johnson, the author of *Blowback: The Costs and Consequences of American Empire* and other great works, was a mentor to me, and I owe him a great deal. In 1996, when I was a reporter at the *Journal of Commerce,* he lifted me up out of obscurity after I broke an important story that revealed for the first time that the United States played a significant background role in a violent 1980 military crackdown in South Korea. A few weeks later, Chalmers sent me a three-page, single-spaced fax praising the piece and inviting me to speak at a conference in San Francisco on the legacy of the Cold War. Later, he told my story about the U.S. role in the 1980 coup in *Blowback*. By making me feel that my years of work and research on U.S. foreign policy were worthwhile, Chalmers helped launch my second career as an independent journalist. He is also noteworthy for his courage and honesty as an intellectual who was able to question his earlier support for the Vietnam War and forge a new way of looking at America and its past.

Professionally and politically, I'm indebted to the many editors I've worked with as I researched and wrote this book. At *Salon,* Mark Follman thoughtfully edited some of my most important articles about intelligence and the phenomenon of outsourcing, and pressed me to write more for that excellent online publication. Monika Bauerlein, the co-editor of *Mother Jones,* published my first article on intelligence and outsourcing, "The Spy Who Billed Me," in 2005, and encouraged me to write about intelligence, national security, and other topics. At *The Nation,* editor and publisher Katrina vanden Heuvel commissioned my 2002 piece on the Carlyle Group, which I started on long before the events of 9/11 thrust that bank into the public eye; I also salute *The Nation*'s managing editor, Karen Rothmyer, and its copy editor, Roane Carey. Though I sometimes disagree with *The Nation*'s editorial judgments, the magazine remains sharp and vital 150 years after its founding, and I'm proud to have been associated with it since 1983.

I seriously doubt that I would have started writing about intelligence contracting if I hadn't met Bill Golden, the founder of Intelligence Careers.com. I first encountered Bill while researching a story on outsourcing for *Mother Jones*. On a whim, I decided to check into one of Golden's job fairs I'd seen advertised on the Internet. When I entered the recruitment building near Dulles Airport in Northern Virginia, everyone had badges draped around their necks indicating the value of their security clearances. A security guard stopped me and, when I told him I was a reporter, directed me to the man in charge: Bill Golden. He was sitting all by himself in a large cafeteria, accompanied only by his laptop. After asking for some identification, Bill loaded my name into Google to check my bona fides, and out popped dozens of articles from *The Nation*, Antiwar.com, and other lefty sites. I thought "uh-oh, there goes my interview"; but Bill just wanted to make sure I was who I said I was. For the next two and a half hours, he explained to me what the outsourcing business was about and gave a concise history of how it began. Bill was my entry into the industry, and made me realize that the people I was writing about weren't so mysterious after all. Since that meeting, Bill has always taken my calls and patiently answered my questions about the industry and the Intelligence Community. Much appreciation, Bill.

As I was writing this book, I was delighted to become acquainted with Raelynn Hillhouse, who blogs from Hawaii on intelligence and outsourcing at *The Spy Who Billed Me*. Raelynn, who writes as R. J. Hillhouse, has been an excellent (if distant) colleague over the past year, offering insight and expertise, particularly in areas where I was in the dark. She and I share a common interest with the business of outsourcing and have, at times, supported and bounced off each other's work. In 2007, for example, we teased out the intelligence budget numbers imbedded in a set of PowerPoint slides I obtained from the Office of the Director of National Intelligence. Raelynn's report on those numbers led the ODNI to issue a formal response—"the only time that office has ever publicly responded to the writings of a private citizen," as she put it. Raelynn took her blog's title from my 2005 article for *Mother Jones,* and thanked me on her site with a link to my own Web site. That one link has driven more traffic to my site than any other. Raelynn's coverage of Blackwater, the private military contractor that provides security for the CIA in Iraq, is the best you'll find. Moreover, her novel *Outsourced* is a gem. If you read that book along with mine, you will have covered most of what you need to know about the phenomenon of intelligence outsourcing.

Thanks also go to the United States Geospatial Intelligence Foundation. In 2006, Steven Jacques of USGIF invited me to attend GEOINT, the foundation's annual conference and exhibition—by far the most interesting unclassified event in the Intelligence Community—despite the group's rule that book writers should not be registered as press. Attending GEOINT in 2006 and 2007 provided insight and information I couldn't have gathered anywhere else. Jordan Fuhr, the USGIF's director of communications, went out of his way to help me understand the imagery part of the intelligence industry. At the National Geospatial-Intelligence Agency, I thank David Burpee, the director of public affairs, for his help. If the rest of the Intelligence Community had press people as accessible and open as Dave is, the public would be much more informed about intelligence, and the nation would be better off.

Inside the industry itself, I thank Leonard Moodispaw, the CEO of Essex Corporation, and John Gannon, a vice president of BAE Systems. They granted me lengthy telephone interviews that helped me better understand the intelligence business and the issues they face as private sector executives working for the Intelligence Community. Jason Kello of the Intelligence and National Security Alliance patiently answered many questions about his organization. Donald W. Tighe, vice president, external affairs, of In-Q-Tel, and Donald L. Black, the chief of public affairs for the Defense Intelligence Agency, provided information that helped me write accurate portrayals of their organizations. Unfortunately, I can't say the same about the ODNI itself, or the NSA and the CIA. Their press people refused to say much of anything for this book and flatly rejected my many requests to interview officials about outsourcing. It's amazing to me that organizations that spend billions of dollars a year in taxpayer money can get away with being so opaque. What the nation spends on intelligence, and how much of that goes to contractors, should not be a state secret.

That's why I thank Steven Aftergood, who edits *Secrecy News* for the Federation of American Scientists. Steven is a national treasure: for years he has been making the case for public disclosure of the intelligence budget. Just as I was closing on this book, his transparency campaign bore fruit when the ODNI (reluctantly and grudgingly) obeyed the will of Congress and declassified the 2007 budget for the National Intelligence Program, which funds the NSA, the CIA, and the other big collection agencies: the total is $43.5 billion. Through his excellent newsletter, Aftergood also makes available scores of reports about the Intelligence Community that would never see the light of day without his perseverance; indeed, several studies that I cite in this book were first mentioned and posted in *Secrecy News*. For his efforts on behalf of the national interest and reporters like myself, Steven deserves a public service medal.

As a journalist and reporter, I owe a great deal to my former colleagues at the *Journal of Commerce,* where I worked for most of the 1990s. Before our staff was scattered to the winds, the *JOC* was a great paper; but in 1998 its British owners decided to downsize, and cut the Washington bureau from thirteen to one in the course of about eighteen months. In particular I want to thank Scott Bosley, who was the paper's editor when it was owned by Knight Ridder, and two reporters I worked closely with in Washington, Bill Roberts, now of Bloomberg, and John Maggs, now of *National Journal.* Though we often disagreed about the politics of trade and other issues, we knew we were good at what we did, and relished the idea of breaking stories that no one else had. The *Journal of Commerce* also holds poignant memories for me. For years, the paper's main office was on the twenty-sixth floor of Two World Trade Center in New York City. In my last several years at the paper, I spent weeks at a time in those offices working on stories, negotiating with management in my capacity as the president of the *JOC* staff union, and staring out the windows at the amazing views of the Hudson River and beyond. Luckily the paper moved out of New York before 9/11; but when I watched the Twin Towers collapse that horrible day, I felt a deep loss that still hurts.

I have many people to thank in Washington, where I lived for nearly twenty-five years and did much of the initial research for this book. Ed Feigen of the AFL-CIO has been a steady friend and comrade for most of my journalism career, as has John Kelly, my oldest friend in Washington, who generously shared his deep expertise on the CIA with me. John Feffer and Karin Lee have worked closely with me on many issues related to U.S. foreign policy and Northeast Asia; they also put me up during many of my visits back to D.C. and have been supportive of my work since I first met them on their way to Korea in 1998. David Isenberg, a colleague from our days together at the University of Oregon, was gracious with his time and editorial advice. David Corn, the longtime Washington bureau chief for *The Nation* who now holds the same position with *Mother Jones,* was helpful with contacts and suggestions, as was Ken Silverstein, the Washington editor of *Harper's*. David Kaplan, one of the nation's top intelligence reporters, helped me understand arcane issues involving the Intelligence Community. On Capitol Hill, special thanks are due to Paul Cox, the press secretary for Representative David Price of North Carolina, and to Representative Price himself, who agreed to several interviews with me about his contractor legislation. In D.C., I also thank Abid Aslam, Alec Dubro, Jason Vest, Nick Schwellenbach, Chris Townsend, John Cavanagh, Sarah Anderson, Bruce Vail, Andy Banks, Bob Guldin, Mary Price, Martha Allen, and my many friends and colleagues at the National Writers Union and in the labor and peace movements.

In Memphis, where I lived while writing this book, I thank Jim Kovarik for reading early drafts of my manuscript. Robert Gordon, the author of *It Came from Memphis* and other fine books on music and culture, gave me excellent advice at a crucial time. Other friends who were supportive in immeasurable ways were Paula Kovarik, Steve Lockwood, Mary Durham, Judy Card, Sandy Furrh, Andy Cohen, Mark Allen, and Rev. Cheryl Cornish. I also want to thank all the great Memphis musicians who make life in the Mid-South a delight, particularly Jim Dickinson and his sons Luther and Cody Dickinson of the North Mississippi All-Stars ("World Boogie Is Coming!"). In the San Francisco Bay Area, where I have deep roots, I thank Pratap Chaterjee and Tonya Hennessee of CorpWatch for their support and suggestions (and Tonya for one favor in particular). Thanks also to my longtime San Francisco comrades Tom Edminster and Ed Kinchley, who've been there for me through thick and thin, and the beatific people at City Lights Books, the greatest bookstore on earth.

Last but not least, there's my family. Roxanne, my precious daughter, is now a student at the University of Maryland. She's been a great support and inspiration to me and is already an excellent writer; I hope that's one thing she's learned from her dad. I dedicate this book to her.

My father, Hallam C. Shorrock Jr., a World War II vet who learned Japanese during the war while serving in Naval Intelligence, has inspired and helped me in every way imaginable. In 1947, he and my mother went to Japan as missionaries, raised a family, and stayed in Asia until 1969. My father was one of the few American residents in Japan to speak out against the Vietnam War, and together we joined the antiwar movement in Japan and, later, back home in the United States. Those experiences altered my life in significant ways and made me who I am today. Yasuko Fukada, my father's wife and companion, has been a big fan of my writing, which she says helped her and my dad get together. Helen Savage Shorrock, my late mother, who died just before 9/11, would have been pleased and proud to see this book in her hands; to her, I owe my love of learning, my fascination with public affairs, and, thankfully, my ability to cook. My siblings, Karen, Terry, Michael, and Judy, and their families, have been steadfast in their love and support. My stepdaughter, Sarah, and her husband, Todd Gill, have been great as well.

It's impossible to summon the right words to thank my wife of seven years, Kathy McGregor, who's an RN, a hospice nurse extraordinaire, a union organizer, and a great storyteller to boot. Kathy supported me in this book project, from my first proposals in 2002 to my last drafts in the autumn of 2007, with jobs that sometimes wore her out. She had to endure a lot during that time—long absences, lost weekends, the stress of deadlines, my jumbled mind after hours of writing. But she never once let me down and bore the pressures with grace, love, and understanding. I hope I can repay her in kind, because she deserves it.

Tim Shorrock
Tahoma, California
February 2008

Notes

PROLOGUE

1. John Humphrey spoke at a session entitled "Supporting the Intelligence Community" at the Intelcon Conference in Bethesda, Maryland, on May 9, 2006.
2. Dave Dragics made this comment at a March 2006 conference for defense investors sponsored by the investment bank Friedman, Billings, Ramsey.
3. "Rumsfeld's Office Streamlines Its IT," UPI, November 10, 2005.

1. THE INTELLIGENCE-INDUSTRIAL COMPLEX

1. For descriptions of the NCTC, see David Martin, "Tour of the National Counterterrorism Center," transcript, CBS News, September 7, 2006; and Kevin Whitelaw, "The Eye of the Storm," *U.S. News & World Report,* November 6, 2006.
2. Mike McConnell, "Overhauling Intelligence," *Foreign Affairs,* Vol. 86, No. 4, July/August 2007.
3. David Hubler, "CACI Pipes Aboard Calland as New VP," *Washington Technology,* August 16, 2007.
4. I was the first journalist to report on this number. I wrote about the ODNI slides in *Salon.* See Tim Shorrock, "The Corporate Takeover of US Intelligence," *Salon,* June 1, 2007, http://www.salon.com/news/feature/2007/06/01/intel_contractors/.
5. Herbert Browne, interview with author, December 18, 2006.
6. Eugene Fidell, interview with author, July 2006.
7. Robert Baer, interview with author, May 2007.
8. Deborah Walker, NSA presentation to Defense Intelligence Agency acquisition conference, May 2007.
9. R. J. Hillhouse, "Corporate Content and the President's Daily Brief," *The Spy Who Billed Me* (blog), July 23, 2007.

10. Jane Mayer, "The Black Sites: The CIA's Interrogation Techniques," *The New Yorker,* August 13, 2007.
11. NRO director Donald M. Kerr, remarks at the United States Geospatial Intelligence Foundation's GEOINT 2006 symposium, November 15, 2006.
12. Tim Shorrock, "The Spy Who Billed Me," *Mother Jones,* January/February 2005.
13. "The US Intelligence Community's Five Year Strategic Human Capital Plan," an annex to the U.S. National Intelligence Strategy, June 22, 2006, http://www.odni.gov/publications/DNIHumanCapitalStrategicPlan18October2006.pdf.
14. Greg Miller, "Spy Agencies Outsourcing to Fill Key Jobs," *Los Angeles Times,* September 17, 2006.
15. Scott Shane, "Government Keeps a Secret After Studying Spy Agencies," *New York Times,* April 26, 2007.
16. Statement by Ellen Cioccio, acting director of Public Affairs, ODNI press release, June 19, 2007.
17. Terri Everett, "Procuring the Future: 21st Century IC Acquisition," Office of the Director of National Intelligence, May 2007, http://www.fas.org/irp/dni/everett.ppt.
18. Reports of our findings quickly made their way into the mainstream press and the blogosphere and, according to industry sources, caused a great deal of angst within the top ranks of national intelligence. "I didn't expect that conversation to dominate the next two weeks of the ODNI public affairs office," an executive who has daily conversations with that office told me. A few days after he made those comments, the ODNI issued a formal statement about our findings, saying that the bar graphs and their underlying data in the Everett slides were based on a "small, anecdotal sample" of a portion of the IC's contracting activities and therefore could not "be used to derive either the overall [IC] budget or a breakdown of any portion of the budget." But that hardly seemed plausible. For one thing, the slides, and their background numbers, had been prepared for more than a year, and imbedded data in Everett's presentation showed that it had been saved 541 times and worked on for over a hundred hours since its original creation ("After 541 saves, you would think the ODNI had it exactly like they wanted it—save for that embedded spreadsheet," Hillhouse commented on her blog). More to the point, the budget numbers in the ODNI's slides matched the estimates of several well-informed intelligence observers. Robert David Steele, a former CIA officer who once directed the intelligence program for the Marine Corps, told me in 2006 that he believed the IC's budget exceeded $60 billion. And a prominent member of the Intelligence and National Security Alliance who didn't want his name used informed me that the contractor and budget numbers in Everett's PowerPoint presentation paralleled his understanding of the Intelligence Community's historical spending, which has typically been equivalent to 10 percent of the defense budget. In 1995, he noted, the IC's budget was $25 billion, or 10 percent of that year's defense budget of $250 billion. Extending that logic, the Bush administration spent, in total, more than $600 billion on defense in 2006 ($669.8 billion, to be exact, according to Winslow Wheeler, a former Pentagon procurement official who directs the Straus Military Reform Project at the Center for Defense Information). Ten percent of that is $66 billion—$6 billion more than the $60 billion estimated by Hillhouse. Considering all that, I think $60 billion is a safe number to use for an estimate of the intelligence budget. See Winslow Wheeler, "Defense Budget Tutorial #1: What Is the Actual Size of the 2006 Defense Budget?," http://www.d-n-i.net/fcs/defense_budget_tutorial.htm.
19. Scott Amey, interview with author, February 2007.
20. Steven Aftergood, interview with author, June 2007.
21. Leonard Moodispaw, interview with author, January 2007.
22. "ManTech Awarded $130 Million in Previously Unannounced Contracts in April for

Support of National Security Programs," ManTech press release, May 15, 2006; and "CACI Awarded $230 Million in Previously Unannounced Contracts to Support National Security and Intelligence," CACI press release, October 31, 2006.

23. Ben Romero made these remarks at an Equity International conference on homeland security in Washington, D.C., on March 3, 2005.
24. "The Private Sector's Role in Building the Intelligence Community of the 21st Century: Increasing Partnering with Industry to Maintain America's Edge," Chesapeake Innovation Center and Equity International Inc., March 2005.
25. Attensity's products are described on Attensity's page on the Booz Allen Hamilton DIESCON 3 Web site, https://diescon3.bah.com/main/index.asp?loc=team&sub=1.
26. John Elstner, presentation to Equity International conference on homeland security financing, Washington, D.C., March 3, 2005.
27. Thomas E. Dunn, presentation to investors conference, Washington, D.C., March 1, 2006.
28. Michael Hardy, "Equity Firm Rolls Three into One," *Washington Technology,* August 20, 2007.
29. Roger Cressey, at panel discussion, "How Former Public Servants Are Doing Good by Doing Well in Business," Intelcon conference, Bethesda, Maryland, May 8, 2006.
30. Joan Dempsey's remarks were printed in the June 2004 issue of *Colloquy,* the newsletter of the Security Affairs Support Association.
31. Lawrence Korb, telephone interview with author, September 2006.
32. R. J. Hillhouse, e-mail interview with author, February 2007.
33. David Isenberg, interview with author, September 2006.
34. T. Christian Miller, "Private Contractors Outnumber US Troops in Iraq," *Los Angeles Times,* July 4, 2007.
35. Scott Shane and Ron Nixon, "In Washington, Contractors Take on Biggest Role Ever," *New York Times,* February 7, 2007.
36. Timothy Sample, interview with author, August 2006.
37. Stan Soloway, interview with author, August 2006.
38. Shane and Nixon, "In Washington, Contractors Take on Biggest Role Ever."
39. Raymond McGovern, interview with author, April 2007.

2. BOOZ ALLEN HAMILTON AND "THE SHADOW IC"

1. President Bush made these comments while introducing McConnell as DNI, January 5, 2007, White House transcript.
2. Matt Kelley and Richard Willing, "Nominee Played Big Role in Outsourcing Intelligence," *USA Today*, January 4, 2007.
3. Viewed on C-SPAN.
4. According to Hoover's Company Records, October 24, 2006.
5. Konrad Ege, "Rutgers University: Intelligence Goes to College," *Counterspy,* June/August 1984.
6. Allen Nairn, "The Eagle Is Landing," *The Nation,* October 3, 1994.
7. Tim Weiner, *Legacy of Ashes* (New York: Doubleday, 2007), p. 138.
8. According to the official biography of Miles Copeland III, Copeland's son and the first manager of the Police, posted on the latter's Web site, http://www.milescopeland.net/content/publish/mc/article_2.shtml.
9. Joan A. Dempsey, "The Limitations of Recent Intelligence Reforms," paper delivered at a seminar on intelligence, command, and control at the Center for Information Policy Research, Harvard University, September 2006.

10. "US Army Selects Booz Allen–Led Team for Strategic Services Sourcing Program," Booz Allen Hamilton press release, March 15, 2006.
11. Eric Chabrow, "Security Contractors Have Military and Intelligence Roots," *Information Week,* February 25, 2002.
12. Siobhan Gorman, "Bush's Choice of McConnell Said to Revive 'Career Model,' " *Baltimore Sun,* January 6, 2007.
13. "Booz Allen GC Keeps an Eye on the Big Picture," interview with C. G. Appleby, Booz Allen Hamilton's chief legal officer, *Legal Times,* July 31, 2007.
14. Civil Applications Committee Blue Ribbon Study, Independent Study Group Final Report, September 2005, www.fasa.org/irpleprint/cac-report.pdf.
15. "R. James Woolsey Joins Booz Allen as Vice President," Booz Allen press release, July 15, 2002.
16. Joan Dempsey's remarks were printed in *Colloquy,* June 2004.
17. Joan A. Dempsey, "The Limitations of Recent Intelligence Reforms," paper delivered at Harvard University, September 2006.
18. James Bamford, *Body of Secrets: Anatomy of the Ultra-Secret National Security Agency* (New York: Doubleday, 2001), p. 552.
19. Stephen F. Hayes, *Cheney: The Untold Story of America's Most Powerful and Controversial Vice President* (New York: HarperCollins, 2007), p. 484.
20. Michael Hirsh and Mark Hosenball, "The Next Top Spy," *Newsweek,* January 4, 2007.
21. Gorman, "Bush's Choice of McConnell Said to Revive 'Career Model.' "
22. Sue Cant, " 'Cyber 9/11' Risk Warning," *Sydney Morning Herald,* April 22, 2003.
23. Lawrence Wright, "The Spymaster," *The New Yorker,* January 21, 2008.
24. This was discovered by the Center for Public Integrity from a Booz Allen Hamilton job posting on the Internet. See Elizabeth Brown, "Outsourcing the Defense Budget," Center for Public Integrity, July 29, 2004. After the job ad was captured by the center, it was removed from the company's Web site.
25. Booz Allen Hamilton, "Delivering Results That Endure," pamphlet handed out at Iraq reconstruction conference, 2003.
26. Michael Hirsh and Mark Hosenball, "NSA: Meet the Next Spy Chief," *Newsweek* Web "exclusive," January 4, 2007, www.msnbc.com.
27. Ibid.
28. David Morse, "What Was Behind the Pentagon's Betting Parlor?," *Common Dreams,* August 4, 2003, www.commondreams.org.
29. Eric Lichtblau, "US May Invoke 'State Secrets' to Squelch Suit Against Swift," *International Herald Tribune,* August 31, 2007.
30. Eric Lichtblau, "Europe Panel Faults Sifting of Bank Data," *New York Times,* September 26, 2006.
31. "PI and ACLU Show That SWIFT Auditor Has Extensive Ties to US Government," memo by the ACLU and Privacy International for the Article 29 Working Party of the European Commission, September 14, 2006.
32. Lichtblau, "Europe Panel Faults Sifting of Bank Data."
33. Vice President Dick Cheney, text of speech to the Heritage Foundation, January 23, 2008.
34. Mike McConnell spoke at the plenary session of the Intelcon conference in Bethesda, Maryland, May 7, 2006.
35. Hayes, *Cheney*; see also "The Cheney Imperative," *Wall Street Journal,* August 15, 2007.
36. Kelley and Willing, "Nominee Played Big Role in Outsourcing Intelligence."
37. Hearing of the Senate Select Committee on Intelligence: The Nomination of Mike McConnell to be Director of National Intelligence, www.dni.gov/testimonies/20070201=transcript.pdf.

38. "DNI Names New Deputy for Acquisition," ODNI news release No. 13-07, May 8, 2007.
39. Leonard Moodispaw, interview with author, January 2007.
40. Jason Kello, interview with author, June 2007.
41. Scott Amey, interview with author, February 2007.

3. A SHORT HISTORY OF INTELLIGENCE OUTSOURCING

1. Stan Soloway, interview with author, March 2007.
2. SASA newsletter, *Colloquy,* 2003.
3. Jeffrey T. Richelson, "US Satellite Imagery, 1960–1999," National Security Archive Electronic Briefing Book No. 13, April 14, 1999.
4. "Declassifying the 'Fact of' Satellite Reconnaissance," National Security Archive Electronic Briefing Book No. 231, edited by Jeffrey Richelson, October 1, 2007, http://www.gwu.edu/~nsarchiv/NSAEBB/NSAEBB231/index.htm#doc32.
5. Robert Baer, interview with author, May 2007.
6. James Mann, *Rise of the Vulcans* (New York: Viking, 2004), p. 144.
7. Ibid.
8. Steven Emerson, "America's Doomsday Project," *U.S. News & World Report,* August 7, 1989.
9. *CNN Special Assignment,* transcript, November 17, 1991.
10. Emerson, "America's Doomsday Project."
11. Ibid.
12. "ACS Wins $45 Million DoD Command Information Superiority Contract," Lockheed Martin press release, October 15, 2004.
13. Emerson, "America's Doomsday Project."
14. According to Citizens Against Government Waste, a Washington nonprofit started by J. Peter Grace and syndicated columnist Jack Anderson.
15. Cass Peterson, "Grace Panel Eyes Savings of Billions," *Washington Post,* January 13, 1984.
16. Peter Fairman, "Privatization of Federal Government Functions: Reagan, Clinton and the Theory/Action Paradox" (Ph.D. diss., University of Massachusetts, 2001).
17. Ibid.
18. Robert W. Poole, "Ronald Reagan and the Privatization Revolution," *Reason*, June 8, 2004.
19. Stan Soloway, interview with author, August 2006.
20. Fairman, "Privatization of Federal Government Functions."
21. Tim Weiner, "Clinton as Military Leader," *New York Times,* October 28, 1996.
22. James Pavitt, "Change and the CIA," *Washington Post,* August 6, 2004.
23. Jacques Gansler, interview with author, November 2006.
24. Al Gore, "The Big Squeeze," *Washington Post*, September 12, 1993.
25. Spencer S. Hsu, "Death of 'Big Government' Alters Region," *Washington Post*, September 4, 2000.
26. Fairman, "Privatization of Federal Government Functions."
27. Ibid.
28. Joshua Wolf Shenk, "The Perils of Privatization," *Washington Monthly*, May 1995.
29. Martha M. Hamilton, "Approaching Critical Mass," *Washington Post*, January 31, 2000; and "Government to Sell U.S. Enrichment Corporation via Public Offering of Securities," USEC press release, June 29, 1998.
30. Bill Clinton, *My Life* (New York: Knopf, 2004), p. 640.
31. Michael R. Gordon, "Campus Activist to Insider: Journey of the CIA Nominee," *New York Times,* January 11, 1993.

32. "Journal in Turmoil; At *Partisan Review*, Intellectuals at War over an Unpublished Article," *Washington Post*, February 16, 1987.
33. "Sid Webb Is Back in the Game Again," *Business Week*, August 24, 1987.
34. Gordon, "Campus Activist to Insider: Journey of the CIA Nominee."
35. David Halberstam, *War in a Time of Peace* (New York: Touchstone, 2001), p. 243.
36. R. Jeffrey Smith, "As Woolsey Struggles, CIA Suffers," *Washington Post*, May 10, 1994.
37. "R. James Woolsey: Uncompromising Defender," Central Intelligence Agency Web site, https://www.cia.gov/csi/books/dci_leaders_us_community_public/chapter_12.htm.
38. Melissa Boyle Mahle, *Denial and Deception* (New York: Nation Books, 2004), p. 152.
39. Smith, "As Woolsey Struggles, CIA Suffers."
40. Ibid.
41. Walter Pincus, "Woolsey Resigns from CIA After Troubled Tenure," *Washington Post*, December 29, 1994.
42. Robert Burns, "Senate Panel Says Woolsey Acted Weakly," Associated Press, October 25, 1994.
43. Michael F. Scheuer, "Bad Intelligence: Two New Books on the Evolution of the CIA Help Explain the Agency's Current Black Eyes," *Washington Post Book World*, November 27, 2005.
44. Final report of the Defense Science Board Task Force on Outsourcing and Privatization, Office of the Undersecretary of Defense for Acquisition and Technology, August 1996, http://stinet.dtic.mil/cgi-bin/GetTRDoc?AD=ADA316936&Location=U2&doc=GetTRDoc.pdf.
45. "Transforming Defense: National Security in the 21st Century," report of the National Defense Panel, December 1997, http://www.fas.org/man/docs/ndp/front.htm.
46. Brian Friel, "The Business of Defense," *Government Executive*, November 11, 1997; and Susanne Schaer, "Gore Endorses Cohen's Call for Further Military Staff, Base Cuts," Associated Press, November 10, 1997.
47. Ann Markusen, "The Case Against Privatizing National Security," *Dollars & Sense*, May/June 2004.
48. Tim Smart, "He's the General Who Calls in the Big Guns," *Washington Post*, December 15, 1997.
49. Ken Beeks, interview with author, September 2006.
50. "Remarks by the Honorable Jacques S. Gansler, Under Secretary of Defense Acquisition and Technology," AFCEA International, September 29, 1999. Gansler has written lucidly on the pros and cons of outsourcing. See, for example, "Transforming Government Supply Chain Management," edited by Gansler and published in 2004 by the IBM Center for the Business of Government.
51. Greg Schneider and Tom Ricks, "Profits in 'Overused' Army; Cheney Slams Deployments That Benefit His Former Firm," *Washington Post*, September 9, 2000.
52. P. W. Singer, *Corporate Warriors: The Rise of the Privatized Military Industry* (Ithaca: Cornell University Press, 2003), p. 145.
53. Schneider and Ricks, "Profits in 'Overused' Army; Cheney Slams Deployments That Benefit His Former Firm."
54. Colonel Herman T. Palmer, "More Tooth, Less Tail: Contractors in Bosnia," U.S. Army Logistics Management College Web site, www.almc.army.mil.
55. Tim Smart, "Lockheed Team Wins Contract," *Washington Post*, February 13, 1999.
56. Stephen Barr, "Federal Union to Represent Big Contractor's Employees," *Washington Post*, February 24, 1997.
57. Ken Silverstein, *Private Warriors* (New York: Verso, 2000), p. 181.
58. Ibid.

59. Ken Silverstein, "Privatizing War," *The Nation*, July 28, 1997.
60. Silverstein, *Private Warriors*, pp. 166–67.
61. Job posting on *IntelligenceCareers.com,* http://www.intelligencecareers.com/jobs/job view.cfm?jobid=272751.
62. "ManTech Telecommunications and Information Systems Corporation Deployments," company Web page, http://www.mantech.com/mtisc/deployments.asp.
63. Michael Pollick, "Taking the Mystery out of Signals," *Sarasota Herald-Tribune,* January 16, 2000; and "Brushing Up the Army's Mental Agility," *Intelligence Newsletter*, September 3, 1998.
64. William D. Golden, interview with author, June 2006.
65. Ibid., April 2007.
66. Jacques Gansler, interview with author, November 2006.
67. Brian Mitchell, "Should America Trust Its Allies? As Friends Sell Arms to Possible Foes, US Gets Nervous," *Investor's Business Daily*, November 24, 1999.
68. Gansler, interview with author, November 2006.
69. "Statement of Principles," Project for the New American Century, June 3, 1997, www .newamericancentury.org.
70. Richard Haver made these remarks at the Intelcon Conference in Bethesda, Maryland, on May 8, 2006. Tape in possession of the author.
71. Bradley Graham, "Iran, N. Korea Missile Gains Spur Warning," *Washington Post,* July 16, 1998; and "Buried Missile Labs Foil US Satellites," *Washington Post*, July 29, 1998.
72. James O. Goldsborough, "Missile Report Vastly Misunderstood," *San Diego Union-Tribune*, July 27, 1998.
73. William D. Hartung, "Rumsfeld Reconsidered: An Ideologue in Moderate's Clothing," *Foreign Policy in Focus*, policy report, January 2001.
74. Robert Dreyfuss, "Orbit of Influence," *The American Prospect*, March/April 1996.
75. "The Ties That Bind: Arms Industry Influence in the Bush Administration and Beyond," World Policy Institute special report, October 2004, http://www.worldpolicy.org/proj ects/arms/reports/TiesThatBind.html.
76. David Jeremiah, interview with *The NewsHour with Jim Lehrer*, June 3, 1998.
77. David E. Kaplan, Kevin Whitelaw, and Monica M. Ekman, "Mission Impossible: The inside story of how a band of reformers tried—and failed—to change America's spy agencies," *U.S. News & World Report,* August 2, 2004.
78. George J. Tenet, *At the Center of the Storm* (New York: HarperCollins, 2007), p. 21.
79. Seymour M. Hersh, "The Intelligence Gap," *The New Yorker*, December 6, 1999. This article, a fascinating and prescient look at U.S. intelligence in the years leading up to 9/11, is available on the Web at www.cryptome.com.
80. All my quotes from William Golden are from an interview with author in June 2006.

4. THE CIA AND THE SACRIFICE OF PROFESSIONALISM

1. Randall Mikkelsen, "CIA Inspector's Report on September 11 Faults Leader," Reuters, August 21, 2007.
2. Michael Rubin, "Privatize the CIA: Our Intelligence Community Could Use More Competition," *The Weekly Standard*, February 5, 2007.
3. Greg Miller, "Spy Agencies Outsourcing to Fill Key Jobs," *Los Angeles Times,* September 17, 2006.
4. R. J. Hillhouse, "The Achilles' Heel of the US War Effort," *The Spy Who Billed Me* (blog), October 4, 2007, http://www.thespywhobilledme.com/the_spy_who_billed_me/ 2007 /10/the-achilles-he.html.

5. Jane Mayer, "The CIA's Travel Agent," *The New Yorker*, October 30, 2006.
6. Miller, "Spy Agencies Outsourcing to Fill Key Jobs."
7. Robert Baer, "Outsourcing the CIA," *Time*, April 20, 2007.
8. Robert Baer, interview with author, May 2007.
9. Robert Baer, *Blow the House Down* (New York: Crown, 2006), p. 88.
10. Melvin Goodman, interview with author, April 2007.
11. "Statement to Employees by Director of the Central Intelligence Agency, General Michael V. Hayden, on Contractor Study," CIA press release, May 30, 2007.
12. Court documents filed by the CIA in response to a lawsuit filed by "Peter B.," a covert contract employee who claims he was unlawfully terminated, obtained by the Federation of American Scientists and posted on the FAS *Secrecy News* Web site, April 11, 2007, www.fas.org/blog/secrecy/.
13. Retired Air Force General Michael V. Hayden, in an interview with C-SPAN's Brian Lamb, April 15, 2007.
14. Hillhouse, "The Achilles' Heel of the US War Effort."
15. Robert Young Pelton, *Licensed to Kill: Hired Guns in the War on Terror* (New York: Crown, 2007), p. 30.
16. Ibid.
17. Larry Johnson, interview with author, April 2007.
18. Ray McGovern, interview with author.
19. At the same time, advances in information technology, and the automation of internal systems at the CIA, provided an opening for IT companies offering data management and information services. At the CIA, "Intelligence reports at the beginning of the decade [of the 1990s] were hand-delivered; by the end of the decade, almost all products were disseminated electronically," Melissa Boyle Mahle, a former CIA Middle East specialist, wrote in her 2004 memoir, *Denial and Deception*. Even so, by the turn of the century the CIA's system was fairly crude compared to what could be found in the commercial world, as Bruce Berkowitz, a former CIA officer and a research fellow at the conservative Hoover Institution, discovered. In 2001 and 2002, Berkowitz was a scholar-in-residence at the Sherman Kent Center for Intelligence Analysis, the CIA's think tank for analysts. Over a six-month period, he was charged with looking at how the Directorate of Intelligence used information technology and comparing the CIA to organizations that performed similar research functions, including the *Washington Post* and the Congressional Research Service. His study, "Failing to Keep Up with the Information Revolution," was published on the CIA's public Web site in April 2007. Berkowitz found that CIA analysts had access to two different computer systems: a classified network for CIA work and for communications with other intelligence agencies, and a declassified network connected to the Internet and public e-mail accounts. Using a switchbox, analysts could move from one system to another; but secrecy protocols at the CIA and its sister agencies made it extremely difficult to access classified documents posted on the CIA's internal Web site, called CIASource. For example, a person could have a non-CIA top secret/SCI clearance and be cleared to read CIASource, but "not have either the CIA network access certification or the equipment able to access the website. The result is that DI analysts work in an environment that is largely isolated from the outside world." He also found that the stringent rules for using classified systems sent "implicit messages to analysts: that technology is a threat, not a benefit, and that the CIA does not put a high priority on analysts using IT easily or creatively." He recommended a new approach that would give CIA analysts easy and quick access to both secret and declassified systems. Only by using IT more effectively could the CIA hope "to provide US officials the intelligence that they are required to detect, understand, and respond to current, emerging, and future threats fac-

ing the United States." See Melissa Boyle Mahle, *Denial and Deception: An Insider's View of the CIA from Iran-Contra to 9/11* (New York: Nation Books, 2004), p. 73; and Bruce Berkowitz, "Failing to Keep Up with the Information Revolution," CIA Center for the Study of Intelligence, May 2007, https://www.cia.gov/library/center-for-the-study-of-intelligence/kent-csi/docs/v47i1a07p.htm.

20. *The 9/11 Commission Report*, p. 90.
21. John Gannon, interview with author, September 2006.
22. According to an NCTC official who testified before the 9/11 Commission. See "Statement of Russell E. Travers to the National Commission on Terrorist Attacks upon the United States," January 26, 2004, http://www.9-11commission.gov/hearings/hearing7/witness_travers.htm.
23. "TAC Gets Work on Terrorist Watch List," *Homeland Security & Defense*, November 2, 2005.
24. Karen DeYoung, "Terror Database Has Quadrupled in Four Years," *Washington Post,* March 25, 2007.
25. Renae Merle, "Fairfax Firm Adds to Its CIA Cast," *Washington Post,* June 22, 2006.
26. Ibid.
27. Ibid.
28. L-1 Identity Solutions Inc., analysts meeting transcript, November 2, 2006.
29. L-1 Identity Solutions Inc., earnings conference call, May 9, 2007 (available on the SEC Web site).
30. Briefing by Douglas Franz, formerly of the Carlyle Group, at an investors forum in Washington, D.C., March 31, 2004.
31. Oynx Garner, "Creating a Win-Win Culture," *Outsourcing Journal*, June 2005, www.outsourcing-journal.com.
32. "Tenet Joins 'James Bond' Firm," Reuters, October 24, 2006.
33. See Laura Rozen, "The First Contract," *The American Prospect,* March 30, 2007, http://www.prospect.org/cs/articles?articleId=12612.
34. "Former CIA Director George Tenet Joins Guidance Software Board of Trustees," Guidance press release, March 22, 2006.
35. General Dynamics, "IT Solutions for Mission Support," publication number 5636, handed out at GEOINT 2006, Orlando, Florida.
36. "Contractor's Rise Shows Blurred Government, Industry Lines," *Government Executive*, July 7, 2006.
37. "Mission-Critical Intelligence Support in War on Terror," *SAIC Magazine,* Winter/Spring 2006, www.saic.com.
38. Donald L. Bartlett and James B. Steele, "Washington's $8 Billion Shadow," *Vanity Fair*, March 2007.
39. Brookes's CIA experience while working at SAIC is mentioned in his biographical information posted on the Heritage Foundation's Web site.
40. Bartlett and Steele, "Washington's $8 Billion Shadow."
41. Dana Priest, "Top-Secret World Loses Blogger," *Washington Post,* July 21, 2006; and Mark Mazzetti, "CIA Worker Says Message on Torture Got Her Fired," *New York Times,* July 22, 2006.
42. "BAE Systems Global Analysis Business Unit: Expert Analysts in Partnership with the Intelligence Community," BAE brochure distributed at GEOINT 2007.
43. "FBI Oversight," testimony before the U.S. Senate Committee on the Judiciary, May 2, 2006, Dr. John Gannon, vice president for Global Analysis, BAE Systems Information Technology, supplied to the author by Dr. Gannon.
44. *Entrepreneur Weekly,* November 8, 2005.

45. Ibid.
46. Greg Miller, "A Bold Upstart with CIA Roots," *Los Angeles Times*, September 17, 2006.
47. "The CIA's Accountants," *Intelligence Newsletter*, July 22, 1999.
48. Linda Robinson and Kevin Whitelaw, "Seeking Spies," *U.S. News & World Report,* February 13, 2006.
49. James Bamford, "This Spy for Rent," *New York Times,* June 13, 2004.
50. Miller, "A Bold Upstart with CIA Roots."
51. David B. Ottoway, "State Dept., Congress in Embassy Row," *Washington Post*, March 4, 1987.
52. "Abraxas Corporation Opens Office in China," Abraxas press release, printed in *Asia Pulse,* October 21, 2004.
53. Ben Hammer, "Abraxas Goes on Shopping Spree," *Washington Business Journal,* December 25, 2006.
54. "One Door Closes, Another Opens," *Montgomery Advertiser*, March 28, 2004.
55. This was posted on a blog called *Enough, I've Had It,* http://blogs.salon.com/0003752/2004/04/14.html.
56. Hammer, "Abraxas Goes on Shopping Spree."
57. Hoskins's name doesn't appear on the company Web site, but his biographical information was posted by his alma mater, Auburn University's School of Engineering, in 2006. See http://eng.auburn.edu/admin/marketing/events/index.html.
58. "McDonald Bradley Participates in Consortium That Lands $250 Million Agreement at DoD," McDonald Bradley press release, October 12, 2007.
59. Stephanie Cline, "Scitor Corp. to Move to Patriot Park in Colorado Springs," *Colorado Springs Business Journal,* May 13, 2005.
60. Eric Winig, "Allied Capital Makes $22 Million Bet on Scitor's Future," *Washington Business Journal,* August 26, 2002.
61. "Employees Acquire Scitor Corp. in 100% ESOP Buyout," press release, Houlihan Lokey Howard & Zukin, July 29, 2002.
62. Nick Wakeman, "M&A Roundup," *Washington Technology*, October 1, 2007.
63. According to the Auburn University Web site, http://eng.auburn.edu/admin/marketing/events/index.html.
64. Stephanie O'Sullivan, remarks to GEOINT 2006.
65. "In-Q-Tel Announced Strategic Investment in Keyhole," In-Q-Tel press release, June 25, 2003.
66. Kim Hart, "Firm to Mine Databases for National Security Threats," *Washington Post,* April 19, 2007.
67. Donald Tighe, interview with author, November 2006.
68. Vernon Loeb, "CIA Adventures in Venture Capital," *Washington Post,* June 3, 2001.
69. Shannon Henry, "In-Q-Tel, Investing in Intrigue," *Washington Post,* July 1, 2002.
70. Donald W. Tighe, In-Q-Tel, e-mail interview with author, January 26, 2008.
71. Olga Harif, "A Start-up's Road to Washington," *BusinessWeek On-Line,* May 10, 2005.
72. Noah Shachtman, "With Terror in Mind, a Formulaic Way to Parse Sentences," *New York Times*, March 3, 2005.
73. I interviewed Tighe at the GEOINT conference in 2006.
74. Joseph Santucci, interview with author, November 2006.
75. According to Stephanie O'Sullivan.
76. Ken Beeks, interview with author, September 2006.
77. Michael Kleeman, interview with author, January 2006.

78. Ken Silverstein, "The JIN: Too Good to Be True," *Harper's*, April 4, 2007. Silverstein also raised serious questions about Ianatron's technology.
79. Chris Byron, interview with author, June 2006.
80. Ray McGovern, interview with author, April 2007.
81. Melvin Goodman, interview with author, April 2007.
82. Michael Scheuer, interview with author, February 9, 2005.
83. Robert Baer, interview with author, May 2007.
84. Timothy Sample, interview with author, August 2006.

5. THE ROLE OF THE PENTAGON

1. "The GIG Vision, Enabled by Information Assurance," National Security Agency Web site, http://www.nsa.gov/ia/industry/gig.cfm.
2. Steven Zenishek made these comments at the Precision Strike 2006 Conference in Silver Spring, Maryland, March 1, 2006.
3. Among other things, the PNAC document proposed that the U.S. Army deploy forward-based units for long-term "reconnaissance and security missions" abroad, to be capable of operating over long distances "with sophisticated means of communication and access to high levels of U.S. intelligence." Looking ahead to the Internet-based systems that would be developed under Rumsfeld, the task force emphasized that these units should be "built around the acquisition and management of information. This will be essential for combat operations—precise, long-range fire requires accurate and timely intelligence and robust communications links—but also for stability operations." The report also foreshadowed the Pentagon's creation of secret human intelligence units. "Especially those forces stationed in volatile regions must have their own human intelligence collection capacity, perhaps through an attached special forces unit if not solely through an organic intelligence unit." Among the members of the PNAC defense task force were three people who would play a key role in the Rumsfeld-Cheney intelligence axis: Stephen Cambone, then affiliated with the National Defense University; Scooter Libby, who would become Cheney's top national security aide; and Paul Wolfowitz, who would become Rumsfeld's deputy. See "Rebuilding America's Defense: Strategy, Forces and Resources for a New Century," a report of the Project for the New American Century, September 2000, http://www.newamericancentury.org/RebuildingAmericasDefenses.pdf.
4. "Intel Reform Clears Congress with Military Chain-of-Command Accord," *Inside the Pentagon*, December 9, 2004.
5. Melvin Goodman, interview with author, April 2007.
6. Joan A. Dempsey, "The Limitations of Recent Intelligence Reforms," paper delivered at a seminar on intelligence, command, and control at the Center for Information Policy Research, Harvard University, September 2006.
7. Douglas Jehl, "Bush Wants Plan for Covert Pentagon Role," *New York Times*, November 23, 2004.
8. Philip Giraldi, interview with author, April 2006.
9. Seymour Hersh, "The Coming Wars," *The New Yorker*, January 24, 2005. The *Washington Post* first revealed the existence of the Strategic Support Branch in January 2005. The Pentagon, *Post* reporter Barton Gellman wrote, was now engaged in overseas missions "that have traditionally been the province of the CIA's Directorate of Operations." That included sending defense personnel abroad under "nonofficial cover," using false names and nationalities—something the CIA's Directorate of Operations had always had exclusive jurisdiction over. Lieutenant General William G. Boykin, the Christian fundamentalist placed in charge of the support branch, confirmed to the *Post* that the Pentagon

was directing some missions "previously undertaken by the CIA," but explained the actions in the context of the secretary of defense's control over the bulk of the nation's intelligence budget. "He has 80 percent of the responsibility for collection, as well," Boykin pointed out, as if this justified Rumsfeld's unprecedented actions. See Barton Gellman, "Secret Unit Expands Rumsfeld's Domain," *Washington Post*, January 23, 2005. Meanwhile, as the secret military intelligence teams grew bolder, they began to alienate U.S. officials in several countries where they were deployed. Edward Gnehm, the former U.S. ambassador to Jordan, disclosed in 2007 that he once discovered that the Pentagon had sent a secret team into Jordan without even telling the CIA station. "The CIA was not happy at all," he said at the time. Later, the *Los Angeles Times* reported that U.S. officials removed a secret Pentagon team from Paraguay after one of its members shot and killed an armed assailant who tried to rob them. And in East Africa, members of another team were exposed by the local government and arrested. The mishaps and clashes prompted a new effort by the CIA and the Pentagon "to tighten the rules for military units engaged in espionage," the paper reported. See Greg Miller, "US Seeks to Rein in Its Military Spy Teams," *Los Angeles Times*, December 18, 2006.

10. "Network-Centric Warfare: Creating a Decisive Warfighting Advantage," Director, Force Transformation Office of the Secretary of Defense, Winter 2003.
11. "United States Network Centric Operations Markets, FY12-22," Frost & Sullivan, www.frost.com. My copy of this report was made available by the Network Centric Operations Industry Consortium.
12. Terence Morgan, interview with author, January 2007.
13. Harry Raduege, interview with author, January 2007.
14. Lt. Gen. William Boykin, speech to the GEOINT symposium, November 2006.
15. Michael Hirsh and Mark Hosenball, "Gates Cleans House at the Pentagon," *Newsweek,* January 9, 2007.
16. "The 2006 Annual Report of the United States Intelligence Community," Director of National Intelligence, unclassified, February 2007; and Gerry L. Gilmore, "DoD to Set Up Joint Intelligence Operations Worldwide," American Forces Press Service, April 12, 2006.
17. This integration was spelled out in a set of PowerPoint slides prepared in 2007 by the Office of the Undersecretary of Defense for Intelligence to explain progress of the JIOC system. One slide, titled "JIOC/DCGS-Joint Concept," stated that the JIOCs are to be integrated with Distributed Common Ground Systems.
18. News transcript, "Press Availability on Joint Intelligence Operations Centers," Department of Defense, April 12, 2006.
19. This contract was disclosed by SAIC during a briefing for investors at the Friedman, Billings, Ramsey Washington, D.C., conference in March 2007.
20. "Mission-Critical Intelligence Support in War on Terror," *SAIC Magazine,* Winter 2006, www.saic.com.
21. Paul Kaihla, "US: In the Company of Spies," *Business 2.0,* May 1, 2003.
22. "Defense Intelligence Agency . . . at a Glance," DIA Web site, www.dia.gov.
23. Robert K. Ackerman, "Defense Intelligence Assumes More Diverse Missions," *SIGNAL Magazine* (AFCEA), April 2007.
24. "Chalabi Meets with Rumsfeld, Cheney," United Press International, November 14, 2005.
25. I am indebted to a colleague who wishes to remain anonymous for her notes on the Defense Intelligence Acquisition Conference, which took place May 14–17, 2007, in Keystone, Colorado.
26. Lt. Gen. Michael Maples, "Consolidating Our Intelligence Contracts," Letter to the Editor, *Washington Post*, August 24, 2007.

27. Donald L. Black, DIA, e-mail interview with author, January 29, 2008.
28. Walter Pincus, "Defense Agency Proposes Outsourcing More Spying," *Washington Post*, August 19, 2007.
29. "Blanket Purchase Agreements," *FedMarket.com*, http://www.fedmarket.com/articles/purchase-agreements-blanket.shtml.
30. "DIESCON 3: Blanket Purchase Agreements/Program Management and Business Process Plan," Defense Intelligence Agency, May 25, 2005.
31. "Statement of Work," DIA Information Technology Acquisition Support Center, www.dia.gov.
32. Clive Thompson, "Open-Source Spying," *New York Times Magazine*, December 3, 2006.
33. All the information about BAE Systems is from the BAE Web site page, "About DIESCON 3," http://www.bae-it.na.baesystems.com/wat.nsf/0/1967DA8A51EA2FFB85256DC200539DE2.
34. Herbert Browne, interview with author, December 2006.
35. Jeff Stein, "In NSA's Shadow, Military Intelligence Rides the Edge of Domestic Spying," *CQ Homeland Security*, January 27, 2006.
36. Stenbit's involvement in CIFA was described in his biography posted on the Web site of ViaSat, a wireless communications company where he serves as a director. "Former Assistant Secretary of Defense John Stenbit Named to Board of Directors," ViaSat press release, August 30, 2004.
37. Walter Pincus, "Pentagon Expanding Its Domestic Surveillance Activity," *Washington Post*, November 27, 2005.
38. Walter Pincus, "Pentagon's Intelligence Authority Widens," *Washington Post*, December 19, 2005.
39. William M. Arkin, "Domestic Military Intelligence Is Back," "Early Warning" column, *Washington Post*, October 29, 2005.
40. Shane Harris, "Signals and Noise," *National Journal*, June 17, 2006.
41. "Counterintelligence Field Activity," House report number 109-411, Intelligence Authorization Act for Fiscal Year 2007, February 2006.
42. Privacy and Civil Liberties Oversight Board, 2007 Report to Congress, April 23, 2007, http://www.privacyboard.gov/reports/2007/congress2007.html.
43. Walter Pincus, "Pentagon Agency's Contracts Reviewed," *Washington Post*, March 3, 2006.
44. Jonathan S. Landay, "Pentagon Contracted for Satellite Photos of US Locations," Knight Ridder, March 18, 2006.
45. Walter Pincus, "Increase in Contracting Intelligence Jobs Raises Concerns," *Washington Post*, March 20, 2006.
46. "Intelligence Analyst Senior Staff," job posting, Lockheed Martin, www.tech-centric.net.
47. Job No. 194272 (Counterintelligence Analyst), Defense Engineers and Intelligence Careers, March/April 2005, www.intelligencecareers.com.
48. "Analex—Major Clients/Defense and Intelligence," www.analex.com.
49. ManTech job posting (Intelligence Analyst, Senior), *BaltimoreAdtaker.com*, August 7, 2007; see also www.mantech.com/alliant-team_cap.asp.
50. "Counterintelligence Field Activity (CIFA)," on Harris Web site, www.govcomm.harris.com.
51. No longer on SRA Web site.
52. Walter Pincus, "Counterintelligence Officials Resign," *Washington Post*, August 10, 2006.

53. Walter Pincus, "Gates May Rein In Pentagon Activities," *Washington Post,* November 14, 2006.
54. Siobhan Gorman, "Imagery Intelligence Agency Chief Being Forced from Post," *Baltimore Sun,* January 6, 2006.
55. Walter Pincus, "Pentagon to End Talon Data-Gathering Program," *Washington Post,* April 25, 2007.
56. "General Who Likened War on Terror to Battle with Satan to Retire," Agence France-Presse, May 21, 2007.
57. Pincus, "Gates May Rein In Pentagon Activities."
58. William Mathews, "Black US R&D Budget Estimated at $17.5 Billion," *Defense News*, August 29, 2007.
59. "Pentagon, DNI Kick Off Effort to Modernize Security Clearance System," *Inside the Army,* June 4, 2007.
60. "Raytheon Team Demonstrates Innovative Technologies at Empire Challenge 2007," Raytheon press release, July 20, 2007.
61. Walter Pincus, "Defense Agency Proposes Outsourcing More Spying," *Washington Post,* August 19, 2007.
62. Steven Aftergood, interview with author, January 2008.
63. Walter F. Roche, "Defense Nominee's Business Ties Raise Concerns," *Los Angeles Times,* December 2, 2006.
64. "Lieutenant General (USAF Ret.) James R. Clapper Joins 3001 Board," CM Equity Partners press release, October 12, 2006.
65. "MoD's Suppliers Target American Market," *Intelligence Online,* February 9, 2007; "Lt. Gen. Jim Clapper and Dr. Jim Blackwell Join DFI Government Services," DFI press release, October 12, 2006; and DFI Web site, http://www.deticadfi.com/.
66. "DeticaDFI Wins Key Position in World-wide US Defense Intelligence Framework," DeticaDFI press release, September 8, 2007, http://www.deticadfi.com/internal.aspx?m=pressrelease&i=47; and "Major US Government Client Awards Contract to DeticaDFI," Detica press release, September 7, 2007, http://www.detica.com/indexed/NewsItem_deticadficontractwin.htm.

6. THE NSA, 9/11, AND THE BUSINESS OF DATA MINING

1. Scott Shane and Tom Bowman, "America's Fortress of Spies," *Baltimore Sun,* December 3, 1995.
2. Peter Spiegel, "U.S. Spy Chief Calls Warrantless Wiretapping Discussion a Threat," *Los Angeles Times*, September 21, 2007.
3. Frank Blanco, interview with author, Fort Meade, Maryland, 2005.
4. Booz Allen Hamilton, "Annual Report 2001," p. 22, available on Booz Allen Web site.
5. Booz Allen Hamilton, "Annual Report 2001."
6. The NSA's contracting out of background checks was described in a Senate Intelligence Committee report in January 2007. See "Intelligence Authorization Act for Fiscal Year 2007," Senate Intelligence Committee, January 24, 2007.
7. Shane and Bowman, "America's Fortress of Spies."
8. Several operations run jointly by the NSA and CIA "caused much friction" between the two agencies, the commission reported. At the mid- and upper-management levels of the CIA and NSA, "struggles developed regarding which agency was in charge . . . when human intelligence and signals intelligence targets overlapped. . . . CIA perceived NSA as wanting to control technology deployment, while NSA was concerned that CIA was

conducting NSA-type operations. See "OIG Report on CIA Accountability with Respect to the 9/11 Attacks," online at www.fas.org/irp/cia/product/oig-911.pdf.

9. Greg Miller and Josh Meyer, "Systematic Breakdown at CIA Before Sept. 11," *Los Angeles Times*, August 22, 2007; and Michael Isikoff and Mark Hosenball, "Terror Watch: The CIA's Withering 9/11 Intelligence Report," *Newsweek*, August 21, 2007.
10. Scott Shane, "NSA Technology Touches Far More than Spy World," *Baltimore Sun*, December 10, 1995.
11. Seymour Hersh, "The Intelligence Gap: How the Digital Age Left Our Spies out in the Cold," *The New Yorker*, December 6, 1999. This article can still be found on the Web at http://cryptome.org/nsa-hersh.htm.
12. Both of these episodes were reported in Scott Shane and Tom Bowman, "Rigging the Game," *Baltimore Sun*, December 10, 1995.
13. Hersh, "The Intelligence Gap: How the Digital Age Left Our Spies out in the Cold."
14. Transcript, 2007 Air Force Defense Strategy Seminar Series, General Michael V. Hayden, Director, Central Intelligence Agency, National Guard Association of the United States, June 19, 2007, http://www.deticadfi.com/Internal.aspx?t=PreviousAirForceSeminars&1=244&s=108.
15. CACI presentation to Friedman, Billings, Ramsey conference on defense investing, March 8, 2007.
16. Statement by Director of Central Intelligence George J. Tenet before the House Permanent Select Committee on Intelligence, as prepared for delivery, April 12, 2000.
17. A year later, in 2002, Beijing discovered that a Boeing 767 purchased for use as President Jiang Zemin's official aircraft contained no fewer than twenty listening devices, including one in the presidential bed and another in the bathroom. The culprit was apparently the NSA's Special Collection Service, a top secret unit within the Central Security Service that is tasked, jointly with the CIA, to eavesdrop on intelligence targets in hostile countries. "China Says President's Jet Bugged," Reuters, January 18, 2002.
18. Michael Isikoff and David Corn, *Hubris: The Inside Story of Spin, Scandal and the Selling of the Iraq War* (New York: Crown, 2006), p. 186.
19. James Risen, *State of War: The Secret History of the CIA and the Bush Administration* (New York: Free Press, 2005), pp. 42–60.
20. Ibid., p. 48.
21. Scott Shane and David Johnston, "Mining of Data Prompted Fight over U.S. Spying," *New York Times*, July 29, 2007.
22. Peter Swire, interview with author, June 2007.
23. Statement of Lt. Gen. Michael V. Hayden, Director, National Security Agency, before the joint inquiry of the Senate Select Committee on Intelligence and the House Permanent Select Committee on Intelligence, October 17, 2002.
24. Bob Graham with Jeff Nussbaum, *The CIA, the FBI, Saudi Arabia and the Failure of America's War on Terror* (New York: Random House, 2004), p. 70.
25. National Security Agency/Central Security Service, Transition 2001, prepared for the incoming administration of George W. Bush, declassified document obtained in 2005 by Dr. Jeffrey Richelson, senior fellow at the National Security Archive. Available at the archive's Web site, www.gwu.edu/~nsarchive/.
26. Graham and Nussbaum, p. 71.
27. The NSA's "Transition 2001" report can be found at the National Security Agency Declassified/National Security Archive Electronic Briefing Book No. 24, edited by Jeffrey Richelson, posted January 13, 2000, and updated March 11, 2005, http://www.gwu.edu/~nsarchiv/NSAEBB/NSAEBB24/index.htm.
28. Stan Soloway, interview with author, February 2007.

29. Statement of Lt. Gen. Michael V. Hayden, Director, National Security Agency, before the joint inquiry of the Senate Select Committee on Intelligence and the House Permanent Select Committee on Intelligence, October 17, 2002; and "The Private Sector's Role in Building the Intelligence Community of the 21st Century," report published by Equity International and Chesapeake Innovation Center, March 3, 2005. The CIC is funded in part by the NSA.
30. James Bamford, *Body of Secrets: Anatomy of the Ultra-Secret National Security Agency* (New York: Doubleday, 2001).
31. Noi Mahoney, "NSA Unveils Private Partnership," *The Capital* (Annapolis, Maryland), August 3, 2001.
32. Ellen McCarthy, "NSA Is Making No Secret of Its Technology Intent," *Washington Post,* June 24, 2004.
33. George Cahlink, "Security Agency Doubled Procurement Spending in Four Years," *Government Executive,* June 1, 2004.
34. "The Business of Connecting Dots: The $1 Billion Intelligence and Security Informatics/Analytics Market," Chesapeake Innovation Center, November 17, 2005.
35. Greg Schneider, "It's Too Soon to Tell, but a Deathly Ill Columbia Company Has Color in Its Cheeks," *Baltimore Sun,* June 28, 1998.
36. Stephanie Wentworth, *Baltimore Business Journal*, October 16, 2006.
37. Paul Richfield, "Northrop Grumman Acquires Essex, Moves Closer to NSA," *C4ISR/The Journal of Net-Centric Warfare/Defense News,* November 9, 2006.
38. Leonard Moodispaw, interview with author, January 2007.
39. "National Security Agency Outsources Areas of Non-Mission Information Technology to CSC-Led Alliance Team," NSA press release, July 31, 2001, http://www.nsa.gov/releases/relea00034.cfm.
40. Dennis McCafferty, "CSC Has a Lock on Government Business," *VAR Business,* September 30, 2002.
41. Anitha Reddy, "Computer Systems Spur Growth for Contractors," Technews.com, May 10, 2004.
42. "National Security Agency Outsources Areas of Non-Mission Information Technology to CSC-Led Alliance Team."
43. "Logicon Brings Key Capabilities, Experience to NSA Groundbreaker Technology Contract," Logicon press release, Northrop Grumman, August 6, 2001.
44. Leonard Moodispaw, interview with author, January 2007.
45. Siobhan Gorman, "Computer Ills Hinder NSA," *Baltimore Sun,* February 26, 2006.
46. "CSC-Led Alliance Receives Three-Year Option for NSA Groundbreaker Contract," CSC press release, June 6, 2007, http://www.csc.com/investorrelations/news/9591.shtml.
47. "Boeing Demonstrates Anti-Terrorism Integrated Tactical Solutions Using Multiple UAV," Boeing press release, June 22, 2006.
48. "Titan Feasts on Defense and Intelligence Budgets," *Intelligence Online*, May 11, 2004.
49. "L-3 Communications Gets $35 Million NSA Deal," Associated Press (via the *Houston Chronicle*), December 21, 2006.
50. Many of these companies were listed in an extensive public release of NSA contractors in 2007. The disclosure came about quite by accident, when the National Reconnaissance Office released its 2005 budget, along with its justification documents, as part of a Freedom of Information Act request filed by Steven Aftergood of the Federation of American Scientists. The document was highly redacted, but most of the pages listing contractors were left untouched, leaving a clean public record of thirteen key intelligence contractors. Specifically, these were companies providing services to the National and Military Operations Support project (NMOS), an effort funded by the classified National Intelli-

gence Program of the IC's annual budget. Its project is a "partnership" between the NRO and three major collection agencies—the NSA for signals, the NGA for imagery, and the DIA directorate for MASINT—and is the key "gateway" used by the NSA to transmit its intelligence to the rest of the government and the Intelligence Community. The NSA contractors are listed as follows: at the top level, three large firms provided the systems integration work for signals intelligence operations. They are Northrop Grumman, General Dynamics, and Booz Allen Hamilton. Below them, providing technical services, are American Management Systems Inc., a subsidiary of CACI International; CACI's Technology Services unit; Electronic Data Systems; BearingPoint, the Virginia consulting company; Northrop Grumman Information Technology, or TASC, the primary intelligence subsidiary of the defense contractor; US Investigations Services (USIS), a wholly owned subsidiary of the Carlyle Group that does background checks on NSA employees and contractors; Boeing Service Company, Boeing's security support company; PricewaterhouseCoopers, the financial auditing company; ManTech Aegis Research, one of the intelligence units of ManTech International; Lockheed Martin, the nation's largest defense contractor; and L-3 Communications, which ranks sixth as a defense contractor.

51. ManTech International Corp., 10-K, filed with the SEC on March 16, 2005.
52. I heard an NSA consultant and two CACI engineers discuss this project at a workshop I attended in Northern Virginia in 2004. David Hall, a former Raytheon engineer turned NSA consultant, harked back to the "good old Soviet Union days," when the United States used to have a huge advantage in IT. Now, he said, "almost anybody can transmit satellite data," and noted that communications technology is even available to "our terrorist opponents."
53. A sound clip of this interview was posted for a time on CACI's Web site, www.caci.com.
54. Patrick Leahy, "Ensuring Liberty and Security Through Checks and Balances," speech delivered to Georgetown University Law Center, Washington, D.C., December 13, 2006, http://leahy.senate.gov/press/200612/121306.html.
55. The subpoenas were announced in a press release from Senator Patrick Leahy, and can be downloaded from that page. See "Senate Judiciary Committee Issues Subpoenas for Legal Basis of Bush Administration's Domestic Surveillance Program," Office of Senator Leahy, June 27, 2007, http://leahy.senate.gov/press/200706/062707a.html.
56. Interview with author, November 2006. For detailed (and contrasting) analyses of the FISA rules, readers should consult two Web sites. One is a podcast from the Federal Law Enforcement Training Center of the Department of Homeland Security that describes the FISA rules for monitoring U.S. persons as understood by the Bush administration. It can be found at http://www.fletc.gov/training/programs/legal-division/podcasts/hot-issues-podcasts/hot-issues-transcripts/foreign-intelligence-surveillance-act-fisa-part-1-podcast-transcript.html. The second analysis, a section-by-section analysis by the American Civil Liberties Union of the 2007 FISA legislation supported by the Bush administration and Senator Jay Rockefeller, the chairman of the Senate Intelligence Committee, can be found at http://www.aclu.org/safefree/general/32524leg20071102.html.
57. Siobhan Gorman, "System Error," *Baltimore Sun*, January 29, 2006.
58. Ariel Sabar, "NSA Awards Pact to Redesign Operations," *Baltimore Sun*, October 2, 2002.
59. "NSA Awards Major Acquisition Contract to Science Applications International Corporation," NSA press release, September 19, 2002.
60. House and Senate Intelligence Committees, Joint Hearing on Pre-9/11 Failures, October 17, 2002.
61. "SAIC Team Wins National Security Agency Trailblazer Contract," SAIC press release, October 21, 2002.

62. "Contractor's Rise Shows Blurred Government, Industry Lines," *Government Executive,* July 7, 2006.
63. Paul Kaihla, "US: In the Company of Spies," *Business 2.0,* May 1, 2003.
64. www.saic.com/products/software/teratext/customers.html.
65. According to a Jordan Becker, an SAIC employee writing on Dr. J. Robert Beyster's blog at www.beyster.com/blog.
66. Doug Beizer, "Array of Tech Products Helps Fight Terrorism," *Washington Technology*, March 9, 2006.
67. "Pathfinder Overview," SAIC Web site, www.saic.com.
68. "Joint Inquiry into Intelligence Community Activities Before and After the Terrorist Attacks of September 11, 2001," report of the U.S. Senate and House Select Committees on Intelligence, December 2002.
69. Pamela Hess, "NSA Intel System over Budget," United Press International, April 19, 2005.
70. Mark Hosenball and Evan Thomas, "Hold the Phone: Big Brother Knows Whom You Call," *Newsweek,* May 22, 2006.
71. "Intel Watch," *Inside the Pentagon*, November 20, 2003.
72. This statement was made in a series of questions posed to Lt. Gen. James Clapper when he appeared before the Senate Intelligence Committee for his confirmation hearing on March 27, 2007.
73. Siobhan Gorman, "Chief of NSA Urges 'Action,' " *Baltimore Sun*, March 10, 2007.
74. Robert David Steele, interview with author, January 2007.
75. John Gannon, interview with author, September 2006.
76. John Pike, interview with author, January 2007.
77. Chris Roberts, "Transcript; Debate on the Foreign Intelligence Surveillance Act," *El Paso Times*, August 22, 2007.
78. Haseltine spoke at GEOINT 2006, the conference organized by the United States Geospatial Intelligence Foundation in Orlando, Florida.
79. Josh Rogin, "DOD Says No to Massive IT Acquisitions," *Federal Computer Week Online*, January 22, 2007.
80. Shane Harris, "Two Controversial Counter-Terror Programs Share Parallels," *National Journal*, June 16, 2006.
81. Quoted in "Total Information Awareness Resource Center," a source of information and action regarding the Total Information Awareness program for concerned citizens, legislators and the media, http://www.geocities.com/totalinformationawareness/.
82. Remarks as prepared for delivery by Dr. John Poindexter, Director, Information Awareness Office of DARPA, at DARPATech 2002 Conference, Anaheim, California, August 2, 2002, http://www.fas.org/irp/agency/dod/poindexter.html.
83. Ibid.
84. Shane Harris, "TIA Lives On," *National Journal*, February 25, 2006.
85. Michael Hirsh and Mark Hosenball, "NSA: Meet the Next Spy Chief," *Newsweek* Web "exclusive," January 4, 2007, www.msnbc.com.
86. EPIC obtained information about the contracts through a Freedom of Information Act request. Copies of the contract letters can be found on EPIC's Web site, at http://www.epic.org/privacy/profiling/tia/#foia.
87. Jeffrey Jonas, interview with author, September 2006.
88. David Morse, "What Was Behind the Pentagon's Betting Parlor?," *Common Dreams,* August 4, 2003, www.commondreams.org.
89. Quoted in "Semantic Analytics on Social Networks: Experiences in Addressing the Problem of Conflict of Interest Detection," paper published by the University of Georgia

(Athens) and the University of Maryland (Baltimore County), 2006, http://www2006.org/programme/files/pdf/4068.pdf.

90. Shane Harris, "Two Controversial Counter-terror Programs Share Parallels," *National Journal*, June 16, 2006.
91. "The Last Tactical Mile . . . and the First," a white paper prepared by the AFCEA Intelligence Committee, October 2006.
92. Siobhan Gorman, "Costly NSA Initiative Has a Shaky Takeoff," *Baltimore Sun*, February 11, 2007.
93. Paul Marks, "Pentagon Sets Its Sights on Social Networking Websites," *New Scientist*, June 9, 2006, http://technology.newscientist.com/article/mg19025556.200-pentagon-sets-its-sights-on-social-networking-websites.html.
94. Jim Dempsey, interview with author, June 2007.
95. James Clapper, confirmation questions, Senate Armed Services Committee, March 28, 2007.

7. INTELLIGENCE DISNEYLAND

1. "Intelligence Officials Say Reform Means a Long, Hard Slog Ahead," *Homeland Defense Watch*, November 1, 2004.
2. These figures were disclosed to GEOINT 2007 by Army Colonel Bill Harmon, the chief of the NGA's forward support team to the U.S. Central Command.
3. NGA director Robert Murrett, remarks at the United States Geospatial Intelligence Foundation's GEOINT 2006 symposium, November 14, 2006. Readers take note: the author was present at GEOINT 2006 and GEOINT 2007. Only the most important quotes from these events will be cited in these endnotes.
4. Robert Murrett, in a speech at GEOINT 2007, San Antonio, October 23, 2007.
5. Donald M. Kerr, speech to the 2006 GEOINT conference and symposium in Orlando, Florida, November 2006.
6. Lance Killoran, in a speech at GEOINT 2007, San Antonio, October 22, 2007.
7. Ibid.
8. Loren Thompson, "Reconnaissance Assets Undercut by Pentagon Infighting," Lexington Institute issue brief, April 2, 2007.
9. "Joint Document Highlights NGA and NSA Collaboration," NGA press release, December 27, 2004.
10. Eric Lipton, "Spy Chiefs Say Cooperation Should Begin at the Bottom," *New York Times*, October 14, 2004.
11. NGA director Robert Murrett, press briefing at the United States Geospatial Intelligence Foundation's GEOINT 2006 symposium, November 14, 2006.
12. Michael Lee, in a speech at GEOINT 2007, San Antonio, October 23, 2007.
13. Richard L. Haver, public speech to intelligence professionals, Washington, D.C., May 2006.
14. "Empire Challenge 2006 Improves US, Coalition Intelligence Support to Troops on the Ground," NGA press release, October 12, 2006.
15. Charles Allen, DHS, remarks at GEOINT symposium, 2006.
16. Steve Jacques, interview with author, September 2006.
17. E-mail from K. Stuart Shea to author, August 11, 2004.
18. Damon Chappie, "Intel Aide's Ties Draw Scrutiny," *Roll Call*, April 1, 2004.
19. These figures are based on USGIF's 2004 tax returns, which as a nonprofit must be made available to the public.

20. Wilson P. Dizard, "Geospatial Intel Moves Out from the Shadows," *Government Computer News,* January 22, 2007.
21. "JFCOM, NGA Finishing Proposals to Enhance Tactical Geoint Capabilities," *Inside the Pentagon,* March 1, 2007.
22. John Pike, interview with author, April 2007.
23. Richard Haver, speech to GEOINT 2007.
24. The Clinton administration's policies on commercial imaging are described in a 2007 report prepared by an independent study group for the NGA, "Independent Study of the Roles of Commercial Remote Sensing in the Future National System for Geospatial Intelligence," completed by the Defense Group Inc. for the NGA in July 2007 and made public by the NGA press office in October 2007.
25. Ibid.
26. "NGA Head General James R. Clapper Answers Wide-Ranging Questions About NGA," *Directions Magazine* (NGA publication), November 10, 2004.
27. ESRI Corporate Profile, *Geospatial Solutions*, December 1, 2004.
28. Sara Kehaulani Goo and Alec Klein, "Google Searches for Government Work," "TechNews," *Washington Post*, February 28, 2007.
29. Information posted on the Web site for the Potomac Institute for Policy Studies, www.potomacinstitute.org.
30. Robert B. Murrett, "10 Years of Geoint," *Pathfinder* (NGA publication), September/October 2006.
31. John Pike, interview with author, April 2007.
32. Karen Walker, "FIRE Allows US Intel Agencies to Learn from 'What-ifs,' " *Defense News,* August 2, 2004.
33. Ibid.
34. Booz Allen's chief subcontractor on the FIRE project is Analytical Graphics Inc., which sells satellite tracking and geospatial software to the NGA, the NSA, the CIA, and the Army Intelligence Security Command.
35. According to "Intelligence Solutions," the SAIC's page for GEOINT on its Web site, www.saic.org.
36. Edmund H. Nowinski and Robert J. Kohler, "The Lost Art of Program Management in the Intelligence Community," CIA Center for the Study of Intelligence, Vol. 50, No. 2, April 2007, https://www.cia.gov/library/center-for-the-study-of-intelligence/csi-publications/csi-studies/studies/vol50no2/html_files/Program_Management_4.htm.
37. "NGA Head General James R. Clapper Answers Wide-Ranging Questions About NGA."
38. Herbert Browne, interview with author, December 2006.
39. Robert David Steele, interview with author, September 2006.
40. "Independent Study of the Roles of Commercial Remote Sensing in the Future National System for Geospatial Intelligence," NGA, 2007.

8. **THE PURE PLAYS**

1. Walter Pincus, "Growing Threat Seen in Afghan Insurgency," *Washington Post*, March 1, 2006.
2. Department of Defense, FY 2006 Supplemental Request for Operation Iraqi Freedom (OIF) and Operation Enduring Freedom (OEF), February 2006.
3. Hearing transcript, Defense Subcommittee of the House Appropriations Committee, February 16, 2006.

4. Tim Lemke, "Veridian Corp. Gets Two Federal Contracts," *Washington Times,* April 22, 2003.
5. Renae Merle and Ellen McCarthy, "General Dynamics to Buy Anteon," *Washington Post,* December 15, 2005.
6. Adelia Cellini Linecker, "IT Firms Get Sales Lift from Military Buildup," *Investor's Business Daily,* February 18, 2003.
7. "L-3 Communications Acquires Titan," *Defense Industry Daily,* June 8, 2005.
8. Lockheed Martin statistics were reported during a presentation for investors at the Friedman, Billings, Ramsey Washington conference, March 8, 2007.
9. "L-1 Acquiring IT Firm That Serves Intel Community," *Terror Response Technology Report,* May 16, 2007.
10. William Conway, interview with author, January 2002.
11. ManTech, Form S-1 prospectus filed with the SEC, November 15, 2002, available at sec.edgar-online.com.
12. "ManTech IPO Rises 14% on First Day," *Daily Deal,* February 7, 2002.
13. CACI's denunciation of Greenwald's film was posted on CACI's Web site, at www.caci.com.
14. Transcript, CACI International analyst meeting, Fair Disclosure Wire, February 28, 2007.
15. 2006 CACI International Earnings conference call, August 17, 2006.
16. These figures, and the statistics on clearances, were provided by CACI officials during a conference call with analysts on March 8, 2007.
17. Kenneth Bredemeier, "Thousands of Private Contractors Support US Forces in Persian Gulf," *Washington Post,* March 3, 2003.
18. "Rumsfeld's Office Streamlines Its IT," United Press International, November 10, 2005.
19. "Dr. London's Radio Interview with Brian Roberts," on CACI's Web site at http://www.caci.com/announcement/radio_interview_7-06.shtml.
20. "Dr. J. P. London Address to Northern Virginia Technology Council, 2/13/02," www.caci.com/speeches/JPl_2-13_speech.shtml.
21. Ibid.
22. Ibid.
23. CACI annual reports, 2003 and 2006.
24. Ibid.
25. "CACI Chairman, President and CEO Dr. J. P. (Jack) London Receives Albert Einstein Technology Award," CACI press release, February 2, 2004.
26. Ali Abuniman, "In Exchange for Interrogation Training, Did Washington Award Security Contracts?" *Daily Star* (Lebanon), May 11, 2004.
27. Company presentation, Friedman, Billings, Ramsey investor conference, Washington, D.C., March 1, 2006.
28. See the transcript of CACI's analyst conference call of February 28, 2007, CACI International analyst meeting, Fair Disclosure Wire, February 28, 2007.
29. Jack London, conference call with investors, May 5, 2004.
30. Ellen McCarthy, "Intelligence Work Comes to CACI via Acquisitions," *Washington Post,* July 8, 2004.
31. Tim Shorrock, "CACI and Its Friends," *The Nation,* June 23, 2004.
32. "CACI Awarded Task Order for DIA," Associated Press, June 7, 2007.
33. "DIA Drafts CACI for Defense Intel Services," *Government Computer News,* May 31, 2006.
34. Ellen McCarthy, "Intelligence Work Comes to CACI Via Acquisitions," *Washington Post,* July 8, 2004.
35. Jay Weaver, "Padilla Was Recruited for Jihad, Document Says," *Miami Herald,* March

16, 2007; and Stevenson Swanson, "Padilla Kept out of Sight, but Case Is Very Visible," *Chicago Tribune*, June 15, 2003.

36. CACI international earnings conference call, April 22, 2004.
37. Telephone interview with the Department of the Interior's Frank Quimby, 2004.
38. Seymour Hersh, "The Gray Zone: How a Secret Pentagon Program Came to Abu Ghraib," *The New Yorker*, May 15, 2004.
39. Maj. Gen. George Fay, report, "Investigation of Intelligence Activities at Abu Ghraib," August 2004, available on many Web sites.
40. Taguba's speech can be heard in the Commonwealth Club's podcast of the event, at http://audio.commonwealthclub.org/audio/podcast/cc_20070625_taguba.mp3.
41. Jim Jelter, "CACI International Warns of Lower Earnings," CBS *MarketWatch*, January 17, 2007.
42. Will Swarts, "Defense Contractor's Stock Under Siege," Smartmoney.com, January 18, 2007.
43. Ibid.
44. Zachary A. Goldfarb, "CACI to Expand High-Security Force," *Washington Post*, September 25, 2007.
45. Kris Osborn, "CACI Feeds Pentagon Hunger for Latest Intelligence IT," *Defense News*, September 3, 2007.
46. Sandra Sugawara, "Air of Mystery Envelops ManTech International," *Washington Post*, October 31, 1988.
47. "ManTech Names Richard Armitage to Its Board of Directors," ManTech press release, June 9, 2005.
48. George Pedersen made these comments in ManTech's presentation at the Friedman, Billings, Ramsey conference, February 28, 2006.
49. This information comes from ManTech's S-1 registration statement with the SEC, filed on November 15, 2002.
50. Thomas Meagher, interview with author, July 2006.
51. "ManTech Acquires GRS Solutions; Deepens Presence Within the Intelligence Community," ManTech press release, October 6, 2006.
52. Transcript, Third Quarter 2006 ManTech International Earnings conference call, November 2, 2006.
53. "Two of ManTech's Employees Presumed Missing," ManTech press release, February 11, 2005.
54. "ManTech Awarded $7.1 Million Contract from DHS," ManTech press release, May 30, 2006.
55. "Homeland Security Information Network Could Support Information Sharing More Effectively," Department of Homeland Security Office of Inspector General, report number OIG-06-38, June 2006.
56. Alice Lipowicz, "Spinning Wheels," *Washington Technology*, May 28, 2007.
57. Charles Allen made these remarks at hearing, House Homeland Security Committee, Intelligence, Information Sharing, and Terrorism Risk Subcommittee, May 10, 2007.
58. Tom Hamburger and Chuck Neubauer, "Democrats Marked by Ethical Questions," *Los Angeles Times*, November 16, 2006.
59. Tim Starks, "Hal Rogers Is the King of Campaign Cash from Homeland Contractors," *Congressional Quarterly Today*, October 6, 2004.
60. Steven Emerson, "America's Doomsday Project," *U.S. News & World Report*, August 7, 1989.
61. Pete Yost, "Whistle Blower Claims Harassment," Associated Press, October 15, 1989; and CNN "Special Assignment" with David Lewis, November 17, 1991.

62. Yost, "Whistle Blower Claims Harassment."
63. "ManTech Wins Information Systems Support Contract," ManTech press release, December 7, 2001.
64. Brody Mullins, "Renzi Under Fire for Defense Provision," *Roll Call,* September 11, 2003.
65. Interview with Brad Antle, *Wall Street Transcript,* August 21, 2006, posted on SI International Web site.
66. Ibid.
67. "Former Assistant Secretary of Defense John Stenbit Appointed to SI International Board of Directors," SI press release, April 26, 2004.
68. Suzelle Tempero, "MTC Chairman Takes Reins," *Dayton Business Journal,* November 20, 2006.
69. Collins spoke at the 2006 investors conference sponsored by Friedman, Billings, Ramsey.
70. Argon, SEC Form 424B4, filed December 13, 2005.
71. "Argon ST," *Washington Technology*, October 30, 2006.
72. While acquisitions enrich the owners of the company being sold, it's not clear that such mergers have been good for the country. On January 10, 2007, shareholders of Essex Corporation gathered at company headquarters for a historic meeting. Northrop Grumman, the nation's third-largest defense contractor, had offered $580 million to buy the company. The offer had already been accepted by the Essex board of directors, so the vote that day was a formality. A reporter for the *Baltimore Sun* recorded what happened. "Wearing a blue dress shirt and a parrot dangling from a green Mardi Gras–style beaded necklace, Leonard E. Moodispaw, the company's unconventional CEO, read aloud the formalities of the proxy vote to the 30 shareholders who attended the special meeting. . . . He confirmed that a majority of the shareholders—most of whom are institutions—had approved the cash-and-debt offer from Northrop Grumman. Despite the magnitude of the sale, the meeting lasted just seven minutes and ended with applause. Afterward, Moodispaw, who is usually quick to quote a line from his favorite singer Jimmy Buffett to sum up his mood, was quiet, almost somber. He called the vote 'anticlimactic.' 'I'm ready to get on with getting operations moving,' he said." The deal was done. (See Allison Connoly, "Essex Sale to Northrop approved," *Baltimore Sun,* January 11, 2007.)

    A few days later, Moodispaw reflected on the sale in a telephone interview with the author. "I didn't really want to sell," he told me. "Some of our employees who've worked in big companies aren't excited about it." But the board, he said, had no choice but to present the offer to Essex's shareholders, 60 percent of whom are large institutions, because "they stand to make a sizable return." In fact, at $25 a share, the Northrop Grumman acquisition was sure to make some Essex shareholders very wealthy indeed, particularly those who bought their stock at its pre-9/11 price of $3. Despite his concerns about the changes sure to be implemented by the giant contractor, Moodispaw vowed to stay on as Essex was absorbed into Northrop Grumman's Mission Systems unit, which employs 17,000 people in forty-seven states. "We try to have fun, and they claim they will continue that tradition," he said. "And I know they mean well."

    Essex's sale closed one of the unlikeliest stories in the intelligence industry. The company was probably the purest example of a pure play: by the time of its sale to Northrop Grumman, it was earning 90 percent of its revenue from the National Security Agency alone. It also held contracts with the NRO, the NGA, the Missile Defense Agency, the Defense Advanced Research Projects Agency, and all four branches of the U.S. armed forces, according to SEC filings. At the same time, Moodispaw, the CEO, was a highly unusual leader for an intelligence company: in addition to his unconventional appearance, he is a lifelong Democrat opposed to the war in Iraq. In our interview, he happily described himself as a "flaming liberal," and wasn't afraid in the least to criticize the commander-in-chief. "The Bush administration is the most vindictive administration I've ever seen," he told me.

Essex was also different in the way it promoted its business. ManTech and the other pure plays advertise heavily and, through their political action committees, hand out tens of thousands of dollars to congressmen in their districts. Not Essex: it expanded largely on the reputation of its technology. Essex never placed an ad, refused to pay lobbyists, and didn't operate a PAC. "I won't play the lobbying game," Moodispaw told me. "That process leads to the [Jack] Abramoffs of the world"—a reference to the Republican lobbyist who was the central figure in a 2006 political corruption investigation in Washington. Moodispaw also takes pride in the fact that he supplied technology to his clients, as opposed to the big contractors who shift armies of cleared employees from agency to agency—a practice that Moodispaw disdains as "body shopping." "We didn't just send fifty people to sit in a building and be the arms and legs of the government," he said.

Now, as tiny Essex is being taken into the huge defense maw of Northrop Grumman, the acquisition is propelling the parent company deeper into the NSA and the market for interpreting signals intelligence. Essex's optical technology will be used by the conglomerate as a door to get into more agencies, and within a few years everything that made it a unique enterprise will be gone. By that time, Moodispaw—who has virtually disappeared from the pages of the industry press since the acquisition—will probably be ready to retire a very wealthy man. At the USGIF symposium in Orlando, I asked a Northrop Grumman executive what might happen to Essex and the entrepreneurs who founded it; will they find a place in the corporation? "It's all part of the negotiating process," replied John Olesak, vice president of space and intelligence in the company's IT sector. "You want to maintain the culture and characteristics of a company, but it doesn't always work because you can't come to terms." In the end, there's "no one model that fits every acquisition." For the employees of Essex, that didn't sound very promising.

The loss of an independent company like Essex may not be the best thing for the IC as a whole or, for that matter, the nation. The mergers and acquisitions boom in intelligence is taking place at a time when the DNI and some officials at the Pentagon have recognized the pitfalls of handing huge contracts to conglomerates like Northrop Grumman and SAIC. A few weeks before the Essex sale went through, a DoD official warned that the systems integrators would no longer get preference in contracting; but if all the middle-sized companies are gobbled up, who's going to take on the smaller, bite-sized contracts that acquisition officials now want to hand out? Another issue, which came to the fore with the sale of Anteon, involves these firms' value to the government as third-party consultants. Anteon, like CACI, partly made its way as a company by providing acquisition oversight to organizations like the U.S. Navy. But once it was acquired by General Dynamics, which has a huge business making surface ships for the Navy, Anteon could no longer provide that service as an uninterested party.

As a result of that conflict of interest, I was told by defense analyst Thomas Meagher, Anteon had to sell off four of its contracts; but in the process, the government lost an important service. That remains a big concern to investment banks, Meagher told me.

Finally, as techno-powers like Essex are sold off, where will new technologies come from? According to a recent study by the Center for Strategic and International Studies, over 50 percent of the key technologies in the defense industrial base come from small companies. Essex itself won its NSA contracts because it was able to get its product to the battlefield quickly—much faster than its larger competitors. The loss of the pure plays, including the ones that were swallowed up in the post-9/11 IPOs that swept through the industry, could dry up an important source of technology. "What is going to be the source of innovation for intelligence and defense after these companies are sold?" Michael Murphy, a securities analyst involved in the Essex IPO, asked at the 2006 Intelcon conference in Bethesda, Maryland. Pointing to General Dynamics again, he wondered aloud: "Is the intelligence community better off with Veridian as part of a giant corporation?" I would say probably not.

9. THE RISE OF THE NATIONAL SURVEILLANCE STATE

1. Michael Hayden, address, National Press Club, January 23, 2006, www.dni.gov/speeches/20060123_speech.htm.
2. This was stated by Assistant U.S. Attorney General Thomas Bondy in open court on August 16, 2007, when the Justice Department argued against the Electronic Frontier Foundation's lawsuit against AT&T before the 9th Circuit Court of Appeals in San Francisco.
3. Eric Lichtblau and James Risen, "Domestic Surveillance: The Program; Spy Agency Mined Vast Data Trove, Officials Report," *New York Times*, December 24, 2005.
4. Chris Roberts, "Transcript: Debate on the Foreign Intelligence Surveillance Act," *El Paso Times,* August 22, 2007.
5. Mike McConnell, "Help Me Spy on Al Qaeda," *New York Times,* December 11, 2007.
6. Lichtblau and Risen, "Spy Agency Mined Vast Data Trove, Officials Report."
7. Helen Fessenden, "Senate Democrats Seek to Regroup Quickly on Surveillance Law Rewrite," *The Hill,* September 11, 2007.
8. Eric Lichtblau, James Risen, and Scott Shane, "Wider Spying Fuels Aid Plan for Telecom Industry," *New York Times,* December 16, 2007.
9. Albert Gidari, interview with author, January 2006.
10. Alan Mauldin, interview with author, January 2006.
11. Leslie Cauley, "NSA Has Massive Database of Americans' Phone Calls," *USA Today,* May 11, 2006.
12. Interview with author, March 2006.
13. The idea that there might have been more than one NSA program largely comes from the Bush administration itself. In his many statements on the legality of the NSA's warrantless eavesdropping, Alberto Gonzales, who was President Bush's White House lawyer and later served as attorney general, was careful to say that he was talking only of programs "described by the President." In one of his first memos on the subject of eavesdropping, drafted when he was White House counsel, he wrote that "as described by the President, the NSA intercepts certain international communications into and out of the United States of people linked to Al Qaeda or an affiliated terrorist organization," and added that "the NSA activities described by the President are fully consistent with the Fourth Amendment and the protection of civil liberties." So it was when he testified before Congress. In 2006, asked during a hearing before the Senate Judiciary Committee if officials in the Justice Department had objected to the NSA's wiretapping program, Gonzales (then the attorney general) denied the reports with this qualified statement: "There has not been any serious disagreement about the program that the president has confirmed." His answers to similar questions from other lawmakers were clotted with phrases like "not under the program about which I'm testifying," or "beyond the bounds of the program I'm testifying about today."

    Those answers left lots of room for the Bush administration. "While Gonzales often seemed to be making wholesale denials, it seems he was only making retail denials, very specific denials, about this one program, and he simply didn't say about the other programs," Peter Swire, Ohio State University law professor and FISA expert, told me in 2007. "Nor was he actually denying the existence of other programs." Jim Dempsey, the executive director of the Center for Democracy and Technology, who has testified in Congress many times about FISA, believes from the evidence that the NSA ran three separate spying programs using the telecommunications system. But the differences between programs may not have been readily apparent to intelligence analysts or companies involved in the data mining.

The government, and particularly the NSA, "were running around frantically post-9/11 doing a lot of things and accessing a lot of data," Dempsey said in a 2007 interview. "Some of it was on an ongoing basis, some of it was on a one-time basis only. In other words, the phone companies might have said, 'sure we'll give this to you today, but we can't let it go on forever.' So one of the problems phone companies faced was, they got sucked into the emergency and it kept going and going and going." As a result, a participant in these programs might dispute the tripartite analysis because it was "subject to evolution over time that may have blurred the boundaries between each program."

Finally, Director of National Intelligence Mike McConnell seemed to acknowledge multiple programs, albeit without any specifics, in a July 2007 letter to Arlen Specter, the ranking Republican on the Senate Judiciary Committee. "A number of these intelligence activities were authorized in one order" by President Bush shortly after 9/11, he wrote. With regard to the administration's Terrorist Surveillance Program, he added: "This is the only aspect of the NSA activities that can be discussed publicly, because it is the only aspect of those various activities whose existence has been officially acknowledged."

14. Rebecca Carr, "AT&T Whistleblower: Say No to Telecom Immunity," *Austin American-Statesman,* November 6, 2007, http://www.statesman.com/blogs/content/shared-blogs/washington/secrecy/entries/2007/11/06/att_whistleblower_say_no_to_te.html.
15. James Risen and Eric Lichtblau, "Ex-Worker at AT&T Fights Immunity Bill," *New York Times*, November 7, 2007.
16. Ellen Nakashima, "A Story of Surveillance," *Washington Post,* November 7, 2007.
17. Ibid.
18. John Markoff and Scott Shane, "Documents Show Link Between AT&T and Agency in Eavesdropping Case," *New York Times,* April 12, 2006; and Robert Poe, "The Ultimate Net Monitoring Tool," *Wired News,* May 17, 2006.
19. Melanie Warner, "Web Warriors," *Fortune,* October 15, 2001.
20. PBS *Frontline*, "Spying on the Homefront," www.pbs.org/wgbh/pages/frontline/homefront/.
21. Nakashima, "A Story of Surveillance."
22. John Pike, interview with author, December 2006.
23. PBS *Frontline*, "Spying on the Homefront."
24. Another knowledgeable source close to the Bush administration is John Stopher, the former budget director of the House Permanent Select Committee on Intelligence. In 2006, in a speech to intelligence contractors and officials gathered in Orlando for the GEOINT conference sponsored by the U.S. Geospatial Intelligence Foundation, he alluded to the NSA surveillance program when he spoke about using computers to do "things humans can't do." Stopher is well informed about the subject. He began working in the IC in 1988 as a systems engineer with Eastman Kodak, a member of the illustrious first generation of intelligence contractors from the Cold War. During the first six years of the Bush administration, he held three positions at the intelligence committee, including staff director of the subcommittee on technical and tactical intelligence and program monitor for the NRO. His budget committee also had jurisdiction over spending on the NSA, the NGA, and the CIA's Directorate of Science and Technology. As a result, he was probably one of the few staffers cleared to learn about the Terrorist Surveillance Program. "In the case of who's calling al Qaeda," Stopher told the GEOINT 2006 conference, "we have to

understand that the power of the algorithms to sort through these problems and identify these sorts of things is really the future. This is what will keep America well ahead of its adversaries. I think we'll see another generation of advancement in that—rather than just sorting through phone calls, if we can structure data correctly, remove barriers that keep people from sharing information, then we can start looking at relationships in multiple dimensions: every phone number has a location; every credit card transaction, every car rental, hotel rental, things like that all have locations as well. You begin to see the power if you can get the data accessible, to where this country can go." These three principles of obtaining huge streams of data, analyzing it with privately developed software, and then using the analysis to zero in on the enemy, are key to the U.S. war on terror as fought by the Bush administration.

25. John Markoff, "Government Looks at Ways to Mine Databases," *New York Times,* February 25, 2006.
26. Walter Pincus, "NSA Gave Other US Agencies Information from Surveillance," *Washington Post,* January 1, 2006.
27. Ibid.
28. Elise Ackerman and K. Oanh Ma, "Wholesale Snooping," *San Jose Mercury News,* May 28, 2006.
29. "Attensity Forms Partnership with IBM," Attensity press release, October 17, 2006.
30. Intelligence page, Visual Analytics Inc., http://www.visualanalytics.com.
31. Laura K. Donohue, "Anglo-American Privacy and Surveillance," *The Journal of Criminal Law and Criminology*, Northwestern University School of Law, Vol. 96, No. 3, 2006, p. 1080.
32. James Bamford, *The Puzzle Palace*, p. 306.
33. Ibid., p. 305.
34. Donohue, "Anglo-American Privacy and Surveillance," p. 1080.
35. Bamford, *The Puzzle Palace*, p. 312.
36. Ibid.
37. Ibid., p. 376.
38. Quoted in Donohue, "Anglo-American Privacy and Surveillance," p. 1096.
39. Kenneth Bass, interview with author, January 2006.
40. Eric Lichtblau, "Key Senators Raise Doubts on Eavesdropping Immunity," *New York Times*, November 1, 2007.
41. Daniel W. Reilly, "Rockefeller predicts win in FISA fight over telecom immunity," *Politico,* January 23, 2008.
42. Glenn Greenwald, "Jay Rockefeller's unintentionally revealing comments," *Salon,* January 24, 2008.
43. Quoted in the Electronic Frontier Foundation's lawsuit against AT&T, www.eff.org/cases/att/attachments/eff/complaint. See also Tim Shorrock, "Watching What You Say," *The Nation*, March 20, 2006; and AT&T's statement to the Senate Judiciary Committee, March 15, 2005.
44. "Strategic Plan 2007–2012: Leading the Defense Intelligence Enterprise," Defense Intelligence Agency, www.dia.mil.
45. "AT&T Government Solutions Wins $14 Million Contract," AT&T press release, June 13, 2005.
46. Shorrock, "Watching What You Say."
47. Michael Isikoff and Mark Hosenball, "Case Dismissed? The Secret Lobbying Campaign Your Phone Company Doesn't Want You to Know About," *Newsweek*, September 20, 2007, http://www.msnbc.msn.com/id/20884696/site/newsweek/page/0/.
48. The correspondence between the telecom companies and the House committee can

be found at "The Public Record" section of the committee Web site, http://energy commerce.house.gov.

49. Ellen Nakashima, "Verizon Says It Turned Over Data Without Court Orders," *Washington Post,* October 16, 2007.
50. Eric Lichtblau, "FBI Data-Mining Went Beyond Initial Suspects," *New York Times,* September 10, 2007.
51. October 12, 2002, letter from Randal S. Milch, Verizon's senior vice president for legal and external affairs and general counsel, to leading Democrats on the House Committee on Energy and Commerce, available on the committee Web site, http://energy commerce.house.gov/Press_110/110-ltr.101207.Verizonrspto100207.pdf.
52. "Full Statement from Attorney of Former Qwest CEO Nacchio," *Wall Street Journal,* May 12, 2006.
53. Nacchio's court filings about Qwest's relationship with the NSA and other government agencies were with a U.S. district court in Colorado in 2006 and released by the court in October 2007. Copies of the documents are available on the Web site of the *Rocky Mountain News*, which first reported Nacchio's contention that he lost contracts due to his refusal to cooperate with the NSA, at http://www.rockymountainnews.com/drmn/tech/article/0,2777,DRMN_23910_5720619,00.html.
54. Shane Harris, "NSA Sought Data Before 9/11," *National Journal*, November 2, 2007.
55. Ellen Nakashima and Dan Eggen, "Former CEO Says US Punished Phone Firm," *Washington Post*, October 13, 2007.
56. Kelly Yamanouchi, "Feds: No Act Existed Against Qwest," *Denver Post*, October 23, 2007.
57. David Milstead, "Assertion Shoots Hole in Nacchio's Secret Info Stance," *Rocky Mountain News*, October 23, 2007.
58. W. David Gardner, "Prosecutors Poke Holes in Nacchio's Last-Ditch Appeal," *Information Week,* October 23, 2007.
59. David Milstead, "Prosecution: No Retaliation Against Nacchio," *Rocky Mountain News,* October 22, 2007.
60. Greg Miller, "Court puts limits on surveillance abroad," *Los Angeles Times,* August 2, 2007.
61. James Risen, "Bush signs law to widen reach for wiretapping," *New York Times,* August 6, 2007.
62. Marty Lederman, "Senate Passes Administration Bill [UPDATED with Link to and Analysis of S.1927]," Balkinization, August 4, 2007, http://balkin.blogspot.com/2007/08/senate-passes-administration-bill.html.
63. Lawrence Wright, "The Spymaster, *The New Yorker,* January 21, 2008.
64. Michael Isikoff and Mark Hosenball, "Terror Watch: A Secret Lobbying Campaign," *Newsweek,* September 20, 2007.
65. Quoted in Lawrence Wright, "The Spy Master," *The New Yorker,* January 28, 2008.
66. Hearing on FISA, Senate Select Committee on Intelligence, May 1, 2007.
67. DNI Michael McConnell, letter to Senator Christopher Bond, January 25, 2008, made public by the Senate Intelligence Committee.
68. Julian E. Barnes, "Air Force Spy Plane to Fly Over Fire Zone," *Los Angeles Times,* October 26, 2007.
69. "NGA Supports Federal Response to California Wildfires," NGA news release number 07–12, October 26, 2007.
70. "Civil Applications Committee (CAC) Blue Ribbon Study," Independent Study Group final report, September 2005, www.fas.usg/irp/eprint/cac=report.pdf.
71. "Fact Sheet: National Applications Office," Department of Homeland Security, August 15, 2007, http://www.dhs.gov/xnews/releases/pr_1187188414685.shtm.

72. Eric Schmitt, "Liberties Advocates Fear Abuse of Satellite Images," *New York Times,* August 16, 2007; and Joby Warrick, "Domestic Use of Spy Satellites to Widen," *Washington Post,* August 16, 2007.
73. Scott Shane, "Shift in Spying Money to Agents from Satellites Is Sought," *New York Times,* June 15, 2005.
74. " 'Satellites Won't Penetrate Homes,' " *Satellite Week,* September 10, 2007.
75. Warrick, "Domestic Use of Spy Satellites to Widen."
76. Jack M. Balkin and Sanford V. Levinson, "The Processes of Constitutional Change: From Partisan Entrenchment to the National Surveillance State," Yale Law School, Public Law Working Paper No. 120; and *Fordham Law Review,* Vol. 75, No. 2, 2006, available online at http://papers.ssrn.com/sol3/papers.cfm?abstract_id=930514.
77. John Ashcroft, Network Centric Warfare Conference, Washington, D.C., January 18, 2006.
78. One of i2's products, a software program called Analyst's Notebook, is one of the most widely used tools in intelligence analysis, and has been praised by U.S. military intelligence officers in Iraq for helping them "visualize relationships and detect patterns." The company is very open about its aims. "To win the war on terrorism," i2 declared on its Web site in 2006, "it is critical to provide analysts with tools that can quickly discern patterns and meaning from large data sets and enable them to effectively share intelligence with a variety of agencies charged with countering terrorist activities and their many related crimes." The article was accompanied by a photograph of President Bush looking over a chart, created with i2 software, depicting Osama bin Laden's financial network; the picture was taken during Bush's 2001 tour of the Department of Treasury's Financial Crimes Enforcement Network in Vienna, Virginia.
79. John Pike, interview with author, April 2007.
80. Robert Block, "US to Expand Domestic Use of Spy Satellites," *Wall Street Journal,* August 15, 2007.
81. Eric Schmitt, "Liberties Advocates Fear Abuse of Satellite Images," *New York Times,* August 16, 2007.
82. Ibid.
83. "Civil Applications Committee (CAC) Blue Ribbon Study/Independent Study Group Final Report," unclassified report released September 2005, http://www.fas.org/irp/eprint/cac-report.pdf.
84. Charles Allen and Robert Murrett, GEOINT 2007, San Antonio.
85. "Domestic spying program detailed soon," United Press International, December 20, 2007.
86. I was present for this speech. A transcript of Kerr's remarks can be found at "Remarks and Q&A by the Principal Deputy Director of National Intelligence Dr. Donald Kerr," 2007 GEOINT symposium sponsored by the United States Geospatial Intelligence Foundation, San Antonio, Texas, October 23, 2007, http://www.dni.gov/speeches/20071023_speech.pdf.
87. "MetaCarta and Mosaic, Inc. Join Forces on the Fight Against Terror," MetaCarta press release, July 16, 2007, http://www.metacarta.com/news-room/press-releases.html?display=detail&id=66.

10. CONCLUSION: IDEOLOGY, OVERSIGHT, AND THE COSTS OF SECRECY

1. Eric Chabrow, "Security Contractors Have Military and Intelligence Roots," *Information Week,* February 25, 2002.
2. "Terrorism: Real Costs, Real Threats, Joint Solutions," *Business Roundtable,* July 23, 2003, www.businessroundtable.org.

3. At this conference, even the most mundane of tasks took on the colors of the new crusade. In one session, Andrew Maner, an official with the Bureau of Customs and Border Protection of the Department of Homeland Security, argued that a new Customs program to download freight information from large corporate importers would be good for business and discourage terrorists as well. "Trade is an ally in the war on terrorism," he declared, adding: "There's a lot of great patriots in this industry." The next day, Michael Meldon, a retired executive from Science Applications International Corporation, the San Diego intelligence contractor, explained his motivations in accepting his new post as CEO of the newly formed Homeland Security Business Council. "I'm not simply responding to the security threat," he said. "I'm really doing something that's going to benefit my business and my bottom line as well as help the security of the United States of America." Introducing the council's vice president, a business lobbyist named Kim Dougherty, he exclaimed: "She's not interested in making money; she's a patriot." There again was that merging of interests. It was as if 9/11 had erased the need for regulation or oversight, or even common sense.
4. Spencer S. Hsu, "Homeland Security's Use of Contractors Is Questioned," *Washington Post,* October 17, 2007.
5. "Information Warfare—Not a Paper War," *Journal of Electronic Defense,* August 1994.
6. "Paladin Secures $150M for Homeland Security," *BuyOuts,* November 15, 2004.
7. "ManTech Names Lt. Gen. Kenneth A. Minihan, Former Director of NSA and DIA, to Its Board of Directors," ManTech press release, June 12, 2006, http://phx.corporate-ir.net/phoenix.zhtml?c=130660&p=irol-newsArticle&ID=871475&highlight=.
8. George J. Tenet, *At the Center of the Storm* (New York: HarperCollins, 2007), p. 516. Others on Tenet's list of "great leaders and friends" included (with their corporate and agency identifications), Jim Clapper (GeoEye/undersecretary of defense), Pat Hughes (L-3 Communications/DIA), Jake Jacoby (CACI/DIA), and Keith Hall (Booz Allen Hamilton/CIA).
9. Minihan delivered this speech at the 2005 Intelcon intelligence symposium in Washington, D.C., on February 8, 2005.
10. These quotes are from earlier chapters, and are sourced there.
11. "R. James Woolsey Joins Booz Allen as Vice President," Booz Allen press release, July 15, 2002.
12. Woolsey made these remarks at a speech I attended on March 19, 2004, in Tysons Corner, Virginia.
13. In a typical public-private partnership scheme, a private company might invest in a hospital or a highway, and then lease the completed projects back to a local government (the London Underground is a public-private partnership, for example). Unions hate them; to save money and maximize their profits, the companies supplying the public services usually pay lower wages and provide fewer benefits to their workers, and often reduce the kinds of services provided to the public. Governments often opt for them as a way to provide services without raising taxes, and companies love them because they offer a guaranteed stream of earnings and profits.
14. Interview with Gilman Louie, *Journal of Homeland Security,* August 2002, http://www.homelandsecurity.org/newjournal/Interviews/displayInterview2.asp?interview=14.
15. J. Michael Hickey, "Improving Emergency Preparedness and Response Capabilities," testimony before the House Committee on Homeland Security Subcommittee on Emergency Communications, Preparedness, and Response, July 19, 2007.
16. "Brief of Amicus Curiae Chamber of Commerce of the United States of America in Support of Appellants and Urging Reversal," filed with the U.S. District Court for the Northern District of California. This and other legal documents in the lawsuits against the

NSA, AT&T, and Verizon can be read at the Electronic Frontier Foundation Web site, www.eff.org.

17. Walter Pincus, "House Panel Approves a Record $48 Billion for Spy Agencies," *Washington Post,* May 4, 2007.
18. Rep. David Price, D–North Carolina, telephone interview, May 2006.
19. P. W. Singer, interview with author, Washington, D.C., May 2006.
20. Tim Sample, interview with author, August 2006.
21. Steven Jacques, now a consultant to the USGIF, telephone interview with author, July 2006.
22. My account of Price's bill and the Bush administration's response is based in part on an article in *Secrecy News* by Steven Aftergood, "Bill on Contractor Liability Raises Intel Agency Concerns," October 8, 2007. For the entire debate, see the Congressional Record, October 4, 2007, page H11261-H11267, at http://www.fas.org/irp/congress/2007_cr/h-meja.html.
23. Aftergood, "Bill on Contractor Liability Raises Intel Agency Concerns."
24. Ken Silverstein, "Six Questions for Marcus Stern on Duke Cunningham," *Harper's Online,* May 22, 2007, http://www.harpers.org/archive/2007/05/hbc-90000141.
25. Greg Miller, " 'Duke' Inquiry Cites Breakdowns," *Los Angeles Times*, August 10, 2006.
26. "Harman Releases Statement and Text of Unclassified Cunningham Report," Rep. Jane Harman press release, October 17, 2006, http://www.house.gov/list/press/ca36_harman/October_17_06.shtml. The actual study, "Report of the Special Council for the Cunningham Inquiry," can be found at http://www.house.gov/list/press/ca36_harman/report.pdf.
27. Marilyn W. Thompson and Ron Nixon, "Even Cut 50 Percent, Earmarks Clog Military Bill," *New York Times,* November 4, 2007.

INDEX

Page numbers beginning with 391 refer to endnotes.

Abraxas, 29, 137–41, 378

Abu Ghraib torture scandal, 3–5, 6, 11, 15, 103, 113, 270–71, 275, 279–82, 369*n,* 370, 371, 378, 381

Accenture, 26, 175

ACS Government Solutions Group, 79

Advanced Concepts Inc. (ACI), 127, 128, 175

Advanced Research and Development Activity (ARDA), 225, 226–27

Advanced Technical Intelligence Association (ATIA), 143*n*

Aegis Research Corporation, 287

Affiliated Computer Services Inc., 267

Afghanistan, 32–34, 166, 187, 231, 265, 269, 276, 297, 304, 347, 367
  battlefield intelligence in, 38, 52, 231, 263, 298, 300, 337, 346, 357
  CIA in, 29*n,* 92, 115, 117, 121–22, 127–28
  contractors in, 12, 14, 33–34, 103, 117, 121–22, 127–28, 177, 272, 285, 287, 289, 370
  insurgents in, 143, 262, 263

Aftergood, Steven, 20, 21, 183–84, 348, 374, 375, 406

AGI, 244, 246–47, 254, 354

Airborne Warning and Control System aircraft (AWACs), 14, 164

Air Force, U.S., 14, 75, 142, 155–56, 167, 238, 240, 265*n,* 277, 297
  contractors and, 40, 43, 101–3, 141, 277, 279, 285, 286
  intelligence service of, 20, 141, 173, 190
  see also specific contractors

Air Intelligence Agency, 141, 360

Albania, contractors in, 99, 102

Alexander, Keith B., 70, 189, 218, 226

Allen, Charles, 62, 122, 236, 291, 339, 348, 351

Allied Capital, 142

Allied Signal, 202

Al Qaeda, 2, 26, 53, 57, 109, 114, 115, 116, 121–22, 133, 167, 186, 189, 190, 191, 193, 200, 204, 263, 274, 276, 305, 306, 335*n*–36*n,* 337, 364, 415, 416

Al Qaeda in Iraq, 212, 233, 347

American Civil Liberties Union, 54, 407

American Enterprise Institute, 116

American Management Systems Inc., 407

Ames, Aldrich, 93–94

Amey, Scott, 21, 71

Analex Corp., 59*n,* 67*n,* 129, 180
  see also QinetiQ Group PLC

Analytical Graphics Inc., 229

Andrews, Duane P., 61, 129, 183, 215

Anteon International Corp., 59*n,* 131–32, 267, 268, 270, 278, 414

antiwar activists, 178, 271, 319

Antle, S. Bradford "Bud," 210, 296

Apollo, 308, 309*n*

Applied Signal Technology (AST), 209, 264, 299–301

Argon ST, 77, 164, 264, 301–3

Armageddon Project, 77–80, 89, 293–94

Armed Forces Communications and Electronics Association (AFCEA), 12, 17, 66, 110–11, 176, 259, 293
Armitage, Richard, 30–31, 94*n,* 96–97, 277, 283, 285–86
arms control agreements, 75, 89, 90
Armstrong, C. Michael, 321
Army, U.S., 190, 265*n*
  Abu Ghraib investigation of, 3, 4, 280–81, 369*n,* 371
  Communications and Electronics Command of, 43, 279, 293
  contractors and, 43, 99–100, 102, 103, 148, 168, 285, 286, 294–96
  Information Systems Command of, 79, 293
  inspector general of, 294
  Intelligence and Security Command of, 103, 190, 268, 286
  Intelligence Center of, 5, 16, 79, 267, 293
  intelligence services of, 20, 66, 111–12, 173
  Signal Security Agency of, 317–18
Army Corps of Engineers, U.S., 243
ARPA, *see* Defense Advanced Research Projects Agency
Arxan Technologies Inc., 361
Ashcroft, John, 315, 342–43, 353
AT&T, 13, 76, 224, 308, 317, 343
  Defense Department and, 164, 175, 307
  Government Solutions unit of, 47, 322–23, 361
  as intelligence contractor, 307, 321–23, 325, 330
  lawsuits against, 305, 366
  NSA access to call records of, 310, 323–24
  and NSA international phone surveillance, 75–76
  and NSA Internet surveillance, 311–13
  and NSA warrantless surveillance program, 26, 197, 305, 333–34, 366
Athena Innovative Solutions, 283
ATK Inc., 96
Attensity Inc., 25, 147–48, 150, 175, 316–17
At the Center of the Storm (Tenet), 130, 170*n,* 362
AWACs (Airborne Warning and Control System aircraft), 14

Baer, Robert, 14, 27, 76, 118, 152–53
BAE Systems, 11, 24, 29, 44, 59*n,* 63, 69, 90, 109*n,* 111, 112, 124, 134–36, 143, 159*n,* 164, 173, 175, 207, 223, 268, 299*n,* 344, 354, 361, 378
Baginski, Maureen, 297, 302
Baker, William O., 61
Balkans wars, 100, 103, 104–5, 235
Balkin, Jack M., 340–42
Ball Aerospace & Technologies Corporation, 247
Bamford, James, 48, 138, 202, 318
Barr, Bob, 194, 381
battlefield intelligence, 38, 52, 67, 145, 155–56, 159, 163, 231, 234–35, 243, 260, 263, 265, 298, 300
  contractors and, 14, 28, 58, 133, 246, 254, 264, 266–67, 286
Baxter, Jeff "Skunk," 249–50, 349
BDM International Inc., 81*n,* 95, 100, 101
bd Systems, Inc., 59
BearingPoint, 26, 175, 209, 359, 360, 407
Bechtel, 33
Beeks, Ken, 97*n,* 98, 149
Beijing, U.S. embassy in, 138–39
Bell Labs, 61, 76, 361
BellSouth, 310
Beltway bandits, 25, 104, 118
Betac Corporation, 79–80, 110, 111, 112, 293–94, 295
Biesecker, Brian V., 231, 233
bin Laden, Osama, 29*n,* 94, 419
biometric identification, 127, 168, 280
Black, Cofer, 29*n,* 121–22
Black, Donald L., 172, 380
Blackwater Worldwide, 29*n,* 33, 34, 118, 122, 270, 358, 370, 381
blanket purchase agreements, DIA and, 173–76, 316–17
Blow the House Down (Baer), 118
Body of Secrets (Bamford), 202
Boeing Company, 47, 77, 80, 95, 96, 98, 108, 110, 117, 118*n,* 142, 164, 208, 237*n,* 240, 359, 378*n,* 407
Booz Allen Hamilton, 6, 11, 37, 40, 50, 51, 59, 63, 66, 69, 73, 76, 80, 112, 116, 127, 142, 209, 215, 224, 229, 240, 255, 266, 321*n*–22*n,* 344, 357, 358, 359, 363–65, 379, 381
  Air Force and, 40, 43
  CIA and, 23, 44, 119, 130, 133, 175
  Defense Department and, 43, 51–53
  DIA and, 43, 173, 174–75, 176, 316–17
  FBI and, 51, 175
  Global Strategic Security service of, 45, 364
  history of, 40–41
  Homeland Security Department and, 42, 360
  Iraq and, 41–42
  NAO proposal and, 339, 348–50
  NGA and, 23, 250, 253, 254, 352
  NSA and, 23, 24, 39, 43, 51, 54–55, 175, 186, 187–88, 222, 308, 316, 352, 407
  ODNI and, 24, 39, 48, 67–68
  "revolving door" and, 43–48, 54, 113
  security clearances of, 43–44, 175, 316
  as "Shadow IC," 47, 363
  as SWIFT surveillance auditor, 53–54
  war games expertise of, 42, 51
Bosnia, 285
  contractors in, 99–100, 102, 103, 272

Bosnian war, 3, 94, 103, 235, 279
Boyd, Charles G., 97*n*, 146
Boykin, William G., 166–68, 171, 182, 241–42, 401–2
Brennan, John O., 11, 63–64, 69, 122–23, 125–26, 175
Bridge Technology Corporation, 210
British Aerospace, *see* BAE Systems
British intelligence, 32, 235–36, 249, 272, 302
Brown, Jody, 5–6
Browne, Herbert A., 12, 13, 176, 259
Burpee, David H., 244, 248, 252, 345
Bush, George H. W., 36, 78, 84, 85, 151, 233
Bush, George W., 10–11, 31, 38–39, 52, 56, 73, 115, 155, 185, 198, 213, 214, 269, 273, 295, 307, 326, 357, 368*n*
  warrantless surveillance authorized by, 304, 305, 308, 334
Bush (GHW) administration, 48–49, 61, 97*n*, 99, 157, 289, 323
  intelligence operations reduced under, 35, 49
Bush (GW) administration, 52, 53, 78, 102, 134, 156, 182, 191, 197, 204, 263
  FISA and, 331–37, 407
  foreign policy of, 106, 151, 272
  intelligence contracting under, 7, 72–74, 104, 113–14, 121, 125, 372–73
  NAO proposal of, 339–40, 348–52
  neoconservatives in, 31*n*, 45, 72, 74, 273, 364
  post-9/11 defense and intelligence budgets of, 19, 35, 392
  preemptive policy of, 272, 273, 342–43
  telecoms and, 306–7, 320–21
  warrantless surveillance and, 26, 54–55, 59, 314–15, 380, 415–16
Business Executives for National Security (BENS), 97–98, 146, 149
Business Roundtable, 321, 358, 362

CACI International Inc., 2–3, 7, 22, 24, 59*n*, 66, 97, 104, 128, 131, 164, 207, 211–12, 233, 268, 270–84, 296, 338, 342, 357, 358, 363, 369, 380
  Abu Ghraib scandal and, 3–5, 6, 11, 103, 270–71, 275, 279–82, 369*n*, 371
  Air Force and, 277, 279
  Army and, 272, 277, 279
  CIFA and, 180, 273
  Defense Department and, 2, 5, 264, 271, 273, 283
  DIA and, 175, 176, 272, 278–79
  Navy and, 276, 277, 279
  NSA and, 15, 188, 194, 271, 316, 407
  "revolving door" and, 29–30, 113
  security clearances of, 27, 112, 272, 277, 279, 283
  stock price of, 282–83
  TIDE database and, 11, 125–26
Caddell Construction Company, 139
California, forest fires in, 337–38, 345, 351
Calland, Albert, 11, 284
Cambone, Stephen, 156, 157–58, 159, 160, 161, 166, 171, 181, 183, 278, 280, 369*n*, 401
Carlucci, Frank C., 98–99, 100, 105
Carlyle Group, 29, 98, 100, 101, 105, 128–29, 159*n*, 179, 210, 269, 407
Carter, Jimmy, 75, 98, 241
Cartwright, James E., 230
Center for Democracy and Technology, 332*n*, 416
Center for International Policy, 119, 151
Center for Responsive Politics, 159*n*, 292, 296, 378*n*
Center for Strategic and International Studies, 52, 414
Central Command, U.S. (CENTCOM), 41, 51, 189, 243–44, 322
Central Intelligence Agency (CIA), 7, 40, 60, 62, 64, 66, 90, 92, 115–53, 167, 191, 246, 271, 323, 378, 398
  in Afghanistan, 29*n*, 92, 115, 117, 121–22, 127–28, 263
  Ames case and, 93–94
  annual budget of, 20, 21
  attrition rate in, 132
  bin Laden unit of, 94, 152
  Booz Allen and, 23, 44, 53, 119, 120, 130, 133, 175
  Bush (GW) administration and, 116
  COG (Armageddon) project and, 78, 79, 293
  contractors employed by, 13–14, 21, 23, 24, 67, 74–76, 80, 114, 117–21, 127–43, 151, 229–30, 264, 298, 301, 302, 337, 360, 376, 378, 380
  cult of secrecy in, 130–31, 149
  extraordinary renditions by, 117–18
  failures of, 109, 124, 286
  HUMINT and, 109, 117, 124, 161, 231
  IBEX project of, 76–77, 80
  in IC turf battles, 93, 136, 156, 159, 182, 235, 401–2, 404–5
  In-Q-Tel investment fund of, *see* In-Q-Tel
  intelligence collection and, 109, 124, 158*n*
  Intelligence Directorate of, 121, 132, 138, 398
  interrogations by, 115, 379
  in Iraq, 92, 115, 118, 254
  loss of authority in, 151–53
  Middle East operations of, 42, 126, 152
  National Clandestine Service of, 14, 117, 121, 374
  National Photographic Interpretation Center of, 134, 235

Central Intelligence Agency (CIA) (*cont.*)
  neocons' unhappiness with, 107, 116
  NGA and, 228, 229, 232
  nonofficial cover (NOC) program of, 138, 401–2
  Nonproliferation Center of, 64, 134
  NSA and, 190–91, 316, 404–5
  Operations Directorate of, 85, 110*n,* 121, 123–24, 132, 137, 152, 317, 374, 401
  politicization of, 151
  post-Cold War budget reductions of, 85, 92
  "revolving door" and, 14, 29, 31, 35, 44, 118–20, 133–35, 137–38
  Science and Technology Directorate of, 16, 119, 121, 132, 141, 144, 244, 416
  Support Directorate of, 121
  SWIFT surveillance program of, 53
  warrantless surveillance and, 316
  war room of, 60, 247
CEO COM LINK, 321
Chain of Command: The Road from 9/11 to Abu Ghraib (Hersh), 4
Chalabi, Ahmed, 94*n*–95*n,* 171
Cheney, Dick, 31*n,* 55, 56, 74, 78, 89, 99, 104, 106, 116, 214, 215–16, 295, 307, 319, 326, 336–37, 342
  as defense secretary, 106–7, 129, 183, 234, 326
  IC turf battles and, 62, 156, 157, 159, 160
  McConnell's relationship with, 38, 48–49
  warrantless surveillance defended by, 306, 333, 334, 379
Chertoff, Michael, 348, 351
Chesapeake Innovation Center, 25, 27, 359
China, People's Republic of, 84–85, 107, 124, 195–97
  Abraxas in, 138–39
  U-2 missions over, 74, 337
ChoicePoint Inc., 343, 353
Cicconi, James, 323
Cingular Wireless, 325–26
Cipher, 317
Cisco Systems, Global Defense, Space & Security Group of, 164
Civil Applications Committee, 348*n,* 349
civil liberties, 68, 339
  NAO proposal and, 348, 351
  warrantless surveillance and, 308, 415
civil rights activists, 319
Clapper, James R., 61, 62, 181–82, 184, 227, 248, 255, 344, 345, 362, 369*n*
Clinton, Bill, 31, 50, 78, 84, 88, 112, 245
  Woolsey's relationship with, 85, 91, 92
Clinton administration, 38, 44, 46, 157, 235
  computer encryption and security concerns of, 49–50
  defense contracting under, 99–105
  intelligence contracting under, 7, 73–74, 88–89, 103–5, 110–11, 123–24, 149, 198–99, 245
  intelligence operations reduced under, 35, 89, 109–10
  Reinventing Government privatization program of, 84, 86–88, 94, 95
CNN, 79, 93, 131, 239, 294
COG (continuity of government) task force, 77–80, 89, 293–94
Cohen, William S., 96, 97
Cold War, 41, 84, 158*n,* 193, 199, 362
  intelligence operations during, 2, 19, 76, 113, 416
Coleman, Robert A., 66, 264, 287–89, 361–62
Collins, Terry, 301, 302
Colombia, 81*n,* 272
Comey, James B., 315*n*–16*n*
Commission on Critical Infrastructure Protection, 50
Committee on the Present Danger, 45
Communications Assistance for Law Enforcement Act (CALEA), 320
communications intelligence (COMINT), 264, 300, 301, 303
computers:
  export restrictions on, 49–50
  security of, 12, 26, 49–50
Computer Sciences Corporation (CSC), 23–24, 47, 59, 63, 283, 296
  DIA and, 173, 175–76
  NSA and, 187, 205–8, 317, 326, 328, 330
Congress, U.S., 83, 185, 186, 187, 194, 204, 225, 235
  defense and intelligence budgets of, 19, 20–21, 35, 46, 93, 107, 110, 113, 124, 199, 230, 265, 366–67, 392
  Democratic control of, 263, 307, 332, 372
  earmarking in, 291, 292, 375–78
  intelligence oversight function of, 7, 21, 57, 65, 70–71, 136, 149, 153, 366–75, 380–81
  missile defense as priority of, 107–8, 124
  NAO proposal and, 348, 351–52
  Republican control of, 73, 86, 95, 105, 108, 112, 124
  warrantless surveillance immunity sought from, 59, 306, 321, 323, 333–34, 379, 380–81
  see also House of Representatives, U.S.; Senate, U.S.
Conrail, 83, 88
Constitution, U.S.:
  Fourth Amendment of, 311, 337, 415
  war powers in, 304
continuity of government (COG) task force, 77–80, 89, 293–94
contractors, *see* intelligence contractors
Convergent Security Group, 27

CORONA satellite, 75, 144, 247
Corporate Warriors (Singer), 100, 282, 370
Council on Domestic Intelligence, 68
Counterintelligence Field Activity (CIFA), 25, 157, 161, 180, 265, 297
 Congressional concerns about, 178, 181
 contractors employed by, 15, 21, 129, 178–80, 183, 283, 344, 376
 domestic surveillance by, 129, 177–78, 338, 344
 Talon database of, 178, 181, 344*n*
Counterpane Internet Security, 309*n*
covert operations, contractors and, 12, 367
criminal law, contractors and, 372–74
Croatia, contractors in, 99, 101
Crowell, William, 67, 312*n*
Crypto AG, 193
CSC, *see* Computer Sciences Corporation
Culver, Walter, 296
Cunningham, Randy "Duke," 21, 179, 283, 375–78
"Curveball," 171–72
Custer, John M., 243
Customs and Border Protection Bureau, U.S., 279, 420
cyber terrorism, 50, 124, 162

Dahlberg, Kenneth C., 34–35, 170, 326
Darby, Joseph M., 280, 282
DARPA, *see* Defense Advanced Research Projects Agency
data mining, 104, 169, 175, 178, 185–227, 285, 311, 313–14, 315–17, 318–19, 324, 326, 338, 340, 342
DC Capital Partners, 30, 31
DeConcini, Dennis, 93–94
Defense Advanced Research Projects Agency (DARPA), 20, 52–53, 56, 103–4, 112, 221, 223, 267, 337, 362, 413
Defense Airborne Reconnaissance Office, 92, 235
Defense Department, U.S., 36, 84, 122, 154–84, 189, 218, 228, 235
 annual budgets of, 19, 20–21, 35, 46, 93, 107, 110, 113, 124, 182, 265, 301, 366–67, 392
 Ballistic Missile Defense Organization of, 204
 C3I operations of, 46, 150, 163*n,* 177
 C4I operations of, 270, 292–93
 C4ISR operations of, 43, 279, 301
 CIFA of, *see* Counterintelligence Field Activity
 COG (Armageddon) project and, 78, 79, 293
 contractors employed by, 2, 5, 13, 14–15, 24, 33, 43, 51–53, 73, 94, 99–105, 131, 142, 161–64, 168, 182–84, 246, 264, 265, 271, 273, 283, 284, 286, 296, 297, 337, 357, 377
 Global Information Grid of, 155, 162, 164, 165, 167, 210, 323
 HUMINT programs of, 156, 161, 278, 401
 in IC turf battles, 136, 156, 158–59, 160–61, 181–82, 401–2
 intelligence collection agencies controlled by, 7, 154, 157, 158, 159, 265
 Logistics Civilian Augmentation Program of, 99–100
 outsourcing task forces of, 95–97
 post-Cold War budget reductions of, 2, 49, 85, 94, 106–7
 supplemental budgets of, 265, 266
 technology emphasis of, 155, 263
 undersecretary for intelligence in, 156, 157–58, 160, 181
 see also Office of the Secretary of Defense
Defense Evaluation Research Agency (DERA), British, 104–5
 privatization of, 105, 128–29
 see also QinetiQ Group PLC
Defense Information Systems Agency, 165, 220–21, 279, 326
Defense Intelligence Agency (DIA), 18, 36, 66, 68, 70, 125–26, 143, 157, 161, 167, 176–77, 181, 235, 360, 364*n,* 378*n*
 blanket purchase agreements of, 173–76, 316–17
 budget of, 20, 21, 170
 contractors employed by, 14–15, 26, 43, 170, 172–77, 183, 209, 272, 278–79, 284, 290, 299, 301, 302, 338, 380
 Defense Human Intelligence Service of, 171
 failures of, 109
 information sharing and, 407
 network centric warfare and, 163
 NGA and, 228, 252
 NSA warrantless surveillance program and, 54, 316
 Solutions for Intelligence Analysis (SIA) contracts of, 172–73
 Strategic Support Branch of, 161, 171, 401
Defense Intelligence Analysis Center, 61, 111
Defense Ministry, British, 128–29
Defense News, 205, 253, 284
Defense Policy Board, 45, 277, 364
Defense Science Board, 95, 302
Defense Security Service, 157, 180
Deloitte & Touche, 138, 165*n*
Dempsey, Jim, 227, 332*n,* 415–16
Dempsey, Joan A.:
 at Booz Allen, 29, 32–33, 46, 47–48, 54, 66, 111, 154, 160, 250, 253
 at CIA, 29, 46, 62, 109, 110, 111, 159, 235–36, 363
Denial and Deception (Mahle), 92
Dennis, William, 237–38

Denver Post, 327, 329
Desert One, 241–42
Desert Shield Operation, 102, 234
Desert Storm Operation, 102, 234
Detica Group PLC, 29, 184
Deutch, John M., 94, 134
DFI Government Services, 184
DIESCON 3, 173–76, 316–17
DigitalGlobe, 229, 240, 247, 251, 340, 354
Director of National Intelligence (DNI), 6, 10, 17, 22, 23, 29, 38–39, 45, 63, 69, 71, 110, 121, 156, 157, 158, 159, 160, 166–67, 173, 176, 181, 186, 230, 288, 325, 332
  congressional oversight and, 367–68, 371
  contractors employed by, 24, 39, 48, 67–68, 136, 349–50, 366
  IC Core Contractor Inventory of, 6, 13, 17–18, 58
  in IC turf battles, 158–59
  INSA and, 59, 64, 67–68, 69–71
  NAO proposal and, 349–50, 351, 365
  PowerPoint presentation by, 9, 18–19, 392
  "revolving door" problem addressed by, 17–18
Distributed Common Ground Systems (DCGS), 155–56, 167, 168, 183, 238
Dodd, Christopher, 334, 381
domestic intelligence, 7, 59, 64, 156, 331, 338, 340–47
  CIFA and, 129, 177–78, 338
  contractors and, 352–53, 355, 367
  integration of foreign intelligence and, 339–40
  NAO proposal and, 339–40, 348–52
  public debate on, 68–69, 348, 350–52
  satellites and, 344, 346, 348, 349
domestic security, *see* homeland security
Dragics, Dave, 3, 276
Dynamic Research Corporation, 59*n,* 265*n,* 268
DynCorp International, 30, 97*n,* 100, 119, 266

Eagle Alliance, 214, 330
Eagle Claw Operation, 241–42
EarthView, 145
Eastman Kodak, 74, 416
East Timor, contractors in, 103
Echelon program, 194–95, 198, 329
Edelman, Eric S., 257, 258
Eisenhower, Dwight, 12–13, 235
Eisenhower administration, contracting under, 74–75
Electronic Data Systems (EDS), 209, 330, 407
Electronic Frontier Foundation, 311, 313
electronic intelligence (ELINT), 300–301
Elk Hills Naval Petroleum Reserve, 83, 88
Elstner, John, 27, 359
Emerson, Steven, 79, 293
Empire Challenge, 182–83, 236
encryption and decryption, 12, 26, 49–50, 76, 103, 162, 200–201
Energy Department, U.S., 88, 139, 286
Engineering Research Associates, 302
Enron, 130, 358
Enterprise Modeling and Simulation, 238
Entrepreneur Weekly, 137
Environmental Systems Research Institute, 229
Environment Protection Agency, 365*n*
EP-3E signals reconnaissance plane, 195–96
Equatorial Guinea, 102
Equity International, 359
Ernst & Young, 138
ESL Inc., 98
ESRI, 242, 244, 246, 353
Essex Corporation, 22, 30, 47, 60, 81*n,* 203–5, 267, 268, 356, 413–15
E-Systems, 77
Everett, Terri, 9, 18–19, 392
EXECUTELOCUS, 218–19
executive privilege, 319

Fallujah, Iraq, 275, 301, 370
Farrar, George, 43, 47, 322*n*
Federal Aviation Administration, 82, 88, 169
Federal Bureau of Investigation (FBI), 24, 51, 66, 146, 175, 176, 319, 324, 335*n*–36*n,* 361
  annual budget of, 20
  in IC turf battles, 93
  intelligence sharing and, 44–45, 236, 344
  National Security Letters of, 324
  NCTC and, 10, 122
  NSA warrantless surveillance program and, 54, 316
Federal Communications Commission, 322
Federal Emergency Management Agency (FEMA):
  COG (Armageddon) project and, 78–79, 293
  domestic surveillance and, 237, 338, 345
Federal Housing Administration, 83
Federal Law Enforcement Training Center, 407
Federal Procurement Data System, 34
Federation of American Scientists, 20, 348, 406
Feingold, Russ, 334, 381
fiber optics, 199, 200
Fidell, Eugene, 13, 379
FISA, *see* Foreign Intelligence Surveillance Act
Flag Atlantic, 308
Ford, Gerald R., 78, 89, 319
Ford, Terrance M., 66*n*
Ford Aerospace, 80

Foreign Intelligence Surveillance Act (FISA), 186, 197, 213, 319–20, 324–25
Bush (GW) administration and, 331–37, 407
NSA surveillance and, 304–8, 320, 327
Foreign Terrorist Tracking Task Force, 177
Forster-Miller Inc., 129
Fort Huachuca, 5, 16, 79, 267, 281*n,* 293, 294–95
Fort Meade, Md., 185, 189, 191, 299
Friedman, Billings, Ramsey investors conference, 261–64, 265, 284, 287, 289, 290, 296, 297, 299
Frontline, 312, 313, 314
Frost & Sullivan, 162*n,* 163–64
Future Imagery Architecture, 47

Gannon, John C., 44, 109, 111, 124, 135–37, 219
Gansler, Jacques, 85, 97, 99, 104–5
Gatanas, Harry, 66, 202–3, 210–11, 297
Gates, Robert:
as CIA director, 44, 91, 106–7, 233–34, 235
as defense secretary, 156, 181–82, 184
Gaza, 274
General Atomics, 93, 159*n,* 168
General Dynamics, 47, 64, 77, 95, 108, 155, 159*n,* 164, 175, 207, 237, 248, 267, 278, 283, 330, 407, 414
General Dynamics Advanced Information Systems, 24, 63
General Dynamics Information Technology, 35, 131–33, 153, 180, 378
General Electric, 74–75
General Motors, 246
General Services Administration, 141–42
GeoEye, 61, 184, 229, 239, 247–48, 251, 252, 340
GEOINT, *see* geospatial intelligence
Geological Survey, U.S. (USGS), 349
GeoScout, 254
geospatial intelligence (GEOINT), 228–60, 351, 352
contractors and, 352–55
Geospatial Operation for a Secure Homeland, 354
Germany, 34, 164, 272, 285
Ghorbanifar, Manucher, 89
Gingrich, Newt, 86–87, 97*n,* 105, 107–8, 110
Global Crossing, 308, 313
Global Hawk unmanned aerial vehicle, 103, 254, 299, 337, 354
GlobalSecurity.org, 21, 163*n,* 245–46
Golden, William D., 103, 111–12, 113–14
Golden, W. Thomas, 293–94
Gonzales, Alberto, 305, 315*n*–16*n,* 415
Good Harbor Consulting, 31
Goodman, Melvin A., 119, 151, 159
Google, 16, 25–26, 174, 248–49, 308, 309
Google Earth, 145, 248, 249, 354
Goolgasian, John, 238, 345–46
Gordon, John A., 29, 140
Gore, Al, 86–87, 88, 92, 95, 97, 235, 245
Goss, Porter, 64, 137
Government Accountability Office, 351–52
Government Oversight Project, 21, 71
Government Secrecy Project, 20
Grace, J. Peter, 81–82
Graham, Bob, 199–200
Graham, Mary Margaret, 167, 230, 256
Gray Hawk Systems, 287
Greece, 99
Greenberg Traurig LLP, 275
Greenwald, Robert, 4, 270–71, 282
Grenada, 167
Groundbreaker Project, 51, 104, 187–88, 205–8, 211, 227, 286, 317, 326, 328–30, 331
GRS Solutions, 287
GTE Sylvania, 77, 300
Guantánamo Bay, 15, 268*n,* 280
Guatemala, 289
Guidance Software, 129, 263
Gulf War, 38, 41, 49, 85, 158*n,* 234
Guyana, 82*n*

Haiti, 41, 85, 87, 94, 100, 102, 289
Halberstam, David, 90–91
Hall, Keith, 44–45, 66, 111, 250, 253, 339
Halliburton, 33, 74, 99, 270, 358
Hamas, 274
Hamre, John J., 216
Harding, Robert A., 68
Harlow, Bill, 33, 170*n*
Harman, Jane, 291, 339–40, 377
Harris, Jeffrey K., 67, 231, 254
Harris Corporation, 79, 80, 180, 293, 359
Haseltine, Eric, 203, 220
Hastert, Dennis, 239
Haver, Richard L., 106–7, 234–35, 245, 250
Hayden, Michael V., 120, 130–31, 137, 181, 188, 193, 196, 199, 200, 201, 202, 204, 206, 215, 217–18, 219, 305, 380
Hazlewood, Leo A., 66, 133–34, 254
Helms, Richard "Hollis," 137–38, 139
Heritage Foundation, 87, 134
Hersh, Seymour, 4, 161, 280, 310*n*
Hewlett-Packard, 63, 66, 164, 175, 207
Hickey, J. Michael, 365–66
Hicks & Associates, 222
Hillhouse, R. J., 15, 19*n,* 33, 117, 373–74, 392
Hitachi, 247
Hizbullah, 274
homeland security, 28, 44, 45*n,* 56–57, 91, 140, 339, 359, 364–65
see also domestic intelligence
Homeland Security Business Council, 420

Homeland Security Department, U.S., 62, 66, 122, 127, 135, 177, 235, 316, 321, 325, 338, 344, 365, 407
- annual budget of, 20, 34, 360
- contractors and, 34, 42, 184, 262, 279, 284, 290–91, 297, 360
- NAO proposed for, 339–40, 348–52
- NCTC and, 10, 122–23

Homeland Security Information Network (HSIN), 290–91, 292
House of Representatives, U.S.:
- Armed Services Committee of, 20, 158–59, 294
- Energy and Commerce Committee of, 323
- Government Reform Committee of, 280
- Homeland Security committee of, 135, 291, 292, 348
- intelligence budgets in, 366–67, 368
- Intelligence Committee of, 20, 64, 178, 186, 217, 229, 239, 240, 295, 296, 316*n,* 339, 366–67, 368, 374, 377, 378, 416–17
- *see also* Congress, U.S.

Hughes, Patrick M., 61, 250–51, 349
Hughes Aircraft, 80
Hughes Electronics Corporation, 101
human intelligence (HUMINT), 92, 93, 242, 244, 253, 265
- CIA and, 109, 117, 124
- contractors and, 13–14, 24, 28, 117, 271, 279, 301
- Defense Department programs for, 156, 161, 278, 401

Humphrey, John, 1–2, 5, 6, 369
Hungary, 99, 272
Hunter, Duncan, 158–59
Hussein, Saddam, 42, 45, 89, 94*n,* 115, 116, 234, 364

i2, 139, 343, 419
IBEX project, 76–77, 80
IBM, 12, 26, 76, 80, 164, 165*n,* 188, 224, 316, 317, 330, 338, 342
IEDs, *see* improvised explosive devices
IKONOS satellite, 248
imagery, 12, 28, 38, 45, 47, 103, 133, 155, 158*n,* 163, 169, 175, 176, 190, 228, 231, 232, 234–35, 243–44, 260, 271, 299, 344, 347, 353–54
- *see also* geospatial intelligence; photoreconnaissance; satellites

imagery software, 244–46
improvised explosive devices (IEDs), 129, 143, 266, 267, 301
India, 109, 249, 286
information overload, 243–44
information sharing, 10, 12, 24, 26, 44–45, 58, 68, 92, 236, 254, 256, 290, 295, 297, 322, 344, 407, 417
information technology (IT), 103, 161, 162, 164, 360
- contractors as suppliers of, 24, 25–26, 30, 111, 117, 131–32, 144, 172–76, 182, 184, 253, 256, 263, 267, 273, 279–80, 289, 308, 331*n,* 379, 398
- In-Q-Tel and, 146–47
- key intelligence role of, 63
- limitations of, 243–44

initial public offerings (IPOs), 269–70
Initiate Systems Inc., 145–46
Inman, Bobby Ray, 60, 134
In-Q-Tel, 16, 25, 26, 143–49, 175, 176, 224, 316, 365
Intelcon, 1–2, 5
Intelink, 134, 174
Intellibridge Corporation, 135, 175
intelligence, surveillance, and reconnaissance (ISR), 263, 265, 298, 301
Intelligence Advanced Research Projects Agency proposal, 58
intelligence analysis, 265
- contractors and, 12, 111, 117, 123–25, 169, 264, 271, 276, 279, 285, 287, 299, 316–17, 367, 379–80, 414
- *see also* Central Intelligence Agency, Intelligence Directorate of; link analysis

Intelligence and National Security Alliance (INSA), 17, 35, 59, 63, 66, 67, 152–53, 203, 351, 371, 392
- board of, 65–66, 297, 302
- CIA and, 64, 66
- nonprofit status of, 70
- NSA and, 64, 66
- ODNI and, 59, 64, 67–68, 69–71
- as successor to SASA, 62–63, 286, 360
- *see also specific contractors*

IntelligenceCareers.com, 112, 279
intelligence collection, 407
- CIA and, 109–10, 117, 124
- contractors and, 111, 255, 271, 287, 367
- Defense Department control of, 7, 154
- integration of foreign and domestic, 339–40, 351
- military operations and, 156
- network centric warfare and, 162
- technology and, 340–41

Intelligence Community (IC):
- Booz Allen and, 43, 47
- contractors employed by, 7, 17–19, 24, 28, 73, 76, 94, 110–11, 113–14, 136, 161, 229, 250–51, 363
- DNI as head of, 39
- failures in, 108–9, 124
- information sharing in, 12, 24, 26, 44–45, 58, 68, 92, 417
- IT services needed by, 25–26, 63, 161
- NCTC as hub of, 9–10

oversight lacking in, 7, 21, 57, 65, 70–71, 136, 289, 363, 367–75
post-9/11 buildup of, 2
post-Cold War reductions in, 35, 49, 85, 94, 106–7, 123–24
turf battles in, 93, 136, 156, 158–59, 160
war games of, 42
see also specific agencies
intelligence contractors:
company loyalty vs. public good in, 36–37, 151–52, 359–60, 365–66, 380
criminal law and, 372–74
government expenditures on, 2, 6, 12, 13, 16, 17, 18–21, 110, 117, 230, 356, 360, 363, 367–68, 381
government oversight of, 1–2, 104–5, 113–14, 367–75, 378–81
government procurement process and, 26–27
information sharing and, 12, 24, 26
IT services supplied by, 24, 25–26, 30, 63
private-public partnership ideology of, 250–51, 256, 356–66
profit motive and, 125, 359–60, 380
proprietary systems of, 255–56
recruiting by, 2
"revolving door" and, 11, 14, 17–18, 28–33, 111, 125, 183–84
security clearances of, 2, 12, 23, 26–27, 28, 64, 110, 112
stockholders of, 21–22
trade associations of, 16–17; *see also specific associations*
see also specific agencies and companies
Intelligence-Industrial Complex, 3, 6, 12, 90, 162, 166, 168
Intelligence Software Solutions Inc., 180
Intergraph Corporation, 242, 354, 378*n*
Interior Department, U.S., 3, 279–80, 351
Internet, 49, 87–88, 144, 155, 165, 174, 197, 201, 226–27, 303, 306, 308, 338, 375*n*
interoperability, 255–60
interpreters, contractors as, 100, 287
interrogations:
contractors and, 12, 13, 15, 132, 267, 268*n*, 367, 369*n*, 379
see also Abu Ghraib torture scandal
Ionatron, 150
IONIC Enterprise Inc., 256
Iran, 42, 53, 76–77, 80, 107, 161, 171, 251*n*, 274
Iran-contra scandal, 53, 89
Iran hostage crisis, 241–42
Iraq, 140
ballistic missiles in, 107
sanctions on, 85
secret U.S. operations in, 32, 42
WMDs in, 115, 171–72, 196, 278
Iraq for Sale: The War Profiteers (film), 4, 270–71, 282
Iraqi National Congress, 94*n*–95*n*, 171
Iraq Liberation Act, 94*n*–95*n*
Iraq War, 33–34, 45, 123, 134, 148, 166, 167, 168, 171–72, 187, 265, 269, 273, 274, 284, 297, 298, 347, 359, 364*n*, 367, 413
battlefield intelligence in, 38, 145, 231, 243, 246, 254, 263, 286, 298, 300, 337, 346, 357, 419
Blackwater and, 122, 370
Booz Allen and, 41–42, 52
CACI in, 212, 272, 275; *see also* Abu Ghraib torture scandal
CIA in, 92, 115, 152
contractors in, 1, 12, 14, 33–34, 113, 118, 177, 370
GEOINT in, 231, 233
insurgents in, 3, 143, 175, 238, 262, 263, 266, 332
ManTech in, 103, 284–85, 287
regime change and, 45, 94*n*, 115
SAIC and, 168
Iridium project, 204
Islamic Jihad, 274
Israel, 164, 273, 274
Italy, 99, 272
Itek Corporation, 74–75
ITT Corporation, 77, 164, 247, 248, 353
ITT World Communications, 318, 319

Jacques, Steven, 239–40, 372
James Bond movies, 128, 146
Japan, 34, 272, 289
Jeppesen International Trip Planning, 117–18
Jeremiah, David E., 31, 109, 146, 286
Johnson, Larry, 123, 125
Joint Chiefs of Staff, 15, 31, 38, 43, 161, 299
Joint Intelligence Operations Centers (JIOCs), 161, 166–68, 171, 182
Joint Intelligence Task Force—Combating Terrorism, 10, 254, 278
Joint Regional Information Exchange System (JRIES), 290
Jonas, Jeffrey, 223–25
Justice Department, U.S., 51, 198, 276, 284, 295–96, 344, 351

Kaman Corporation, 98
Katrina, Hurricane, 34, 237, 238, 345–46
Kello, Jason, 63–64, 65, 67, 70
Kellogg Brown & Root (KBR), 99–100
Kenya, U.S. embassy attack in, 109
Kerr, Donald M., 16, 70, 232, 242–43, 352
Kerr, Richard J., 31, 134–35, 286
Keyhole Inc., 16, 145
Klein, Mark, 311–13
Kosovo, 85, 102, 272
Krongard, Buzzy, 146

Kuwait, 103, 234, 272, 285
Kyrgyzstan, 285

L-1 Identity Solutions, 127–28, 175, 263, 266, 268
L-3 Communications Inc., 47, 59*n*, 61, 73, 90, 96, 102, 127, 164, 173, 176, 188, 209, 250, 266, 267, 317, 349, 352, 377*n*
Laird, Melvin, 216
Language Weaver Inc., 149
LaPenta, Robert, 127–28, 268
Latent Semantic Indexing (LSI), 216–17
law enforcement agencies, 139, 177, 312, 342
  intelligence sharing and, 10, 24, 44–45, 236, 290–91, 344
Leahy, Patrick, 212–13
Lebanon, 42, 152, 274
Lee, Michael G., 234, 243
Leonard Green and Partners LLP, 142
Levinson, Sanford V., 340–42
Lexington Institute, 232
Libby, I. Lewis "Scooter," 45*n*, 401
Liberation Tigers, 274
Liberty, USS, 191–92
Lichtblau, Eric, 305, 329*n*
link analysis, 316, 324
Lockheed Corporation, CIA and, 74–75, 80, 95, 119, 337
Lockheed Martin, 12, 23, 24, 47, 61, 63, 67, 79, 81*n*, 95, 96, 97*n*, 104, 108, 112, 127, 142, 146, 155, 159*n*, 164, 207, 208–9, 223, 229, 231, 240, 266, 267, 286, 300, 326, 359
  CIFA and, 179
  Defense Department and, 101, 163–64
  DIA and, 173, 175, 316, 378*n*
  NCTC and, 11
  NGA and, 243, 254, 353
  NSA and, 188, 202, 330, 407
Lockheed Space and Missile Corporation, 194
Logicon, 206
London, J. P. "Jack," 4–5, 131, 212, 271–77, 282, 283–84, 356–57
London subway bombings, 347
Loral Defense, 95
Los Alamos National Laboratory, 168
Los Angeles Times, 18, 117, 138, 356, 402
Louie, Gilman, 147, 365
LPA Systems, 354
Lucent Technologies, 52, 95*n*

McConnell, J. Michael, 10*n*, 186, 220, 222–23, 326, 333, 380
  at Booz Allen, 17, 23, 29, 39–40, 50–51, 53, 54, 62, 339, 358
  Cheney criticized by, 55
  Cheney's relationship with, 38, 48–49
  as DNI, 6, 17, 23, 29, 38–39, 45, 47, 54–55, 57–60, 63, 69, 71, 173, 181, 230, 365, 367, 369
  DNI confirmation hearing of, 56–57, 351, 379
  IC Core Contractor Inventory report suppressed by, 6, 18, 58
  as INSA chairman, 17, 62, 63, 64, 68, 126, 351
  Intelligence Advanced Research Projects Agency proposed by, 58
  at JCS, 38
  in Naval Intelligence, 48–49
  as NSA director, 29, 38, 49–50, 190
  Powell and, 48–49
  warrantless surveillance defended by, 305–6, 307, 331–32, 334–37, 416
McDonald Bradley, 142, 287
McDonnell Douglas, 79, 81*n*, 119, 293
McGovern, Raymond, 36–37, 123, 151
McNamara, Barbara, 29–30, 66, 278
Mahle, Melissa Boyle, 92, 398
ManTech International, 7, 22, 24, 29, 47, 59, 63, 66, 69, 80, 97, 146, 207, 211, 224, 264, 268, 284–96, 317, 338, 342, 357, 358, 361–62, 363
  Aegis Research unit of, 287, 407
  Air Force and, 102–3, 285, 286
  Army intelligence and, 102, 285, 286, 294–96
  CIFA and, 180
  Defense Department and, 284, 286
  DIA and, 175, 284, 290
  Homeland Security Department and, 284, 290–91, 292
  intelligence sharing software of, 24, 290–91, 292, 295
  IPO of, 269–70
  in Iraq, 103, 284–85, 287
  lobbying and campaign contributions by, 291–92, 296
  Navy and, 285
  NSA and, 102–3, 188, 203, 264, 284, 286, 290, 330, 407
  "revolving door" and, 28, 30, 31, 135
  security clearances of, 269–70, 287, 288
Maples, Michael, 70, 167, 171, 172, 173, 262
maps, mapping programs, *see* geospatial intelligence
Marine Corps, U.S., 139, 243, 272, 275, 286
  intelligence service of, 20, 173, 260, 354
Martin Marietta, 90, 92, 95
  see also Lockheed Martin
MASINT (measurement and signatures intelligence), 68, 143, 163, 171, 175, 350, 351, 354
MASINT Association, 143
Mayer, Jane, 15, 117–18
MCI, 321, 323

Meagher, Thomas, 287–88, 414
measurement and signatures intelligence (MASINT), 68, 143, 163, 171, 175, 242, 253, 298–99, 350, 351, 354, 407
MetaCarta, 353
Microsoft, 26, 63, 66, 69, 164, 229
Middle East, 33, 42, 126, 152, 262, 266, 273–74, 275, 285, 337
military contractors, *see* intelligence contractors
Military Extraterritorial Jurisdiction Act, 372
military-industrial complex, 12–13
Military Professional Resources Inc. (MPRI), 101–2, 176
Minihan, Kenneth A., 29, 134–35, 286, 299, 328, 360–63
missile defense, 107–8, 124, 157, 169, 171
Missile Defense Agency, 297
Mobile Integrated Geospatial-Intelligence System (MIGS), 237–38, 346
Mohammad Reza Pahlavi, Shah of Iran, 76–77
Mohammed, Khalid Sheikh, 169
Moodispaw, Leonard, 22, 60, 203–5, 207, 413–14
Moscow, U.S. embassy in, 138–39
Mossadegh, Mohammad, 42
Motorola, 204
MTC Technologies Inc., 29, *59n*, 265, 268, 270, 297–99, 361
multiple spectrum imaging, 242
Munson, Alden V., 58–59, 70
Murrett, Robert B., 70, 230, 231–32, 233, 236, 242, 247, 251, 347, 351, 352
Murtha, Jack, *159n*, *378n*
MZM Inc., 21, 130, 178–79, 283, 375–78

Nacchio, Joseph P., 327–30, 331
NAO, *see* National Applications Office (NAO) proposal
Narus Inc., 67, 312
National Aeronautics and Space Agency (NASA), 36, 239, 349
National and Military Operations Support (NMOS) project, 406–7
National Applications Office (NAO) proposal, 339–40, 348–52, 365, 381
National Business Parkway, 208–9
National Commission on Terrorist Attacks Upon the United States, *see* 9/11 Commission
National Correlation Working Group, 67
National Counterterrorism Center (NCTC), 9–11, 35, 134, 176
  contractors employed by, 11, 23, 123, 136
  "revolving door" and, 11
  terrorist database of, 10, 11
  Threat Matrix produced by, 10
National Cryptological Museum, 191–92
National Defense Industrial Association (NDIA), 66, 67
National Defense Panel, 96–97
National Economic Council, 85
National Foreign Intelligence Program, 46
National Geospatial-Intelligence Agency (NGA), 44, 46, 47, 70, 145, 166, 181, 228–60, 302, 416
  Advanced Geospatial Intelligence Office of, 242
  annual budget of, 20, 21, 228
  CIA and, 228, 229
  classified operations of, 251–55
  contractors employed by, 14, 17, 23, 24, 26, 39, 131, 133–34, 154, 156, 169, 184, 229, 243, 244, 248, 250, 253–54, 265, 272, 298, 352, 353–54, 357, 362, 413
  Defense Department control of, 7, 154, 157, 158, 159, 228, 231, 254
  DIA and, 228, 252
  domestic surveillance by, 236–38, 338, 351
  Future Intelligence Requirements Environment of, 253
  GeoEye and, 247–48
  GEOINT 2004 and, 229–30
  GeoScout project of, 254
  intelligence sharing and, 45, 236, 407
  Katrina and, 237, 238, 345–46
  network centric warfare and, 162–63
  NextView program of, 247
  9/11 attacks and, 237, 345
  NRO and, 229, 231–32, 242–43, 252
  NSA collaboration with, 231–33, 242–43, 346–47
  origins of, 233–36
  "revolving door" and, 61
  satellite industry and, 247–48
  supplemental budgets of, 265, 266
National Guard, 43, 237
National Imagery and Mapping Agency (NIMA), 44, 94, 228, 235–36, 244–46
National Institute for Military Justice, 13
National Intelligence Council, 44, 111, 124, 135, 184
National Intelligence Estimates, 135
  on ballistic missiles, 107–8
  on Iran nuclear program, 55–56
  on Iraq WMDs, 115, 171–72
National Intelligence Program (NIP), 20, 406–7
National Interests Security Company LLC, 30–31
National Program Office, 79, 80
National Reconnaissance Office (NRO), 31, 44, 46, 47, 58, 60, 67, 70, 75, 92, 105, 108, 111, 140, 166, 250, 407, 416
  budget of, 16, 20, 21, 265

National Reconnaissance Office (NRO) (*cont.*)
contractors employed by, 16, 26, 39, 90, 129, 131, 142, 154, 239, 267, 271, 286, 298, 301, 322, 406–7, 413
Defense Department control of, 157, 158, 159
domestic surveillance by, 344
information sharing and, 407
network centric warfare and, 163
NGA and, 229, 231–32, 235, 242–43, 252
NSA and, 190
National Security Agency (NSA), 7, 25, 46, 60, 100, 130, 134, 138, 141, 150, 157, 166, 167, 176, 182, 185–211, 231, 268, 297, 303, 359, 362, 416
ACI and, 128
Advanced Research and Development Activity of, 324
annual budget of, 20, 21, 186–87, 193, 199, 201–2
Central Security Service of, 190
CIA and, 190–91, 404–5
computer systems crash at, 199–200
contractors employed by, 14, 15, 23, 24, 26, 30, 39, 43, 51, 67, 75–76, 80, 98, 102–3, 112, 131, 133, 142, 154, 156, 169, 175, 184, 186, 187–88, 203, 208–12, 246, 247, 264, 265, 272, 284, 286, 290, 296–97, 298, 300, 301, 308, 316, 317, 322, 326, 330, 338, 352, 353–54, 360, 379, 406–7, 413
data mining effort of, 185–227
Defense Department control of, 157, 158, 159
domestic surveillance by, 59, 250
early computer development supported by, 192
Echelon program of, 194–95, 198, 329
GEOINT 2004 and, 229–30
headquarters of, 189
IBEX project of, 76–77, 80
information assurance directorate of, 188
Information Warfare office of, 46
INSA and, 64, 66, 70
Internet surveillance by, 303, 310, 311–14
Minaret program of, 319
National Reconnaissance Office and, 190
Naval Security Group conflict with, 32
NCTC and, 10
network centric warfare and, 162
NGA collaboration with, 231–33, 242–43, 346–47
outsourcing as failure at, 214–15
post-Cold War transition of, 193–94
Powell's UN presentation and, 196–97
PR campaign of, 202–3
President's Daily Brief and, 189
private sector dependence of, 185–87, 201–2
Project Groundbreaker of, 51, 104, 187–88, 205–8, 211, 214, 286, 317, 326, 328–30, 331
Project Trailblazer of, 24, 214–21, 254
public's education about, 196–97
responsibilities of, 189–90
"revolving door" and, 29–30, 133
Shamrock Operation of, 317–18
Signals Intelligence Directorate of, 188–89, 203
Soft Landing program of, 202
Soviet codes broken by, 192
supplemental budgets of, 265, 266
telephone call record access of, 310–11, 313–14
warrantless surveillance program of, *see* warrantless surveillance
see also specific contractors
National Security Archive, 75, 200
National Security Council, 31, 85, 89, 289
National Security Letters, 324
National Security Telecommunications Advisory Committee (NSTAC), 307, 325–27, 366
National Special Security Events, 236
"national surveillance state," 340–41
National Vigilance Park, 191
NATO, 104, 132, 235, 289
Naval Air Warfare Center, 101, 236
Naval Petroleum Reserves, 83, 88
Naval Security Group, 32, 190
Navy, U.S., 101, 276, 277, 279, 285
Argon ST and, 265, 301
battlefield intelligence and, 155
imagery collection and, 232
intelligence service of, 20, 30, 46, 48–49, 173, 190, 354
outsourcing of cargo and tanker ships by, 83
SIGINT and, 232
NCI Information Systems, 27, 265*n*, 268, 283*n*
NCTC, *see* National Counterterrorism Center
Negroponte, John, 22, 38, 47, 58, 230, 255, 259, 326
neoconservatives, 31*n*, 45, 72, 74, 89, 94*n*, 106, 107, 116, 157, 273, 364
Network Centric Operations Industry Consortium (NCOIC), 164–65
network centric warfare (NCW), 161–66, 182, 183, 263–64, 279, 296, 297, 323, 342
Network Solutions, 87–88
Newsweek, 49, 53, 217–18, 334
New Yorker, 10*n*, 15, 117–18, 161, 310*n*, 335*n*

New York Times, 36, 54, 55, 69, 89, 90, 198, 315
on warrantless surveillance, 304, 305, 306, 308, 309–10, 315, 329*n,* 332
NGA, *see* National Geospatial-Intelligence Agency
"NGesture" video table, 238–39
Nicaragua, 53, 289
9/11 Commission, 68, 124, 156–57, 191
Nortel Networks, 207
North American Aerospace Defense Command, 165
Northern Alliance, 122
Northern Command, U.S. (NORTHCOM), 25, 142, 177, 268, 316, 338, 344
North Korea, 87, 94, 107, 337
Northrop Grumman, 22, 23, 29, 64, 66, 73, 79, 80, 81*n,* 93, 95, 106, 108, 127, 139, 142, 155, 159*n,* 205, 234, 238–39, 246, 256, 266, 297, 300, 317, 349, 359
Defense Department and, 163–64, 337
DIA and, 173, 175, 322
Essex acquired by, 267, 413–15
NGA and, 229, 352
NSA and, 15, 187, 203, 215, 322, 330, 352, 407
Nottingham, Edward, 329–30
NSA, *see* National Security Agency

OAO Corporation, 286, 330
Odeen, Philip A., 95–96, 98, 100
Oehler, Gordon, 134
Office of Strategic Services (OSS), 42
Office of the Director of National Intelligence (ODNI), *see* Director of National Intelligence
Office of the Secretary of Defense, 5, 43–44, 66, 184, 286
Olesak, John F., 256, 414
Omen Inc., 30, 209
optical processing, 203–5
Oracle Corporation, 47, 175, 229
Orion Center for Homeland Security, 180
O'Sullivan, Stephanie, 144–45, 148

Pakistan, 32, 118, 169
Paladin Capital Group, 45*n*–46*n,* 91, 328*n,* 356, 361
Palestinians, 273, 274, 275*n*
Pathfinder (software), 217
PCI Geometrics, 353
Pedersen, George, 261, 270, 284–85, 287, 288–89, 292, 357
Pelosi, Nancy, 367
Pentagon, 9/11 terrorist attack on, 2, 51, 113, 345
Perle, Richard, 89, 94*n*
Perry, William J., 95, 98, 216, 267
Philippines, 41, 161, 347
photoreconnaissance, 75, 90, 105
see also geospatial intelligence; imagery
Pike, John, 21, 163*n,* 219–20, 245–46, 252, 313–14, 347
piXlogic, 148
Plame, Valerie, 30, 45*n,* 116, 138
Poindexter, John, 52–53, 56, 221–22, 312
Polaroid, 74
Politico, 321
Poole, Robert, 83–84
Potomac Institute, 63
Powell, Colin, 30, 31, 38, 48–49, 196–97, 235, 249*n,* 326
Power Marketing Administrations, 83, 88
Predator unmanned aerial vehicle, 92–93, 103, 133, 231, 254, 299, 354
Premier Technology Group (PTG), 3, 103, 279
President's Daily Brief (PDB), 15, 36, 85, 189, 199, 379–80
President's Foreign Intelligence Advisory Board (PFIAB), 31, 62, 146, 160, 286
Price, David, 369–73
PricewaterhouseCoopers, 137, 209, 407
Privacy and Civil Liberties Oversight Board, 178
Privacy International, 54
Private Sector Survey on Cost Control, 81–82
Professional Services Council, 36, 73
Project for the New American Century (PNAC), 94*n,* 105–6, 107, 157, 364*n,* 401
Protect America Act, 331–34
pure plays, 227, 261–303

QinetiQ Group PLC, 29, 61, 67, 128–29, 180, 183, 263, 359
see also Defense Evaluation Research Agency, British
Quadrennial Defense Review, 51, 163
Quadrennial Intelligence Community Review, 64
QuesTech Inc., 277
Qwest Communications International, 309, 323, 327, 328–30, 331

Raduege, Harry D., 165–66
Raytheon, 23, 69, 95, 146, 159*n,* 164, 223, 239, 240, 264, 266, 301, 302, 330
Defense Department and, 155–56, 163–64, 167, 182–83
Intelligence and Information Systems of, 238
NGA and, 229
NSA and, 188
RCA Communications, 318
Reagan, Ronald, 53, 73

Reagan administration, 32, 98, 289
COG (Armageddon) project of, 77–80, 89, 293–94
Iran-contra scandal and, 53, 89
military buildup of, 95
privatization and, 73, 81–84, 88, 99
Reason Foundation, 83, 87
Renzi, Eugene, 79–80, 292–95
Renzi, Rick, 292, 294, 295–96
Research and Development Experimentation Capability (RDEC), 225
Reyes, Silvestre, 316, 367
Rice, Condoleezza, 257–58, 326
Ridge, Tom, 140, 150, 165*n*
Risen, James, 198, 305, 329*n,* 332
Rockefeller, John D. "Jay," 57, 218, 321, 333, 334*n,* 407
Rockwell International, 76–77
Rumsfeld, Donald, 89, 94*n,* 106
as defense secretary, 3, 45, 51, 78, 136, 154, 156, 157, 159, 160, 171, 181, 234, 265, 266, 273, 278, 280, 282, 319, 344, 364, 369*n,* 401, 402
in intelligence turf battles, 160–61
network centric warfare and, 162, 401
as OEO director, 51
technology emphasized by, 155
Rumsfeld commissions, 107–8, 157
Russia, 124, 249

SAIC, *see* Science Applications International Corporation
Sample, Timothy R., 35, 62, 64–65, 68–69, 152–53, 371–72
satellites, 12, 16, 25, 44, 47, 74–75, 77, 89, 90, 93, 103, 105, 108, 119, 129, 141, 144, 154, 155, 163, 183, 190, 205, 228, 229, 231–32, 244, 245, 246–49, 252, 353, 379
domestic surveillance by, 344, 346, 348, 349, 365
Saudi Arabia, 32, 101
SAVAK, 77
SBC, 322
Scheuer, Michael, 94, 152
Science Applications International Corporation (SAIC), 80, 96, 98, 110, 116, 127, 129, 142, 143, 155, 159*n,* 168, 184, 237*n,* 240, 255, 264, 265*n,* 266, 299, 322, 326, 338, 342, 349, 357, 363, 365, 380, 381
CIA and, 23, 34, 59, 119, 130, 133–34
CIFA and, 180, 344
Defense Department and, 166, 168, 323
DIA and, 175, 176
Homeland Intelligence Solutions group of, 180
INSA and, 59, 63, 67, 69
Intelligence and Security Group of, 169
Mission Integration unit of, 134
NCTC and, 11
NGA and, 23, 24, 133–34, 169, 229, 253–54
NSA and, 15, 23, 133, 169, 187, 202, 214–21, 222, 308, 330
Project Trailblazer and, 214–21
"revolving door" and, 28, 61, 113, 133–34
Saudi military training by, 101
security clearances of, 23, 169, 170
and TIA plan, 53, 222, 223
Scitor, 12
CIA and, 137, 141–43, 378
Defense Department and, 142, 184
Secret Service, U.S., 236
Securities and Exchange Commission, contractors and, 21–23
Security Affairs Support Association (SASA), 60–62, 80, 286, 360
see also Intelligence and National Security Alliance (INSA)
security clearances, of intelligence contractors, 2, 12, 23, 26–27, 255
see also specific contractors
Seidenberg, Ivan G., 325
Senate, U.S.:
Armed Services Committee of, 89, 227
Church Committee of, 317, 319
intelligence budgets in, 93, 367
Intelligence Committee of, 44, 56–57, 93, 109, 217, 218, 223, 306, 335
Judiciary Committee of, 136, 213, 315*n,* 320–21, 323, 343*n,* 416
McConnell's DNI confirmation hearing in, 56–57, 369*n,* 379
see also Congress, U.S.
sensors, 253, 262, 264, 267, 299, 301, 302
Sentia Group, 139–40
September 11, 2001 terrorist attacks, 2, 14, 35, 45, 73, 78, 111, 112–13, 115, 121, 137, 144, 172, 191, 204, 236, 285, 337, 339, 341, 342, 351, 354, 357
Booz Allen and, 51
Shamrock Operation, 317–18
Shea, K. Stuart, 229, 239–40
Shelton, H. Hugh, 267, 278
Shrader, Ralph, 51, 363–64
signals intelligence (SIGINT), 38, 48, 76, 105, 155, 182, 185, 211–12, 227, 233, 242, 252, 260, 297, 344, 351
contractors and, 12, 14, 15, 24, 28, 103, 131, 141, 169, 264, 266, 271, 285, 299, 300, 301, 302, 330–31, 354, 414
SI International, 27, 66, 142, 210–11, 265, 268, 270, 296–97, 302
Silverstein, Ken, 102
Singer, Peter, 4*n,* 100, 282, 370–71
SkyBuilt, 148
Smith, Hedrick, 314
Smith, R. Jeffrey, 31, 91

Social Network Analysis, 274–75
social networking sites, 226–27
Soin, Raj, 299
Soloway, Stan, 36, 73, 84, 201
Somalia, 32, 99–100, 161, 167, 171
South Korea, 166, 249, 272, 285, 289
Soviet Union, 139, 192
  collapse of, 49, 84–85, 124, 233
  photoreconnaissance of, 75, 252*n*
  U-2 missions over, 74, 337
Space Foundation, 239
Special Forces, U.S., 122, 241
Special Forces Operating Command, U.S., 241
Special Operations Forces, 298
SpecTal, 12, 127–28, 130, 175
spy planes, 47, 74, 119, 144, 155, 205, 228, 235, 254
  domestic surveillance by, 337–38, 346, 365
SRA International, 66, 173, 180, 265*n*, 268, 353
SRD, 26, 223–25
State Department, U.S., 78, 125, 127, 235, 284, 286, 299
  Blackwater and, 122
  Counterterrorism Office of, 123
  Intelligence and Research Bureau of, 20, 177
Steele, Robert David, 219, 259–60, 392
Stefanowicz, Steven, 4–5, 281
Stenbit, John, 177, 297
Stopher, John, 239–40, 416–17
Studeman, William O., 29, 49
submarines, 169, 232
Sun Microsystems, 164, 175
supercomputers, 76
SWIFT surveillance program, 53–54
Swire, Peter, 186, 199, 375*n*, 415
Syntek Technologies, 221
System Engineering & Development Corp. (SEDC), 203–4
systems integrators, 23–24, 104, 130, 131–37, 163, 253, 266, 308, 407, 414
Sytex, 268

TAC, *see* The Analysis Corporation
Tacit Knowledge Systems Inc., 149
Taguba, Antonio, 281, 282
"tail to tooth" commission, 98, 100
Taliban, 29*n*, 122, 263
Talon robots, 129
Tanzania, U.S. embassy attack in, 109
Taxpayers for Common Sense, 378
technology:
  Clinton administration emphasis on, 85–86
  domestic surveillance and, 340–41
  export restrictions on, 49–50
  Rumsfeld's advocacy of, 155
  shift from public to private sector in development of, 35–36, 103, 144, 174, 362, 379, 414–15
  Woolsey's advocacy of, 92–93
  see also information technology (IT)
telecommunications companies, 197, 213
  call records of, 310–11, 313–14, 338, 341
  campaign contributions by, 334*n*
  global transit traffic and, 307, 309
  immunity for, 59, 306, 321, 323, 333–34, 343*n*, 379, 380–81
  as intelligence contractors, 307–8, 336–37
  warrantless surveillance and, 305
  in World War, II, 317–18
  see also specific companies
Telecordia Technologies, 326
TeleGeography Research, 309
Tenet, George J., 7, 32, 45, 62, 170*n*, 172, 195, 262, 263, 362
  Brennan's friendship with, 126
  as CIA director, 94, 109–10, 115–16, 133, 151, 157, 230, 246, 254, 263
  In-Q-Tel started by, 16, 143, 146
  on intelligence contracting, 74
  post-CIA career of, 28–29, 126–30, 175, 263, 268
  on QinetiQ board, 128–29, 183
  as rainmaker, 32–33, 126
TeraText, 216, 217
Terrorist Identities Datamart Environment (TIDE) database, 11, 125–26
Terrorist Surveillance Program, 305, 331, 416
  see also warrantless surveillance
Terrorist Threat Integration Center (TTIC), 122–23, 125
The Analysis Corporation (TAC), 63, 66, 263
  CIA and, 130
  DIA and, 175
  NCTC and, 11, 125
  "revolving door" and, 126
  TIDE database maintained by, 11, 125–26
Thompson, Bennie G., 348, 352
Tighe, Donald W., 146–47
Titan Corporation, 90, 92, 119, 159*n*, 173, 207, 209, 267, 270, 281*n*
  see also L-3 Communications Inc.
T-Mobile, 309
Total Information Awareness (TIA) plan, 52–53, 56, 221–26, 227, 311–12
Trailblazer Project, 24, 214–21, 227, 254
"transaction space," 222–23
Transportation Security Administration, 285, 359, 360
TrapWire software, 139, 140
Treasury Department, U.S.:
  intelligence budget of, 20
  SWIFT surveillance program of, 53–54
Truman, Harry, 318
TRW, 58, 74, 79, 80, 81*n*, 90, 98, 108, 110, 119, 177, 184, 202, 207, 224, 245, 293, 297, 330
  Information Technology Group of, 107*n*

Tucker, Chris, 224, 256–57, 259
Turbulence, 226–27

U-2 spy plane, 47, 74, 144, 155, 208, 235, 254
  domestic surveillance by, 337–38, 346
  MTC and, 265, 298
Unified Combatant Commands, 39, 166, 167, 299
United Defense Industries, 100, 269
United Nations, 196–97
United States Geospatial Intelligence Foundation (USGIF), 17, 66, 145*n*
United Technologies, 98
unmanned aerial vehicles (UAVs), 12, 92–93, 103, 155, 169, 183, 254, 265, 299, 301, 337, 347, 353, 354
URWARS (Urban Warfare Simulation), 275
U.S. Chamber of Commerce, 365–66
U.S. Enrichment Corporation, 88
U.S. Geospatial Intelligence Foundation (USGIF), 228–29, 239–40, 254, 353
US Investigations Services (USIS), 100, 179, 209–10, 407
U.S. News & World Report, 79, 230, 293

VENONA program, 192
Veridian Corp., 64, 223, 267, 270
Verint Systems Inc., 361
Veritas Capital, 30, 31, 100, 283
Verizon, 197, 207, 308, 313, 330
  campaign contributions by, 334*n*
  Defense Department and, 307
  FBI and, 324
  as intelligence contractor, 307, 321, 325, 365–66
  NSA access to call records of, 310, 323–24
  warrantless surveillance and, 305, 324–25, 333–34
Veteran Intelligence Professionals for Sanity, 151
Vietnam, 41*n,* 167
Vietnam War, 48, 84, 235
Viisage, 128
Vinnell Corporation, 101
Viper Networks Inc., 308*n*–9*n*
Visual Analytics Inc., 317

Wade, Mitchell J., 283, 376–78
Waechter, Steven, 27, 264, 283
Wakefield, Todd, 147–48
Wall Street Journal, 340, 352
Walt Disney Corporation, 11*n,* 202, 203
war games, 42, 51
Warner, David, 221
war on terror, 44, 45, 51–52, 115, 268*n,* 269, 271–72, 274, 275, 285, 287, 299, 300, 341, 342, 347, 350, 357, 370, 417
warrantless surveillance, 7, 26, 54–55, 59, 69, 194, 197–98, 207, 304–5, 314–15, 331–34, 338, 342, 416
  AT&T and, 26, 305, 366
  Booz Allen and, 54–55
  Bush (GW) administration and, 26, 54–55, 59, 314–15, 380, 415–16
  CIA and, 316
  civil liberties and, 308
  corporate immunity for, 59, 306, 321, 323, 333–34, 343*n,* 379, 380–81
  DIA and, 54, 316
  FBI and, 54, 316
  of global transit traffic, 307, 309
  and IC reputation, 213–14
  NSA and, 185–211
  Qwest and, 309, 323, 327
  Verizon and, 305, 324–25
  see also Terrorist Surveillance Program
Washington Post, 4*n,* 77*n,* 88, 91, 93, 101, 126, 134, 147, 172, 173, 178, 183, 273, 277, 282, 283, 285, 316, 401–2
Washington Technology, 22, 142, 302
Watts, Wayne, 323–24
Waugh, Billy, 121–22
Weekly Standard, 55, 116
Welch, Larry, 277–78
Western Union, NSA and, 75–76, 318, 319
Westinghouse Electric, 98
William O. Baker Award, 46, 61–62, 72
Wilson, Joseph, 30, 116
Windsor Group, 58
Wolfowitz, Paul, 45, 106, 177, 326, 401
Woodward, Bob, 31*n,* 77*n*
Woolsey, R. James, 52, 78, 107, 108, 195*n,* 361
  at Booz Allen, 29, 42, 45, 47, 54, 78, 322*n,* 364, 365*n*
  as CIA director, 85, 90–94, 245
  Clinton's relationship with, 85, 91, 92
  pre-CIA career of, 89–90
WorldCom, 323, 330
World Trade Center:
  9/11 terrorist attack on, 2, 113, 236–37, 345
  1993 terrorist attack on, 109
WorldView-1 satellite, 247, 353–54
World War II, 40, 317–18
Wright, Lawrence, 10*n,* 335*n*–36*n*
Wyden, Ron, 56, 218, 369*n,* 379

Yancey, Gary L., 299–301
Yoo, John, 314–15

Zachary Construction, 139
Zarqawi, Abu Musab al-, 212, 233, 347
Zinni, Anthony, 31, 243–44
Zollars, Ronald M., 133, 219

About the Author

Tim Shorrock is an investigative journalist who has been writing about U.S. foreign policy, national security and business for more than twenty-five years. His articles have appeared in dozens of publications, including *The Nation, Mother Jones, Salon,* and *The Progressive.* For most of the 1990s, Shorrock was a reporter in the Washington bureau of *The Journal of Commerce.* He lives in Tahoma, California, in the Sierra Nevada mountains, and can be reached through his blog and Web site, www.timshorrock.com.